Afghan Expedition

Notes and Sketches from the First British Afghan War
of 1839-1840

James Atkinson

SUPERINTENDING SURGEON OF THE ARMY OF INDUS, BENGAL ESTABLISHMENT

Copyright © The Long Riders' Guild Press

All rights reserved. Without limiting the rights under copyright reserved above, no part of this publication may be reproduced, stored in or introduced into a retrieval system, or transmitted, in any form or by any means (electronic, mechanical, photocopying, recording or otherwise) without the prior written permission of The Long Riders' Guild Press.

The Long Riders' Guild Press

www.classictravelbooks.com
www.horsetravelbooks.com

The Long Riders' Guild Academic Foundation

www.lrgaf.org

ISBN: 1-59048-280-8

First published by Wm. H. Allen & Co. in 1842, with the title *The Expedition into Affghanistan: Notes and Sketches descriptive of the country, contained in a personal narrative during the campaign of 1839 & 1840, up the surrender of Dost Mahomed Khan,* from which the text for this edition is taken. The author's original spelling has been left unchanged except in the title.

The cover image, in the author's own words, "represents a Den in the Mountains of the Bolân Pass, with a party of Beloochees ready to commence a cowardly and murderous attack on the British troops."

CONTENTS

FOREWORD by Jules Stewart .... Page i
INTRODUCTION by Merlin Hanbury-Tenison .... Page iii
AUTHOR'S PREFACE .... Page ix
CHAPTER I. – Causes of the Expedition. .... Page 1
CHAPTER II. – History of Shah Shoojah. .... Page 6
CHAPTER III. – History of Shah Shoojah continued. .... Page 20
CHAPTER IV. – Journey of the Author to join the Army. .... Page 31
CHAPTER V. – Journey of the Author continued. .... Page 43
CHAPTER VI. – Advance of the Army of the Indus. .... Page 52
CHAPTER VII. – Advance of the Army to Candahar. .... Page 65
CHAPTER VIII. – Occupation of Candahar. .... Page 81
CHAPTER IX. – March from Candahar to Ghizni. .... Page 91
CHAPTER X – Attack and capture of Ghizni. .... Page 101
ILLUSTRATIONS .... Pages 115-168
CHAPTER XI. – Ghizni. .... Page 169
CHAPTER XII. – March to Caubul. .... Page 180
CHAPTER XIII. – Caubul. .... Page 192
CHAPTER XIV. – Caubul. .... Page 204
CHAPTER XV. – Caubul. .... Page 217
CHAPTER XVI. – Caubul. .... Page 228
CHAPTER XVII. – March to Jellalabad. .... Page 240
CHAPTER XVIII. – Journey from Affghanistan, through the Punjab,
   to Ferozepore. .... Page 248

APPENDIX.
THE CAPTURE OF GHUZNEE – A British Army Report by Lieutenant-General Sir John Keane and other English Officers. .... Page 265

LIST OF ILLUSTRATIONS

With the exception of the first and last drawing, the captions all appear on the facing pages.

Beloochees in the Bolân Pass .... Page 115
Scene on the River Sutledge, near Pauk-Puttun in the Punjaub .... Page 117
The Town of Roree and the fortress of Bhukker, on the Indus .... Page 119
The Encampment at Dadur, with the entrance to the Bolân Pass .... Page 121
View of the mountain Baba-Naunee .... Page 123
Entrance to the Bolân Pass from Dadur .... Page 125
The Wild Pass of Siri-Kajoor .... Page 127
The opening into the narrow pass above the Siri Bolân .... Page 129
The approach to the fortress of Kwettah .... Page 131
Entrance into Kojak Pass from Parush .... Page 133
The troops emerging from the narrow part of the defile
    in the Koojah Pass .... Page 135
The first descent through the Koojah Pass .... Page 137
The second descent through the Koojah Pass .... Page 139
The third descent through the Koojah Pass .... Page 141
The City of Candahar .... Page 143
The Fortress and Citadel of Ghuznee and the Two Minars .... Page 145
The Valley of Maidan .... Page 147
The Village of Urghundee .... Page 149
Entrance into Caubul from Killa-Kâzee .... Page 151
The main street in the Bazaar at Caubul in the fruit season .... Page 153
The Balla Hissa and city of Caubul, from the upper part of the Citadel ... Page 155
Caubul from a burying ground on the mountain ridge,
    North-East of the city .... Page 157
The Durbar of Shah Shoojah-ool-Moolk, at Caubul .... Page 159
The Avenue at Bâber's Tomb .... Page 161
The Tomb of the Emperor Bâber .... Page 163
Portrait of His Majesty Shah Soojah-ool-Moolk .... Page 165
Caubul Costumes .... Page 167
Sketch Map of Afghanistan .... Page 168

FOREWORD
JAMES ATKINSON
By Jules Stewart

Dr. James Atkinson, surgeon, Orientalist, soldier, artist, was also a man of extraordinary luck. Bearing the grandiloquent title of Superintending Surgeon of the Army of the Indus, in 1838 Atkinson set out from Ferozepore to accompany a doomed army on its march into Afghanistan, a 'wild, ill-considered and adventurous scheme of far-distant aggression', in the words of Sir Henry Marion Durand, one of the officers who took part in the initial stages of the campaign. The result was the massacre of an entire British force of some 16,000 souls, a catastrophe which the historian Sir John Kaye described as 'something terrible to contemplate', in the wake of which 'there had ceased to be a British Army'.

But as stated, Atkinson was lucky, for he was one of the few outstanding figures of that terrible Victorian drama who escaped the wrath of the avenging Afghans that pursued and cut down the entire retreating force in a week of merciless carnage. Atkinson was relieved in the ordinary course of routine shortly after the surrender of Dost Mohammed, the Afghan ruler who was unceremoniously unseated by the British for allegedly conspiring with the Russians. Atkinson returned to Bengal in 1841, and how fortunate for us that he was spared the fate awaiting the army of occupation.

Atkinson, who was 61 at the time, retired in 1847 after forty-two years of service. His experiences in Afghanistan left us with a personal narrative that provides an extraordinary first-hand description of the events and leading players of Britain's first disaster in Afghanistan. The book is supplemented by his *Sketches in Affghanistan*, containing a series of lithographed drawings that complete the picture of what was then an unexplored country. Atkinson's collection of twenty-five drawings depicts the march of the Army of the Indus from Sindh to Kabul in Afghanistan via Quetta and Kandahar in 1839 and 1840. He also had a talent for portraiture and several of his works, including a self-portrait, are in the National Portrait Gallery.

Atkinson was famed in his day for his immense knowledge of Persian literature. He was as an accomplished Persian scholar and served as Deputy Professor of Persian at Fort William College. Atkinson was a model for an array of later British administrators and soldiers who found themselves captivated by the people of India and in particular, the lands beyond the North-West Frontier. The name of Major George Roos-Keppel comes to mind, the man who produced a grammar of Pashtu, translated Pashtu historical works and co-founded Islamia College, now the undergraduate school of Peshawar University. Sir Olaf Caroe, the last British governor of the North-West Frontier Province, was another scholarly civil servant who wrote a seminal work on the history of the Pathans.

Atkinson was himself an accomplished poet who published his first verse at the age of 21, a romance called *Rodolpho*. His love affair with Italian poetry was cut short in 1813 when the Viceroy Lord Minto invited him to Calcutta to take up the appointment of assistant assay master at the mint. In addition to this position, he held the post of superintendent of the Government Gazette which, under his editorship, published valuable statistical and topographical information on little known parts of India. Atkinson's death of apoplexy in 1852 deprived the world of a scholar, artist and intellect in the true mould of the Renaissance Man.

Jules Stewart is the author of a history of the First Afghan War, *The Crimson Snow* (Sutton Publishing Ltd.) to be published in February 2008.

INTRODUCTION
By Merlin Hanbury-Tenison

It has always been a soldier's privilege to avoid the complicated aspect of the decisions behind a conflict or war. When asked whether or not I agree with the war in Afghanistan I have always been able to nimbly side step the question by pointing out that, as a soldier, I simply do my duty and carry out my orders as long as they are morally justifiable. The army is an instrument of policy and it is not our place to question the 'why' but merely to implement the 'how'. Normally soldiers are not particularly interested in these issues anyway. We are simply people doing a job to the best of our ability in situations that are relatively testing. Of course more recently the situation has become extremely testing in the arena of Helmand Province.

This argument is very effective when back in Britain dodging the interrogation of prying aunts and curious godparents all keen to know how the young man is turning out and how he views the world. When one is actually deployed in the desert deep in Southern Helmand we are daily answering for the decisions, made in the comfort of the United Kingdom, with hard work and considerable amounts of danger. Whilst we are all very aware that the situation in Afghanistan is very complicated and that there are many diplomatic, historic and tribal factors at play; it is still obvious that when we are at the cutting edge every soldier from the 18 year old trooper with two GCSEs to the sergeant major who has served for twenty years will form some kind of political opinion. This is only natural when the army goes to great lengths these days to ensure that every soldier from general to rifleman has some understanding of the political and social factors at play in Afghanistan. With so much at stake in the conflict we all form an opinion.

As a tank commander in command of a troop of four scimitar light tanks, I am on the front line in this conflict and am deployed for weeks at a time into the area around the Helmand River to reconnoitre and destroy Taliban strongholds and interdict their supply lines. On a daily basis we see the oppression and devastation that these so-called freedom fighters have brought upon their country. In a startlingly similar way to Dost Mohammed's regime they have pillaged the local countryside to the extent where the locals now live in conditions almost unchanged to those 170 years ago when Dr Atkinson was writing his journal. It is quite fascinating to see quite how similar the conditions really are. It was the main factor that really struck me in Atkinson's papers. With the addition of a few Massey Ferguson tractors and the exchange of the jezail for the AK47 and RPG, he could very well have been writing about Afghanistan in 2007, not 1840. His illustrations confirm this and could have been of the very enemy that I am engaged against today.

www.classictravelbooks.com

This is largely because in the intervening years, times when the country was not plunged into conflict of some sort or the other were the exception, not the rule. After Atkinson left in 1841 the country was subjected to several years of British occupation before they finally managed to expel and destroy our Army of the Indus in an infamous manner under the Dost's son, Akbar Khan. Following this was another British invasion some years later and a third in the early 20th century. Adding the Soviet invasion and occupation in the 1980s, the on-going Shia and Sunni hostilities and the civil power wars in the 1990s and it is clear to see that with Afghanistan's coloured past not much time has been available for economic growth and development.

The coalition effort (of which the British mission forms a considerable part) is currently doing its best to rectify this problem through aid programs and development projects. In Helmand the Kajaki dam project is an example of this. By repairing an old Soviet dam and installing new turbines we would be able to supply power to the whole Helmand basin; bringing them out of the dark age they have lived in since the dam stopped working in the early 90s. Unfortunately the Taliban are intent on preventing anything that they deem as 'infidel interference' from succeeding and it always seems ironic that the people whom we are intent on helping are those who harbour our enemies who employ all their energies in arresting this assistance.

There are many similarities between the invasion of 1839 and our present conflict. Atkinson writes of the excitement of all of the soldiers partaking in the invasion at the time, and the disappointment of those left behind. In the same way I remember clearly in the months approaching our deployment the pride and tangible excitement in my own troop as they prepared to go and play their part in an episode in British history that would be remembered forever. It is the light at the end of a long tunnel of training and preparation. Of course when one has arrived in theatre the light switches to the 'end of tour' date when we can all return home to see our families and loved ones. We appear to have a similar level of local support as that which Atkinson experienced. The Taliban may use local villages along the river as hideouts and supply depots. But the locals provide this facility more through fear than a belief in their cause. They are just farmers who want peace so that they can tend their crops and look after their families. They generally appreciate that our army could bring that peace in the same way that Shah Shoojah offered it to their great grandfathers who were fed up with Dost Mohammed's oppression. There are always those who are willing with information and advice to help us as we try and move the Taliban away from their villages in order to allow them to return to that very peace they all crave for.

But the main similarity in the two conflicts is one which has been overlooked by onlookers in almost every war ever fought. Hollywood is the great deceiver when it comes to accounts of campaigns. They would have us believe that every war from the siege of Troy, through both world wars and up to the current insurgencies is a non stop, action packed roller coaster ride. The reality is that ninety percent of war is an extremely tedious waiting game and Atkinson makes it clear that long periods were spent in between each skirmish and battle; during which time the troops would wait in anticipation and find ways to distract themselves from the ever present threat on the horizon.

The scene, I am sure, hasn't changed in 170 years and won't change for another 500. As I write this I am sitting with my own troop on the eastern edge of the Dasht-i-Margo (The Desert of Death, aptly named) doing what soldiers have done since time immemorial. Some tarpaulins have been hastily erected to throw some shade over our boiling bodies; the temperature is approaching 50 degrees centigrade. My troopers sit huddled in a corner with a well thumbed pack of cards. They play poker or gin rummy, using pebbles or cigarettes as counters to be exchanged for real money when we are back at camp and throwing obscenities and accusations of cheating back and forth as propriety dictates. The corporals and sergeant sit a little apart, smoking and chatting, reminiscing about their families back in England and occasionally getting up to inspect some niggling problem with one of the vehicles that the troopers should have repaired. Of course they are always quick to point out that when they were troopers work was harder and done in a less complaining manner and junior soldiers had more respect for their non commissioned officers. The view, if it were anywhere else in the world, would be described as exquisite. We are in your classic desert with pale, creamy coloured dunes all around us and not a hint of vegetation in sight. To the west is a large plateau which stretches to the horizon and is as flat as a snooker table. As the sun sets in the evening a deep orange and then purple glow is projected over everything and everyone in the troop pauses and goes quiet as we all feel the presence of the tens of thousands of soldiers from dozens of armies, both private and national, who have sat on this plain and felt these same emotions and seen this same view. The landscape of Europe and the Americas may have changed countless times in the last 170 years but that of Afghanistan remains a constant, beautiful wasteland. The life of a soldier is an ageless one and we are just one more chapter in an endless history.

There are, however, many differences in our purpose, methods and reception in Afghanistan from the army that Atkinson accompanied so many years ago. Back then the army was invading to install a ruler on the throne of Afghanistan. We had concerns over Russian, Persian and French interests in the country and needed to secure a buffer between these potential enemies and British India with it's warm-water ports. These issues are no longer valid and the appearance of the terror threat has become a much greater stimulant for our presence in the country. As a result of this we are no longer fighting the whole scale battles which Atkinson witnessed between the British army and the men of Dost Mohammed. We are now engaged in a long-term counter-insurgency campaign which has reshaped the face of warfare meaning that the classic image of two vast armies marching across a plain toward each other has probably been lost forever. We are now in the era of the IED, the suicide bomber and the hidden sniper. All threats which are just as dangerous but far harder to counter. Our methods have changed accordingly which has resulted in units like mine being utilised far more often. A highly manoeuvrable force, such as ours, is ideal for dashing up and down the irrigated areas within the Helmand river basin, fighting the serpent wherever it cares to raise its head. The enemy are able to fade in and out of existence like ghosts; retreating at ease into the green zone to either side of the river where they can blend in with the local population in a way that we will never be able to, or retiring to 'safe' areas where there is no governmental control whatsoever and they can rest and resupply at their leisure. We are fighting to reduce these areas in size and number but an army can never be everywhere at once. They can then race back at high speeds to show us that every village and every window is a possible hiding place and that every corner has a possible hidden bomb just waiting to catch you off guard.

Of course another considerable difference in the management of our army in this day and age is that all soldiers know that they will only be deployed into a conflict zone for six months. In Atkinson's day you marched with the army until the campaign was complete and were then often stationed in the conquered country for months or even years afterwards. This would have had a profound effect on the soldiers and on the environment in which we are all based. Every camp in Afghanistan has a very fluid population with men constantly arriving and departing as people's tours begin and end. This brings with it fresh minds and enthusiasm but it also means that no one is ever anywhere long enough to really become an expert in the local area. Atkinson recounts at one point meeting a subaltern who had been posted to a camp in Northern India for six years. He would have become an unquestioned expert on his area and the local tribes. These days that would be unthinkable and, certainly for a subaltern, the maximum amount of time in any post is unlikely to exceed eighteen months, even in the UK.

The final difference which I found extremely interesting in Atkinson's account is the amount that a surgeon is able to travel with a Victorian army. To travel with the Army of the Indus from port all the way to Kabul and back again by horse would be a journey that with transport aircraft and heavy-lift helicopters would be unthinkable today. In a brigade of 5,000 soldiers approximately 1,000 will see the outside of the two or three major bases within Afghanistan. The remainder will arrive on their flight from England, work for six months within a sprawling metropolis of a camp with high walls and bunkers on every corner, and then return to the UK with little experience of the country other than that it is hot and sandy. Their jobs are often equally as dangerous and even more demanding than ours. When you are in a camp the enemy know where you are and casualties have been sustained due to the enemy targeting these locations. A surgeon today will work as hard if not harder than Atkinson did; it is simply that the opportunity to see the country to the extent that was possible in the nineteenth century has diminished. Those few soldiers who do leave the camp and conduct the combat operations on the ground are the few who are privileged enough to view the true beauty and diversity of this vast and exciting country. Regrettably the sketches of a surgeon in Camp Bastion would not compare in interest or spectacle to those of Dr Atkinson.

My own ancestor, William Williams, served alongside Dr Atkinson for much of his time in Afghanistan. He was also sent as a lieutenant in 1841 when only 20 years old as a reinforcement to his regiment, the 13th Light Infantry, in Kabul. While plagued by ill health (malaria, dysentery and perhaps tuberculosis) at a time when infections ran rife through the garrison he was nevertheless engaged in numerous battles and writes eloquently in letters home to his brother of excitements and frustrations that I know to be all too familiar. He travelled through to Jallallabad with General Sale's army in advance of the Army of the Indus in that ill-fated expedition where almost 16,000 British and native troops were slaughtered by the Afghans. He writes at one point of a skirmish in a village on the way through the Tezin Valley. The enemy were hiding in the village and my ancestor's company pushed in to flush them out and got into some major fighting. He writes, "After a few volleys I saw them fall by the dozen. They fell more like rain. I set fire to some straw and some of the enemy came out and were killed by the men. Some of them preferred being burnt alive than being gentlemanly killed. I mean being shot or having a sword politely put through him or having his head easily taken off by a trooper at a blow." I can't help feeling that our expectations of Afghan conduct have changed somewhat in the intervening years!

Another ancestor of mine on my father's side of the family fought in the next Afghan campaign in 1876. William Tenison was 19 when he was sent as a young lieutenant to the 59th (Manchester) Regiment then on active service in Afghanistan. He was shortly caught up in the Battle of Ahmed Kheyl and would always recall in later years that however tough conditions and fighting were, the regimental elephants would follow the army with the silver on their backs and all of the officers would get changed every night for dinner. I'm afraid that standards have definitely slumped in that department and as I sit huddled with my troop around a tin of spam in the evenings I chuckle to imagine my ancestor, possibly in the same patch of desert, dining in style 130 years earlier.

So as the sun sets over another day in the Dasht-i-Margo and my troop and I prepare for another night spent lying in a hole in the ground next to our tanks, with a rifle or machine gun within easy reach in case of inquisitive, sleep-walking Taliban. It is clear that in the years between Dr Atkinson's stay in this troubled country and my own sojourn little has changed in the way the people, the enemy or ourselves live and go about our daily business. The technology has changed and the purpose for our being here is different too. But soldiers, on both sides, remain by nature the same creatures; with the same priorities, concerns and dreams. All we can hope is that this conflict will end in a manner which suits the Afghan people the best. They have suffered hardship and oppression for centuries now and there are many nations who must accept a part of the blame for this. Currently the reconstruction of the country is being conducted with the view to righting many of these wrongs. I just hope that the social and spiritual rift which has developed between our two nations can be healed in the process.

Lieutenant Merlin Hanbury-Tenison is a troop leader in a formation reconnaissance regiment in the British Army called The Light Dragoons. He was deployed in Helmand Province on active service for six months in 2007.

AUTHOR'S PREFACE.

The occupation of Affghanistan forms, no doubt, an important era in the annals of British India. Nearly thirty years ago, it was asserted that, if Napoleon could have passed the winter at Moscow with his four hundred thousand men, it was his intention, as his scheme *viâ* Egypt had failed, early in the following spring to have marched that number through Caubul, upon our Indian possessions; whilst the remainder, strengthened by powerful reinforcements, were to have pressed on to St. Petersburgh. In this design he was supposed to be encouraged by the recollection that, a few years before, Shah Zemaun, then King of Caubul, had put his army in motion towards the East for the conquest of Delhi. Zemaun assembled a large army for that purpose in 1796, and advanced as far as Lahore; but disorders in his own capital, which threatened the subversion of his power, and hostile demonstrations from Persia, compelled him to relinquish the enterprise at that time. He made a second and a third attempt, in the two succeeding years, and with a similar unfavourable result. A correspondence between him and Tippoo Sultan, on the subject of the invasion of India from the west, was found among the papers of the latter after the capture of Seringapatam.

Long before that period, intelligent travellers and emissaries from the courts of Europe had been making their way among the native princes of India in every quarter; and subsequently, when Mr. Elphinstone was at Bikaneer in November, 1808, proceeding on his mission to Shah Shoojah, the Rajah of that remote place appeared to be aware of the secret object of our visit, and the state of political affairs in Europe. "He shewed," says Mr. Elphinstone, "a knowledge of our relations with France, and one of the company asked whether my mission was not owing to our wars with that nation." It was certainly the arrival of the French embassy in Persia, in 1808, with other indications of Bonaparte's designs on Hindoostan, which occasioned the mission in question.

The western powers have, however, failed in their object. The views of France were frustrated, and Russian diplomacy, with an invading army, directed by the emperor in the first instance against Khiva, was equally unsuccessful. The resources of the British Empire in India have been more efficiently applied, and have placed us in possession of Affghanistan in the name of Shah Shoojah-ool-Moolk. But a semi-barbarous country newly conquered, and semi-barbarous it is compared with European civilization, can never be retained without the continuance for perhaps many years of nearly the same amount of military force by which it was acquired. There must always be a commanding power to repress the ever-vigilant and turbulent chiefs of the endless plundering tribes which inhabit the Affghan Empire. Unless, therefore, the contingent of Shah Shoojah be increased by the addition of several regiments, and those composed mainly of

Hindoostanees, officered by Europeans, it seems impossible that the British force can be withdrawn, without risking the safety of the Durranee monarchy, and abandoning a policy considered to be of the highest importance to the best interests of our vast possessions in the East. Like Sisyphus, we have rolled up the huge stone to the top of the mountain, and if we do not keep it there, our labour will be lost.

In the few works that have appeared since the restoration of Shah Shoojah, different tastes have been consulted. Plain unembellished details — commentaries on the military operations, and the gossip of the camp, have all put in their claim to favour and approbation. Yet the subject is not exhausted, nor is it likely to be, as long as British India requires Affghanistan as a barrier against the encroachment of more western potentates. Many important particulars connected with the campaign are still very imperfectly understood. Among other things, the character of Shah Shoojah, as well as that of Dost Mahomed Khan, has been greatly misconceived and misrepresented. But when facts become better known, the relative qualities of these two personages will be more correctly appreciated.

Many inveigh against the principle of the invasion in favour of Shah Shoojah, and are of opinion that gaining over Dost Mahomed to our interests would have answered every useful purpose, and at a thousandth part of the expense to the state. But Sir Alexander Burnes could make nothing of the Barukzye Ameer, who was one of the *non fits*, and, truly, taking the whole proverb, *Ex quovis ligno non fit Mercurius*, he was materially unsusceptible of being converted into the substantial bulwark required at the time by the British Government.

But however politicians may differ, nothing could well exceed the enthusiasm which prevailed among the troops on being ordered on the expedition, or the deep regret of those who had not the good fortune to belong to the Army of the Indus. There was something in the north-west — something beyond the Indus — in Khorassan and Affghanistan — which operated like a charm. A colder climate was inviting to sojourners near or within the tropics, and the valley of Caubul had been lauded to the skies for its romantic scenery, its salubrity, and its beauty. For my own part, arduous and harassing as the whole campaign was, I shall always remember having shared in its novelty, excitement, and success, with strong feelings of pride and satisfaction.

Then there was something in the supposed origin of the Affghans which invested them with a good deal of historical consequence. Hindoo and Persian traditions go so far as to state that the progenitors of mankind lived in that mountainous tract, which extends from Balkh and Affghanistan to the Ganges: a pretty extensive range for the Garden of Eden! And the river Pison of Scripture is said to compass the whole country of Havilah, and Havilah is supposed to be Caubul.[1]

Ferishta[2] gives the people a very respectable antiquity, derived from a work he had consulted in the composition of his history, in which they are said to be Copts, of the race of Pharaoh! Others think them descendants of the Jews. Subsequent and recent writers give them no such lineage, and Professor Dorn, who sees farther into a mill-stone than anybody else, concludes, from all *he* has read and studied on the subject, that they cannot be referred to any tribe or country beyond their present seats, and the adjoining mountains; and that they are in fact, as far as history goes, an original people: that they had, in other words, an Adam and Eve of their own! Tacitus pronounced the Germans *Indigenæ* or natives of the soil. But upon this Gibbon remarks:- "We may allow with safety, and perhaps with truth, that ancient Germany was not originally peopled by any foreign colonies already formed into a political society; but that the name and nation received their existence from the gradual union of some wandering savages of the Hercynian woods. To assert those savages to have been the spontaneous production of the earth which they inhabited, would be a rash inference [like that of Professor Dorn], condemned by religion, and unwarranted by reason."[3]

The expedition of Alexander the Great had also given to Caubul and its provinces a deep interest among men of antiquarian inquiry, and Kafiristan was long supposed to be peopled by the descendants of a colony of Greeks, though the Greeks were perhaps never so far north as that portion of Asia. Their fair complexions, and sitting upon chairs, unlike the tribes and nations that surround them, *seemed* to indicate a European race, and curiosity was awakened to ascertain the truth or otherwise of that hypothesis by a more close examination. But this classical phantom has now, I apprehend, "vanished into thin air." There is nothing Greek or Greekish in any of their vocabularies I have met with, but enough to shew that the dialect of Kafiristan partakes of Sanscrit, Persian, and Hindoostanee. A Kafiristanee, a female slave, was sent, among other diplomatic presents, according to the custom of the country, by the Shah of Kooner to Jellalabad when I was there. She was said to be a beautiful specimen of the softer sex. On her arrival, she was made free, and given in marriage to the servant of an

---

[1] Tradition further declares, "When Satan was ejected or kicked, as they say, out of the Garden of Eden, where he first lived, he leaped over the mountains, and fell on that spot where Caubul now stands;-hence the origin of the well-known proverb, that the inhabitants of Caubul are truly the offspring of this prince of darkness. Those of Caubul do not deny his having been at Caubul; but say, he had no offspring, was soon conjured away, and withdrew into the district of Lamgan!"- *Asiatic Researches,* vol. vi. 492.
[2] *Editor's note*: A noted Persian historian, (c. 1560-c1620), whose given name was Muhammad Qasim Hindu Shah. He wrote a popular and well-regarded history of India.
[3] Chap. ix.

Affghan in the service of the mission. I had an opportunity of seeing this imputed descendant of the Greeks. She had, as is usual among her tribe, blue eyes and brown hair, but her complexion was dark, though the general "tincture of the skin" in Kafiristan is comparatively fair. She appeared to be about forty, and had ordinary features. I was of course disappointed. and further inquiry and investigation in other quarters produced nothing to convince me that any characteristic remains of a Greek colony existed in Kafiristan.

The immense number of coins found at Eagram, in the Kohistan, near Caubul, conjectured to be the site of *Alexandria ad Caucasum,* was another attraction to many with classical recollections, anxious to traverse and explore the land which had been trod by the Macedonian hero and his victorious legions. Yet the inhabitants of that plain have never been, like the Kafiristanees, suspected of being descended from the Greeks, perhaps because they do not sit upon chairs! In 1836, Mr. Masson had procured at Bagram above thirty-five thousand coins, comprising Greek, Indo-Scythic, Bactrian, Parthian, Guebre, Brahminical, and Mahomedan, and the whole plain is said still to teem with Grecian relics, seal-rings, medals, &c., of the olden time.

Every thing, indeed, promised novelty and gratification as to personal feeling, independent of the more powerful stimulus produced by a great public enterprise, which, in breaking the wearisome monotony of military life in cantonments, pointed to a scene of active operations, from which triumph and renown might be safely predicted.

* * *

The aforegoing Preface, as well as the work itself, was written and despatched to England from India, prior to the insurrection which broke out at Caubul in November last.

It is proper likewise to state, that the original and highly-finished drawings by the author, consisting of views of the scenery and passes, representations of occurrences during the campaigns, of the costumes of the natives, &c. (referred to in the work), which have been lithographed in England, are published in a separate volume, as a distinct work.

Editor's note to the 2007 Classic Travel Books Edition: This edition of *Afghan Expedition* is the first in which the author's text and dramatic drawings have been presented together in one volume.

EXPEDITION INTO AFFGHANISTAN.

CHAPTER I.

CAUSES OF THE EXPEDITION.

Russian Influence in Central Asia — Runjeet Singh's Conquests in Affghanistan — Dost Mahomed Khan — His position and policy — Objects of the Anglo-Indian Government — Preparations for the Expedition — March of the Bengal and Bombay Columns.

The siege of Herat by the Persians, the interference of Russia in the affairs of Central Asia, and the proceedings, hostile to our interests, of the rulers of Candahar and Caubul, which threatened the peace and security of our north-west frontier, were the immediate causes of the expedition into Affghanistan, undertaken by the British Government in India to restore Shah Shoojah-ool-moolk to the throne of his ancestors.

Russian influence had been busy in Persia, and the government of Persia had not only introduced a Russian agent to Dost Mahomed Khan of Caubul, with letters from the Emperor Nicholas, but sent emissaries in furtherance of its own affairs connected with the siege of Herat.

Runjeet Singh, the sovereign of the Punjab, had, in 1834, secured among his conquests the territory of Peshawer, forming a part of the Caubul dominions, and this acquisition Dost Mahomed Khan peremptorily demanded to be given up to him, although Peshawer never was in his possession, but fell, subsequent to the dismemberment of the kingdom, to his brother, Sultan Mahomed Khan, who in lieu of it received a jagheer worth about four lacs of rupees per annum from the Sikh government. He nevertheless, in 1837, attempted to wrest the province by force from the Maharajah, and having equipped a large body of troops, which he led through the Khyber Pass, encountered the Sikh army at Jumrood, a few miles from the city of Peshawer. The action was obstinately fought, and had nearly terminated in the total discomfiture of the Affghans; but Shumsoodeen Khan, a nephew of Dost Mahomed, headed, at the critical moment, a charge of cavalry, and so formidable was the onset, that it at least equalized the fortunes of the day, both claiming the victory, and both keeping their own ground. But the effect was sufficiently conclusive; the Maharajah, however, deemed it necessary to set other engines at work more powerful than those of war, and there was no more fighting for the disputed territory.

At the time this attempt on the part of Dost Mahomed Khan was made, Sir Alexander Burnes was at Caubul, on a commercial mission, and received instructions from the Governor-General to endeavour to promote and establish an amicable understanding between the neighbouring states; but Russian and Persian interests appeared to prevail over the Caubul ruler, or his own ambition had become too inordinate to admit of the mediation. and accommodation. suggested. The Russian agent, Vicovich, was then at Caubul, received and treated by Dost Mahomed Khan in the most flattering manner; and Sir Alexander Burnes, having failed in attaining the object of his original mission, as well as the end of his further instructions, immediately took leave and returned to India.

Upon the unsuccessful termination of those negotiations, and the apparent impossibility of bringing Dost Mahomed Khan to a due sense of the dangerous policy he was pursuing, and to an adequate appreciation of his own interests, it became imperative on the government of India to act with energy and decision. There can be no question that it was the obstinacy and infatuation of Dost Mahomed which precipitated the subsequent scheme of policy; but had he been less impracticable, it is improbable that much reliance could have been placed on the stability of his power. His position as a usurper, or a conqueror, or whatever designation may be applied to seizing the government of Caubul, an integral part only of the old empire, was surrounded with great difficulty; and the questionable nature of his authority, added to the deficiency of his resources, compelling him to commit many acts of oppression, could not invest him with much substantial national power to resist any hostile encroachment from the west. He was even too weak to repress the turbulent and refractory spirit of the chiefs in remote districts, addicted as they were to plunder and rapine, so that their outrages became not only overlooked but sanctioned, on the reluctant and occasional payment of a precarious tribute, whilst the petty landholder was subject to every species of vexatious exaction. In fact, his comparatively substantial and undisputed rule did not extend further than from Mukoor, below Ghizni, to Dhukka, near the Khyber Pass; and long as he had managed to preserve his own equilibrium among contending and restless factions, it is not likely, from the fresh and powerful impulse given to the intrigues undertaken to acquire and maintain Russian and Persian ascendancy in Central Asia, and having himself, as well as his Candahar brothers, already sought the protection of Russia, that any friendly relations, which might have been entered into with him by the British Government, could have been either permanent or safe.

It will be remembered, too, that the siege of Herat was being vigorously carried on by the King of Persia, and that his successful operations might be expected to be followed by a movement further east. Even the Ameers of Sinde had been influenced by his intrigues, and the three brothers of Candahar, Kohn Dil Khan, Rehim Dil Khan, and Mehr Dil Khan, had combined with Dost Mahomed Khan for the purpose of assisting Persia in the siege. The measure resorted to at this juncture to frustrate the combination in question was one of momentous importance. It was to restore and consolidate the old kingdom, for the defence of the British empire in India, by bringing Caubul, Candahar, and Kelat into one legitimate government under Shah Shoojah-ool-moolk, then a voluntary exile at Loodianah, one of the military stations of British India. Runjeet Singh was referred to on the occasion to be a party with the British government in enabling the Shah to recover the throne of his ancestors. But Runjeet, with his usual rapacity, and not satisfied with the possession of Peshawer, required a large accession of Affghan territory to the westward, extending to Jellalabad, as the price of his co-operation. This inordinate claim, however, was at once refused, and the Maharajah at last, with apparent cordiality, united to carry the proposed measure into effect.

The geographical position of the Punjab, lying as it does between the provinces of India and Affghanistan, rendered the aid of Runjeet Singh of great importance, whether passive or active, as among other points it secured a ready transmission of our supplies to the army, and enabled us to penetrate Affghanistan from the east with a small force, whilst the grand army entered the country, *viâ* Shikarpore, from the south.

The scheme of policy once formed, and promulgated by the Governor-General, there could be no question about the promptitude necessary to mature its details. Two regiments of regular infantry, two troops of horse artillery, and two regiments of irregular cavalry, were raised with almost unprecedented celerity, under the command of British officers, in the service of the Shah, and in November, 1838, his Majesty left Loodianah in progress to Shikarpore, where the British army, already assembled at Ferozepore for the support of his cause, was ordered to join him.

It is proper to remark that a few weeks before the march, intelligence was received of the Persians having raised the siege of Herat, an event no doubt occasioned by the well-timed occupation of the island of Kharak in the Persian Gulf by a detachment of Bombay troops. But this single circumstance, important as it was, could have no effect in checking the enterprise, already agreed upon in the tripartite treaty, signed by Shah Shoojah-ool-moolk, Runjeet Singh, and the Governor-General of India.

The Bengal column of the army of the Indus marched from Ferozepore, early in December, through the territory of the Khan of Bhawulpore (who had shortly before concluded a treaty with the British Government, and had acknowledged its supremacy) to Bhukker, where an admirably constructed bridge of boats was formed by our Engineers, to cross the Indus at that point, and thence to

Shikarpore, about twenty miles west of the river. Meer Roostum Khan, of Khyrpore, one of the Ameers of Sinde, surrendered the island and fortress of Bhukker into our hands during the military operations of the campaign; but the other Ameers, who, it was believed, had actually sworn fealty to Persia, and who concluded that Sinde, which had been formerly an appanage of Caubul, might be resumed on the restoration of Shah Shoojah, thought proper to dispute our progress. In anticipation of this disposition of the Ameers, as well as to cooperate with the Bengal troops in Affghanistan, a force under Lieut.-General Sir John Keane had been ordered from Bombay, and had advanced into Sinde. The Ameers, however, soon saw the overwhelming extent of our military means, the folly and uselessness of resistance, and signed the treaty, which allowed a free navigation of the Indus, and admitted a subsidiary force within the Sinde territory, the expense of part of which to be defrayed by themselves; besides, they consented to the payment of twenty-eight lacs of rupees to Shah Shoojah, in consideration of the Shah relinquishing in future all claims of supremacy, and arrears of tribute, over the country held by them.

But before they submitted, a considerable part of our troops had been directed to march along the left bank of the Indus towards the capital, Hyderabad, with the view of bringing them more immediately to terms. The expediency of this flank movement in Lower Sinde has been questioned, on the ground that it endangered the accomplishment of the grand object of the expedition, when no loss of time ought to have been permitted in establishing the Shah's ascendancy in Affghanistan. No doubt we had good cause, from the faithless and hostile conduct of the Ameers, and power enough with so fine an army, to have levelled Hyderabad with the ground; but delay would have lost us the season to advance, and very probably would have robbed us of many of the advantages we have since obtained. Singly, and unconnected with other arrangements, the capture of the Sinde capital might have been of great moment; but compared with the comprehensive scheme of the Governor-General, it became of minor importance.

The Governor-General had appointed W. H. Macnaghten, Esq., envoy and minister at the court of Shah Shoojah, and that officer, having completed some important preliminary arrangements with the Maharajah at Lahore, hastened down the Indus to join the Shah at Shikarpore, and arrived there early in February. The flank movement had then taken place, and instructions were forthwith issued for the return of the troops which had been detached on that duty, upon the previously settled principle, that no avoidable military operation should be allowed to interfere with the great object of the campaign already stated. Sir John Keane did not appear to have required the aid of more than one brigade, and that only conditionally. Had the flank movement been continued even a few more days, considerable difficulty would have arisen, for it soon became necessary to break up that portion of the bridge of boats which stretched from Rohree to Bhukker, half-way over the Indus, in consequence of the sudden rise and rapidity of the stream. However, the troops got back to Rohree in good time, and passing over to the right bank of the Indus, were ready to advance. The Shah with his contingent crossed the river higher up, at Goth-Amil.

The Bombay column was still at Larkana, when the two brigades of the Bengal division, under Major-General Sir Willoughby Cotton, moved from Shikarpore, in the latter part of February, 1839, *en route* to Candahar. On the 4th of March, however, Sir John Keane assumed command of both columns, and the troops of the two presidencies united at Quetta, in the province of Shaul, in the beginning of April.

CHAPTER II

HISTORY OF SHAH SHOOJAH

Origin of the Durranee Empire — Ahmed Shah — Tymoor Shah — Dismemberment of the Empire on his death — Its re-union under Shah Zemaun — Assassination of Pyndah Khan — Proceedings of his son, Futtih Khan, and Shah Mahmood — Defeat and capture of Shah Zemaun — Shah Shoojah proclaims himself King — Is defeated — Raises a Force of Khyberees — Is again defeated — But at length gains the Capital and the person of Mahmood — Shah Mahmood takes the field again — Mission of Mr. Elphinstone — Defection of Muddud Khan and of Saloo Khan — Flight of Shah Shoojah — Conflicts and intrigues — The Shah imprisoned in Cashmeer by Atta Mahomed Khan — Liberated by Shah Mahmood — Designs of Runjeet Singh — The Shah proceeds to Lahore — Runjeet gets possession of the *Kohinoor* — The Shah escapes from Lahore — Makes an unsuccessful attempt upon Cashmeer — Takes refuge at the British Cantonment of Loodianah.

BEFORE entering upon the events of the campaign, it may be acceptable to the reader to be furnished with some account of Shah Shoojah, the remarkable adventures of his life, and his legitimate claim to the Durranee Empire.[4]

The monarchy of the Suddozyes, or that of Shah Shoojah's ancestors, commenced with Ahmed Shah. Nadir Shah, the celebrated conqueror, was assassinated in June, 1747, upon which Abdullah Ahmed Khan, an Affghan officer of the first rank, and distinguished by the high favour and partiality of Nadir, proclaimed himself king of the Affghans, under the name of Ahmed Shah; and the chiefs and people of the different provinces readily settled under the dominion of a man so well known for his enterprise and valour. Tymoor Shah succeeded his father in 1773. At his death, in 1793, the whole fabric of the government fell to pieces. Shah Zemaun, the son of Tymoor, mounted the throne of Caubul, whilst Humayoon seized upon Candahar, Abbass on Peshawer, and Hajee Feroz-oo-deen and Mahmood on Herat, all sons of Tymoor by different mothers.

The state of things which followed the separation of the provinces and the dismemberment of the empire did not last long, for in a short time Shah Zemaun succeeded in dispossessing Humayoon of Candahar, and, having taken him prisoner, cruelly put out his eyes; an expedient commonly resorted to effectually to destroy political rivalry without taking life, though allowing the victim to live may be considered more the effect of caprice than of any disposition to spare on the score of humanity. Caubul, especially, may be justly apostrophized thus:-

---

[4] *Durrane* is derived from *Durr* 'a pearl;' *Durri Durran,* which is the Shoojah legend or motto, meaning 'the pearl of pearls.' The name appears to have originated in the Affghans being accustomed to wear a pearl in one of their ears.

> Caubul, proud Affghan city! change and crime
> Have been thy stigma from remotest time;
> Dark, bloody, thy career, to treason prone,
> Thou'st banished sons and brothers from the throne;
> Tortured them, seared their eye-balls, as if strife
> Unnatural was the chief pursuit of life,
> And human suffering mockery. Power supreme
> In Asiatic bosoms is the theme
> Most cherished, hardening every heart to guide
> The treacherous sword of some fierce homicide.
> The softer virtues never yet controlled
> Ambition's rage — the tide has ever rolled
> With force resistless; one, one only aim,
> Possession of the throne, whate'er the claim,
> Distant or near; —and he, whose conquering might
> Seemed to secure him in his boasted right,
> Has felt, in turn, by rival vengeance sped,
> The bolt of Fate on his devoted head.

And thus it was when Shah Zemaun deprived Humayoon of his sight, he little thought that retributive justice would so soon inflict upon himself the same barbarous punishment. For a time fortune was in his favour, and Abbass was compelled to relinquish Peshawer; but he was only thrown into prison, his punishment being apparently meted out in proportion to the value of his possessions. At a subsequent period, upon receiving secret information from Wuffadar Khan, that a conspiracy existed among the nobles and chiefs at Candahar to dethrone him, and set up Shah Shoojah, his full brother, in his place, Shah Zemaun put to death Pyndah Khan, a man of distinction, who had been honoured with the surname of Ser Fraz Khan, by Tymoor Shah, together with several others, ascertained or supposed to be connected with the plot.

After the assassination of Pyndah Khan, and the confiscation of his property, always the greatest inducement to strangling or decapitation, his son, Futtih Khan, sought an asylum with Shah Morad Beg at Bokhara, accompanied by Shah Mahmood, the half-brother of Shah Zemaun. But on their arrival at that place, Morad unexpectedly betrayed a disposition to place them in confinement, and was only diverted from that act of tyranny by Meer Fazil Ahmed Sahib-zada, Serhindee, his minister, who not only succeeded in changing the king's purpose, but induced him to receive the fugitives with favour. Inaction, however, was not suited to the temperament either of Mahmood or of the renowned Vizier, and their next step was a journey to Persia, in the hope of furthering their ulterior object, and being revenged for the cruel murder of Pyndah Khan. They soon set out, and seeking an interview with Futtih Ali Shah, succeeded in obtaining a military force, with which they were enabled to proceed against Candahar.

In the mean time, Shah Zemaun had gone to Caubul, and left the government of Candahar in the hands of Meer Ali Khan, Meer Akhor, believed to be a man of the strictest fidelity and honour, who, without hesitation, however, at once betrayed his master, and gave up the city to Mahmood and Futtih Khan. Encouraged by this success, they pushed on towards Caubul, and were met by Shah Zemaun at Ghojan, where a very short conflict ensued; the treachery of Muddud Khan and all the Durranees, who fled from the king to join the standard of Mahmood, put an end to the fight. Shah Zemaun and Wuffadar Khan, in despair, then returned to Caubul, and were afterwards compelled to seek refuge in the Khyber mountains. Harassed with fatigue, and sinking for want of food, they stopped for a little refreshment at a fort near Pesh-bolak, belonging to Moollah Ashak, a Shinwaree chief, by whom they were betrayed, and delivered into the hands of their enemy. It was on his way back, a prisoner, to Caubul, at Jugduluk, that Shah Zemaun received the same punishment he himself had inflicted on his brother Humayoon! Wuffadar Khan, who had been mainly concerned in the assassination of Pyndah Khan, was tortured, and put to death.

Shah Shoojah, the full brother of Shah Zemaun, now comes on the field of action. He was then about twenty years of age, in charge of Peshawer and of the royal treasury, and, proclaiming himself king, assembled a considerable force and marched immediately towards Caubul. Midway, he found himself opposed to Mahmood's cavalry and infantry, amounting together to about three thousand men, under Shahzada Kamran and Futtih Khan. A severe contest took place, but the attack of the enemy was so overwhelming, that the Shah's ranks, after a severe struggle, gave way and were put to flight, he himself escaping with fifty horsemen in the direction of the Sufeid Koh. For two days he wandered in sadness and sorrow among the mountains, and afterwards fortunately received the hospitality of the Khyber chief, Mahomed Ameer Khan. In that asylum he remained some time; but, finding that Kamran, after taking possession of Peshawer, had, on returning to Caubul, left it in the hands of a Nazim, named Abdul Wahid Khan, his friends and the Khyberees raised and furnished him with five thousand foot, for the purpose of recovering that city. With the best promise of success, however, he was again defeated. He then retired to Choora, among the Afreedee tribes, and subsequently among the Ghiljies, suffering from the extremes of poverty and distress, but still, in his melancholy exile, cherishing the hope of ultimate success. His patience and perseverance, under circumstances of adversity and bitterness which might have discouraged the most resolute, and with a constancy and integrity of character rare indeed among his countrymen, at length received their reward.

The life of Shah Shoojah has truly been a chequered one, the principal events of which he has himself recorded with infinite frankness and candour. From the small autobiography, in the Persian language, now before me, most of the preceding facts have been drawn, and from which the following remarkable particulars are also chiefly derived.[5]

The oppressive administration of Shah Mahmood having dissatisfied and given great offence to the people, the term of his government was pronounced to be at hand, and amidst the commotion and distraction that prevailed, he at last found himself besieged in the citadel, or Balla Hissar. The air rung with uproar and confusion, and Mahmood, aware of his desperate position, with the aid of his Arabs and Hubshees, kept his cannon incessantly firing upon the town, to give an appearance of being prepared for any extremity. In the mean time, Shah Shoojah had arrived in the neighbourhood of the capital, when several chiefs, headed by Sheer Mahomed Khan, the Mooktar-oo-doulah, joined him, and urged him to enter the city immediately, the whole population being ready to receive him. But the Shah was cautious, and it was not before the second day that he moved forward, and then encamped near the Emperor Bâber's[6] tomb, where he devoted himself to prayer, and from whence, having been subsequently joined by a powerful reinforcement of horse and foot, he entered the city, and occupied the garden house of Sirdar Muddud Khan. The Arabs and Hubshees were still firing from the Balla Hissar, and the arrival of Futtih Khan, with about ten thousand men, from Candahar, at Killa Kâzee, promised for a moment relief to Mahmood; but the Vizier's force was soon dispersed, and the Shah took possession of the Balla Hissar in triumph.

This event, the accession of Shah Shoojah ool-Moolk to the throne, occurred in July, 1803. Mahmood was taken prisoner, and immured in the upper fort, but no injury, according to Affghan usage, was inflicted on his person, the Shah, from motives of humanity, disdaining to act as he had done towards his brother Shah Zemaun, whom he now immediately released from confinement and received into his family, where he still remains. He thus "scotched the snake, not killed it," and to his clemency may be attributed the subsequent loss of his throne, for Mahmood, after having been treacherously liberated from his prison, became again the triumphant rival of Shah Shoojah. It was Syud Ahmed, known also by the name of Meer Waez, the head of the Mahomedan priesthood, who performed this service for Mahmood, on the alleged plea of revenge for the death of his friend, the Mooktar-oo-doulah, who, becoming a rebel, had been killed at Peshawer, whilst in arms and fighting against the Shah. He at the same time released Kamran and other princes of the blood from confinement, and having thus "let slip the dogs of war," retired to the Kohistan, where he continued to

---

[5] The Shah never uses the equivalent to the pronoun I; but always, Humayoon-i-ma, 'our royal self.' In conversation he speaks of himself in the third person, *Sirkar,* which means 'the Government.' Sirkar heard, or ordained, or did, such a thing.

[6] *Editor's note*: The author writes a short biography of Emperor Bâber in Chapter XIV, page 212.

resist the king's authority. But condign punishment overtook the rebel; for, though a Syud, and steeped in professed holiness, as chief of the Moollahs, his head paid the penalty of his crime.

A short time before Mr. Elphinstone arrived at Peshawer, which was in March, 1809, the Shah had despatched a body of troops to recover the revolted province of Cashmeer. Attah Mahomed Khan was the rebellious Nazim, and son of the Mooktar-oo-doulah, the same Mooktar who promoted the accession of the king, became his minister, and afterwards changing sides, with the hereditary facility of an Affghan, was, as just stated, slain in arms against him. With this force, consisting of twelve thousand horse, he sent Shahzada Munsoor, Mahomed Akram Khan, and Muddud Khan, amply supplied with stores and treasure.

A few days after the departure of the Shahzada, a messenger arrived with the astounding intelligence that Shah Mahmood and Futtih Khan had captured Candahar, and that Shahzada Yusef, and Mahomed Azeem Khan, previously in charge of the government, had been obliged to fly. Indeed, Azeem Khan himself shortly joined the Shah at Peshawer and confirmed the whole disaster.

At this period, the embassy from the Governor-General of India was at hand. "I now," says the Shah, "received information that an envoy had arrived at Kohat from the *Angreez Cumpanee Bahauder* (the British Government in India), and in the usual terms of hospitality and etiquette, I gave him permission to come to me. He brought magnificent presents conformable to European taste and oriental custom, elephants, gold embroidered broad cloths, splendid mirrors of large dimensions, telescopes, and other surprising and wonderful productions of art, impossible to describe. I appointed a suitable number of persons to wait upon him and the gentlemen of the embassy, and, agreeably to the practice of Eastern Courts, every thing that would contribute to their convenience and pleasure was promptly supplied."

But the times were unpropitious, and ill-suited to the objects of the mission, the Shah's mind being occupied and distracted by the alarming state of the kingdom.

> When sorrows come they come not single spies,
> But in battalions.

And presently arrived the tidings of Akram Khan having reached Muzufferabad, among the mountains of Cashmeer, where a decisive battle had been fought and the victory obtained by the rebels. Akram Khan attributed this failure to the treachery of Muddud Khan, who had abandoned his post, and as the troops under his command were broken and dispersed, he hastily returned with a few followers to Peshawer.

No sooner had these tidings produced their discouraging effect, than accounts of Shah Mahmood having got actual possession of Caubul, and his intention to advance upon Peshawer, were received. The people were filled with amazement and indignation, and impatient to engage and punish the invader; and the Shah, with all the celerity circumstances would allow, collected new levies, and with the remnant of the troops which had by that time returned from Cashmeer to Peshawer, proceeded out of the city and encamped near the garden of Ali Merdan Khan,[7] preparatory to a movement on Caubul. It was now rumoured that Mahmood had already got to Jugduluk, about a third of the way. "Seeing that at this juncture the safety of the British mission could not be secured, and that in these troubled and treacherous times Peshawer was an unfit place to reside in, I explained," says the Shah, "in all respect and friendship, the circumstances which compelled me to suggest that the envoy should retire to Attok, till a more prosperous opportunity would permit our amicable intercourse to be renewed."

The Shah had taken the precaution to send his harem for safety towards Rawil Pindee, in the Punjab, accompanied by the blinded Shah Zemaun, and every thing being now ready, the march commenced on the 15th of June, 1809. He first encamped at Dhukka, in the Khyber Pass, sending in advance Azeem Khan and Muddud Khan, with four thousand horse, — the reported misconduct of the latter seeming to have been overlooked or forgiven. But the Shah had soon to repent this error. A communication from Azeem Khan in progress informed him, that Muddud Khan appeared to be so dejected, and expressed himself as so overwhelmed by the disgrace and disaster at Cashmeer, that nothing could raise his spirits, and that, in fact, from various other unfavourable indications, he (Azeem Khan) had no dependence on his loyalty. The Shah, in consequence, directed him to remain where he then was, till he came up with the guns and the rest of the army; but Muddud Khan, upon being made acquainted with this order, was not to be diverted from his long-meditated purpose, and moved off at once with the whole of the cavalry as far as Nimlah. From thence he corresponded with Mahmood, who had been afraid to advance further than Jugduluk from a supposed deficiency of means; but now, encouraged by the defection and advice of the traitor, pushed on with confidence to Gundumuk. There Muddud Khan joined him, and having arranged and matured their plan, returned to Nimlah.

The Shah was then at Ali Bagan, about thirty miles to the eastward of Nimlah, and when he became aware of these facts, he immediately ordered Akram Khan and Ghufoor Khan, accompanied by his own guard, to lose no time in cutting off Muddud Khan, and preventing, if possible, the effects of his treason. On coming

---

[7] At that period, the garden of All Merdan Khan was a collection of villas, divided by trees and parterres, and of great extent, situated a few miles west of Peshawer. The whole is now in ruins, and the parterres turned into corn-fields. The remains of the buildings indicate as much splendour, according to Mahomedan taste, as the remains of Adrian's villa at Tivoli, according to the Græco-Roman style of architecture.

up with him in the little valley of Nimlah, they found him with his rebel force drawn out ready to oppose them. This was on the 29th of June. The moment Akram Khan beheld this foul treachery, he imprudently, at the head of only five hundred horse, rushed impetuously down upon the enemy, and fought with such bravery, that numbers fell beneath his sword; but, unfortunately, in the midst of his intrepid career, a ball struck him through the chest, and falling lifeless to the ground, "he drank," says the Memoir, "the glass of sherbet from the hand of the Cup-bearer of Death. At the same time, Ghufoor Khan was taken prisoner, sacrificed, and attained the rank of martyr:" so says the Shah.[8]

The loss of Akram Khan seems to have paralyzed the king's efforts, for though merely an engagement with his advance, he deemed it decisive that further resistance would be vain. Submitting, therefore, with patience to what he looked upon as his destiny, he turned off towards the skirts of the Sufeid Koh, and passed a brief space among the Shinwanee tribes. At Choora, in the Khyber mountains, he remained five days; after which he was induced by the representations and advice of his people to advance on Candahar, and proceed circuitously by the way of Peshawer and Kohat. But the horizon of his fortune was again clouded; Shah Mahmood and Futtih Khan, with six thousand horse, met him at Jakan near Candahar, and both immediately prepared for action. The contest was sustained with great spirit, and the loss was considerable on both sides, but the fate of the day was decided by the defection of Saloo Khan Astikzye, on whose firmness and valour, after Akram Khan was slain, the Shah had placed his greatest dependence, and who had the command of seven hundred horse, which of course followed the example of their leader. In a moment, all was confusion and defeat, and the Shah, hurrying from the scene, pursued his way by Arghestan, and from thence towards the Indus, which he crossed near Leia, taking temporary refuge in the territory of Mahomed Khan, Suddozye.

As soon as the Khan heard of the Shah's arrival, he waited upon him, and presented him with an elephant, tents, and money, and zealously performed all the hospitable service in his power. He also gave the Shah the satisfactory intelligence, that, since the fall of Peshawer, his family had found a safe retreat at Rawil Pindee.

Runjeet Singh, ever ready to profit by the vicissitudes of fortune, now eagerly seized the opportunity of ministering to his own cupidity, by offering to aid the Shah in the conquest of Mooltan, and expressing a great desire to be honoured with an interview. This communication was accompanied by loads of presents, which were received, and a suitable return made; but no answer was given on the subject of the offer that corresponded with the cunning despot's wishes. He

---

[8] Dost Mahomed Khan is said to have been in the battle, under his brother Futtih Khan, who, for his conduct on that occasion, raised him to the rank of Sirdar.

therefore wrote again, and proposed to capture Mooltan himself, and present it to him, to prove incontestably his friendship and devotion in his service. But the Shah was unwilling to forward Runjeet's own views in this respect, and, evading the question at issue, proceeded to his family at Rawil Pindee. A short time afterwards, influenced by deliberations with his Khans, he determined to make an effort for the recovery of Peshawer. He crossed the Attok with his force, at a time, too,. when the river was full, and running with great rapidity, which might have deterred a less determined and resolute man. Mahomed Azeem Khan, brother of Futtih Khan, was then the Naeb, and on being apprized of the Shah's advance, headed his troops to meet him at Chumkunee. The two armies continued ten days within a few miles of each other, as if waiting to see what chance or accident might produce, during which period numbers deserted from the Naeb's ranks to the Shah, and Mahomed Azeem Khan and his brother, Peer Dil Khan, despairing of success from an engagement, considered it best to retreat, and pursue their course back to Caubul, leaving the Shah to take quiet possession of Peshawer.

This was a bright gleam of sunshine, but as transient as it was bright, for, in September of the same year, Mahomed Azeem Khan returned from Caubul, with a chosen force, to retake Peshawer in Mahmood's name. The battle that ensued was well contested, and the Shah's troops are said to have fought nobly; but it ended, as usual, in his defeat. After the engagement, he retired to Attok, where he stayed four days unmolested, and from thence proceeded back to Rawil Pindee.

The Shah, however, was not discouraged, and he again endeavoured to get possession of Peshawer. The renewed tyranny and exactions of Mahmood, and Futtih Khan, his minister, had more than ever exasperated the people, and a fair opportunity presented itself to risk another trial. He again crossed the Attok, and Mahomed Azeem Khan hastened again from the city to meet him. In the fight that took place, great numbers were killed on both sides. The brother of Mahomed Azeem Khan received a matchlock ball in his mouth, and died of the wound. "The Seal of Silence," says the Shah, "was placed upon his lips." The chiefs, however, seeing pretty clearly the aspect of affairs, and the little chance of a favourable result, observed to his majesty, that it was then the hour of evening prayer, and their camp at a distance in the rear. They, therefore, proposed to fall back and "fight another day!" Accordingly, the force withdrew towards Muzar-Shaik Rehimgar, and next day, instead of renewing the contest, marched to the fort of Attok, where the Shah remained for some time, and then receiving no inducement to encounter the enemy again at that time, returned to Rawil Pindee.

After he had resided a year, in undisturbed tranquillity, at that place, several of Shah Mahmood's supporters, Jehan Dad Khan, brother of Atta Mahomed Khan of Cashmeer, Semunder Khan, Bamizye, and Noor Mahomed Khan Alkozye, joined him on the plea of being disgusted with the injustice and oppressive administration of Futtih Khan. They had with them about a thousand horse, intended for the support of the Shah's interests, and, almost simultaneously, Atta Mahomed Khan sent to him, for the same professed service, fifteen hundred more, under the Dewan, Nund Ram. The Shah might have suspected, from such a combination, something treacherous; but he appears to have had no doubt of their sincerity in espousing his cause. He consequently made another bold struggle to regain Peshawer. Mahomed Azeed Khan seemed to be equally energetic, and equally prepared to contest the field; but fortune was against him. A detachment of three hundred men, which he had sent in advance towards Kerowlee, was cut off by the Shah's troops, and from this unexpected disaster he deemed it advisable to return towards Caubul, and the Shah again entered Peshawer in triumph.

Jehan Dad Khan, Semunder Khan, and Nund Ram had previously received secret instructions from Atta Mahomed Khan of Cashmeer, by every exertion in their power to get possession of the Shah's person, and, in the first place, to imprison him in the fort of Attok. There seems to have been treason on all sides, and the stratagem employed by the conspirators, or the instruments of Atta Mahomed, was a rather extraordinary one. The Khans represented to the Shah, that the horses of his troops were in a sorry condition, and now, that fighting was over, proposed that they should be sent out in different divisions to the villages about Peshawer to graze; to which all parties agreed, and the horses were distributed in various quarters accordingly. By another crowning manœuvre, the Khans secured the Shah's personal escort (whose horses were also at graze) and deposited them safely in the fort of Peshawer; whilst by a further outrage the Shah himself was put in durance by Jehan Dad Khan, kept for some time in the fort of Attok, and afterwards conveyed under that chief's own eye to Cashmeer, where he was imprisoned on the mountain called Maran! All this, detailed at length in the autobiography, looks more like a fictitious tale than an actual occurrence, and exhibits another instance of the romance of real life. The object of this train of deception and treachery was soon apparent. Atta Mahomed Khan, the Bamizye, boldly visited the Shah, on his arrival at that place of his confinement, in quest of the Kohi-noor![9]

Of this daring outrage Mahmood himself would seem to have felt the shame and the disgrace; for to such a degree was his indignation roused, when the

---

[9] The *Koki-noor,* or mountain of light, is a large diamond, said to be valued at three millions and a half sterling. This splendid gem appears to have been among the plunder taken by Nadir Shah from Mahomed Shah, when he invaded Hindoostan. From him it came into the possession of Ahmed Shah, the founder of the Durranee empire, from whom it descended to Shah Zemaun, who, when in prison, had it secretly built up in the wall of his apartment, and it was afterwards discovered on Shah Shoojah's accession to the throne, in 1803.

circumstance came to his knowledge, that he ordered five hundred horsemen to proceed forthwith against the villages of the tribe of Bamizyes, located near Candahar, to dishonour their families, and deliver up their houses to plunder and devastation. But Mahmood saw no chance of effecting the Shah's release, unless he equipped an expedition to take possession of Cashmeer; and Futtih Khan, accompanied by Dost Mahomed, was sent in command of the troops for that purpose. On his arrival at Shubyan, Atta Mahomed made a show of resistance, and a considerable display of troops; but, on further weighing the chances in favour of and against his success, he determined to fall back and retire to the fort of Sheergur, on the plains of Buttamaloo. He there pondered on the difficulties of his situation, and came to the resolution of throwing himself at once on the clemency of the Shah, as the only probable way of escaping from the peril to which his base conduct had exposed him. Accordingly, becoming his own advocate, he appeared before his majesty in miserable plight, with a rope round his neck, and solicited pardon for his great crime in the most abject and urgent manner. His supplication was dexterously preferred, and rendered more impressive by being well garnished with suitable passages from the Koran. The Shah listened patiently to the earnest and impassioned appeal to his humanity, surveyed him with an eye that penetrated his soul, and then, in the spirit of forgiveness, "commanded by God and the Prophet, acceded to his prayer." These are the words of the memoir.

Futtih Khan had now taken possession of the city, where the Cashmeer troops, deserting from Atta Mahomed, joined his standard. Soon afterwards, he paid an honorary visit to the Shah, accompanied by Mokum Chund, Runjeet Singh's sirdar, and both were graciously received; but the ill-starred king never seems to have been free from the machinations of his false friends or of his open enemies. At the time the expedition proceeded from Caubul against Atta Mahomed for his liberation, Runjeet Singh had secretly a stake in the deep game that was playing. He had already effected the removal of the Shah's family from Rawil Pindee to Lahore, on the pretext of greater safety, and it was part of his scheme, in concert with Futtih Khan, to induce the Shah to make choice of the same place. There was no difficulty in accomplishing this object; for the moment he knew that his family was there, he expressed a strong desire to be with them; and the two chiefs, pleased with the success of their manœuvre, facilitated his departure for Lahore with the greatest alacrity.

On his way to Lahore, the Shah was frequently besought by the chiefs of the places he passed through to take possession of Cashmeer in his own name, and they engaged to supply the means; but he replied, with proper feeling, "Shah Mahmood sent Futtih Khan to release me from prison, and I cannot return evil for good."

Upon Runjeet Singh hearing of his approach to Lahore, he sent his son,

Kurruck Singh, with Ram Singh, and other chiefs, to meet him on the road, to give his illustrious guest an honourable welcome, and to escort him into the city. Two days after his arrival, he was visited by Ram Singh, whose sole object appears to have been a sight of the *Kohi-noor!* But the Shah said that he had it not then by him. In two days more, Ram Singh went again, and again requested to be allowed to see the *Kohi-noor,* and received the same answer as before. The words had scarcely been uttered, when he heard a voice, saying, " Sometimes bread is denied, and sometimes water," and his people from that moment looked upon him as a prisoner.

In this manner, a month passed away, and every time the *Kohi-noor* was demanded, the answer was to the effect of "any thing in kindness, but nothing by force." After that, about fifty thousand rupees were at different times presented to the Shah, in the name of *nuzurs;* but this was only the prelude to another demand for the *Kohi-noor,* which was met as before. In a few days, Runjeet Singh himself paid a visit to the Shah, professed for him the warmest friendship and esteem, and, for the purpose of producing a favourable impression upon him, entered of his own accord into a written agreement, under the most solemn asseverations, calling upon the spirit of Baba Nanuk,[10] and of every thing sacred among the Sikhs, that the lands of Kotkamaleea, Jungsyal, and Kalla-noor should be settled upon him for his expenses for life, and that for the recovery of his kingdom he would gladly furnish both money and troops to any extent. The crafty Sikh succeeded in his purpose by a constant application of flattery, and the Shah, deceived and cajoled by his empty promises, at length gave up to him the *Kohi-noor.* After this, he soon discovered that the revenues of the three villages assigned to him had been for the current year already exacted, and in aggravation of that base transaction, he found himself strictly guarded on every side. "Despair," says the Shah, "betrays the soul of an infidel; my freedom is still within the scope of possibility, and if not obtained by my own efforts, it may be granted by the goodness of God."

---

[10] Nanuk Shah was the founder of the Sikh religion. He is said to have been born in 1469, in the province of Lahore, and led a life of extreme austerity. His doctrine inculcates devotion to God, his perfect unity, and peace towards man. The form of ceremony established by Nanuk in congregations, consists of a hymn in praise of the unity of the Deity; then a prayer against temptation; for grace to do good; for the general benefit of mankind, and for a particular blessing on the sect which he denominated *Sikh,* or devoted followers. He travelled much, visited the most famous places of sanctity among the Hindoos, and the temple of Mecca, and died at an advanced age at Kertipore; and was burned near the river Ravi, the Hydraotes of the Greeks. The object of Nanuk, living as he did in times of furious animosity between Hindoo and Mussulman, appears to have been a sort of amalgamation of the doctrines peculiar to each. But practically the Mahomedan is perhaps more hostile to the Sikh than even to the Hindoo, and he again is equally despised and detested by the Sikh.

His first object, under this misfortune, was to secure the safety of his family. He had several friends who resided at Loodianah, and his wish was to have the zunana conveyed thither, and placed under their protection. But how? Every kind of scheme was thought of, and nothing seemed to promise success. Four different times had the women disguised themselves in the dress of the common people of that quarter, and failed as often. At last, however, they effected their escape from the city of Lahore. "A thousand thousand times," says the Shah, "did I thank God for their happy deliverance from the grasp of the tyrant."

When Runjeet Singh was informed that the family of Shah Shoojah had escaped, he was exceedingly enraged, and immediately doubled the sentries over the king. Eight armed men were placed at the door of his prison-room, and, during the night, four of them stood with lighted torches in their hands. The Shah passed months in this ignominious thraldom, with a very scanty allowance of food. After a variety of stratagems had occurred to his mind, and proved fruitless, the means of escape dawned upon him. He raised up a few boards of the floor of his room, and tried to squeeze himself through the opening. He effected that object, and cautiously dropped down below into a lumber-room. Groping about, he discovered a succession of seven other small rooms, and having ascertained that success was within his reach, he returned to his prison to make the necessary preparations. At night, he put a servant in his bed, disguised himself in other clothes, and then descended in the dark through the aperture, followed by four domestics habited like fakeers. Having passed through the seven rooms, he came to the public drain of the city, through which he crept on all-fours, and emerging from it, reached the bank of the Ravi, where the boatmen, previously. bribed, were in waiting. The boat was rapidly pushed across, and as soon as the Shah landed on the other side, he journeyed on, and, sometimes on horseback and sometimes on foot, with great fatigue and difficulty, reached Seealkote, about seventy miles to the northward of Lahore. From thence he moved on to Jummoo, where he took refuge in the obscure hovel of a dyer.

Rest had now become necessary from the weariness and indisposition produced by the long and rapid journey; but the Shah had scarcely been seated half an hour, before a person, favourably known to him in other times, discovered him, and recommended his instant departure, as it would be dangerous, he said, to remain a moment longer at Jummoo, well aware as he must be of the vigilance and activity of Runjeet Singh, who had no doubt sent parties in all directions to intercept him. This warning was sufficient to rouse the wearied Shah to pursue his now more difficult way, for the flat plains of the Punjab had disappeared, and stupendous mountains were before him. Crossing one of them, he descended into the valley of the Cheenab, and remained at a village belonging to the son of the Rajah of Jummoo till a *jalah,* or float, made of inflated skins, could be prepared for crossing the river. Next morning, the raft being ready, he passed over with his four domestics. A few miles ahead, he observed a fort, which he was told belonged to the Rajah of Bimber, and the troops of Runjeet Singh were actually besieging it at the time for arrears of revenue. The Shah, in great alarm, altered his course to another village, and, on the seventh day, reached Rajour, where Rajah Akeer Khan, being informed of his arrival, waited upon him, and hospitably furnished him with every thing that under his pressing circumstances could be required.

During his stay at Rajour, he happened to be joined by the train of household followers he had left behind him at Lahore, so that he had now with him not less than a hundred horse. No mention is made in what manner this cavalcade eluded the vigilance of Runjeet's myrmidons, after the escape of the Shah had been known; but the city and suburbs of Lahore are so populous, and the crowds passing in and out of the city generally so dense, that a few scattered horsemen would scarcely be noticed.

With this reinforcement, and the anticipated assistance of the Rajah, whose hospitality and apparent zeal in his service had filled his mind with visions of prosperity, he now seriously meditated the recapture of Cashmeer; but the Rajah was apprehensive of the consequences to himself in the probable event of failure, and declined all co-operation in that design. He was, notwithstanding, strongly encouraged in the projected enterprise by a deputation from the Rajah of Kustwar, who promised to further his views' with hand and heart; and the Shah, gladly accepting the proffered assistance, immediately moved back towards Badrowar, and recrossed the Cheenab. On his approach to Kustwar, the Rajah gave him a most flattering welcome, and honoured him with presents of great value. After remaining at that place about three months, constantly receiving the most cordial and distinguished attention that could be paid even to a reigning sovereign, he set off, accompanied by the Rajah, in progress to Cashmeer. The Rajah had raised money by disposing of all his jewels, which enabled him to take the field with two thousand Hindoostanees and fifteen hundred of his own men.

Mahomed Azeem Khan was at that period naib of Cashmeer, and, perfectly informed of the intended attack, had prepared for a vigorous resistance. The Shah's troops, notwithstanding the heavy falls of snow and rain that occurred at the time, dispersed the enemy on several occasions; but the intense cold was fatal to numbers of the Hindoostanees, and entirely paralyzed their exertions. "Nothing," says the Shah, "could transcend the valour of the Rajah in leading on his men," and, in the warmth of his gratitude, he thus addresses him in verse;-

> Heaven's blessing upon thy noble sire,
> Who filled thy mind with martial fire,
> Placing example great before thee;
> And blest the mother, too, who bore thee!

But the struggle was of no avail; three more days of incessant rain and snow, and a deficiency of supplies, compelled the Shah and the Rajah to give up the contest, and return to Kustwar.

The Shah continued nine months more the Rajah's guest; after which, the desire of visiting Loodianah, and seeing his family, came over him with irresistible force, besides the unexpired hope of being able to make a further effort to regain his kingdom from that quarter. The communication of this apparently sudden resolution was heard with tears by the Rajah of Kustwar, who tried to dissuade him from the journey, on the urgent ground that he could not venture through the territories of Runjeet Singh, and that the route over the mountains towards Tibet was beset with still greater danger. But the Shah replied, "There may be hardship and peril among the mountains, from fatigue and difficulties of the way — my own country is a country of mountains; but I shall meet with no enemy to molest me:" and he made preparations for his departure. He took with him a hundred men, and the Rajah accompanied him two stages, parting from him with tears and boundless expressions of attachment to his cause. The Shah travelled fifteen stages, night and day, with but few and short intervals of repose, suffering extremely from cold, frost, and snow; and, almost exhausted by the inclemency of the weather, he arrived on the borders of Tibet. From thence he sent back the confidential followers of the Rajah, who had appointed them to attend him thus far, and now employed the people of the country to carry his baggage and supplies over the hills. Pursuing cheerfully and without interruption his journey, he crossed the Sutledge, passed through Subathoo, and arrived in safety at the British cantonment of Loodianah, where he was united with his family. This was in November, 1815.

CHAPTER III.

HISTORY OF SHAH SHOOJAH CONTINUED.

State of Affghanistan — Inroads of the Persians — Hajee Khan Kanker — Dost Mahomed Khan — His outrageous conduct at Heart — Futtih Khan imprisoned, and his eyes put out by Shah Mahmood — His brothers resolve on revenge — They espouse different causes — Azeem Khan treacherously induces Shah Shoojah to make another attempt to regain the throne — The Shah defeated and returns to Loodianah — Atta Mahomed punished with loss of sight — Proceedings of Shah Mahmood and Prince Kamran — Futtih Khan cut to pieces — Shah Mahmood, abandoned, flies to Candahar — Sultan All Shah strangled — Designs of Dost Mahomed Khan — He obtains possession of Ghizni — Conflict between Azeem Khan and the Sikhs — Disunion of the Barukzye brothers — Dost Mahomed Khan secures the supremacy at Caubul — Shah Shoojah makes another effort to recover his power — Is defeated before Candahar — Returns to Loodianah.

THE Shah had resided quietly two years at Loodianah, when he received intelligence from Affghanistan, which gave new encouragement and energy to his hopes. At Herat, Futtih Khan had been plotting the seizure of Kamran, and the Shahzadah, made aware of the circumstances, soon found the means of being revenged upon his enemies.

When Futtih Khan and Dost Mahomed returned from Cashmeer, after the liberation of Shah Shoojah, they learned from Shah Mahmood, that Futtih Ali Shah was perpetually making hostile inroads near Herat, and keeping Hajee Ferozdeen, his brother, in a constant state of alarm. A council being held upon this state of affairs, the Vizier undertook to make the king's mind easy, and immediately set off with a strong force towards Herat. The Affghans and Persians met, and a sanguinary encounter is said to have taken place, in which vast valour was displayed, as usual; but, strange to say, in Oriental warfare, neither claimed the victory. Both thought themselves defeated, and ran off in opposite directions. Futtih Khan was slightly wounded in the conflict. On his return, Mahmood was at Candahar, where a new course of policy was immediately hatched, for the removal of Hajee Feroz, on the plea of his being unequal to the government of Herat, and unworthy of trust. Futtih Khan proceeded forthwith on this expedition, and the instrument employed was Hajee Khan Kauker, of whom more hereafter.

The Hajee was equal to any thing for which circumvention, cunning, and treachery were the predominant qualities required, and plans were easily laid by him to seize and imprison the unsuspecting governor, whom he delivered into the hands of Dost Mahomed Khan. The Dost, with the ball at his foot, only thought of turning it to the most advantage. He lost no time in penetrating into the zunana and the Harem Serai, in search of jewels and treasure. From the arms, ears, and neck of a daughter of Mahmood, given in marriage to the son of Hajee Feroz

Deen, he with his own hands dragged off ornaments of great value, and otherwise disgraced the family. This outrage excited the strongest indignation in the breast of Futtih Khan, who determined to punish the offender severely; but Dost Mahomed, apprized of his intention, fled to Caubul with his plunder. Instructions were, however, sent to apprehend him there; but again the wily depredator escaped, and sought security with his brother, Mahomed Azeem Khan, at Cashmeer. Azeem Khan at first pretended to be as angry with Dost Mahomed as Futtih Khan, but matters soon became accommodated.

When this infamous transaction was heard of at Candahar — particularly infamous in the East, where the Harem Serai is universally looked upon as a sacred retreat — Kamran said to his father Mahmood, "This, I have no doubt, is the work of Futtih Khan — he is at the bottom of this shameful violation of the zunana, and has himself urged Dost Mahomed to commit the outrage. If you do not visit the crime and the criminal with just punishment, your own family and mine may be treated to-morrow in the same atrocious manner." In reply, Mahmood assented to whatever course Kamran might deem it proper to pursue, and the Shahzadah was soon on his way to Herat, with Atta Mahomed Khan, by whose advice Futtih Khan was apprehended, thrown into prison, and his eyes put out.

Upon this intelligence reaching the brothers of Futtih Khan, they all resolved on revenge, and throwing off their allegiance to Mahmood, thought of nothing but deposing him, and raising one of his brothers to the throne. Yar Mahomed Khan espoused the cause of Shahzadah Ayoob; at Peshawer. Nawaub Sumud Khan, Sultan Ali Shah, at Caubul, and Peer Dil Khan went towards Derajat, to bring in Shah Shoojah. Each party began to coin money in the name of the new king, and had his accession proclaimed in the mosques. Amidst this turbulence and rivalry, Kamran's son, Jehangeer, and Atta Mahomed Khan, marched from Herat to Caubul, and endeavoured to crush the rebel authority there; but they were unequal to tHe task, and compelled to return back to Candahar. Mahomed Azeem Khan, who had amassed great wealth at Cashmeer, also hearing of the misfortune that had happened to his brother, sent Dost Mahomed in advance towards Caubul with a small force, and followed himself with an army of horse and foot, appointing another brother, Jubbar Khan, to take charge of the province. Before leaving Cashmeer, that insidious Barukzye had written in strong terms to Shah Shoojah, advising him to embark in another expedition for the recovery of his throne; and the Shah, always eager to accomplish the object nearest his heart, and at such times apparently as inaccessible to suspicion as regardless by whom the ever welcome stimulus might be applied, readily made another effort.

He proceeded this time by Bhawulpore, the Khan liberally assisting him with troops and money, and crossing the Gharri at that point, he passed circuitously through Dera Ismael Khan towards Peshawer. Peer Dil Khan joined him at the former place, and attended him on his route. Shahzadah Ayoob, becoming alarmed by the formidable accounts which reached him of the Shah's force, fled from Peshawer, and left the city unprotected. Shah Shoojah, however, had not been long there, before his pretended friend, Mahomed Azeem Khan, approached from Cashmeer, and it was then rumoured that, instead of coming to assist him, his expedition had a far different object; in short, the capture of Shah Shoojah himself. His majesty in consequence retired towards the mountains, and was again unfortunate; for, after halting and giving battle to Azeem Khan, his magazine by some accident blew up, and killed or disabled his gunners, putting his whole force into inextricable confusion, which obliged him to quit the country by the way of Kohat. He stayed a considerable time at Shikarpore, where he was well received by the Ameers of Sinde, and returned through Ajmeer and Delhi to Loodianah.

The real object of Mahomed Azeem Khan was further shewn by the recal of Ayoob to Peshawer, and it is also said that Dost Mahomed, even then averse to Shah Shoojah's restoration to the throne, was mainly instrumental in producing the catastrophe just described.

Shah Mahmood and Kamran were now on their way from Candahar towards Ghizni, and Sultan Ali Shah directed Sumud Khan, Yar Mahomed Khan, and Dost Mahomed Khan, who had proceeded to the capital, to arrest their progress and bring them to action. Atta Mahomed Khan had at that time abandoned Jehangeer, and going to Caubul, was well received by Sultan Ali Shah; but Yar Mahomed, ascribing to him solely the cruelty exercised on Futtih Khan, was resolute in advising a similar infliction on Atta Mahomed, whose "visual ray" was accordingly extinguished, and with at least equal torture. Whilst this retributive act was being perpetrated, an additional atrocity was on the eve of commission.

Mahmood and his son Kamran soon arrived at Ghizni, and proceeded from thence onwards to Hyder-khail. They were enraged at the hostility displayed by the Barukzye brothers in support of Sultan Ali Shah, and, determined to make a terrible example of the blinded Vizier, who was carried along with them in fetters, called together all the Durranees, and mercilessly commanded them to cut him to pieces alive. Populzye, Noorzye, Alikozye, Ishakzye, and other classes of the same race, performed this horrid deed. Ears, nose, arms, and legs, were severed from the body of the miserable man, so that each might have a share in his destruction, with the view that none of them might afterwards be received as partisans of the rebel brothers. The remains of Futtih Khan were collected together and buried at Ghizni. The tomb, bearing an inscription on white marble, is situated in a walled garden about a mile on the east side of the fortress.

Shaghasee Dilawer Khan, whose share in that dreadful mutilation consisted in depriving Futtih Khan of his ears, suddenly left the camp of Mahmood, and joined Dost Mahomed Khan at Chahardeh, declaring that it was wholly on compulsion that he had participated in the mutilation and murder of Futtih Khan. The politic and timely pardon of this chief led to the junction of others, and Mahmood soon found himself abandoned by the Durranees, and compelled to retreat with his son Kamran to Candahar. Ghizni thus fell into the hands of the Barukzye sirdars.

Mahmood's flight and the fall of Ghizni having come to the knowledge of Mahomed Azeem Khan, that ambitious sirdar marched at once from Peshawer with Shahzadah Ayoob on Caubul, and urgently advising the deposal of Sultan Ali Shah, the prince readily concurred in the necessity of the measure, and felt no compunction in ordering him to be seized and strangled! This obstacle being removed, Ayoob and Azeem Khan turned their attention to the sirdars in possession of Ghizni, and were in their turn successful. But Dost Mahomed doubled back on Caubul, and there industriously stirred up the Khizzelbashes in his favour, his mother being of that tribe. The numbers which flocked to his standard corresponded with the indefatigable exertions he made to oppose his brother Azeem and Ayoob, both of whom he publicly represented as his bitterest enemies, and whom he threatened to destroy if their hostility continued. Of this state of things Mahomed Azeem Khan soon became aware, and returned to Caubul to punish his rebellious brother, and secure Ayoob on the throne. Whether it was that the Khizzelbashes repented and abandoned Dost Mahomed, or that he despaired of success, the restless chief deemed it expedient to fly on the approach of his brother, and take refuge at Kohat. But he did not stay there long. Ghizni was again the object of his ambition, and seeing no impediment to his progress in that direction, he proceeded with a few followers across the mountains. At that juncture, the fortress was in the hands of Abdoo Rohman, on the part of Mahomed Azeem Khan, with a tolerably good garrison, and therefore, like the Persian heroes of old, recorded in the *Shahnameh,* who had recourse to every stratagem to compass their ends, the Dost is said also to have manifested his superior cunning by entering the fort in disguise, under the pretence of buying and selling. He had little difficulty in getting introduced to the governor, and, while in the act of carrying on his assumed traffic, seized the favourable moment, and shot him through the head! Then, throwing off his disguise with melodramatic effect, he declared himself, and again became master of Ghizni. So goes the story; and this exploit is called one of Dost Mahomed's most remarkable achievements! Azeem had in the meanwhile settled at Caubul, and though he received the account of the outrage above described with great indignation, the times were so much "out of joint," that he thought it advisable to overlook the recent violence of Dost Mahomed, to whom he despatched a messenger, saying, "I cannot forget that you are my brother, but you have indeed acted ungratefully towards *me;* and yet I cannot refuse to pardon you." The Dost, however, not satisfied with forgiveness, demanded to be continued as governor of Ghizni, and his demand was complied with.

At a subsequent period, Mahomed Azeem Khan, elated with his prosperity, and aspiring to attain the distinction of a conqueror, meditated a descent on the Punjab, to snatch the sceptre from Runjeet Singh. For this purpose, he embodied a large army, consisting of Khizzelbashes, Durranees, and all the Faithful of Peshawer, Candahar, and Ghizni, and proceeding to Peshawer, issued orders for the siege of Attok. Breathing vengeance against the Sikh infidels, and in the name of the Prophet proclaiming his expedition a holy war, he got as far as Noshera, which is situated between Peshawer and the Attok, with his reputed Ghazees, or champions of the faith. Runjeet Singh, informed of the intended attack on his territory, moved from Lahore, with unparalleled celerity, to oppose Azeem Khan, and is said to have accomplished the march in the short space of six days, a distance of two hundred and sixty miles. The conflict which followed was, according to Affghan report, disastrous to the Sikhs, from whom several guns were captured, and Phoola Singh, a principal sirdar, was slain. Night stopped the battle, but not the vigour of the Maha Rajah's resources in times of need. Other instruments than guns and swords were put in requisition, and so admirable were his tactics, that the weathercock brothers, Dost Mahomed, Yar Mahomed, Sultan Mahomed, and Syud Mahomed, were bought over, and rendered useless to Mahomed Azeem Khan, who, disappointed and disgraced by the failure of his enterprise, upon the success of which he had so confidently relied, retired to Caubul, and is said to have died of grief.[11] His son, Hubeb Oolah Khan, then became Naib of Caubul, and soon found himself in a position of great difficulty, for Dost Mahomed marched from Peshawer against him, and though the nephew for some time had sufficient force to resist the uncle's invasion, he was at last obliged to succumb. The immense wealth of his father, obtained in Cashmeer, said to be about three millions sterling, was secured by Dost Mahomed and his confederate brothers, reserving the largest share to himself, together with the great object of his ambition, supremacy and sovereignty at Caubul.

His first care, after his self-elevation, was to prevent the chance of his brothers disturbing his dominion, and as the chiefs of Kohistan were the most powerful and influential in that quarter, he was unceasing in his exertions to win them to his favour. Some he gained by promises, and others, who resisted his authority, were terrified by most unwarrantable severity. Beheading, hanging, and strangling were promptly resorted to, and among the victims are numbered

---

[11] The battle took place in 1823. Dost Mahomed and Yar Mahomed deserted in the night, and took with them the whole of the artillery, with which they had been entrusted, back to Peshawer. Dost Mahomed shortly afterwards visited Runjeet Singh.

Khajah Khanjee, Sahibzadah Oosben, Mazoo of Tagaw, and Mohamed Shah Khan, the father of Meer Musjidee Khan.

But to return to Shah Shoojah. It might be supposed that the unvarying repetitions of discomfiture and misfortune would have completely subdued his spirit, and induced him to repose, during the remainder of his life, in the security and quiet of a domestic home, protected and pensioned as he was by the British Government. And this peaceful state of mind may have been presumed from the fact of the succeeding fifteen years, a long interval, having elapsed without one outward appearance of his contemplating the possibility of entering upon another campaign. But his spirit was not to be conquered, and in February, 1833, he was again in arms with the same object in view, invited by chiefs and heads of tribes on whom he as usual placed full reliance. Ghilzyes and Durranees were equally pressing, and the Ameers of Sinde tendered their most zealous support in the event of his making another effort for the recovery of his dominions. Indeed he was encouraged on all sides, and even Runjeet Singh presented him with a lac[12] and twenty-five thousand rupees to assist in carrying on the war, but not without the prospect of ample compensation, for it was stipulated that, on the king's re-ascending the throne of Affghanistan, Peshawer should be added to the Punjab.

The Shah left Loodianah with two guns drawn by bullocks, and about four hundred men. At Malar-Kotela, where he continued a month, his little army became increased to one thousand, horse and foot, all of them Sikhs, Rohillas, and Hindoostanees; he then moved to Bhawulpore. From the Khan of that province he received an old gun, fifteen camels, and four thousand rupees in cash. With this further accession to his means, he proceeded onwards, and having arrived at Subzulkote, which is the boundary of the Sinde dominions, he crossed over the Ghurra towards the left bank of the Indus. At that season, the river was full and rapid, and great difficulty arose from the reluctance of the boat-people to venture upon the foaming flood. On that account, the passage of the troops occupied several days.

When the Shah arrived at Shikarpore, the Ameers of Sinde sent their Vakeel, Kazim Shah, with five thousand horsemen, to meet and give him welcome. His army now amounted to thirty thousand, and remaining at Shikarpore several months, the number was augmented to fifty thousand. The Ameers presented him with four guns, fifty camels, and about two lacs of rupees; but this was not quite sufficient to satisfy the Shah's expectations; and the Ameers preferred fighting to making any further payment. Accordingly, war was declared, and the field of battle was at Sukher-Bhukker, on the right bank of the Indus.

It is so common a thing with Affghans to see the most enthusiastic friends

---

[12] *Editor's note:* A lac was 100,000 rupees, a rupee being with about a tenth of a pound until 1870.

faithless, and the most atrocious traitors trusted, that consistency of principle and all honourable feeling must be by them considered non-existent among mankind. On the Shah's arrival at Shikarpore, he was joined by Jehan Dad Khan, from Candahar, and Semunder Khan from Hydrabad, as his devoted adherents; the very men who treacherously carried off his majesty from Peshawer to Cashmeer, and imprisoned him, at the instance of Atta Mahomed Khan, on Mount Maran. Having now taken them into his full confidence, he entrusted them with twelve thousand of his picked men, horse and foot, and six guns, to attack the Sindian force, said to amount to between sixty and seventy thousand. The engagement which followed was one of the most fierce and sanguinary that had occurred during his repeated struggles for his crown. The Sindians were defeated; two thousand were drowned in endeavouring in their flight to get across the Indus, and about fifty chiefs on the enemy's side were killed in the action.

After this brilliant result, the Shah turned his views towards Larkana, about fifty miles to the southward of Shikarpore, and had begun his march, when the Nawaub Bahader Khan averted the dreaded invasion by a timely present of a lac of rupees to the Shah, and another lac between the two profligate chiefs, Jehan Dad Khan and Semunder Khan.

The Shah had now eighteen guns, and, elated with past and present success, proceeded towards Candahar. He crossed the desert called the Put, a march of twenty-eight miles, by night; in four days he got through the Bolân Pass, and from Dusht-i-bedoulut advanced on Shaul Mustoong. From that place, he sent Semunder Khan with a communication to Mehrab Khan, of Kelat, summoning that chief to his presence, and requiring the customary offerings. In the meantime, he directed the whole army to move on under his eldest son, Shahzadah Tymoor, and remained himself at Mustoong with a body of horse, to receive Mehrab Khan and his presents. Mehrab Khan, however, being radically rebellious, did not make his appearance, but, after a week had elapsed, sent, not in loyalty, but in bitterness, and on compulsion, a lac and a half of rupees, twelve camels, and two fine horses for his majesty's use,

The Shah then pushed on and overtook his army in the Pisheen Valley. He crossed the Kojak Pass by the same route as that afterwards taken by the Army of the Indus, and arrived before Candahar with his army, increased by daily accumulations to upwards of 60,000 strong. An Asiatic force cares not to carry forward any supplies. Commissariat arrangements are wholly unknown. The soldiers are everywhere at free quarters, and the country through which they pass is consequently subjected to the most wanton spoliation. This accounts in a great measure for the continual increase of numbers on the march of an Asiatic army, a license being thus easily obtained by the unprincipled for all sorts of pillage and devastation.[13]

Several marches before the Shah reached Candahar, he had to encounter parties of the enemy, which he overpowered and dispersed as often as they presented themselves. On his arrival, he encamped close to where the old city of Nadir Shah stood, and consumed two months in preparations for the siege. He invested the three sides of Candahar on which the Herat, Shikarpore, and Caubul gates are situated, and in the meantime, the three brothers were not inactive in resisting his efforts. After a severe conflict, however, the Shah secured possession of two important positions, the Rouza-i-Hizrut, and the garden of Rehim Dil Khan, outside, but near the city walls.

He now received intelligence that Dost Mahomed Khan had left Caubul with a large army, but the news was qualified by the information that the troops were scantily provided with supplies, and that the movement was likely to lose him the capital, when left to itself. Numerous councils of war were held in consequence, aud various opinions delivered, when tidings suddenly arrived that Dost Mahomed Khan was actually within a march or two of Candahar. Some of the Khans now advised that the Shah's army should retire on Bala-Kerz and other contiguous villages; others that the army should take up a position at Abbasabad, where grain, water, and all kinds of fruit abounded; and others advised the old city, then, as now, desolate and abandoned, as the best calculated for the protection of the camp. Every man clamorously expressed himself according to his own views, and in the end the ground decided upon was Abbasabad, commonly called Abba-Saba, near the Chehel Zeena, and under the mountains Kohi-nigar.

The day after the Shah had changed his position, Dost Mahomed arrived, and was saluted from the fort with fifty guns. On the following morning, at eight o'clock, he advanced against the Shah's army, with his Jezaelchees and camel guns, and was met with determined bravery by the Rohillas and Hindoostanees. The Shah encouraged his men incessantly; he was richly dressed, armed with bow and arrows, sword, shield and dagger, and mounted on a white charger splendidly caparisoned. He was surrounded by his Khans, and the battle raged in every quarter, sometimes favourably, sometimes adversely, to either party. At last, Dost Mahomed's force gave way and fell back towards the Herat gate, in spite of his threats and exhortations not to abandon the field. He bore the Koran, his constant resource, high in the air, imploring the flying troops to turn back, but in vain. He is said to have lost four guns in that panic; after which, a sudden change of fortune took place. "Destiny, which confounds the vigour of the

---

[13] But this remark does not strictly apply to the advance of the Shah. There were contending parties in the field, and the superior numbers which flocked to his standard shewed at least that *his* cause was not unpopular.

strong, gives energy to the weak—who can control destiny!" So says the Persian writer from whose description this account is drawn. The fugitive army, ashamed of their cowardice, stopped short under the walls of Candahar and turned round to resume the fight. At this moment, the shock was great, and confusion seems to have fallen equally on both sides, for the Caubulees, on recovering from their fright, found to their surprise that the troops of the Shah were in their turn retreating. This is said to have arisen from an injudicious movement made by Mr. Campbell, an Indo-Briton, in his majesty's service, on whose experience and gallantry he relied. He had fearlessly charged with his infantry a large body of the enemy's cavalry, and in the *melée* received several desperate wounds, which brought him to the ground. The Hindoostanees, seeing him fall, lost heart, and a general rout took place among the royal troops. Still, it is presumed, there must have been treason in the camp, for the numbers opposed to the Shah's immense force were only three thousand under the Sirdars, and sixteen thousand, with twenty guns, under Dost Mahomed Khan. The Shah's army immediately dispersed in all directions, he himself having quitted the field with about one hundred horsemen.

On the morning after the fight, which took place on the 2nd July, 1834, he had already crossed the river Helmund, and at midnight was at Kareez. Next day, hungry and fatigued, he reached Do-sung, the fort of Muddud Khan, Durranee, who received him with respect and kindness. At the village of Gudda he was hospitably received by Ali Khan, Belooch, and Gholum Rus Khan, eldest son of Saloo Khan, Astikzye. In a few days, Saloo Khan himself waited on the Shah, and offered the use of his residence at Lash, as long as he desired it, which he accepted, and from thence communicated to Kamran at Herat the disastrous state of his affairs. He remained two months with Saloo Khan, and all the chiefs in the neighbourhood vied with each other in hospitable attentions to the unfortunate king. When he had received a reply to his letters from Herat, he was anxious to proceed towards Ferrah, but changed his purpose in consequence of a suspicion of fresh perfidy. Saloo Khan, the same chief who betrayed him at Jakan, had been written to by Prince Abbas Mirza of Persia, requiring him by every exertion in his power to seize and convey the Shah to Meshed, and deeming compliance of importance to his own interests, he endeavoured to persuade the Shah that his proceeding to Meshed would be advantageous to his prospects of future success. But the Shah thought otherwise, justly apprehensive of treachery, and therefore departed in a different direction, adopting the route by the Dusht-i-Bhukwa, though it exposed him to great inconvenience and peril. It was a burning desert, which he had to cross, the water bad, to be obtained only at distant stages, and the whole party suffered greatly from exhaustion, hunger, and thirst. The Persian writer, in describing it, says: "The halting places were so remote from each other, and the atmosphere so like fire, that another step would have reached to the day of resurrection!"

The first village he came to was Munkoocher, bordering on the territory of the Khan of Kelat, Belooch, where, under a shed, he sought protection from the intense heat of the sun. In the evening, he set off again and marched all night, and next morning was within a few miles of Mehrab Khan's fort. He was in great danger of being intercepted there by the Belooch, who, in apprehension of worse consequences, had been induced to contribute a lac and a half of rupees to the Shah when on his march to Candahar; and now, had it not been for the intercession of his women, who anxiously implored him not to be guilty of so foul an act, he would have made the Shah a prisoner at once. He still, however, breathed vengeance against him, and when he found the Candahar Sirdar, Rehim Dil Khan, with five hundred horse, endeavouring to overtake the fugitive king, he sent out a party to effect the purpose he had before contemplated; but fortunately the Shah escaped from the toils spread out for his capture. He passed in safety through the narrow and perilous defile of Derrah-moola, with mountains on each side so high that they "shut out sun, moon, and stars," in Persian phrase; then through Bhaug, and as far southward as Larkana, where, notwithstanding the hostile proceedings on his advance to Candahar, he was welcomed by the Ameers of Sinde, and invited to Hydrabad. He remained there for some time, treated with the highest respect and consideration, and then returned, *viâ* Jessulmeer, to Loodianah, after an eventful campaign of two years.

This rapid sketch, mostly from his own materials, exhibits the Shah in a remarkable point of view. The recovery of his throne was, not unnaturally, the dearest wish of his heart; it was his ruling passion, ever present to his imagination, ever promising success, and to such a degree of intensity had his anxiety on that subject arisen, that he never appears to have distrusted the principles or questioned the objects of those artful men who, at different periods, urged, him to a new enterprise. It would almost seem, too, that professed zeal and apparent co-operation in forwarding his claims on Caubul were sufficient to atone for the most atrocious duplicity and villany, such as were manifested by Atta Mahomed Khan, and others whose names are recorded in the course of this brief biographical notice.

In preparation and pursuit, he "screwed his courage to the sticking-place;" but in actual conflict, and at the critical moment, some fatality always occurred to deprive him of that victory which his conduct otherwise deserved. We see this strongly exemplified on two memorable occasions. At Nimlah, his troops, under Akram Khan, were defeated, owing to the imprudence of that chief, who was killed, and by the defection of Muddud Khan. At Candahar, too, he lost the day owing to the brave but rash conduct of Campbell, and before, at Jakan, by the treachery of Saloo Khan.

But it was imagined that the decrees of fate or Providence had placed an insurmountable barrier against the Shah's success in Affghanistan. He had, indeed, been long looked upon as a man on whom adversity had set its seal, and was universally believed to be peculiarly the victim of misfortune. But, as he said, when lingering in the prison of Runjeet Singh, "Despair betrays the soul of an infidel," and as time produces mighty changes in the world, with him "Hope travelled through." Only four years after his last calamitous campaign, the bright star of England illuminated his path, and placed him on the throne of his ancestors.

CHAPTER IV.

JOURNEY OF THE AUTHOR TO JOIN THE ARMY.

The Author's personal movements — Ferozepore — Its classical associations — Rude navigation of the Punjab rivers — The. Gharra, or Hyphasis — The shores scantily peopled — Indolence of the Puujabees — Intoxicating effects of food — The river which bore the fleet of Alexander — Bhawulpore — The Author robbed — Ahmidpore — The town and people — Aga Rufli, a wealthy Jew — Wretched character of the houses — The Great Desert — Khanpore — Nowshera — Another Ahmidpore.

WE may now return to the Bengal division, which left Shikarpore in the end of February, 1839. But before I come to that starting point in the narrative of the march, I may be allowed to take a brief retrospect of my own personal movements, in journeying from Sylhet, in the lower part of Bengal, to join my appointment as superintending surgeon of the army of the Indus.

Passing without comment over the intermediate space, which is so well known, it will be sufficient to observe that, having left Sylhet on the 15th of October, 1838, and proceeded by water as far as Allahabad, I arrived at Loodianah by dawk on the 7th of January, 1839. I had expected to obtain a boat at Falour, on the Sutlege, to enable me to drop down the river expeditiously as far as Bhukker; but not one was procurable, and I therefore had to push on by land to Ferozepore, a further distance of about eighty miles.

Ferozepore has some slight pretensions to classical associations. Alexander the Great is said to have erected twelve altars on the banks of the Hyphasis, to perpetuate the memory of his expedition to India. "These altars," says Quintus Curtius, "were of hewn stone," and, according to Diodorus (lib. xvii.), seventy-five feet high. Arrian says, "they were equal in height to so many fortified towers, but far exceeding them in bulk. On these he (Alexander) offered sacrifices to the gods, and gave them thanks for making him thus far victorious, and consecrated them as eternal monuments of his labours." Major Rennell concludes their situation to have been near the junction of the Hyphasis and the Hesudrus, and as Pliny, citing the letters of Alexander, informs us that the king passed to the eastern bank of the Hyphasis to erect them, they must have stood, I think, in the neighbourhood of Ferozepore. Diligent search may yet discover some traces of these buildings, the foundations of which, being of "hewn stone," can hardly have wholly mingled with the dust.[14]

---

[14] When I was at Ferozepore, in January, 1839, the streets were narrow, and in the filthiest state imaginable; the houses all huddled together. When I was there in February, 1841, on my return from Affghanistan, a totally new prospect presented itself — the fort and town had been new-modelled, indeed rebuilt of burnt brick — wide streets, with colonnaded rows of shops, had been constructed, and the whole exhibited the promise of

On my arrival at Ferozepore, on the 12th of January, also, not a boat was to be procured, every one available being employed to carry down grain and other stores to the army. Shah Shoojah's horse artillery contingent was under orders to march next morning towards Shikarpore, but I had not the means of embracing that favourable opportunity, my camp equipage being on its way from Delhi, across the desert, to Bhawulpore. At length it was suggested that I might be able to find room in one of the grain boats, and to ascertain this point, and the description of boats used in this quarter, I went to the ghaut, five miles off, and thought that, after inspecting them all, some sort of accommodation might be contrived. On the 14th the grain bags were so arranged as to allow "ample room and verge enough" for my purpose. But the floor was a rush mat, laid upon thin elastic sticks, irregularly placed, so that every time I moved I was reminded of Belzoni, making his way among the crackling mummies in the catacombs of Egypt, and it required great caution to avoid a twist and sprain of the ankle. But I cared little about the discomfort to which I must be necessarily exposed, anxious as I was to overtake the army, already halfway to Shikarpore. Having travelled by dawk, I had no servant, and the only one I could pick up at Ferozepore was a wretched Khidmutgar, of miserable appearance, so that I commenced my stream voyage under no very favourable auspices.

The river at Ferozepore is commonly called the Sutlege; by ancient authors the Hesudrus; but after its junction with the Beyah or Beyas, near the village of Hureekee, some miles higher up, it has also the name of Beyas, which continues as far down as Pagputten, where it is called the Gharra, till it unites with the Chenab or Acesines, at Ooch.

January 16th.-The fleet, consisting of eighty-one boats, started from the ghaut this morning. That on which I embarked was, like the rest, flat-bottomed, with flat sides and ends, and planked all round about eighteen inches high. In their indigenous state, these boats have no covering, nor protection of any kind from the weather, but everyone of the present fleet, for the safety of the stores, had a covering made of reeds and straw. The management of them is the rudest that can be conceived. They are merely permitted to drop down the stream — no effort is ever made to keep clear of others or of the shore, the crew, four men and a boy, being too lazy to do any thing by way of prevention. It was a most ridiculous sight to see the rafts, for they are simply rafts, whirling round in all directions, stern foremost, head foremost, and cross-ways; the men screaming at the top of

---

an extensive mercantile city. For this improvement, we are much indebted to the zeal and exertions of Capt. H. Lawrence, the assistant Political Agent. The native merchants of India and the Punjab. seeing distinctly the dawn of commercial prosperity in that quarter, at once entered into the speculation of erecting long lines of shops and warehouses, and increasing the town; and there can be no doubt that in a very short period Ferozepore will become one of the most important mercantile *entrepôts* in the north-west part of India.

their voices, pushing on and pushing off the sand-banks in the greatest confusion. I had fancied, on leaving Delhi, that a Punjabee boat would pass down the river with the same facility and expedition as one on the Ganges; but, alas! the boats employed now, and the only boats procurable, were obliged to be taken from the ferries, used for crossing over cattle as well as men, in different parts of the river, and the boat people, five in each, were accustomed to no other labour than poking their vessel along with a long pole, or jumping over the side and dragging and pushing it to its destination. Pulling an oar with any degree of effect was beyond their skill; each punt is supplied with two, at what may be called the bows. They are long and heavy, with a flat board tied to the end in the clumsiest manner. These oars are lifted up and dropped down again, perpendicularly, as if to chop the water, but they add little or nothing to the forward portion of the vessel, which has no rudder, a bamboo or long pole badly managed does duty for that. On one occasion, the boat struck on the stump of a large tree under water, and could only be moved in circles as on a pivot. We were several hours in this ridiculous condition before we got released. The difficulty was not a small one, considering that the planks of the raft were rather loose; that we were a good distance from the shore; and that the stream was deep and rapid. The scene was varied one night by a huge rat, which had been fattening on the grain, jumping on me in bed, and by one of the boats being on fire, which, however, was got under without much damage.

The guard consisted of a jemadar and twenty sepoys, with twenty others, proceeding to Shikarpore, and the fleet was under the direction of a commissariat gomashta, who never allowed the boats to start early, and always came to after five or six hours, so that the day's work was over at about 2 P.M. In consequence, our progress was slow and tedious, and I did not reach Bhawulpore till the 5th of February, having been three weeks in the boat. The distance is now usually run in a few days.

The Gharra, or Hyphasis of the Greeks, is a noble river, even at this season, when it is daily falling, and leaving large islands, with perpendicular sides, some of them ten or twelve feet high. The view being thus shut in, the right or nearest course could not always be distinguished, and generally we unluckily hit upon the most circuitous. The villages, up to which the river rises after the melting of the snows on the mountains to the north, were now about two or three miles from its present margin, so that when full, it must be of great width, and, from its rapidity, dangerous to navigate in such boats as the country can produce. We were at least a dozen times aground or on shore every day, the channel being often very narrow, though "the waste of waters" was considerable on either side.

The shores had a dreary appearance, mostly covered with low jungle, and it was only a scanty clump of trees, very rarely seen, that marked the site of the villages. Seldom it happened that a fowl or an egg was procurable, ottah, ghee, oil, and tobacco being the sum-total of articles to be found in any of them, and these only in small quantities. The turnips growing on both sides of the river, for the use of the cattle, are of a most excellent kind, large and well tasted. Irrigation is carried on by the Persian wheels erected on the banks, and their squeaking noise may be heard miles off, indicating a village at no great distance; but the whole range of shore on either side is very scantily peopled, and days now passed away without man, woman, or child, being seen. It is extraordinary, too, that nobody thinks of fishing in the Gharra. I am told, that a fisherman once did set up at Mumdote, but was obliged to relinquish his occupation, as the sale was insufficient to support him. Whilst we remained near Pagputten, one of the sepoys brought me a large fish, a sort of whiting, which was very good, and I think it was the only one I had, though upon a magnificent river two and twenty days, in which abundance of fish might have been caught; but the people have no "appliances or means," no nets, no hooks, nothing.

My four men and a boy, all Punjabees, were perfectly uncivilized, and the laziest of mortals.[15] Hardly an hour had passed, after starting, before they began to ask at what time we should come to again, and this occurred every day. The moment the boat was secured, they jumped on shore, and then all was cooking, smoke, and gabble. At dusk, a large fire of jungle wood was kept up, which they sat round, screaming wild songs, like as many jackals, till eight o'clock, the hour at which they crept to their dens to sleep.

On two occasions during the passage, I witnessed the intoxicating effects of food. To induce the Punjabees to exert themselves a little more, I promised them a ram, which they consider a great delicacy for a feast. It must be premised that their common fare consists of rice and vegetables made palatable with spices. The ram was killed, and they dined most luxuriously, stuffing themselves as if they were never to eat again; after an hour or two, to my great surprise and. amusement, the expression of their countenances, their jabbering and gesticulations, shewed clearly that the feast had produced the same effect as any inebriating spirit or drug. The second treat was attended with the same result. One day, the boat people observed a large species of crane, which had struck a

---

[15] The first drawing of my collection in the course of publication, represents a scene on the river not far from the village of Pagputten. A number of the Punjabees occupy the fore-ground, some of them cooking, others in conversation, the boatmen in the boats peculiar to the Punjab are seen on the left hand, and on the middle bank is the delineation of the Persian wheel, turned round by a couple of bullocks — the driver on a seat carried forward at the end of a beam supported over the horizontal wheel. At a little distance are two females in crimson dresses, the usual colour in this part, carrying water-pots on their heads, for household purposes. The softer sex in the East, among the lower orders, are usually employed in this drudgery. *Editor's note: The author's illustrations can be found between page 115 and 167.*

fish in the shallow edge of the stream; and was flying away with it in his beak, and two or three of them instantly sprang into the water to get on shore to chase the bird with hallooings to make it drop its prey. This is said to be often done with success, and they never fail to try their luck. In this instance they were disappointed.

The buffaloes along the Sutlege are of various shades, from dirty black to a whitish colour; some were spotted, and their horns curled, and annulated like those of a ram. About a week before my arrival at Bhawulpore, large flocks of pelicans, as white as snow, began to appear occasionally in the water; but they took flight as the boats approached them. These were agreeable sights when so little of either human or animal nature was to be seen. Even a crow was a *rara avis,* and the jackals were seldom heard. There was in fact nothing for them to eat, the thinly peopled villages being so remote from each other.

Tuesday, Feb. 5.-I arrived at three P.M. at Bhawulpore. The Gharra at that point was only about eighty yards wide. Mr. Elphinstone says; "After crossing a small canal, and passing through some fields, we left the woods, and at length reached the banks of the Hyphasis. I was much disappointed in the breadth of the river, as well as with the appearance of its shores; but it was impossible to look without interest on *a stream which had borne the fleet of Alexander.*" But here Mr. Elphinstone has fallen into an error. Alexander's fleet did not pass down the Hyphasis, but the Hydaspes, the modern Jelum. Arrian says distinctly, "he (Alexander) then returned (from the Hyphasis) to the river Hydraotes, and thence to the Acesines; he again offered sacrifices upon the banks of the river Acesines, which river after having passed over, he came to the Hydaspes. When he had made all things ready for conveying his army upon the banks of the Hydaspes, he resolved to sail down that river, till he came into the ocean." Curtius is also precise on this point:

"After ordering twelve altars to be erected, he went back and encamped near the Acesines, *ad flumen Acesinem locat castra,* till he embarked on the second river," the Hydaspes, the Indus being the first, reckoning of course from the west.

My object now was to procure a boat to convey me down to Bhukker, but I was as unsuccessful here as at Ferozepore, the only one at the ghaut being laid up for repairs. However, more favourable resources presented themselves than I could have expected; my baggage-camels had most opportunely just arrived from Delhi, without the least accident. My protracted voyage down the river was not, therefore, unproductive of good. Had I arrived earlier, and been still without the means of water conveyance, I should have had to wait for my Kafila at Bhawulpore. But as it happened, I had reason to rejoice, for the Shah's artillery contingent, commanded by Capt. W. Anderson, which commenced its march when I was at Ferozepore, was under orders to proceed next morning.

The space left by the river from the town of Bhawulpore was about three miles. The first part was loose sand, then a belt of thin feathery jungle, about five feet high, sufficiently separated to be threaded without much difficulty; nearer the town there was no jungle, but the ground was cracked into various large shapes, and the openings so wide and deep as to render it dangerous to walk over in the dark, for it had become dark some time before I reached the mud walls of the town. The deep irregular fissures in the alluvial soil, produced by the heat of the sun, furnished me with a miniature resemblance of the *Mer de Glace* at Chamouni, in Switzerland. Bhawulpore, though it gives the name to the state, is not the residence of the Khan, who only visits it occasionally. I did not enter the town, but proceeded direct to camp, where I was most hospitably received by Captain Anderson and his two officers, Cooper and Turner.

Feb. 6.-At four A.M. I was summoned to my Toorkee charger! This animal had crossed the desert with my camels from Delhi, where I purchased him from a Bokhara horse-dealer, who had just arrived with him and some others from Toorkistan, and was called a *chahar-gosh* (four-eared), each ear being according to custom slit down, to give the appearance of two. I note this said Toorkee most gratefully, because he bore me nobly throughout the whole campaign, without any other assistance, a distance of nearly two thousand miles!

The road was in the first part a tolerably good one, but the guides missed their way. The guns had consequently come along the wrong side of a deep nullah, dug for the purposes of irrigation, but at that time dry, with high ridges on each side. It was therefore necessary to cut through them, to allow the guns to go across, and this was done with great promptitude and alacrity. We did not reach the ground near Khyrpore till near ten o'clock, only eleven miles, and suffered a little inconvenience from the heat of the sun. In the evening one of the camels, which had been left behind to bring on my baggage from the boat, arrived, and, snugly ensconced in my tent, I congratulated myself on having all my travelling accompaniments about me again, including my whole kafila from Delhi, and all my servants. I slept well that night.

Feb. 7.-I awoke between four and five in the morning, and observed one of my servants examining every part of the tent; on asking him what he was about, he replied that he could not find my clothes where he had left them, in a corner, the night before. The whole had disappeared; wearing apparel, shaving apparatus, writing-case, with all my memoranda, lists, receipts, letters, spectacles, sketch-books, journal, and a variety of small trifles, but important considering the impossibility of replacing them on the march. My annoyance and vexation at the loss of my drawings and papers was extreme, and I could not help indulging a suspicion that some of my servants had assisted in taking them away, for I had repeatedly mentioned my anxiety about the safety of my paper-case, from which he and all around might have supposed it contained money. But it contained none. I might say, parodying a few lines of Goldsmith,

"Bright uniforms may flourish or may fade,
Tailors can make them, as a tailor made;
But drawings, journals, scraps, the author's pride,
When once destroyed, can never be supplied."

I offered a reward and had it proclaimed through camp, but it was of no use; the clothes had been, no doubt, conveyed far enough, and the papers, of no value to the thief or thieves, destroyed. This was my first loss. Our march to-day was to Hussain-ke Wassy, a mud village, nine miles and a half; the greater part of the way through tamarisk jungle.

Feb. 5.-Proceeded at five A.M., and arrived at Ahmidpore at nine. Near Ahmidpore is Dhurra, the usual residence of Bhawul Khan, the chief of Bhawulpore.[16] We were encamped about a mile from the town, in which there is a mosque with four minarets, the largest building I have seen in this quarter. The houses and the fort are all of mud or unburnt brick, the streets very narrow, and the bazaar has covered shops on each side; but the articles for sale are of the worst manufacture, and the rudest imaginable. We were surrounded by the gaping inhabitants; fish and kid were selling in a state of rich decomposition, and in very small pieces, almost like mince-meat. The women, the most horrid beldames ever seen, covered with rags and dirt, and the men remarkable as much for their filthiness, as for their black bushy beards, and an expression of countenance of the brigand or assassin cast. They are said to be as cowardly as they are boastful, and grossly illiterate. We met with men and boys playing at marbles in the town; they hold them in a different way to the European fashion, but effect their object with great expertness. They had holes in the ground, in a straight line, and avoided a stroke (as we do at billiards) when they thought proper.

The well-known Jew, named Aga Ruffi, said to be the wealthiest dealer in Ahmidpore, having a capital of several lacs of rupees, had called upon me in the morning, and accompanied by Capt. Hay, one of our party, I paid him a visit at his own house in the town. We found him in a wretched mud hovel, about eighteen feet by seven; at one end was a common cot, or bedstead, covered with a dirty counterpane, on the edge of which, as there were no chairs, we were asked to sit, whilst he dropped on the ground, and crossed his legs, together with seven or eight of his relations and friends present. He had on a rich variegated silk dress, and a huge turban; he shewed us several articles of Russian manufacture, made-up dresses, silks, &c., for he was said to be the only person at Ahmidpore who had any thing of the kind; he is also said to have some influence with the Khan. His two brothers, a Candahar friend, and the rest, were all seated on their haunches, smoking, and I was surprised, knowing the existing prejudices in

---

[16] He has no aristocratical pretensions, being by caste a weaver.

India, to see Mussulman and Jew pass the hookah from one mouth to another, without the least hesitation. On the ground, in the middle of the hovel, was a hole full of wood-ashes, in which they all continually spat. Their rich dresses and the miserable domicile in which they were huddled afforded a strange contrast. Within the mud wall which surrounded the dwelling there was an unprotected deep well; the ground was covered with filth, and the disgusting picture was completed by a number of dirty old hags and squalling children, who seemed to form part of the Aga's establishment. The worst native hut in India could not exhibit a more striking appearance of poverty and wretchedness.

Aga Ruffi and his friends accompanied us to see the town, and we must have been objects of curiosity, for we were followed by a crowd of the idle inhabitants wherever we went. Nothing valuable in the way of manufacture is produced at Ahmidpore. Their matchlocks are sold at from eight to ten rupees each. We met in the streets several women, whose faces were hidden under a patch of net-work let into a large robe or gown which falls from the head to the feet. They are beggars, called Syud-zadees, but the form of their ugly features may be easily distinguished when the net-work is drawn closely over them, as it usually is. The robes were perhaps originally whitish, like unbleached linen, but those we saw had a deeper tinge, and were just as filthy as the heat of their bodies and dust could make them. Beggars *without* disguise were sufficiently numerous.

The approach to Ahmidpore on our march was of a favourable description; the dome of the mosque with its four tall minarets shone conspicuously; there was an appearance too of high cultivation, the ground in its immediate vicinity being divided into beds of about twenty feet square, with a narrow ledge on every side, to keep in the water poured into them by irrigating wheels from a canal, and also from the wells which abound there. The verdure of each bed was of the brightest hue, the trees were numerous, roundly formed, and full of foliage, which gave a richly picturesque garden look to the view. We passed along a lofty mound on the west side of the city, which seemed to have been once a boundary wall, and about a mile beyond it was our encamping ground. On our way we heard the roll of the drum, and afterwards were told that the Khan had three regiments — one of a thousand men, in the course of preparation, at drill, commanded by a European, named Macpherson, who, as I was told, receives five rupees a day. The second and third consisted of about fifty men each! The specimen we saw of the Khan's soldiers was a poor one. He was on guard near the fort, black-belted and musketed (such a musket!), and the brass breast-plate had on it the number 24, surrounded by an oval wreath; it was more than two inches wider than the black belt on which it was fixed. His habiliments, excepting a sort of cap which it would be difficult to describe, were those usually worn by a palankeen-bearer in India, and he was strutting consequentially before his hut, which did duty for a sentry-box, as if he was a functionary of vast importance. The breast-plate, it appears, was copied from one brought to the Khan by a deserter from the 24th Regt. N.I., and as the figures were no doubt considered a part of the ornament, 24, I am told, figures away in every breast-plate that has been made for the Bhawulpore army.

Amidst this novel scene, we were pleased to see a house about a mile from Ahmidpore, built at the expense of the Khan for Mr. Mackeson, the assistant political agent; with white-washed walls and green Venetian windows; it did not seem to belong to the place, but to have been brought away, and dropt there, from the provinces.

The Khan's principal residence is called Dirawel, situated in the desert; it is also called Dilawer (the *r* and *l* being interchangeable, as in *tulwar,* 'a sword,' *turwal);* it contains his zunana, and is an undoubted place of safety for the frail sisterhood. His treasure in gold and jewels, said to amount to about seventy lacs, is also kept there; the women who are once introduced to the zunana of the desert are, like the poor nuns who take the veil, doomed to remain there for life. The population of Ahmidpore is between nine and ten thousand, and the revenue of Bhawul Khan's territories is said to be nine lacs.

Feb. 10.-Our march this morning was along the skirts of the great desert of Bhawulpore, and the tract is but partially cultivated, the greater part of it being sand-hills, interspersed with the tufts of jungle called jahoo, or tamarisk; the road generally good, excepting that in many places, and often to a considerable distance, the loose sand is deep and heavy for the loaded cattle. At a quarter past eight we reached Chundi Khan-ka-kote, said to contain a good bazaar. In the evening we went into the village, and found a mud Burlington Arcade, with mud shops on each side of a street, about six feet wide; it was covered over with long sticks, over which mud, again, had been thrown to keep off the heat of the sun; but this careful arrangement was only to be met with in a few places. The articles for sale were coarse blankets, salt, sugar, and grain. The paths of the village were like sand-pits, more than ankle-deep.

I saw some boys and girls at a novel sort of amusement; the instrument was formed by a perpendicular post of wood, crossed over by a bar of the same material near the top, giving the whole the shape of a T. Through this transverse bar is a hole, into which the upper part of the post is pushed, and the horizontal part turns on the pivot. Six inches from the extreme ends of the upper part of the T, there are two pegs. The urchins wrap a part of their clothes round the pegs, and one of them is mounted astride on each side. Thus placed, three or four of their companions seized the two arms of the machine, and ran it round with as much rapidity as they could; they then quitted their hold, allowing it to spin round itself, and it continued to do so for some time, to the loudly expressed delight of the whole assembly, as well as of the riders, who had a most difficult position to maintain, I should think; but it was evidently to them a pleasure of the most agreeable kind.

Feb.11.-March to Chowdree, ten miles and a half, where there is an old mud fort in ruins, and a deserted village; road through tamarisk jungle.

Feb.12.-March to Mahmood-ke-kandi, eleven miles and a quarter, still in the skirts of the desert; road level and good.

Feb. 13.-Halt. Intelligence has been received that the Ameers of Sinde have come to terms, and that our troops in advance to Hydrabad will return, and proceed immediately to Shikarpore.

Feb. 14.-Marched to Khanpore, seventeen miles and a half; road crossed by a great number of rather deep nullahs, which had been, however, filled up or bridged over, for the convenience of the troops, to a sufficient breadth. The appearance of Khanpore was more town-like than any I had yet seen in that part of the world; there is a bright sparkling mosque, white, and rather richly ornamented with coloured masonry. The houses at a distance, lit up by the ruddy morning sun, had a good substantial effect; but it was "distance" that "lent enchantment to the view," for, on a nearer inspection, they were found to be rudely built of mud, and not of burnt brick, as they at first seemed to be. Near the entrance of the town, the camels of the columns in advance appear to have perished in great numbers, exhausted, no doubt, by one of the longest marches on the road.

The villages, close to which we passed, within a few miles of Khanpore, were more like *bustees* in the lower provinces of India than any I had previously noticed, the men and women in considerable numbers being actively employed in their agricultural occupations, and merely looking up as we passed. To the west of the town is a brick bridge, with a pointed arch, striding over the canal called Ihtyarwah, which is supplied from the Sutlege. Khanpore is a commissariat depot for the grand army; the extensive fields of young corn on every side are as brilliant as the hue of the emerald, and most agreeable to the sight, after seeing nothing but stunted grass, brown jungle, and sand, for so many days. Khanpore is also a considerable market for indigo and cotton, great quantities of which are exported to Mooltan and other parts of the Punjab, and as far as Affghanistan. The indigo is packed in large cloth bales; they have no wooden boxes.

Feb. 15.-Halt. Lieutenant Mackeson dined with us in camp; he has been in this country about six years, and on his arrival black-mail was universally levied, but the people are now in a better condition. The military road, recently constructed by him for the march of our troops, is the first ever made through the Bhawulpore state; kafilas used to skirt the river over a sort of foot-path by a very circuitous route. Several Beloochees are here buying up matchlocks, preparing, no doubt, for some outrage we shall hear of by-and-by. Plenty of hare and black partridge, and with the aid of Anderson's capital cook, we fared sumptuously.

Feb. 16.-A man, who arrived this afternoon from Herat, on his way to his home at Mooltan, says that the tribes are ready to aid Shah Shoojah, but first require our presence to secure their own safety, and adds that Dost Mahomed had not above a thousand well-disciplined and trustworthy horsemen about him. He brought despatches from Lieutenant Pottinger, of Herat, to the envoy and minister at Shikarpore, from whom he had a letter, stating that he had done good service to our Government. A few marches on this side of Bhukker he and his party had been attacked by twenty mounted Beloochees; two of his followers were wounded, and all of them robbed of their clothes and property.

Feb.19.-After halting from the 14th, we marched this morning to Samakhan-ka-kote, fourteen miles. It began to rain about three A.M. lightly, and now and then we had good pattering showers; but as the people declared it never rained here, I expected every moment that it would cease. It, however, came on in earnest, and long before the march was over, I was drenched through and through; but it never rains at Khanpore! Camels are bad travellers in rain, sliding and slipping with their long legs at every step; great numbers fell on the road, and some could not be got up for a long time, even after their loads were taken off; many of the grain camels stopped half-way, unable to go on; loads of hay, grain, and camp equipage lay scattered on the road as I passed, the mud fetlock-deep, and worse in many places. The foot camp-followers — men, women, and children — were in a deplorable condition, several abandoning their shoes, which became so clogged and heavy with clay as to prevent their being able to walk at all. The rain continued the whole day, and it was not till late that we had the shelter of a tent from "the pelting of the pitiless storm." On the 20th, the mess-tent, and a considerable number of other things, like Gilpin's hat and wig, still on the road. On the 21st a heavy fog, but the evening was clear and fair, and the moon, about a week old,

"Through heaven's pure azure spread her sacred light."

Feb. 22.-Marched to Nowshera kelan, thirteen miles and a half. The fog at starting was very heavy, and fell like small rain, continuing all the way; route through tall jahoo jungle. Met 400 grain camels returning empty from Shikarpore. The village of Nowshera contains about a thousand inhabitants. Explored the old mud fort, and found in the gateway two men in the stocks — asked them the cause of their being in confinement, when they promptly replied, in a careless, good-humoured tone, that it was merely a quarrel about land, and the boundary of their property. The guard, however, deprived them of this flourish, by declaring that they were confined for theft! Every thing in a sad state of dilapidation; the children of the place, however, were playing about with great glee, and some of them riding on planks see-saw fashion, as the youngsters do in England.

Feb. 23.-Marched to Kattie-ka-bustee, fourteen miles; road good, but through jahoo jungle, and over sand-hills, peculiar to the margin of the desert. Information received in camp, that a detachment from the army at Shikarpore was under orders to proceed in advance on the 1st March, in consequence of the commissariat officer at Bhaug reporting the necessity of a force to insist on the native authorities there, under the rule of Mehrab Khan, of Kelat, producing supplies of grain;— the Shah, with his troops, to move on the 5th, and the army a few days afterwards.

Feb. 24.-From Kattie-ka-bustee to Sarwahi, ten miles and a half. About three miles and a half on the road is another Ahmidpore, a walled and fortified town; the wall on the road-side is nearly all down, but there are two mud bastions, or rather piles of mud, upon each of which is a gun mounted on a crazy carriage, and the guard-house, behind, a miserable grass hut: no living soul was there. A great number of the inhabitants had gathered together, and were standing at one of the gateways, or rather where a gateway had been, for it was an open breach, to see our cavalcade. A villager told me there were plenty of wild-hogs and tigers in the jungle we had passed through, and a variety of game. Passed immense crowds of camels employed in conveying grain to the army.

About a mile south-west of the camp to-day is a mound, fifty or sixty feet high, with a plateau six hundred feet by four hundred; the ruins of two circular bastions clearly indicate it to have been a fort, and the whole surface and sides are scattered over with loose burnt bricks. It is now a Mussulman burying-ground, and contains many hundred graves. There is in one part a mosque of recent construction, and contiguous to it a covered building, with an open space walled round, in which are four neatly made tombstones, no doubt the final resting-place of some family of consequence in the neighbourhood: it is this mound that is called Sarwahi. To the north, again, about two miles off, is a fort called Fazilpore, the old route of the kafilas.

Close to the west of the camp is the village of Sinjarpore, with a wretched bazaar; here I met with a jemadar of Skinner's horse, who said he had come with 2,000 camels for grain, flour, &c., to take to Shikarpore; and here I learnt the use of the *machāns* (raised platforms, fourteen or sixteen feet high), which I had observed in front of almost every straw hovel we had lately passed. They are used in the rainy season, when, like the Nile, the Sutlege overflows the country, and muskeetos and other insects are most annoying. There is a sort of fireplace below, in which they burn straw to fumigate and destroy the enemy, which being done, wholly or in part, the whole family — husband, wife, and children — all repair to the horizontal roof for repose, as sleeping in the huts below is impossible.

CHAPTER V.

JOURNEY OF THE AUTHOR CONTINUED.

Subzelkote — Robbery of the dawk — Dirty condition of the town — Belooch robbers — An alarm in the camp — Visit to Gotekee — Mosque — The Author reaches the Indus, at Roree — And joins the army.

FEB. 25.- To Subzelkote, six miles and a half. About four miles from Sarwahi, at a small village, is the boundary between the territory of Bhawul Khan and one of the Ameers of Sinde; still jungle on all sides.

The Hydrabad Ameers have been brought to their senses, but the people do not seem disposed to be very civil yet; the dawk was robbed some days ago near Subzelkote, and the despatches carried off; in consequence of which, inquiry was now to be made on the spot. The Killadar, named Futteh Khan, was sent for, but he refused to appear, saying he never quitted his fort on such occasions; the threat of coercive measures, however, induced the functionary to trot over to the camp on horseback, with about a dozen followers on foot. He was told that the four horsemen who had committed the robbery had been traced to Subzelkote, and he immediately replied, that the robbers must have been Meer Roostum Khan's men, but he knew nothing of the matter. Meer Roostum Khan is the Khyrpore Ameer, to whom we were indebted for the temporary cession of Bhukker during our operations, his flag and that of the English flying in the fort in amity at the same time. The Killadar's reply was doubtless a mere subterfuge. It is more probable, that his own master, one of the refractory Ameers, who had been forced to terms, was anxious to discover our further policy, and with that view had the dawk plundered. Common robbers seek for other booty. He promised, however, to do his utmost to discover what was lost. He had on a pale green silk embroidered jacket, a white loose robe thrown over his shoulders, with wide blue trowsers, a red Belooch cap, and was mounted on a scraggy white nag.

In the evening, we visited the town, *ciceronied* by one of the Killadar's men. Its population is between 4,000 and 5,000. The two bazaar streets, which cross each other at right angles, were crowded with people; a small part is covered in, but in a straggling, insufficient way. The whole place is like a dirty stable, asses, tattoos, and men, all accommodated together. Every hut is half-full of dried grass. They keep their grain in perpendicular mud cylinders, with a hole at the lower part to let it out as wanted. For other household matters, they have a similar receptacle, about six feet high, but with a small door and lock in front. Saw hemp and the white poppy growing under the walls of the fort; from the latter they make their opium, and an intoxicating beverage of the other; they also make a strong liquor from *gour* (molasses). The Killadar's mansion is of mud, like the rest, with a large compound full of straw, and the accumulated filth of animals; and in picking your road even through the streets, it is difficult to avoid defilement. On the broken wall, near the principal gate-way, is a piece of iron ordnance, upon a rudely constructed carriage, the mouth of the gun blown off, and the whole utterly useless.

Feb. 26.-From Subzelcote to Oobarah, eleven miles; fine hard road, generally through jahoo jungle, but with many intervals of rich cultivation; herds of cows; the horns of the buffaloes, as before remarked, are curled round and annular; their colour blackish, brown, dun, and whitish. The asses in this part, which are of a very small size, are said to be able to carry very heavy burthens. A man in the bazaar at Sarwahi, where a number were collected, told me that they were equal to five maunds (above twenty-eight stone) weight, to a moderate distance. Certainly we had a dozen, and small ones, too, taking flour from Oobarah to Bagoodrah, fourteen miles and a half, and their load was two maunds each, (nearly thirteen stone), which they carried with ease. The price of the donkeys is only four rupees. Oobarah has about five hundred houses, and they say five thousand inhabitants. The bazaar is like all the rest, corn, oil, gour, ghee, ottah, almost the sole articles for sale; except, however, spirits made from gour, and nearly equal to our commissariat rum. It is four annas the seer, being sold by weight.

Feb. 27.-Marched to Bagoodrah, fourteen miles and a half; this place has not even a mud edifice, all the huts being of straw; supplies scanty. At Bagoodrah several robberies were committed in the camps of the preceding columns: horses carried off from where they were picketted, and other property plundered.

Feb. 28.-From Bagoodrah to Gotekee, sixteen miles and a half, situated about six miles from the Indus; the road still through wild jungle. Gotekee is a town of mud houses. On our arrival, found that the quarter-master serjeant, who goes on in advance the day before to mark out the encamping ground, had been attacked and wounded at four P.M. yesterday, within three miles of that place. He was proceeding considerably ahead of his small party, excepting one man, when he met eight or ten armed Beloochees on tattoos, who in passing uttered the *salâm aliekum,* 'peace be upon you,' and he supposed them to be sepoys of some native prince. But very shortly after, he heard the sepoy behind him, on horseback, scream out," Don't kill me, I am a Mussulman!" and was himself assailed at the same moment by two ruffians, whilst the third seized the bridle of his horse. In the scuffle, in which many blows were struck, he was driven from his saddle, but got hold of one of their swords; upon which they fell back, and he immediately, for safety, rushed into the thick jungle which lined the road. Finding, however, that they were in pursuit, probably to recover the sword, he flung it down, and succeeded in secreting himself. He remained about an hour in his hiding-place, and then, cautiously peeping out, discovered that the robbers had decamped, no doubt from apprehension of his party coming up. The sepoy also escaped with his life. The Belooch had gone quickly up to him, and taking hold of his horse's head, looked into the mouth, and familiarly asked him how old it was. Seeing the sepoy off his guard, he in an instant dexterously caught him by one leg, and flung him to the ground. With the same alacrity, the sepoy sprang up, called out, "Don't kill me, I am a Mussulman," and ran away into the jungle. The two horses, rather of a sorry description, and a bundle of clothes, were secured by the captors. The serjeant's wounds were inconsiderable except one, but that one, in his side, had nearly been fatal. A stout sword-belt prevented the sword from penetrating his bowels; as it was, the muscles were nearly cut through. At noon, my servants arrived, with the two camels which daily bring on my sleeping tent and bed, and informed me, that a Sikh, not belonging to us, was lying on the road, about a mile off, bleeding from wounds recently inflicted. He himself stated that he had been overpowered by five horsemen, plundered of all he had, forty rupees, and his clothes, and then, after the infliction of several deadly wounds, left to his fate. He, too, was accosted with the ominous "*salâm aliekum!*"

It appears that the road between Sirhud and Gotekee is notorious for similar scenes of blood; that there are two or three villages, adjacent to each other, which harbour bands of Beloochees, who have emigrated from their own mountains and wilds, and settled in that quarter; and that they have spies who reconnoitre the passengers, and ascertain the chances of success. One of my servants, in charge of the two camels, was drinking at a well, when a man came up to him, and asked him "If he had any muskets or pistols with him?" The reply was, "Several." "If any troops were following?" "Yes, plenty." "Let me see that sword," he said. "No," was the reply; "I keep that for my own defence." From all this, no doubt, the man was in league with the robbers, and my servants and property must have had a narrow escape, for it was not above half an hour after this colloquy, that the outrage just described took place. An easy conveyance was sent out for the wounded man, and a party of Skinner's horse in quest of the miscreants. Two of them were brought in, and a tattoo, recognized and owned by the serjeant. A sword belonging to the wounded Sikh was also found on the culprits. A third was shot through the leg, and could not be brought in; a dhooly was afterwards sent out for him, but he had been carried off in the meantime. Evidence was taken, the prisoners secured, and the whole affair reported to the superior authority. In the afternoon, twelve other suspected individuals were taken in the jungles, but when confronted, they were not recognized, and therefore allowed to depart. Only four of them had swords, from one of which fresh blood appeared to have been wiped. The owner admitted it at once, and, smiling, said it was the blood of a goat he had just killed!

The Beloochees have borne the same character for centuries. The *Boorhani Katia,* a celebrated Persian dictionary, gives the following definition of *Kooch* and *Belooch*:- "The names of certain races of barbarous people, who inhabit the mountains on the borders of Kerman. It is said they are descended from the Arabians of Hejaz. Their employments are fighting, and shedding blood; thieving and robbery on the roads. If at any time it happens that they cannot find strangers, they murder one another, plundering and destroying each other's property. Thus even brothers, near relations, and friends quarrel; and they consider this as a pleasant occupation." Their habits will soon be more fully developed.

When the wounded Sikh was brought into the camp, the continuance of life, even for an hour, seemed impossible; he had been hacked all over in the most savage manner. His forehead was cleft to the brain, one arm hung by a slip of skin, the shoulder-blade was laid open, and the bowels were bare, from a dreadful gash in the side. The camp was now in a great bustle, in consequence of a rumour that parties of horsemen had been seen stealing from the villages to the town, and it was supposed that some further outrage might be either attempted, or be in contemplation. Though no faith was placed in this rumour, it was thought best to be well on our guard; the sentries were doubled, and three guns (six-pounders), with grape ready in the muzzle, were brought to bear on the town, and the other nine equally prepared, should any thing of a hostile nature occur. All was quiet during the night.

March 1.-Halt. The Sikh still alive; the utmost attention had been paid to his wounds. Notwithstanding all that had occurred, a party of us visited Gotekee this evening, attended by a man named Delawer Khan, in the employ of Sir Alexander Burnes. Between the camp and the town, there is a thick plantation of Kajour trees, several hundred yards wide. The bazaar has had some pretensions to be showy, the fronts of the shops, under the open verandahs, being decorated with diminutive human figures, flowers, trees, fruit, and animals. In going along, we met one of the *Mureeds*[17] of the principal mosque, who invited us to see it, and we readily accepted the invitation.

Looking in at the door, we found the interior was spread over with fine grass, for a carpet, and a great number of the faithful prostrating themselves in prayer. Among them were several women, also at their devotions. The Mureed begged that we would take off our shoes; but this was obviated by saying it was the custom in our places of worship only to take off our hats, which we did, and then entered, though he still kept looking at our shoes with apparent concern. The Peer or Saint of the mosque, named Salik Shah, was sitting on a mat, with several other persons, to whom we were introduced by the Mureed. He is a benevolent, venerable-looking man, broad and corpulent, with a white flowing beard; he had

---

[17] *Mureed* is an Arabic word, meaning scholar, disciple, follower, of the Mahomedan faith.

a most agreeable smile, and spoke with much gentleness. The Mureed took the opportunity of pleading for the man wounded in the leg, and one of the others in confinement on account of the outrage already described, saying they were simple villagers and innocent of the charge. His importunity was got rid of, by assuring him that the culprits would be handed over to Sikunder Burnes, who would, of course, act in the case according to the evidence adduced, and the law of the state. The building was arcaded, and the walls and ceiling inlaid with little square tiles, like the Chinese, on which small blue ornaments were burnt in. On a sort of pediment, the year of its erection was inscribed (1148), and a Persian distich informed us that it was beautiful as the garden of Eden — مثل جنت عدن

We were then asked if we would like to see the burial-place of the Saints, situated on one side of the quadrangle; to which I assented; but that spot was much too sacred to be trod upon with shoes, and I was, being the first, anxiously solicited to comply with the usual ceremony. I therefore put off my shoes, the Mureed actively assisting, and followed him into the *sanctum sanctorum,* very dimly lighted, through a low doorway. The middle space was surrounded by a wall, or rather curtain, breast-high, and inlaid with vitrified blue tiles, inscribed everywhere with أي محمد "O Mahomed," and passages from the Koran. There were about a dozen tombs, all covered over with the tiles already mentioned; their first Saint, after the foundation of the mosque, was buried there, and others who followed him. One of the Mahomedans, who was describing every thing, asked me if I thought it true, as written in their books, that Jesus Christ would appear on earth again in twelve years! He spoke Persian, as they all did, not seeming to be familiar with Hindoostanee. The Mureed kept my shoes in his hand all the time outside, and when I had finished the survey, he placed them beyond the precincts of the holy place for me to put on again. Just as we were returning, the Muwuzzen walked up the flight of stairs which led to the top of a gateway, highly decorated with the same sort of tiles as the mosque, and called, with a loud shrill voice, his brethren to their evening prayers; before he had done, we were out of the Moslem temple. Outside it was plastered with a composition of mud and chopped straw, and had a glittering cupola, shaped like a pigeon-house, embellished with the same eternal vitrified tiles, but variegated at the top with green circular pottery ornaments, of a spiral form. The people were all very civil. The brother of the Saint, or Peer, an old fat man, having just joined the party, begged to be introduced to me, and we embraced in the customary way. He understood that we had a medicine which, taken internally, cured all sorts of wounds and broken limbs, and was desirous of obtaining some of it, such as Roostum sent for to cure Sohrab! But I told him it was always indispensable that the patient should be first seen by the doctor. At Kohat, near Peshawer, a black substance, called momya, is dug out from the hills there, and is believed by the natives, when eaten, to unite broken bones in a few days! In this promenade, we were surrounded by about fifty men.

The town of Gotekee is as much a piggery as any other I have seen on this side of the Indus, I had forgot to mention that the Mureed boasted of relics in the mosque not to be inspected or seen but by the orthodox. The wooden pillars which support the roof were said to be brought from a far distant region, and when about being put up, one of them had disappeared. The next day, a pillar fell from heaven to supply its place, and no one but the Peer knows which it is. If anyone has the good fortune to find it out, and embraces it in secret, his every wish, even of the most extraordinary kind, will be fulfilled. Many have successively embraced the whole, thinking by that means to receive the boon; but that will not do, the boon is not to be obtained by that sort of artifice, the pillar must be hit upon at once. It was not asserted, however, that the Peer had invariably all *his* wishes accomplished, although believed to be possessed of the important secret!

Moved to Dadoola, ten miles and a half, on the 2nd, the road still through everlasting jungle on both sides; and on the 3rd to Azeezpore, fourteen miles. Started at four A.M., the road fetlock-deep in dust. At six, I perceived on my right what appeared to be a horizontal line of fog, but on nearing the place, I was delighted to find it unexpectedly a branch of the Indus. The sight of it, after so much wild jungle, was most refreshing, and, associated as that celebrated stream is with the glory of Alexander the Great, I felt almost as much exhilarated, on seeing the classical stream, as the soldiers of Xenophon, when the sea burst on their view, and they exclaimed with joy to their comrades, *"Thalasse! Thalasse!* 'the sea, the sea!'" The branch I allude to reunites with the Indus three or four miles further down. Our customary prospect of ruggedness and withered green we have lost. The peasants are ploughing, and sowing tobacco all round us.

On the 4th of March, we moved on to the encamping-ground, about a mile east of Roree, where a fine view presents itself of the town, the island fortress of Bhukker, and the further shore of Sukkur on the Indus.[18] In Alexander's time, this was the country of the Sambracæ, "a nation not governed by kings, but by as many democracies as tribes." The Indus, however, at this point, displays none of its magnificence. The jutting out of Roree into the stream, and the middle space being so largely occupied by the fort of Bhukker and the other islands, esteemed of peculiar sanctity, it has but two comparatively narrow channels, over which the bridge of boats for the army was thrown. One of the islands is consecrated to the renowned Saint in Mahomedan countries, Khaja Khizzer, and on that island a fakeer shews a most sacred relic, one of the hairs plucked from the beard of the

---

[18] The second drawing of my collection represents the town of Roree and the fortress of Bhukker.

Prophet, which is said to be of a bright red.[19]

After breakfast, I proceeded towards the ghaut, on the west side of Roree, passing through the town. The streets are the narrowest I have seen, only wide enough for one horseman, the laden camels having to make a long detour to the southward to get to the bank of the river. The ascent from the east side is very considerable, mounting a sort of apex, and the descent on the ghaut side very precipitous; the ground hard flinty rock, which resounds sharp under the horses' feet.

The ferry-boats are of a most inconvenient description, with sides about five feet out of the water, so that getting camels on board is a most tedious and difficult operation. The portion of the bridge on the east side of Bhukker had been removed in consequence of the sudden rise and rapidity of that part of the river, which was productive of much delay and trouble to those who did not arrive in time. The portion across the channel between Bhukker and Sukkur continued in a perfect state. Whilst crossing over in a boat, I observed a man, said to be fishing; he was supported on a flattened water-jar, peculiarly constructed for that purpose. The mouth, which is on the upper part, is covered by the belly of the man stretched over it at full length, and he floats on the stream, or propels himself forward or sideways with his feet, like a frog, at pleasure. As the fishes are caught, he places them in the jar; if he has to carry any thing across the river, it is put on his back, or between his feet, raised up, and he paddles himself along with his hands.[20]

Bhukker, according to Ferishta, was formerly the capital of Sinde. The fort stands on a flint rock, more than twenty feet above the level of the river, and the walls are between thirty and forty feet high; its extent is about eight hundred yards by four hundred. The interior is full of mounds and hollows, and trodden by a hundred crossing paths. The only habitable place, is the small house previously occupied by the Killadar, of two stories, the lower one arched; it has windows, with shutters that slide up and down like a sash, and when used, are kept at the height required by hooks, at different distances, which go across the groove

---

[19] A hair of the Prophet's beard is a choice relic. At Cudapah, in the Deccan, a temple was erected in honour of one, which was preserved in a golden casket, with a crystal lid. When Hyder Ali captured Cudapah, he carried off the precious trophy to Seringapatam. It is said that Mahomed had a habit of stroking down his beard, in familiar conversation with his friends, and every hair that fell off was instantly seized by his disciples, and kept with care, which accounts for the number existing in every part of the Mahomedan world.

[20] Humboldt gives an account of *swimming couriers,* who are employed in conveying letters between the shores of the South Pacific and the province of Jaen de Brancamoros. These men, known by the name of *el coreo que nada,* wrap the letters in a cloth, which they bind round the head, and to assist in swimming, provide themselves with a log of wood, generally the trunk of the bombax.

on each side. The surface of the walls is divided into blank compartments, and when an opening is necessary for air, the space is filled up with open latticework, in angles, like Chinese paling, very minutely and well executed. With regard to heat, Bhukker is now a very oven. There are remains of a great number of mosques, all ornamented with the sort of vitrified painted tiles, used at Gotekee, but in a superior manner. On the Roree and Sukkur sides of the river, too, the neighbourhood abounds with ruined mosques of a similar kind, which indicate considerable Mahomedan magnificence in former days. The walls of the fort are now broken down in many places, and there is but one remaining gateway; the Sindian flag, a square of red silk, is flying close to ours. On the northeast side of the fort, beyond the wall, is a luxuriant grove of kajour or date trees, the fruit of which is said to be remarkably fine. This grove is skirted by an outer wall, resting on the external margin of the solid flint rock, that forms the base of the fortress. The garrison consisted of the 35th Regt. N.I, commanded by Colonel Monteath, who resided in the Killadar's house, but the officers and sepoys, for want of other accommodation, were necessarily under canvass. The wounded Sikh before mentioned was left in the regimental hospital, and, *mirabile dictu,* I was afterwards told that up to the 24th April he was still alive, and doing well!

An idea was entertained that the Hindoo sepoys might refuse to cross the Indus, because it was supposed that a Brahminical prohibition existed on that subject, which it would be a sin and dangerous to disregard. But the sepoys themselves do not seem to have given it a thought. *Attok* certainly implies 'prohibited' or 'forbidden,' and as the Attock flows into the Indus, the same interdiction is applied to its whole course. There are other rivers which bear the same name, and are of the same forbidden character. The Helmund is said to be often called Attock, and also the Mahanuddy, near Cuttack. But the interdiction may have arisen from some local prejudice or objection, or more probably a boundary question, wholly independent of any religious consideration. Brahmins and Hindoos of every description abound west of the Indus, so that the prohibition we are adverting to is "more honoured in the breach than in the observance." Besides, it is historically shewn that Affghanistan was, before the Mahomedans invaded the country, inhabited by Hindoos, which countenances the conclusion that the prohibitory obligation, if it ever virtually existed, had reference to a civil and not a religious object. "I cannot help taking notice," says Captain Wilford,[21] "of a curious observation made by a learned Brahmin, that whosoever prohibited the crossing of the Attock, meant only that nobody, making use of the usual modes known at that time, should presume to cross it; but if he could leap over it, or cross it in a balloon, or astride a wild goose, or any other bird, which may be effected through magic, there would be no harm whatever! This strange idea

---

[21] Asiatic Researches, vol. vi. p. 534.

brought to my recollection a whimsical story of the Mussulmans who inhabited the country of Sinde or Tata: they fancy that Alexander by magic art conveyed his whole army over the Indus, every man of his riding astride a wild goose. As Alexander was pretty successful in India, they conceive that this would not have been the case if he had crossed the Indus either in boats or by swimming; and the most obvious method he could adopt, in their opinion, was to convey his soldiers in the above manner!!" A *very learned* Brahmin!

March 6.-Left my kind friends of the artillery contingent, as they were obliged to halt, and I was anxious to get up with the army. My tent for sleeping had been pitched on the beach on the Sukkur side, as higher up the ground was covered with dead camels, which produced an intolerable stench. The country was said to be more cultivated on the west side of the Indus, towards Shikarpore, than on the east; but I found it generally much worse, and much more wild and desolate. I started at four A.M., and for the first four miles, where the advance columns of the army had halted for a short time, the effluvia from the dead camels in a state of decomposition was dreadful, pungent and fœtid beyond description; it exceeded any thing that can be conceived. At one P.M. I arrived at Shikarpore (twenty-four miles), where I joined the 2nd brigade of the Army of the Indus, then under orders to march on the 10th, right glad that my long pursuit was at an end. Sir Willoughby Cotton with the advance had moved forward in the latter part of February, as before stated.

CHAPTER VI

ADVANCE OF THE ARMY OF THE INDUS

Shikarpore — The *Put,* or desert — Shah Shoojah — Belooch robbers — Nowshera — Desolate and arid country — Affairs with the Belooches — The Bolân Pass — Beebee Nânee — Conflict with the Belooches — Bold Scenery — Plain of Dushti-be-doulut — Sufferings of the camp-followers — Loss of camels — Siriab — Kareezes, or subterranean aqueducts — The troops unite at Quetta.

THE town of Shikarpore, excellently situated as it is for commerce, has not much claim to antiquity, as its existence cannot be traced beyond the beginning of the seventeenth century. Its monied population consists of Hindoos, originally introduced there in the reign of Tymoor Shah; the total amount of souls is said, by Sir Alexander Burnes, to exceed thirty thousand.

March 7.-This afternoon, a commissariat officer arrived with despatches from Sir John Keane's camp, requiring all the camels with the 2nd brigade, and countermanding the march on the 10th. This produced a deep sensation of regret, but the measure seemed to be unavoidable, as Sir John was unable to get on for want of carriage. He goes by the Gundava Pass, and the commissariat officer is to take seventeen hundred camels, in a day or two, laden with grain, in that direction, and all the rest, available, are to be sent to Larkana, where the Bombay camp now is. This of course paralyzed the 2nd brigade, and therefore my intention of remaining with it, as my object was to reach head-quarters as soon as I got to Rojan.

I left Shikarpore on the evening of the 9th, in progress to the brigades in advance; passing through Jagan[22] and Janeedera, about noon on the 10th, the whole distance thirty-six miles, where I overtook the park of artillery, under Major Pew, and Captain Watt with commissariat stores. The march of twenty-six miles and a half over the *Put,* or desert, was now before us, and at this season, could only be undertaken by night. The march could not be divided, in consequence of there being no water on the route; we therefore started at seven in the evening. It was a most arduous task. For about three miles, the road was through scattered low jungle, but afterwards the prospect was, like the calm sea, a smooth unbroken expanse, only bounded by the sky. The surface seemed to be hard tenacious clay, or a stony substance, which rung under the horses' feet. It was a brilliant star-light night; frost seemed to be in the air, it was so cool and bracing. Our friends grilling at Shikarpore would have been delighted to feel its refreshing influence. Some time after midnight, there was a halt to rest the cattle,

---

[22] The boundary between the territory of the Sinde Ameers and that of Mihrab Khan, of Khelat.

and in that interval our servants made up a blazing fire, for the north wind was blowing bitter cold. A little Hunter's beef, portable soup, and hot brandy and water, produced their usually goodly effects on such occasions, and enabled us to pursue our route with improved spirits.

March 11-It was near eight o'clock in the morning before we got to Barshoree. We had two guides, the foremost with an armed sepoy on each side of him, with the view of preventing treachery,[23] and the whole line of march was well guarded against any attack by the predatory Belooches. Our guide took us a roundabout way, making the distance at least thirty miles; the guide in the rear kept the right direction over the desert, and arrived at Barshoree before us. A great number of camels broke down on the road, and were left to die, among them two of my own. Our tents did not come up before the afternoon, so that, worn out with extreme fatigue, I was glad to take up my "lodging," not "on the *cold* ground," but on the hot sand, for a few hours. The water at Barshoree was scanty and bad, drawn from innumerable small wells. The town is surrounded by a wall, and the interior as full of filth as all the rest. The head-man presented himself for any service that might be required of him; he was a Belooch, of most unpropitious aspect, loaded with murderous weapons, which he displayed successively, and described with great complacency. He had on a prodigious silk turban of bright yellow and orange silk, which had been given to him for some good service by Sir Willoughby Cotton, and of which he seemed mighty proud. The poor fellow was some time afterwards killed by mistake; he had been enjoying the festivities of a wedding in the neighbourhood of Barshoree, and was returning late at night, when, in the dark, he and his friends were taken for robbers by a party of horsemen on duty, and in the conflict that followed he lost his life.

March 12.-Marched from Barshoree to Meerpore, fourteen miles. Pass dead camels continually. The road through a desert-like country, with an unbroken line of horizon, till within a few miles of Meerpore, when a few stunted bushes and trees were visible at an extensive abandoned Belooch village of mud huts, with shattered walls and bastions, called Shoree. Meerpore is also a fort-like village of mud; the people had assembled on the walls to see us. The sun was oppressively hot, but in the afternoon a thick haze with thunder came on from the westward, which brought a refreshing shower, and the cool drops fizzed as they fell on the burning sand. The atmosphere was soon clear, and shewed to our delighted eyes

---

[23] In Mahmood of Ghuzni's journey through the country of Sinde, the army was misled for three days and nights by one of the Hindoo guides in a sandy desert, so that many of the troops died raving mad from the intolerable heat and thirst. The guide, on being tortured, confessed that he was a priest of Somnat, who, to revenge the injuries done to the temple, had thus endeavoured to bring about the ruin of the Ghiznivide army.

a high blue range of the Gundava mountains.

The dawk-runner has just come in with a loose bundle of packets; he says he has been attacked by Belooches, who tore open the papers, destroyed some, and carried off his horse! I had the good fortune to find six letters to my address. The chill wind of the desert has occasioned an affection of my eyes and swelling of the lips to a painful degree. Another of my camels *hors de combat.*

March 13.-From Meerpore to Ustàd, fifteen miles. The range of Brahooee mountains seen rather indistinctly all the way on our left, with chalky precipitous sides like the Dover cliffs, conjectured to be about 30 miles off, and on our right a lower range of hills at a greater distance; the intermediate country perfectly flat. We are on a wide plain, and the site of the camp takes its name from a remote village, and only a few hundred yards from the Naree river, which rises in the hills to the North of Dauder, and loses itself in the plains to the westward of Shikarpore. Ustàd is notorious for thieves, and the column in advance had suffered much from their depredations.

March 15.-From Ustàd to Bhaug, ten miles. The hills only dimly visible for a short time, and then totally obscured by the haze. Passed three deserted mud villages, all with mosques, some flat-roofed, and others with domes. The town of Bhaug is a sorry place, similar to those on the other side of the Indus, the bazaar-streets covered over in the same slovenly way. On the southwest side of the town is an extensive burying-ground; some of the tombs are mounds of earth, and some of brick, and near is a large mosque, the dome white, and adorned with green, shining, pottery minarets. There are also several mosques in the town. The women in the streets, the ugliest in creation; the men like assassins.

There is a sulphur mine at Bhaug, where gunpowder is manufactured, but of an inferior kind; the composition is sulphur and saltpetre, one part each, and two of charcoal made from a wood called *ak.* The governor of Bhaug is noted for his excessive love of spirituous potations, and, consequently, for being almost always drunk. This afternoon, a great number of armed horsemen passed by our camp, said to be a relative of Mihrab Khan, with his followers, going to wait on the Shah at Kassim shah-ka-jouk, which is about five miles to the south-east of Ustàd.

The Shah had made two marches on each of the two preceding days, of twenty-six miles, the first, over the *Put,* and had almost knocked up all his cattle. He was compelled to come into our route for want of water and supplies, having left Shikarpore in a more westerly direction. He was to halt three days at Kassim shah-ka-jouk. Soon after, a flock of cranes were seen in the sky, flying in that direction, and this was considered by the people a happy omen. Mihrab Khan's tactics will be seen presently.

March 16. - Marched from Bhaug to Myhesir, fifteen miles and a half. The whole prospect entirely flat, and not a tree to be seen.

Though so near the mountains, the haze rendered them totally invisible, but on approaching Myhesir, some low hills peeped out right in our front of a red, rugged, and barren appearance; but in an hour the haze shut them out again. Three Belooch robbers were brought in, two of them manacled in a curious way. The arms of the third, a young man, were secured behind his back with ropes. The handcuffs consisted of a log of wood, about two feet long by three inches wide; there was a square hole in the middle of it, which the hands are first put through, and then a wooden pin is driven through the centre part of the hole, between the wrists, which effectually prevents either hand being withdrawn. I made a sketch of the three prisoners as they stood before me. The name of the eldest was Dost Mahomed Khan, which he pronounced with a smile of complacency, as much as to say, "I too am a Dost Mahomed Khan." A party of the 4th Local Horse captured six mounted camel-stealers, and brought them into camp. Permission applied for to hang them, but, should it be granted, not a tree is to be found to fix them on *in terrorem.* Myhesir has a mosque similar to that at Bhaug, but is a much smaller village. Halted on the 17th, to refresh the cattle before the trying marches through the Bolân Pass.

March 18.- From Myhesir to Nowshera, fourteen miles and a half. About a mile from the camp, came to a belt of jungle or scattered bushes; passed a deserted mud hamlet, and at the fourth mile came to the stony hills, some an aggregation of pebbles, and some in large masses of rock, the path between them being simply the plain, excepting at two or three places, where a ridge had been made passable, which occasioned a little acclivity and descent; it was in other parts threading hills as we do trees in a jungle. At the ninth mile, came to the wide bed of a mountain torrent, about a foot deep, tumbling and glittering along, which we had to pass. Beyond this, an extensive plain opened, edged with distant hills, and five miles further was the walled and bastioned town of Nowshera. The camp was in an amphitheatre, hemmed in with wild and rugged mountains, lofty to the west, but rather low on the north side, not a speck of verdure on them, all red and brown, but finely variegated in tint by sunshine and distance.

March 19.-From Nowshera to Dauder, between six and seven miles. There was a good deal of thunder and lightning last night, with showers of rain; hail-stones of considerable size appear also to have fallen, as they have left their marks distinctly on the sand we are passing over this morning. The wind from the north-west, cold and bracing, and reminds one of an English day. Passed two small streams, and about halfway the bed of a river, a hundred feet wide, with high steep sides; the two narrow streams brawling along the middle part over stones and pebbles, quite delightful to see after the dull monotonous scenery we had been accustomed to. The lofty mountains on our left looked boldly out, and, though bleak and sterile, had a fine effect. Our camp is about a mile from the town of Dauder, and the Bolân Pass almost in sight. In that direction the tops of the mountains are covered with snow. This morning an order was received from Sir John Keane (who had assumed command of the Army of the Indus on the 4th), directing Captain Watt to halt, and send one thousand gallons of rum, and all the camels available, for the use of the European troops with him. The rum and two hundred spare camels were immediately forwarded to Gundava, where the Bombay column was reported to have been on the 16th, and was coming on by the Damin-i-koh route, *viz.* along the foot of the hills. The Shah's camp was at Bhaug by the last accounts.

On the 21st, another requisition was received from Sir John Keane for more camels, as he could not move from Gundava without them.

March 23.-Desolation has certainly put a mark on this arid spot, that is, as far as the eye can reach from camp. Looking back, our progress has been an arduous one, water only met with in small quantities, and forage equally scarce. The latter evil could only be remedied, in some degree, by carrying on large supplies, which involved another difficulty, that of additional carriage, not always to be obtained.[24]

Marched from Dauder to Kundye, eleven miles and a half. I now accompanied the park of artillery, and five companies of the 37th Regt. N.I. Leaving Dauder, the road was skirted with low jungle for two or three miles. We then entered the Bolân Pass, a rough and pebbly road, between sand-hills, studded with flint and lime stones, small and large, the space in breadth between the hills varying from 300 or 400 yards to about 30. As the torrent runs deviously from one side of the gorge to the other, we had to cross it six or seven times. The bottom consisted of large round loose stones, which gave an uncertain footing for a horse, though the camels with their large spread of foot got through without much difficulty. The depth was not more, generally, than eighteen inches, and the water bright and transparent. At the place called Kundye (the village from which it is named is at some distance in the hills), our tents were pitched on a hard bed of large stones and pebbles, surrounded by sand-hills, presenting an oval surface about 600 yards by 400, on the south side of which the stream is deep and clear, and some of the European soldiers very soon seized the favourable opportunity of enjoying a good bathe in it.

As the rear-guard was coming along, in charge of baggage, &c., a number of Belooches fired at them from the hills, about a mile from the ground, and then rolled down stones, but without effect. In return, they had a dozen shots from the sepoys and sarwans (camel-men), which proved equally harmless, it being their

---

[24] The third drawing of my collection represents the entrance to the Bolân Pass from Dauder. The view affords no indication of the rugged nature of the Pass, the hills for the first few miles being of an undulating character. The mountains at Siriab, still covered with snow, are seen in the distance. On the foreground is Khalik Dad, Belooch, Governor of Dauder, and his attendant, and some of our camp-followers cooking.

wont to skulk behind pieces of rock; but they were soon seen flying from the ridge of the hill down the other side. Their strategy is to fire, and disappear.

This was the first day of excitement. The moment the circumstance was known in camp, a party of the 4th Local Horse was despatched to the spot, accompanied by several officers, anxious to have a brush with the Belooches, who had previously succeeded in carrying off eight of the park bullocks. The marauders were presently found, and hunted among the hills, but none of them were killed, though many must have been desperately wounded, quantities of blood being observed on the rocks over which they were followed. They were indeed seen dragging off the wounded, and in a short space, joined by at least a hundred more, who, after pausing a few minutes, fled together down the further hills. One of our sarwans was slightly wounded, and also a sepoy of the 37th. Three prisoners were taken and brought into camp. We could see distinctly through a glass the Belooches, with their matchlocks, creeping and doubling over the hills, watched and pursued by our people, who after great fatigue in climbing up crumbling acclivities, came back a little before sunset.[25] Many of the artillery waggons did not come up till midnight.

March 24.-From Kundye to Kirtah, ten miles and a half. The village a few miles over the hills. At day-break, a number of armed Belooches were discerned on the ridge of the mountain, close to our camp; but, on seeing a party after them, they instantly fled. The first third of the road is through a rather narrow defile of bold and abrupt sandstone rocks, of considerable height, and in that third we crossed the torrent eight times. Further on, the hills on each side were more sloping, and afforded a tolerably open view, and the intermediate flat became gradually much wider. Altogether we crossed the torrent sixteen or seventeen times; the thirteenth or fourteenth was the deepest, the water coming over the stirrup-irons. All the way there was but one narrow path. In one of the shallow torrents, a little off the road, was found the dead body of a European soldier, one of the 16th Lancers, with his regimentals on, supposed to have fallen down drunk in the rear of the brigade in advance. The body was conveyed to camp, and, after an inquest, buried. We are pitched in a stony place, about a mile in diameter, surrounded by lofty mountains. The dead camels seen on this day's march more numerous than usual. Many had laid down, and been drowned in the torrents, emitting a most horrid effluvia.

March 25.-In consequence of the extreme difficulty of the road yesterday, a halt was rendered unavoidable, inconvenient as this place is for one in every respect, where no forage is to be procured, in addition to the little we had the

---

[25] There are two castes of plunderers in the Bolân Pass, much dreaded by the kafilas, the Doda Marees, amounting to 3,000, under Doda, and the Dhumad Kakads, amounting to 5,000, under Tanias Khân. — *Leech.*

means of bringing on from Dauder. Under these circumstances, a day's stoppage in the Pass is a serious concern. It was near four o'clock this morning before the whole of the hackeries[26] were up. After retiring from the hills yesterday morning, the Belooches followed and harassed the rear-guard all day and all night. They carried off one hackery and bullocks, and wounded a sepoy severely in several places; two of the villains, however, were killed, and their arms and plunder taken. The hills being wider apart, they descended in the night, and tried to get away the cattle, in front and rear of the line of hackeries, as opportunity seemed to offer, dodging them incessantly. The wounded sepoy was left on the ground for dead, but afterwards found and brought into camp. One party of Belooches had got hold of a hackery loaded with charcoal, and cutting off some steaks from a camel, were discovered busily roasting the flesh at a charcoal fire; but their savoury repast was unceremoniously interrupted by the sudden approach of some sepoys, who turned it into "the banquet of death!"

March 26.-From Kirtah to Beebee Nânee, eight miles and three-quarters. Yesterday afternoon, several camels were missing. After an active search, they were found in a hollow, tied down in a setting posture, and the mouth of the cave covered over with branches of jungle to hide them. The road good compared with that of the two preceding days, and not one water-course to cross. The surface was pebbles and stones of various sizes, but not so loose as before, and two or three lines of camels could go abreast of each other. The space between the hills much wider, and the hills themselves of a sloping and undulating character. At two-thirds of the way, we passed through an artificial opening in a transverse range, called Jillowgheer, which led into another sort of basin surrounded by hills, the farthest of which was Beebee Nânee. A quarter of a mile before arriving at the ground, we passed by at least a hundred graves within a small circumference on both sides of the road, some simple heaps of stones rising to a point, and others of a more regular form, constructed in square rows. There were two circular places, about sixteen feet in diameter, surrounded by a wall of loose stones two feet high; a space was left to enter, and opposite to it a recess, probably meant for a religious purpose. It is said that Beebee Nânee has been the scene of many a sanguinary conflict, this part of the pass being notorious for attacks on the kafilas from Korassan. This very spot is called *Kutl-gah,* 'the place of slaughter,' and tradition says that here a kafila was destroyed, and here the slain were buried.

The mountain of Beebee Nânee, under which we encamped, has also its tradition. Beebee Nânee, an old crone, was making *chapatties* (wheaten or barley cakes), one day, when she discovered a formidable band of Belooch robbers descending upon the plain. In the great terror into which she was thrown, she

---

[26] *Editor's note:* a cart drawn by bullocks.

prayed fervently to the Prophet to open the mountain close by for her refuge, and lo! her prayer being heard, it opened and swallowed her up. The *chapatties* were at the same moment turned into stones. Another version states that Beebee Nânee was also turned into stone, and that the petrifaction of the lady of the *chapatties* may be found by digging into the bowels of the rock, but, unfortunately, the particular part of the rock is not yet ascertained.[27]

From Beebee Nânee to Abigoom, eight miles and a quarter. The road very fatiguing to man and beast, all loose stones and pebbles, which give way to the feet, and this was the case for nine-tenths of the distance. The encamping ground here is more uneven and more covered with large stones than at the three former places. The Belooches were seen in great numbers, and they had fallen upon and wounded two sepoys of the rear-guard. The water at this place only shews itself in very shallow rills in the hollows of the stony surface, in parallel courses, sometimes rippling a little, and sometimes unseen. The water thus loses itself, and the spot is, therefore, called Abi-goom, two words expressive of its disappearance.

March 28.- Abi-goom to Siri Bolân, nine miles and a half. Passed closer among the hills than before, and the march less fatiguing in consequence of the footing being firmer. Two-thirds of the way is the date-tree, on the right hand; which gives the name of Siri Kajoor to that part of the pass. The road is hemmed in by wild and rugged mountains, which afford numerous inaccessible positions for the predatory and murderous Belooches. Their Jezails, the native rifle, with a fixed rest, are formidable weapons, and are said to carry about eight hundred yards. They are often seven feet long. A dead camel and a camp-follower, with his throat cut, and otherwise cruelly mutilated to death, were lying close together on the middle of the road.[28] The ascent from Abi-goom is considerable; we passed through numerous little rivulets which water the defile, undefined and straggling in their course.

Yesterday, at Abi-goom, we were informed by Major Craigie, the Deputy Adjutant-General, on his way back from Sir Willoughby Cotton's camp at Siriab, to meet Sir John Keane in the rear, that six troopers belonging to the 3rd Cavalry had been left at Siri Bolân, in charge of a tent and other property, the carriage camels being knocked up and unable to proceed along with the regiment. Till the day before yesterday, another party was with them, and afforded sufficient

---

[27] The fourth drawing of my collection represents a view of the mountain called Beebee Nânee, from Kutl-gah, or the place of slaughter. In the fore-ground is a camp-follower asleep, and three Belooches about to murder him; a piece of ordnance, drawn by camels, on the line of march.

[28] The sixth drawing in my collection represents the wild Pass of Sirl Kajoor; a den of Belooches is exhibited in the fore-ground, which overhangs the road traversed by the army. A party of sepoys is seen on the heights above, ready to punish the murderers.

protection even at a place notorious for the depredations of Belooch robbers. It was naturally apprehended that the troopers would be destroyed if left alone, and in consequence Colonel Herring promptly despatched a duffadar and ten suwars of the 4th Local Horse, as a reinforcement, and they arrived at Siri Bolân before sunset.

Our advanced guard got there at a little before daylight this morning, when they first heard of the conflict which had taken place on the preceding night. I arrived on the spot at about eight o'clock A.M. The stony ground then bore witness of how much blood had been spilt. The Belooches, perhaps not aware that the six troopers had been reinforced, proceeded to attack them, with the view of carrying off the tent and camels, about eleven o'clock, but they met with a hot reception. The attacked, however, were in a bad position, their tent being pitched in a hollow commanded by high banks on either side, and at a short distance. One party of Belooches rushed on it at the right, and another on the left, sword in hand, having fired their match-locks only once or twice, probably having no more powder, a dilemma to which they are often reduced. The troopers and suwars were not less on the alert against fearful odds, for the assailants are said to be very numerous. The fight was with the sword, and the struggle appears to have been dreadful. One of the suwars was killed by a deep gash in the neck, close to his father, also a suwar, each urging the other on in the most intrepid manner. Only one of the suwars escaped unhurt, nine of them having been severely wounded in several places; one trooper had a slight cut in the head. The Belooches, however, suffered most; several were killed, but taken up, and carried off at once by their friends. I saw pools of blood in every direction. The dead body of one of them, a lad about eighteen or twenty, was still lying on the ground, his brethren being unable to recover it, though they had made strong efforts to do so. I was told that there were continual wailings and cries in the night for "Fyzoolah, Fyzoolah!" but Fyzoolah was deaf to the call. A second attempt was made at an early hour this morning, and the small band was again triumphant, defeating the marauders, now amounting to about two hundred men, who, upon being driven off, had recourse to pelting with stones from the high spots on either side. When our advance-guard arrived on the ground, while the atmosphere was still thick, and objects indistinctly seen, the troopers, supposing them to be the enemy again, challenged them, and if a satisfactory reply had not been immediately given, they would have been fired upon. Such was the gallant achievement and determined spirit of this little party. After this, they joined us on the march.

The lofty mountain, which crosses in front, is every now and then enveloped in dark clouds, and the wind blows very strong at intervals, with alternate showers and sunshine, producing rainbows, which beautifully embellish the stern grandeur of the scene. Halt on the 29th. It has been blowing hard all night, and my tent, held by large stones, to which the ropes are fastened, is quivering in the wind, and threatening to come down. In the afternoon, a loud shout rung through the camp, and on inquiring, I found that another exploit had been performed among the Belooches, and two heads had been brought in. A party of them had been carrying off some camels at graze, after attacking and wounding the sarwans. Four suwars were immediately despatched to the spot, and overtook the robbers, who fired at them twice, but without effect; the suwars then rode up to them, and closed, to prevent a third loading. The Wurdee major, who commanded, now got into a parley with one of the Belooches, who had the vantage-ground, flourishing his sword on an eminence, and uttering words of defiance. The suwar, as shrewd as he was fearless, suddenly dismounted, and springing up the rock, called out, as if to his comrade, "Shoot him!" The Belooch, turning round to see what threatened him, his bare neck became exposed, and the suwar, seizing the opportunity thus contrived, with one furious stroke of his heavy sword, severed his head from his body. He was a young man, about twenty, and his countenance handsome. Its stern expression and character, as the head lay on the ground, very much reminded me of Leonardo da Vinci's Medusa, in the Florence gallery. The other head was that of an older man, the hair being grey; a third was killed, but the sword broke short in the skull, and, tumbling down the crags, the head could not be got at to be brought into the camp. The rest escaped among the hills. These are revolting sights, but the murderous habits of the Beloochees extinguish every feeling of commiseration for their fate.

March 30.-March from Siri Bolân to Dushti-be-doulut, eleven miles; our last, and the most arduous march through the pass, the ascent being the most considerable. At about two miles from Siri Bolân, a beautiful spring gushes from the rock on the left hand, whose sparkling and meandering streams water the road as far as Abi-goom, and there disappear. Near this place there has been many a conflict with the Beloochees. Not far from it, the rear-guard of one of the regiments was attacked by a great number, between 200 and 300. They rushed down the hills, and after firing their match locks, came forward sword in hand. The officer who commanded promptly collected his sepoys together (about eighty); made them keep quiet and reserve their fire till the Beloochees approached well within gun-shot; they did so, then gave them a volley, and immediately afterwards charged them rapidly with the bayonet. Fifty-one, killed and wounded, were left on the ground, besides a number with slighter wounds; carried off by their flying companions. The rear guard was not troubled again that day.[29]

---

[29] The sixth drawing in my collection represents the opening into the narrow pass above the Siri Bolân, and a skirmish with the Beloochees.

After three miles of very rugged road, the windings of the pass begin. The rocks on each side are projecting and stupendous, and in the narrowest passages almost perpendicular. Immense blocks of stone are scattered about all the way, and the scenery is of a more magnificently wild character, and of a bolder form, than any we have yet met with. The summits of the mountains have numerous small bushy trees upon them, and near the road, and on the towering rocks, are many of a large size; the foliage a most brilliant green, and the trunks of a silvery whiteness. As we passed along, the singing of birds greeted our ears, a sound not heard for many a day. Underfoot, we had still loose stones and pebbles, and where there happened to be a little patch of earth, it was covered with a white efflorescence like snow. About the seventh mile, there was a higher ascent for half a mile, and then a gentle descent till we came to the most difficult part for the cattle to get over — the westerly boundary of the pass. The acclivity is steep, but only about one hundred yards long; great pains had been taken by the engineers to make it more practicable, and many impediments had been removed, but it was still an arduous task to surmount; in proof of which it need only be mentioned, that twelve dead camels were found lying on the road, half-way up, within the small space of thirty yards, which had belonged to the preceding column. When at the top of the ridge, the eye was gladdened with beholding immediately below an extensive plain of at least three miles by two, level as a bowling-green, and not a stone upon it, surrounded by mountains of a moderate height.

The descent is of similar extent to the other side, and equally, if not more steep. This plain is called Dushti-be-doulut, and here we encamped. The animals were not less delighted than ourselves with the change. My Toorkee, finding himself so suddenly on a smooth surface, after the fatiguing obstacles of the pass, frisked about in the most amusing manner, and camel and gun-bullock seemed equally delighted with the change. The plain was covered with herbage, and flowers of various hue. There were small tulips of exquisite scarlet, some of a bright yellow, daisies, cowslips, and a sort of wild thyme and marjoram, which scented the whole air. Our camels revelled on fresh forage in our sight. The only drawback was a deficiency of water, which had been foreseen; and in consequence, we brought on with us as much as we could carry, so that we were exposed to no inconvenience in that respect. Dushti-be-doulut is rendered by Mr. Elphinstone 'the unhappy plain,' decidedly a misnomer, for we found it any thing but that. There is snow upon the heights to the north, ten or twelve miles from us; the wind chill and sharp all the morning, enough to benumb both feet and hands.

The camp followers in the rear suffered severely during the march through the pass. We were continually shocked with dreadful tokens of the barbarity of the people, manifested by the mangled bodies, so frequently met with, of those who belonged to the column in advance. Indeed, the whole range of territory, beginning in Sinde, is infested with hordes of the same murderous, the same ferocious, yet cowardly character. The stragglers were generally the victims, and male and female equally the objects of attack, plunder, and destruction. Many of the instances are too horrible, too refined in atrocity, to be described, for, not satisfied with the extinction of life, the miscreants mutilated the dead bodies in the most savage manner. Firing their matchlock from behind rocks, in the defiles of the mountain tract, it was frequently impossible to discover where they were, and, when discovered, as impossible to get at them with any good effect. It was at first supposed that robbery was their chief or only aim, and they succeeded in carrying off at times considerable booty, but their wanton treatment of those who fell into their hands, fully shewed an exasperation of spirit which must have been excited by the superior authority in the districts through which we passed. That authority was afterwards found to be Mihrab Khan, the chieftain of Kelati Nusseer, on whose promises we had relied for supplies! Further, to shew the difficulties of the road, the dead camels seen on the whole route to-day were innumerable. The loss in one brigade only from Dauder to Dushti-be-doulut is said to have been 2,000.

March 31.-Moved from Dushti-be-doulut to Siriab, seventeen miles. Heard the lark for the first time carolling sweetly at dawn. Road between two ranges of mountains varying from four or five miles to half a mile apart, the ground covered with detached tufts of aromatic herbs; the latter part pebbly and rough, at the foot of a rugged mountain on the left hand.

We encamped in a spacious valley with plenty of herbage for the cattle. At Siriab, the subterraneous aqueducts are very numerous, dug deep, and in lines according to the course of the water, which runs from eight to ten feet, and often more, below the surface, and are used for the purposes of irrigation. These *Kareezes,* as they are called, are of ancient invention and ascribed to Hoshung, the second king of Persia, of the Peshdadian dynasty[30]. Commencing at a spring, they are constructed by a succession of wells at some distance from each other, and of such depths as the level and soil require. They are connected at the bottom by a channel sufficiently large for a man to pass through, to keep them clear. Quintus Curtius, in describing the richness and luxuriance of the pasturage between the Tigris and the Euphrates, says, "The cause of this fertility is the humidity circulated through the soil by subterraneous streams, replenished from the rivers."[31]

On the 6th of April, the whole of the troops united at Quetta, a large fortress or town in the province of Shaul, with interior and outer walls, situated on a wide plain. At a distance it looks like a lofty mound. There are several small villages

---

[30] *Editor's note:* Approximately 10,000 B.C.
[31] Lib. v. c. 1

in its neighbourhood, marked by clumps of trees and strips of cultivation, of a beautiful green, rendered more brilliant by the greys and browns of the surrounding surface. There is a pretty grove of poplar and mulberry trees near the fort, but the ground is much cut up by deep watercourses.[32]

---

[32] The seventh drawing in my collection represents the approach to Quetta.

CHAPTER VII.

ADVANCE OF THE ARMY TO CANDAHAR.

Diminution of rations, owing to want of provisions — Territory of Kelat — Mihrab Khan — His duplicity and hostility — Not without excuse — Outrages of the natives at Quetta — March to Candahar — Harassed by the Kaukers — Punjabee traders — Treachery of Mihrab Khan and the Candahar Sirdars — Beloochees — Valley of Pisheen — Kaukers — Difficulties of the road — Loss of cavalry horses — Dung-beetle — Robbers — The Kojuk Pass — Loss of cattle and stores — Proceedings of the Candahar Sirdars — Hajee Khan Kauker — Earthquakes — Deficiency of water — Whirlwind — Arrival at Candahar.

IT was at Quetta that the state of the army, for want of a sufficient supply of grain and ottah, became alarming, for it was at Quetta that abundant resources were promised and expected, and when the sad reality was made known, the whole camp was filled with disappointment and dismay. It therefore became absolutely necessary to adopt some prompt measure, and, however painful the expedient imposed upon the chief military authority on the spot, Sir Willoughby Cotton, by the pressure of circumstances, a reduction of the daily expenditure became imperative. Accordingly, the rations were at once reduced to half the usual quantity. The European soldier's loaf suffered that diminution — the sepoys seer of ottah became half a seer, and the camp-follower's half-seer became a quarter of a seer. The prospect was gloomy and threatening enough, but the measure of limiting the allowance to the smallest possible amount no doubt averted from the troops a more awful and tremendous visitation, that of actual starvation. The quantum of allowance thus reduced was not, however, of short duration, for it was nearly three months before the commissariat was enabled to supply full rations.

Quetta is part of Mihrab Khan's territory. Ahmed Shah installed Nusseer Khan, said to be descended from an Arab stock, in the government of Kelat, thence called Kelat-i-Nusseer, imposing the condition of furnishing 12,000 fighting men whenever the exigencies of the state required them. The province was thus made dependent on Candahar, and it was not till the accession of Mihrab Khan, the grandson of Nusseer Khan, that the allegiance to that state was wholly thrown off. The sirdars of Candahar, upon this defection, assembled a force, intended for the invasion of Kelat, and the punishment of the imputed rebel; but it was to no purpose, the means being totally inadequate to the accomplishment of that end, and Mihrab Khan continued to set them at defiance. It is said that, about ten years ago, he put to death his brother, the Khan of Sarewan, who had, in his turn, revolted, and imprisoned the son, Meer Nawaz Khan, who succeeded in effecting his escape, and subsequently joined Shah Shoojah on his last unsuccessful expedition against Candahar.

A friendly correspondence was opened with Mihrab Khan, at the commencement of the present campaign; and whilst the army was in progress, Sir Alexander Burnes was deputed to him at his capital, for the purpose of obtaining his good services, and of prevailing upon him to wait upon the Shah. He seems to have had a morbid dread of his majesty, and could not be brought to promise that he would see him, without the assurance that the British Government would stand his friend, and guarantee his safety. He trusted that, if his enemies succeeded in driving him from Kelat, an asylum and bread would be afforded him in our provinces. He was informed that he need be under no apprehension on that head, but that he should hold the territory dependent on Kelat on the same terms on which it was held in the reign of Ahmed Shah, and that, so long as the British army should be engaged in operations in the direction of Khorassan, he should receive a subsidy of one lac and a half of rupees per annum, payable half-yearly, and in consideration of that subsidy, he was only required to furnish supplies, carriage, and escorts, to the utmost of his ability, all of which would be separately and punctually paid for. To this effect, a treaty was prepared, which, after a good deal of shuffling and subterfuge, he at length signed; but it appears that he never intended to fulfil its obligations. It was, indeed, obvious, from the strong language he was accustomed to use to those about him, that the heart-burning and hostility produced by our expedition were not to be appeased by either words or money, although he did hold out the hollow promise of waiting on the Shah to tender his allegiance.

In November, 1838, the crooked policy of Yar Mahomed drove Colonel Stoddart and Lieut. Pottinger from Herat, and this event, being communicated by the Vizier throughout Affghanistan, roused the hopes of the disaffected, who on that ground felt assured of the co-operation of both Kamran and Persia in opposing the declared object of the British Government. Mihrab Khan, in common with the brothers of Candahar and the Ameers of Sinde, received the same tidings, and his first secret proceeding was to order the hakim of Gundava, a part of the Kelat territory, to prevent the purchase of grain and camels by the agents of our government, then employed there in the provision of stores and carriage for the troops. These facts came subsequently to our knowledge, which shew that, at the very period adverted to, whilst communications of an amicable nature were going on between him and the authorities of the advancing army, he, on the other hand, was doing his utmost to impede our march.

In the last conference with Sir Alexander Burnes, Mihrab Khan informed of our embarrassments for want of grain, and throwing off the caution he had before observed, not only denounced the Shah, but prognosticated with confidence the disorganization and ruin of our army. He, too, seemed to plume himself on a correspondence with Russia and Persia, and affected to deprecate their displeasure. "Wait!" said he, "till sickness overtakes your troops, till they are exhausted with fatigue from long and harassing marches, and from the total want of supplies; wait till they have drunk of many waters, and wait, too, till they feel the sharpness of Affghan swords." In perfect accordance with this bitter feeling, it was Mihrab Khan himself who had stimulated and directed the Beloochees to attack our baggage on the plains and in the Bolân Pass, made the villagers withhold supplies of every kind, and commanded them to do us all the injury in their power. This they certainly did to the utmost extent of their means, which happily were not of a sufficiently formidable nature to arrest our progress, though they did expose the army to many distressing privations.

Finally, Mihrab Khan refused to wait upon the Shah, then at Quetta; Sir Alexander Burnes withdrew from Kelat; and the treaty became a dead letter. The mask of duplicity being thus removed, the obvious course would have been to punish the deceiver at once; but there was no time to waste on this minor consideration, and the punishment was only deferred to a more fitting period. The hostility of Mihrab Khan, however unwise, impolitic, and destructive of his own interests, was not without some shadow of excuse. During the domination of the Barikzye rulers of Candahar, the Kelat territory, with all its accretions, had been entirely independent, and he could not but anticipate the reduction, at least, of his existing possessions, to their former limited boundary under the Suddozye monarchy. To a man, therefore, of a turbulent and tyrannical disposition, as he is represented to be, the vindictive course he pursued, under the wild impression of surviving the tempest rolling over his head, was not much at variance with the usual habits of mankind under similar circumstances. Open warfare was out of the question, and his only hope rested in professions of amity and zeal in our cause, and at the same time secretly exerting every nerve to obstruct our progress. His guilt lay in his treachery. He was undoubtedly the source of the greatest inconvenience and obstacles that occurred to the army during its long march, and they were of no ordinary magnitude. In an intercepted letter, dated after the signature of the treaty above adverted to, which was addressed to a Meer Kasim Khan, he says, "What is the use of your treaties and arrangements? All child's play. There is no relief but in death; no cure but in the destruction of the English. Their heads, goods, and bodies must be sacrificed. Strengthen the pass! Call on all the tribes to harass and destroy!"

At Quetta, repeated outrages were committed by the villagers. Not a day passed without fresh instances of their atrocious conduct. They used to come into camp with articles for sale, inveigle men out to their fastnesses, on the pretence of selling their grain cheap, and then murder them. One day, an officer of the 16th Lancers and a party of his men were fired upon by some Kaukers, from the loop-holes of a mud round tower, situated on the skirts of a hill, a short distance from camp, and one man was wounded. The Lancers rushed forward and surrounded the place, but not before several had escaped. They then dismounted, seized the end of the matchlocks which were pointed through the loop-holes, and wrung them out of the hands of the assailants, now six in number. Some of the lancers mounted upon the roof, formed of branches and a layer of mud, and, getting at the enemy, a deadly struggle ensued; the Kaukers resisting till five of them were killed, and the sixth, unequal from his wounds to any other effort, was brought into camp, and on the decision of a military tribunal, hanged next day on a tree in front of the walls at Quetta. On the following morning, the body was quietly taken down by the inhabitants of the town, and buried close to the fort gate.

Whilst in the province of Shaul, Syud Muheen Shah, who figures prominently in Conolly's interesting Narrative of his Overland Journey, arrived in camp from the sirdars of Candahar, with the view of arranging terms for them, and preventing any act of hostility. A letter had been despatched to the sirdars in February from Shikarpore, by Sir John Keane and the Envoy and Minister, advising them to tender their immediate submission to their lawful sovereign, and apprizing them that any other course would involve them in disgrace and ruin. Muheen Shah brought with him a written communication in reply to that letter, in which they said they had fulfilled all the obligations and duties of friendship with the English whenever any of their nation visited Candahar; that they had no quarrel with them, but were alarmed at the presence of their ancient enemy, Shah Shoojah, in our camp, and that Muheen Shah was deputed in the hopes of having their fears removed. The proposals he was instructed to make were said to have been of too extravagant a nature to be acceded to, and the answer returned engaged that the sirdars, on submission, should be allowed to retain all the jagheers and means of subsistence enjoyed by their ancestors; and the Shah further promised to reward them on the performance of their duties towards him with zeal and fidelity. These terms were rejected by the agent in behalf of the sirdars, whose submission was not considered worth a higher price, for, in fact, there was not the least likelihood that they could bring into the field an adequate force to embarrass our movements, even if they had the courage or the temerity to offer any resistance.

After this, an attempt was made to create and nourish a religious feeling, and exhortations and injunctions were circulated to destroy the infidels, whom, it was said, the Shah was bringing into the country to extinguish the holy Mussulman faith. But the Shah was not backward in addressing his friends at Candahar on the subject, and as no demonstration contemplated by the sirdars followed their exertions, the communications of the Shah had doubtless the intended effect.

On the 7th of April, Sir John Keane, the first brigade of the Bengal column, and the Shah, proceeded *en route* to Candahar, leaving a portion of his Majesty's troops, and the 43rd N.I. at Quetta. Orders have been given by the Envoy and Minister to raise a corps of eight hundred men, called the Bolân Rangers, on the principle so successfully adopted by Mr. Cleveland at Bhaugulpore.

The fourth brigade marched on the 9th from Quetta to Kuchlak (eleven miles), the northern boundary of the Kelat territory. As we are approaching Candahar, no part of the baggage or tents is now allowed to go on ahead, as before; a more cautious mode of proceeding on the march being required on entering Khorassan. For about six miles, the road through the valley is good; then a deep but narrow watercourse intervenes, the mountains on each side closing to within a quarter of a mile of each other. There is then a gradual ascent for about a mile over stony ground, to a considerable height, and the descent from that point is rather abrupt and dangerous. It brings us into a deep hollow or gorge between high and craggy mountains, from which, protected in convenient and well-concealed positions, the Kaukers, a tribe inhabiting that range, harassed and wounded our people on many occasions. We had a sergeant shot through the leg, and a sepoy through the shoulder. The ground is as stony as any part of the Bolân Pass. Turning round the base of the mountain to the right, we come to a spring, flowing through two parallel channels a few yards asunder, the water of which, as it gurgles over the stony bottom, is as clear as crystal. Beyond these channels is a sandy plain, bordered by mountains, but of less magnitude than those we have passed. There are several walled villages, with the usual accompaniment of orchards, in this valley, called Kuchlak, but totally deserted. We are encamped near two extensive burial—places, both with numberless graves, some of the ornamented with rows of small stones in fanciful shapes and stems of now withered plants. They have all head and foot stones, the largest at the north end; the position of the graves in Affghanistan being invariably north and south, whilst in Christian countries they are universally placed east and west.

On the 10th, a party of Punjabees, well armed, arrived. They came across the mountains from Mooltan, with camel loads of unbleached cloths for sale, and yesterday several Affghans were in camp selling raisins, almonds, and tobacco, which they had brought on asses from Candahar, one hundred miles, in only four days. We had a number of whirlwinds to-day in different parts of the camp, sending dense columns of dust perpendicularly to the sky, but without doing any damage. The dust here is very fine, and as pungent as snuff. Some of the soldiers in roaming about found accidentally the doors and fastenings belonging to the deserted hovels, underground, and heaped over with rubbish. The inhabitants had left nothing but the mud walls, and retired to the mountains, and there kept their flocks of sheep and goats, descending below daily to feed them, but rarely within sight of the troops. They could only judge of an English army from the ample experience they must have had of their own military marauders.

A correspondence has been intercepted between the Sinde Ameers, Mihrab Khan of Kelat, and the Candahar Sirdars, fully developing their hostile intentions and the perfidious nature of their conduct.

The distance from Kuchlak to Hyderzye is ten miles. The road lies through the space between low hills of red earth, without one particle of vegetation. Crossed the Logar river three times in the march. As we approached Hyderzye, and not till then, we meet with green fields of young wheat; the villagers have brought into camp loads of ottah and ghee for sale, but at a high rate, five pounds and a half for one rupee, of the former, and two and a half of the latter, made from the *Doomba* sheep tails! Plenty of Doomba sheep are also procurable at two, three, and four rupees each. The people here are Syuds, but those on the hills of the Kauker tribe.

From Hyderzye to Hykulzie, ten miles. After six miles of tolerably even ground; the road is over low hills, and then descends into an extensive valley edged with mountains. There are several villages in sight, built of mud, and apparently with more squareness and neatness than those we have passed; but I do not see the picturesque little orchards which are met with in Shaul. Whilst fancying we had escaped from the further annoyance of Beloochees, I was told that three heads had been found in a hollow close to my tent. They all bear the marks of deadly wounds both by sword and bullet. It appears that a party of Local Horse had been sent out against the marauders, and, as usual, had brought in the heads of the slain, when the first brigade was here, three days ago. They had all the sharp Beloochee nose drooping to a point, not to be mistaken, and no doubt belonged to men who continued following our track from the Bolân Pass. A venerable-looking Affghan, with a long white beard, "that swept his aged breast," an inhabitant of the neighbouring village, called Tunghi, came up to me, in a respectful manner, and entering into conversation, informed me that the principal people of that quarter had, a few days before, waited on the Shah, and joined his camp.

This is the valley of Pisheen, inhabited chiefly by Syuds, who are favourable to the Suddozye dynasty. It runs from the north-east to the south-west, and presents an immense expanse of unbroken plain, the border mountains in the extreme distance being only dimly seen. This morning, a number of Kaukers, unarmed, hovered about the rear, and at length had the confidence to walk up to the officer of the rear-guard and ask for a few articles that had fallen to the ground, and could not be taken on; these they thankfully received, and departed. This promised a better state of things; but we soon afterwards found that one of our camel-men had been cut down and murdered, whilst drinking at a well!

Marched from Tunghi, on the 13th, to a mile and a half north of the river Lora. No village near. The road crossed continually by deep fissures and dry watercourses. On both sides, plenty of cultivation. The path close to the Lora is on a ledge, of about ten feet wide, and on the right a high perpendicular bank of earth; on the left a chasm twenty feet deep, into which a waggon with six bullocks tumbled headlong, without the animals being hurt by the fall. The descent to the river, thirty feet wide and two feet deep, is very steep, and the opposite side equally precipitous. Notwithstanding the difficulties of the passage, greatly exaggerated as they have been, they were surmounted by the camels and waggons without much effort, and the park of artillery, with the four long eighteen-pounders, got over without one accident.

At Quetta, and after leaving that place, a great number of the cavalry horses had been shot, in consequence of being in an exhausted state from over-fatigue and deficiency of grain; and whenever we passed the carcases on the road, left by the column in advance, we invariably found the natives busily employed in skinning them, which they managed very dexterously. The dead camels, too, were treated in the same way, besides furnishing the hungry with a savoury repast.

In riding along, I had often observed the large black beetle trundling in the dust a round piece of cow-dung, with wonderful activity. In my walk to-day, I had an opportunity of watching the animal. After rolling the ball, three times the size of itself, to some distance, he quitted it, and began burrowing in the ground, digging away with his claws, and throwing up the loose earth incessantly, till a hole he supposed sufficiently large was made, and then he tried to push in the ball. It did not quite enter, and therefore, pushing it aside, he set to work again, and threw up more earth from below. This being done to his liking, using his head for a shovel in a very surprising way, the ball was finally deposited inside, and himself arched in. During the operation I have described, which lasted nearly one hour, the sagacity and alertness of the insect were astonishing. I have just watched another, and with precisely the same result, with this addition, that I saw him pick out and form the ball from the fresh heap on the ground. He only rolled it, however, a short distance, before he commenced upon the customary excavation. The ball is used as the nest for the insect's eggs. The British insect, the dor, clock, or dung-beetle *(Geotrupes stercorarius)*, has different materials for burying along with its eggs. It digs a deep cylindrical hole, and carrying down a mass of dung to the bottom, in it deposits its eggs. And many of the species of the genus *Ateuchus* roll together wet dung into round pellets, deposit an egg in the midst of each, and when dry, push them backwards with their hind-feet into holes of the surprising depth of three feet, which they have previously dug for their reception. The proceedings of the tremble dung-beetle of America *(Scarabæus pilularius,* Linn.) are thus described by Catesby:— "I have attentively admired their industry, and mutually assisting of each other in rolling their globular balls from the places where they made them to that of their interment, which is usually the distance of some yards. This they perform breech foremost, by raising their hind parts, and forcing along the ball with their hind-feet."

Scorpions are said to abound in all the valleys, but I have only seen one. It had been caught, and was preserved in spirits. Porcupines' quills are found in all directions, and small tortoises; these are roasted alive in their shells, and their flesh picked out and eaten by the natives. The burnt empty shells, near a quantity of wood ashes, are constantly seen on the road. Two nights ago, the 1st Brigade was under arms, upon information that a chuppao, or night attack, would be made on the camp, but nothing occurred. Fowls, eggs, grain, ghee, asses, and camels, brought in for sale. The camels are led by Hubshees, who are, in a Mahomedan country, slaves, of course. Affghans on horseback, gaily dressed, and armed with sword, dagger, shield, and matchlock, with attendants, are moving about the tents, seeing and examining every thing. This may be considered a questionable proceeding, and not much in accordance with the caution proper to be observed in a country still in possession of an enemy. Abdoolah Khan, the chief of Pisheen, is said to have laid the whole valley under contribution, plundered the refractory or those who resisted his exactions, and ran off, to aid the cause of Dost Mahomed.

We are surrounded by robbers and murderers, carrying off our camels and horses whenever an opportunity occurs. The forbearance in letting utter strangers traverse the camp, "with curious eye" armed or unarmed, is doubtful, for till Shah Shoojah is proclaimed, and there are unequivocal manifestations of the nation's allegiance to him, we cannot do otherwise than consider ourselves in an enemy's country. The people cannot oppose us by a military force, but they can annoy and harass us, and cripple our means of getting in our supplies by stealing our cattle; and they do this from day to day with increasing vigilance and perseverance. The character of those we are among is of the most diabolical kind. Treacherous and blood-thirsty, they are always ready to take life, even without the stimulus of provocation.

Cunning, too, is an equally prominent feature in their conduct. An officer purchased a donkey at Quetta, and this morning it was claimed while at graze, and nearly taken away, by an Affghan, as his own, having just brought it, he said, from his village in the mountains. A man, who had sold all his wheat, left his empty bag on the ground, and returning soon after, accused two women with having stolen his corn. The parties were brought forward, and on the examination of evidence, the Affghan's rascality was at once ascertained and exposed. The Bengallees and Hindoostanees are sharp, but they acknowledge themselves beaten by the Khorassanees.

April 15.-Marched from the right bank of the Lora to Arumbee, near the Killah of Abdullah Khan, six miles. About a mile before coming to the ground, is a circular mound with a plateau about eighty feet diameter, and thirty feet high, with sloping sides. It is full of graves, like those at Kuchlak, the position north and south, the people always preferring lofty situations for interment. In the whole extent of this valley, as far as I can see, there is scarcely a tree; it is perfectly flat. A correspondence has been just intercepted in the pass by the engineers, who are making the roads practicable for the guns, addressed by the Candahar chiefs to the chief of the Tull Chintiali country, exciting him to oppose us with all his means. It seems they imagined we were still at Quetta. The Chintiali state lies to the east of the Bolân Pass, so that the requisition of the sirdars would have been rather too late to be of use. The rapacity of the Beloochees, however, could hardly have been exceeded if the chief of Chintiali had known the wishes of his friends at Candahar. The inhabitants, mounted and on foot, with camels, asses, and grain, are more numerous in camp than yesterday, and estimated at three hundred. A party of horse ordered out to recover camels which had been carried off at graze. After a hard ride of six miles, the thieves were overtaken, three of them killed, and the camels brought back. It was dark before the party returned.

April 16.-From Arumbee to the commencement of the Kojuk Pass, seven miles. After crossing about a mile and a half of the Pisheen plain, our course lay among the low hills to the north, over a stony road, which continued to the encamping ground, about four miles to the east of the Killah of Abdullah Khan. The fort appears to be a large one, in fine order, with bastions, and beautifully situated on the long slope from the hills. It is well stocked with fine fruit-trees, and has stabling sufficient for a hundred and forty horses. One of the Shah's regiments and some cavalry are ordered to garrison the fort, in addition to which, a body of Achekzyes, or men of the neighbouring hills, two hundred strong, is to be raised for the protection of this part of the country.

Since leaving Quetta, we have had good grazing ground, and the mortality among the camels is greatly decreased. The horses seem to have taken their place in the ranks of death from want of grain. We have had frequent whirling gusts of wind, which last for half a minute, to-day, filling the tents with clouds of dust. They are limited to a small circumference, and ascend spirally to a great height. The soldiers call them "Devils." The tops of the adjacent hills are covered with graves, piled over with stones, as before described.

April 17.-We have crossed the Kojak Pass in the Khojeh Amraun range of mountains. This has been a day of days. At the foot of the hills on each side of us, going up to the pass, were regular rows of middling-sized trees, of a similar form to those in the Bolân Pass, with thick silvery trunks, and a round body of foliage. In several parts they were very numerous, but still in line, and gave an idea of former care having been taken in embellishing the ground. They had all the appearance of a mall, or boulevard, and must have been a favourite spot in times gone by. The cuckoo and noisy magpie were now heard, I think for the first time. The bordering of trees lasted all the way, the intermediate track lessening, till we got to a part of the pass called Purush, six miles and three-quarters from where we started. At Purush, stupendous masses of perpendicular rocks, which form the commencement of the narrow part, fronted us, and on a nearer approach, we found two paths, only a few yards wide; that which branched off on the left was watered by a trickling rill, and was the common kafila route — that on the right, or rather straightforward, was dry, but rarely used, and had been cleared and made practicable by the engineers for the passage of the troops and artillery.[33] It was while reconnoitring in this defile that Brigadier Arnold and his aide-de-camp were fired upon from the heights by a Peshkhidmut, or look-out party, under Ibar Khan, said to be in the service of the Candahar sirdars; but upon some sappers and miners shewing themselves prepared to attack them, they rode off, and were not seen again. The road up to the defile had gradually increased in steepness, and diminished in width, and now the ascent became still more difficult. The tediousness of the march, therefore, may be easily conceived. The very narrow part is about two miles, and then it widened a little to a tolerably open space, where the old path to the left was so steep as to be quite impracticable for our purpose, and in consequence the engineers, taking a wide sweep, had cut another less abrupt upon the brow of the hill on the right hand. It was not, however, above eight or ten feet in breadth, and the upper part was still, owing to the projection and some rocks, difficult of access, but it was overcome.[34] The descent from that point for a considerable distance was very abrupt, precipitous, and winding, and the bottom crossed by a small torrent. The view up to the next portion of the pass was rather frightful, both on account of its altitude and the broken course to be pursued in toiling up to the summit. The first slope was strewed with dead camels; I counted sixteen together on one precipitous spot, and the face of the whole acclivities exhibited similar evidence of the peril which attended our progress. The column diverged, following different paths, and at length accomplished its task.[35] The top commanded a fine view of the encampment of the 1st Brigade, in the remote distance, at a place called Chumun, but no more meriting that name, which means 'a garden,' than Salisbury plain. The descent[36] threatened disaster among the camels, and it was not long before a great number of them tumbled headlong down into the ravines. Over Mount Cenis or the Simplon, the road is good in the most difficult parts, but here, it may be said, there was nothing of the kind, added to which the earth was soft and loose, and afforded but an insecure footing. The column and its innumerable followers took three different routes. We encamped near the bottom of the hills, but still on the slope, about two miles from the commencement of the plain of

---

[33] The eighth drawing in my collection represents the entrance into this pass.
[34] The ninth drawing in my collection represents the troops emerging from the narrow part of the defile, and the old and newly-constructed roads up the ascent.
[35] The tenth drawing of my collection shews the first descent, and the direction of the troops upwards.
[36] This descent is represented in the eleventh drawing of my collection

Chumun. Our position is as if we were in the lower part of a bowl, being closely surrounded by hills, rising in rather a concave form upwards, from which the hereditary robbers, the Achikzyes, may, in the night-time, do great injury by firing on the people, scattered as they are on the cliffs in all directions. But, from the first, the marauders have shewn no predilection for night work. Daylight and the rearguard have almost in every instance constituted the time and object of their depredations.[37]

Only two of the long 18-pounders belonging to the park were got over yesterday, assisted by a detachment of fatigue-men from the European Regiment, the 13th Light Infantry, and 48th N.I. Our loss in public cattle, ammunition, and stores, has been great. It is said that twenty-five thousand rounds of ball-cartridge had fallen into the hands of the Achikzyes, in consequence of the camels on which they were loaded having died on the road. Some of the officers with a few sepoys chased a band of the robbers over a second range, and came to a place where their plunder had been collected, consisting of three barrels of gunpowder, tents cut to pieces, boots, shoes, a prayer-book, uniforms, trunks, swords, tea, coffee, cigars, &c. &c. Several of the robbers were shot in the pursuit. The gunpowder was blown up, and the other articles were too much damaged and torn to be of use. It was not before the 21st, that the whole park of artillery and train of waggons were got over the pass-five days of indefatigable exertion, performed by the troops, under a burning sun, with the utmost cheerfulness. In returning to camp, the 1st European Regiment, which had distinguished itself by extraordinary efforts on the occasion, gave a joyous "Huzza!" The mountaineers are constantly committing outrages, rolling down heavy stones from the crags which overlook the regimental bazaar, and firing into the camp. Indeed firing into the camp was a nightly practice. Stragglers are often cut off in the daytime, and a ruffian was hanged a few days ago for having wounded a water-carrier dangerously, whilst drawing water at a well. Several Europeans have been murdered under similar circumstances. The guards in the pass, however, have done considerable execution among the merciless wretches.

We hear from the camp ahead, that the Affghans have cut off the supply of water at Dundi-golai, and that a body of invulnerable horsemen, with charmed lives, are determined to come to action, and destroy the infidel Ferenghees! The 1st Brigade will no doubt be delighted at their resolution. A cossid had just been taken, with letters from Kohn Dil Khan, urging the chiefs in this quarter to assist him in exterminating the English, and informing them that he had 12,000 foot and 5,000 horse ready to fight us. The boast looks like a *ruse-de-guerre,* and the

---

[37] The twelfth drawing in my collection represents the third descent of the Kojak Pass, looking back from three parts down, where the 1st Bengal European Regiment had encamped, to assist in bringing over the artillery.

cossid was doubtless sent, like another Sinon, on purpose to be taken. *Nous verrons.*

April 21.-We now hear upon good authority that Rehim Dil Khan and his brother, Mehr Dil Khan, accompanied by several other chiefs, had left Candahar with 3,000 cavalry, with the professed intention of opposing us, and had actually got as far as Killah Fut'oolah. Kobn Dil Khan had remained in the city, as well to protect the interests of himself and family as to watch over the suspected disposition and motions of the inhabitants. Some of the small parties detached by Rehim Dil Khan and his brother had distinguished themselves by an achievement or two, having carried off two elephants belonging to the envoy and minister, which had been taken too far from camp for forage, and plundered and killed some of our helpless camp followers. But this was the sole amount of their warlike operations. The flimsy nature of the combination soon became apparent. Resolutions were formed to attack us by night, a *shub-khoon,* or *chuppao,* being a favourite military tactic among themselves, and among themselves it commonly succeeded. But they discovered that we had vigilant sentries and picquets, and they despaired of producing any effect on our camp. They had many a consultation, many a counsel, on the posture of affairs, which ended in Hajee Khan Kauker, one of the most influential chiefs in their interests, quitting them on some plausible pretext, and coming quietly into our camp on the 20th, with about two hundred followers, to tender his allegiance to the Shah! On the same day, Abdool Mujeed Khan, the son of Shah Pusund Khan, Governor of Lash, and Gholam Akhoond-zadah very loyally followed his example. The defection of these men from the combination was fatal to all further hope, if hope ever existed, among the sirdars. Rehim Dil Khan and Mehr Dil Khan, accompanied by their invincible cavalry, then rode precipitately back to Candahar.

The name of Hajee Khan was originally Taj Mahomed Khan, a Kauker by tribe, of humble birth; by his craftiness and talents, he rose to be a personage of consequence in times of political strife and revolution. He had often distinguished himself, not only as an intrepid soldier, but as a politician of the most versatile class. He had intrigued even in favour of the Sikhs during their hostilities with the Affghans, when Peshawer fell into their hands, and at the present time he had a nominal allowance of 60,000 rupees per annum, and the command of some hundred cavalry, under Rehim Dil Khan, whose sole object in employing him was, it is said, to prevent the accomplished intriguer from falling into other hands. But we shall see more of the Hajee by-and-by.

April 22.-The laborious duties at the pass being finished, we marched to Chumun, the first brigade having moved in advance from that place on the 19th. *Chumun* implies a garden, a meadow land, or a piece of ground luxuriant with rich vegetation; but here we have a sterile, dirty surface, which must have received its name in derision. The hills on the north side of the Kojak even have better claims to the appellation. They abound with wild thyme, rosemary, flowers like pinks and daisies; hyoscyamus, leeks of a mild flavour, and the rhubarb plant (the *rawash*) grow thick all over them. The leaf is something like that of a large cabbage, projecting from the root, near the surface of the ground; the stem and flower about three feet high, and the root as thick as the wrist, running and branching out several feet deep in the earth. It is surprising to see flowers of the brightest tint peeping up singly on arid, parched, and stony ground.

April 23.-Upon the probability of finding no water at Dundigolai, we are directed to march this evening, and should the information prove correct, we can push on ten miles further, to Killah Fut'oolah, where no deficiency is apprehended. The march of ten miles will then be more conveniently effected than during day, in the present hot weather. At 9 A.M. a smart shock of an earthquake was experienced in a direction from south to north. There was a rumble in the ground; fifteen minutes after, another shock with rushing noises was felt, of longer duration and greater force. The heat was very intense at the time, and had been for some days.

April 24.-Our multitudinous brigade, now consisting of the European Regiment, the 35th, and 37th N.I., the park of artillery, and the 4th Local Horse, marched yesterday evening exactly at six. The road descends considerably, but without abruptness, and decreases in elevation to the extent of two thousand feet. About midnight we came to a shallow basin of water, but only fit for cattle. There we halted an hour, and four miles further on, between hills, we arrived at the place designated Dundigolai. Search was immediately made for water, but the reservoir was perfectly dry, and not a drop to be found anywhere; we therefore pushed on. The moon was but a week old, and only gave us a dim light till three, up to which period we were obliged to have numerous halts, to allow time for the park of guns and waggons to come up. After that, another long halt to the break of dawn, and we finally reached Killah Fut'oolah at seven.

This was a most tedious and harassing march, and far eclipsed, in every thing that was disagreeable, the fatigues of the past. The termination of this night's exertion, too, was not of a nature to soothe the distressed mind, but to sharpen disappointment; for what were our surprise and vexation on discovering that, instead of good water, none drinkable was to be found, the villagers having filled the wells with the limbs of murdered men, earth and stones; and a little nullah, flowing beautifully a few days before; was now quite dry. The distance marched was, I think, full twenty-six miles, at the lingering rate of two miles an hour. We were, however, not to be foiled by this device of the enemy, and every exertion was forthwith made to restore the water to its usual channel, and the object was effected, but only in a limited degree. The water of the nullah just mentioned was derived from a mountain-spring ten miles to the east of the camp. Killah Fut'oolah is merely a mud-wall enclosure for a collection of hovels, called a village, and is situated near two hills, opposite to each other, and between which the road to Candahar lies. The place was entirely deserted, and not a native to be seen.

April 25.-In consequence of the small quantity of water, the 35th was ordered to go on in advance this morning to Melamundee. Since we left Arumhee nothing has been brought into camp for sale; in the pass nothing but hostility was met with, and on this side, so near Candahar, the threats of the sirdars will probably keep the people aloof. Sir John Keane, with the first brigade, was at Fut'oolah on the 21st, and would be at Melamundee on the 22nd, Deh Hajee on the 23rd, Khooshab on the 24th, and probably at Candahar on the 25th. From this movement, so many days in advance of us, it is to be inferred that the Shah and our authorities are pretty sure of a satisfactory reception there; nothing else would seem to account for such a straggling disposition of our army. The Bombay troops are as many days in our rear as the first brigade are ahead of us, they being at the Kojak Pass to-day. A *badi-gird,* or whirlwind, has just rushed over the plains at a rate of no less than four miles an hour, presenting its perpendicular compact form, like a flying column, and leaving not a trace of dust behind. In noticing this curious effect of wind and dust, called the "devil," on a former occasion, I omitted to mention its horizontal progression.

There are rumours of camels carried off to the hills, and several officers and sepoys have started to overtake the robbers. No quarter. The loss of camels is the loss of the sinews of war in this country. Treasure, ammunition, grain, baggage, cannot be moved without them. The loss is, therefore, three-fold; the value of the animals, the value of the loads, and the want of means to get on. But robbery is said to be the first step in the march of civilization: it may be equally said to be the last. Gibbon remarks that "the sober historian is forcibly wakened from a pleasing vision, and is compelled with some reluctance to confess that the pastoral manners, which have been adorned with the fairest attributes of peace and innocence, are much better adapted to the fierce and cruel habits of a military life."[38] One of the officers, whose horse was more fleet than the rest, overtook the robbers, fired his pistol, but missed, and they, with the activity of monkeys, escaped into the hills. Twenty camels, however, were recovered.

In the evening, a respectable-looking man, declaring himself to be a dependent of Hajee Kauker, brought into camp several bullock-loads of flour for sale, which were eagerly bought up at four pounds the rupee. He says he has a little fort over the adjacent mountain, and understands that the sirdars have abandoned Candahar.

Marched on the 26th at half-past two A.M. from Fut'oolah to Melamundee, eleven miles and a half. The road between mountains all the way, and the whole

---

[38] Decline and Fall, chap. xxvi.

more or less stony. The last mile and half is through a hollow, like a watercourse, where we found a number of graves. The middle of the hollow had a line of wells, at short distances, not more than a foot or two deep, and eight or ten inches in diameter, from which excellent water was obtained. The bodies of two Hindoostanees, hacked almost to pieces, were seen on the road. Murdered men and dead camels are constantly brought to our view on the march. The scenery, rugged mountain and plain, and rarely a tree to be found. No town or village that deserves the name. The troops harassed by long marches, with limited food, and no chance of relief even at Candahar. The weather, too, as hot as in the provinces at this season of the year. The thermometer 92° in tents, and the high wind keeps us in a cloud of dust. The inhabitants in most parts freebooters. The plains we have passed over, narrow or wide, are not like the plains of Europe, but an expanse of stony or sandy earth, studded or scattered over with tufts of herbs and wild grass, each small tuft two or three yards from its fellow, and hardly fit for the camels to browze upon. At Melamundee, like most other places where we halted, there is no appearance of any thing to give it a name.

Again, at half-past two A.M. from Melamundee to Tuktapool, fourteen miles. On the road, within two or three miles of the latter place, is a detached rock, from which issues a clear gushing spring, called Lylee Mujnoon, a name of course simply in honour of the two lovers celebrated by the Persian poets, the scene of their passion having been Arabia. There is a fine river called the Doree, within a hundred yards of camp, from which we have got a few small trout, very good. Still mountains on every side, but at a considerable distance. The villagers have come in with dry tobacco, selling it at four rupees the pound. Scarcely were our tents pitched this morning, when there was a cry of camels being carried off on going to graze as usual. A party of horse forthwith proceeded to the spot, and found the missing camels among a herd of fifty others. Two men and a boy were taken prisoners, the men kept in custody, and the boy sent back to tell his friends that if another camel was touched during our stay, the men would be immediately shot. This answered the purpose, for no further attempt was made to disturb the camp.

Marched from Tuktapool to Deh-Hajee, eight miles, road good. Still mountains, "rude, barren, and bare," on either side. We are now only sixteen miles from Candahar, and letters from thence tell us that, on the approach of the Shah, the three brothers with their families, and about two hundred followers, fled from the city on their way to Grishk, a small fortress on the river Helmund, which belonged to them, and formerly to their brother, the Vizier Futtih Khan. The two elephants belonging to the Envoy and Minister, which were carried off at Fut'oolah, became useful, and supplied a conveyance for the wives and family of Rehim Dil Khan to their place of refuge.

The Envoy and Minister, in his official letter to the Government of India, dated the 24th of April, thus describes the approach of the Shah to Candahar:-

"This morning, we marched upon Candahar, a distance of about eighteen miles, and we are now encamped within two miles of the city. The spectacle which presented itself on the road was the most interesting one it ever fell to my lot to witness. His Excellency Lieut.-General Sir John Keane, with the Army of the Indus, was one march in our rear, our advance having been made on an erroneous calculation of the distance, which was too great to be performed by the European troops from the heat of the weather. The Shah's disciplined troops were behind us, and his majesty advanced, attended only by the officers of the mission and his own immediate retainers. At every hundred yards of our progress, we were met by bands of well-mounted and well-armed men all tendering their allegiance to his majesty, whilst the peaceable inhabitants of the city assembled in crowds, and manifested their joy at the Shah's restoration in the most unbounded terms. Tranquillity is restored, the people flock to our camp with the greatest confidence; there is no longer any apprehension of scarcity, and even the confidential servants of the sirdars, several of whom have visited me, declare their satisfaction at the change of Government, and state that they would sooner have joined the Shah, but for the dread that some evil would have been inflicted on their families, whom they must have left in the city."

On the morning of the 25th the Shah entered Candahar.

CHAPTER VIII.

OCCUPATION OF CANDAHAR.

Appearance of the city on approaching it — Its siege by Nadir Shah — The interior of Candahar — Tomb of Ahmed Shah — The houses mud hovels — The habits of the inhabitants filthy — Inauguration of Shah Shoojah — Grand spectacle — Apathy of the people — Assassination of a British officer — the Kelat Chief — Letters from Dost Mahomed Khan — Atrocious murder of camp-followers — Sickness of the troops.

UPON the flight of the sirdars, the Shah wished to send a detachment of his own troops immediately in pursuit; but the Envoy and Minister, considering the excitement that prevailed, and that, in the event of their being overtaken, they might be subjected to insult and injury from the Shah's over-zealous horsemen, deemed it advisable to make another offer through Mullah Nassoo, a confidential adviser of Kohn Dil Khan, which he thought would be accepted. The kind intervention of the Envoy, however, was of no avail; the terms were rejected, and, in consequence, a strong detachment, under Brigadier Sale, was ordered to proceed towards Grishk; but, on reaching the Helmund, they found that the sirdars had not stopped there, but continued their route towards Meshed.

On the 29th of April, we marched to Khooshab, ten miles, a flat extensive plain all the way. In the neighbourhood of Khooshab are immense fields of wheat ripening fast; an abundant harvest is now of the utmost consequence to us. The village is a large one, and almost every mud hovel in it is covered with a dome, half of them in ruins. The inhabitants, men, women, and children, are sitting, some standing on the tops of their houses to see the troops pass; all laughing gaily, and seeming quite at their ease. Our camp is at the foot of a lofty mountain to the north.

Started at day-break on the 30th for Candahar. Passed over the slope of the mountain on our right; the ascent was not difficult. We then descended into a plain, passed over a large burying-ground, and through the village called Kerz, celebrated for the peculiar excellence of the grapes produced there. Our course lay through a very narrow street between broken mud walls. Most of the hovels are dome-built, a cheap mode, requiring no wood-work, and the entrances more like holes leading to a cave than door-ways. The inhabitants were, here too, on the tops of their dwellings, and their features appeared more of the Malay cast than I had conceived of Affghans. They were dirty in the extreme.

Over the plain in front of us, and under a rugged mountain to the north, was seen the longthought-of city of Candahar, a lofty dome, the dome of Ahmed Shah, being the most remarkable and conspicuous object that rose above the long horizontal line of mud wall which encompasses the western capital of Affghanistan. The distance from our last ground is about six miles, and we are about four miles to the southward of the city, on a fine spacious plain, the very spot on which the battle was fought between Shah Shoojah and Dost Mahomed Khan in 1834. Not far from us is the old city of Candahar, said to have been founded by Hussain Shah Ghilzye, by whose name it is generally known among the Affghans. The crumbling walls are of uncommon thickness, entirely formed of mud, and though some parts of the buildings are still in a tolerable condition, the whole presents a melancholy picture of ruin and decay.

Contiguous is the renowned Chehel Zeena, or rock of forty steps, which lead to a small arched structure on the summit, not above eight feet square, adorned with numerous inscriptions. The principal one informs us that it was begun by order of the Emperor Bâber, in commemoration of his having conquered Candahar, on the 13th of Shawul, 928, Hijra (A.D. 1522), and that it was completed in 953 (1547), seventeen years after his death; so that the work must have been a quarter of a century in hand. They are hewn out of the hard flinty rock, as well as the two lions which stand at the top. They are exceedingly difficult to ascend, but the labour is well rewarded by a most extensive prospect. Indeed, the inscription states that it was intended to be a *jehan noomah,* or a summer-house, for enjoying the surrounding scenery.

Nadir Shah carried on the siege of Candahar upwards of a year, Forster says eighteen months, Hussain Shah holding out with unconquerable firmness. But when famine had committed great ravages among the people, his daughter, moved to compassion by the constant sight of their sufferings, privately sent a messenger to Nadir, to point out the place from whence he might readily put an end to the contest. This was near the Chehel Zeena, the path to which was entered by the road from the city. Tradition also gives a wonderful account of this affair, and says that Nadir's guns were dragged up the almost inaccessible mountain which overlooked the capital by means of cotton and grape-stalks being thrown under the wheels to secure them in their progress! The enterprise was successful, and Candahar was annexed to the dominions of Persia. This was in 1738.

Sir John Keane, who arrived with the 1st brigade on the 26th, had encamped half a mile west from the Herat gate, in a grove of mulberry trees, and surrounded by fields of clover.

May 1.-Yesterday, our accounts from the city of what was procurable were very gloomy. Nothing but ice and vegetables; neither tea nor sugar. To-day, there is every thing in abundance, except grain, but very dear — sugar five rupees per seer, and tea, bad too, sixteen rupees. We had boiled beans and lettuce at dinner, which was a great treat, after *doomba* mutton, fowls, and chupattees, for such a long period. This morning, we had a dish of beautifully ripe mulberries on our breakfast-table.

On the 3rd of May, we moved forward to within a mile and a half of the city, on the south-east side, near the ruins of the capital built by Nadir Shah to supersede the old one. The fragments of mud still bear his name.[39] The present city was founded by Ahmed Shah, not many years afterwards. It is situated on the north side of an extensive plain, about two miles from the lofty mountain called Baba Wulee,[40] and it is surrounded by a high mud wall, with numerous bastions. It is an oblong square; the length about five thousand feet, and the breadth four thousand. A small stream runs across the interior, north and south, called the Abipatoo. The walls are about thirty feet high. To the south is the Shikarpore gate, to the east the Caubul gate, and to the west the Herat and Tope-khana gates. To the north is the Eed-gah gate, which leads to the palace, arg, or citadel, occupying that side. There are four principal streets, about thirty or forty feet wide, sometimes called bazaars, being lined with shops. They cross the area at right angles, from the different gates, and at the centre there is a covered building, called the Char-soo, in diameter fifty or sixty feet, surmounted by a dome, under which dealers and traders expose their wares and commodities for sale. Others, again, are squatted, selling their goods, on each side of the streets, some having little holes of shops, and the greater number on the bare ground, — swords, shields, knives, horse-furniture, fruit, small looking-glasses of the most common kind, flat oblong cakes of bread, like saddle-flaps, kabobs, &c., form a part of their varied stock. At the end of the street, running north from the Shikarpore gate, is the palace, hidden by a rude building of mud. The interior, however, is spacious, of light summer-house architecture, and embellished with trees and fountains, in accordance with the taste and customs of the Affghans.

On the north-west side of the city is the still unfinished tomb of Ahmed Shah, the grandfather of Shah. Shoojah. It is octagonal, with minarets, and is surmounted by a smaller octagon, also with minarets, and then a dome; the height may be about eighty feet. But the whole is of indifferent workmanship. The blue and white glazed tile predominates on the outside surface, and another tile, variegated with yellow, in imitation of gold, is employed for the embellishment of the inside. The diminutive wooden doors, clumsily constructed, with little padlocks of the coarsest kind, are more fitting for a beggar's hut than a temple. The grave of Ahmed Shah is not in the middle, but awkwardly on one side of the pavement, and there are several others, smaller and of different dimensions, scattered as it were between it and the wall, belonging to the same family. The dome outside is roughly plastered, with parts of the scaffolding still sticking in holes of the brick-work, though nothing could have been done to it for the last

---

[39] The thirteenth drawing in my collection represents the distant city of Candahar, taken from the camp of the 4th brigade.
[40] Baba Wulee was a Mussulman Saint, who lived about four centuries ago, and his tomb, a place of pilgrimage and of great sanctity, is upon this mountain; an annual fair is held there, which is attended by crowds of devotees from all quarters.

thirty years, that is, since the Barukzye rule, succeeding that of the Suddozye monarchy. The precincts of the tomb are said to be still a sanctuary for the guilty, as sacred as ever was the Holy Rood. Near the palace were six old guns, supported on trucks, left by the sirdars, in a most useless condition. The quadrangle in front was full of the Shah's suwars and body-guard, as slovenly as can well be imagined. In going along, the passenger is jostled everywhere by Affghan horsemen, who throng the streets, with huge folds of cloth on their heads and backs, armed with shield, matchlock, spear, sword, and dagger. Without all these accompaniments, an Affghan cannot move from his hovel; indeed, as Minerva sprung fully equipped from the head of Jupiter, so an Affghan springs from his resting-place in the morning, armed at all points. Their mud houses are more like places for cattle than the habitations for men. Not only in every corner, but all along the sides of the mud walls in the street, are the filthy habits of the inhabitants brought to view. The women of the lower sort go about unveiled — their features large and masculine. The better sort, or those in better circumstances, cover themselves with a chadder, or sheet, peeping through a piece of net-work, already described in the notice of Ahmidpore. The men are neither disrespectful nor the contrary, but indifferent. The only mark of wonder and curiosity I observed was displayed in a crowd of them minutely examining and feeling every part of a buggy, belonging to an officer of the army. Doubtless, they had never seen such a vehicle before at Candahar.

May 8.-This has been a grand day for the Shah. In honour of his restoration, all the troops were out, Bengal and Bombay cavalry, horse artillery and foot, European and Native, about eight thousand men. They assembled at daylight on the plain north of the city walls. After going through sundry manœuvres, they passed successively in review-order before his majesty, and it was truly a magnificent sight to see so noble a force in so admirable a condition, after so long and arduous a march. The scene was highly exhilarating. The Shah was seated on a musnud, raised on a platform four or five feet high. Two chowrie-burdars, meanly dressed, stood behind him, waving the cow-tail chowries over his head, a part of royal etiquette. A common-looking hookah-burdar took him a *kazyan,* of common shape, except the *surpoos,* which was in the form of a peacock, and apparently made of gold. The Shah smoked only a few whiffs, according to custom, and then sent it away.[41] The Shah and his chowrie-burdars only on the platform, the construction of which was not very appropriate accommodation for a king. What a contrast! The brilliant scene before him, and the simplicity of his appearance, for his whole attire was as remote from regal

---

[41] Mr. Elphinstone says, in 1809 "the Kalyân was of gold, enamelled, and richly set with jewels; the part where the tobacco was placed was in the shape of a peacock, about the size of a pigeon, with plumage of jewels and enamel."

splendour as the humble throne upon which he reclined. The throne, as it may be called, consisted of a carpet and three large pillows, one on each side, and one at his back. In front, below, sat the British mission, and on the left Sir John Keane. A canopy covered the whole, and shaded them from the sun.

I cannot say much about the Affghan multitude. The walls of the well-raised tombs in the great burying-ground, between the city and the military spectacle, were crowded with thousands of spectators, but upon the spot there might not have been above five hundred, which was occasioned by guards of local horse being stationed at some distance to keep off the pressure of the people. A loud shout was raised, "May the king live for ever!" but not quite in the *"Vive le roi"* fashion. We must not, however, judge an Affghan, a Candaharee Affghan, by a European standard. He is a solemn animal, and not addicted to enthusiastic public rejoicing on any occasion. The people do not understand it; even the marvellous sight of a British army, such as was never either seen or could be imagined in this part of the world, seemed, from external appearances, to produce no symptom of excitement or surprise among them.

They gazed on without emotion of any kind, "dull as the fat weed that rots on Lethe's wharf." The drawing up of such a force was, indeed, a puzzle to them, and they viewed quietly and patiently the scene before them, as if uncertain what would be the result, or what sort of *hikmut* (manœuvring), formidable or otherwise, might be displayed by the Feringhees! It might almost be supposed that they were influenced by an impression similar to that described by Mr. Elphinstone, in his account of Caubul: "They believed," says he, "that we carried great guns packed up in trunks, and that we had certain small boxes so contrived as to explode and kill half-a-dozen men each, without hurting us; and there was a story current, that we had made and animated a wooden ram at Mooltan; that we had sold him as a ram, and that it was not till the purchaser began to eat him, that the material of which he was made was discovered!"[42]

May 29.-A dreadful event occurred last night. Lieuts. Wilmer and Inverarity, 16th Lancers, had been out fishing in the Argundab river, a distance of some miles from camp, and were returning late; it was about nine o'clock, but bright moonlight. Lieut. Wilmer happened to have been a good deal behind, when Inverarity, walking on, and just descending the declivity towards Candahar, along a rugged path, not more than three feet wide between the ridges, under the buffalo-hump-looking mountain, called Baba Wullee, was struck by a heavy stone, and knocked down. He was then attacked by a band of miscreants with swords, and cruelly murdered. Lieut. Wilmer was also attacked, but warding off

---

[42] The population of Candahar at this time was reported to me by a Moollah, as consisting of twelve thousand Durranees, twelve thousand Gholam Khanahs, and twenty-four thousand Ghilzes; making a total of forty-eight thousand.

the first blows with a stick, succeeded in effecting his escape. He ran back to the camp of one of the Shah's regiments, and, returning immediately with a party, proceeded to the place where Inverarity had fallen. Poor fellow! he was still alive, but died on the spot, and the murderers had disappeared.

Accounts just received, mention that the Kelat chief is utterly confounded by our successful march to Candahar. His treachery had been nourished by the conviction that we should never be able to surmount the difficulties so formidable at the Kojak Pass, defended as he expected it would be by the boasted vigilance and bravery of Kohn Dil Khan and his troops with "Affghan swords." He also anticipated that fatigue and sickness would wholly paralyze our efforts, and "keeping the word of promise" for supplies "to our ear," continued to stimulate his Beloochees to harass our march at every accessible point. Whilst he fancied that he was deceiving others, he was industriously bringing on his own ruin.

The war-cry begun by the sirdars was now vehemently re-echoed by Dost Mahomed Khan, as the tempest drew nearer to the capital, and he addressed the following letter to Mihrab Khan of Kelat: "I constantly hear of your good faith and attachment to me. Do not trust the words of the accursed English. You are not to be deceived by their knavery and money. You have a high regard for the Mussulman laws, and have not forgotten the friendship between us. The English have made the name and presence of Shah Shoojah a tool to carry on their designs, and to deceive the good and true Mahomedans. The infidels have put disgrace upon the inhabitants of Candahar, and they have killed the people by famine. Thank God! the Brahooes, champions of the faith, have plundered them in the Bolân Pass, and the Ghiljies are also destroying them, and carrying off their camels at Candahar. I have now four thousand horsemen, one thousand matchlock men, and ten pieces of artillery, commanded by my sons, Mahomed Afzul Khan, and Mahomed Azim Khan, and when joined by Gool Mahomed and Abdoo Rohman, they will attack and plunder the suburbs of Candahar. Gholam Hyder, the Governor of Ghizni, will be ready with four thousand horsemen for their assistance, and I myself, after keeping all the affairs of the Peshawer infidels under the management of Mahomed Akber, my son, aided by Momens, Khalîls, and Afreedees, will proceed to fight the infidels towards Candahar. Wade, the Feringhee, with the son of Shah Shoojah, is at Peshawer, and cannot, dare not, oppose my son. When I get to the ground of conflict, I will wage desperate war, to preserve the faith and laws of the Prophet, against the infidels, and sacrifice sons, relations, friends, Affghans, and myself in the glorious cause. Make the Brahooes and Beloochees harass and plunder in the Bolân Pass. I hope Almighty God will deliver us from this unclean crew of infidels, and put all their riches into the possession of the Mussulman champions of the faith!"

Dost Mahomed at the same time sent another fulmination to Abdoo Rohman, the Ghiljie chief, as follows:— "Your letters have reached me. If God favours me, you shall share my honours and riches. Every thing shall be sacrificed for the protection of the faith. May the Kafir-Feringhees[43] be the food of the sword, and all their property and wealth be ours! Yesterday, the 20th of Rubbi-ool-awul, I sent forth my sons, Afzul and Azim, with four thousand horse, experienced warriors, ten pieces of artillery, and five hundred matchlock men. They have been instructed on every point, and will receive your assistance to shed the blood of the accursed English, and plunder their baggage. I am satisfied the Sikhs will not aid the English against me. All the tribes of Momens, Khalîls, Afreedees, and Bajorees, have joined my son. Gholam Hyder, with two thousand horse, is ready at Ghizni, and I am also engaged in preparations to march. The accursed nation, the English, have done good to nobody. The capture of Candahar has been to them an ominous event. It has bound the chain of malediction round their necks, and they will never get rid of it. May God destroy Hajee the infidel (Hajee Kauker), and my shameless brothers, who abandoned Candahar without a struggle. However, praise God, you and I will leave a good name in the world. Rest assured that my sons and army will follow this letter; and, after them, I will also join you in person, and sacrifice myself in defending the faith of the Prophet against the infidel English. Write to me till we meet."

Such were the frenzied ebullitions of Dost Mahomed, "full of sound and fury," and in the true Bobadil spirit of a vain Affghan.

We have now to describe another scene of blood, one of the most atrocious character. It had long been the intention of many of the campfollowers to quit the army, whether with or without permission, and strike across the country *viâ* Dera Ismael Khan, through the Punjab, back to India, and on our arrival at Candahar, that intention was attempted to be carried into effect. Of course, they had enough money to support themselves on the long journey, and several, satisfied to remain with the army, entrusted what they had accumulated in the hands of those that went, for the purpose of being delivered to their families or friends. In one instance, a sarwan, or camel-driver, one of the home-goers, is said to have had a hundred gold mohurs in his possession. At this time, a kafila was reported to have just arrived at Candahar from Herat, and was proceeding towards India. This was deemed a fortunate opportunity, and it was immediately agreed that they should go under the protection of the kafila-bashee, or head of the caravan. Accordingly, the camp-followers, amounting, it is said, to above two hundred, all pretty well armed, placed themselves under the kafila-bashee, who had moreover,

---

[43] *Kafir-Feringees,* or infidel Europeans. In India, the Portuguese are usually denominated Feringhees; but in Central Asia, as well as further to the westward, all Europeans are called Feringhees, a name which came into use after the Crusades, the chief part of the armies being Franks, Ferrings (French), *k* and *g* being interchangeable in the East, and indiscriminately pronounced one for the other.

on the payment of a few rupees each, engaged to ensure their safety as far as he went, and to see them well supplied with food.

During the first march, all went on well; but, in the evening, the kafila-bashee required them to give up their arms, on the plea that it was the custom in that country, he being himself responsible for their safety, and that their continuing armed might alarm the inhabitants of the villages at which they halted. He promised that in the morning, the swords, pistols, shields, matchlocks, &c., should be always returned to them. The camp-followers, however, stoutly refused for a while, but at last consented, and they were then placed in a sort of *serai* for the night. The kafila-bashee was faithful to his promise, and, in the morning, every man of the camp-followers was delighted to see his arms again. Another day passed, and at night the same ceremony was observed. The people, being now under no alarm, expressed no reluctance to obey the kafila-bashee. The third and fourth day came, and the same course was pursued. But on the fifth or sixth night, in a part of the country notorious for robbery and murder, they were, on pretext of keeping them out of danger, assembled in a mud fort, called Maroof, situated on the estate of Huboo Oolah, a Barukzye. In the morning, however, a different scene ensued; one by one the poor wretches were brought out through the gate, and savagely murdered! This dreadful slaughter had gone on for some time, when the shrieks and groans of the victims reached the ears of those still within the fort, and told them of the fate that awaited them. In the agony of horror and despair, they clambered up the walls to escape; many had their limbs broken in wildly springing down outside, and thus disabled, they were cut to pieces. In the frightful struggle for life, very few are understood to have got back to Candahar to tell the horrid tale. It is said the murderers first deliberately made Mahomedans of the Hindoos, and then cut their throats. The Mahomedans were put to death outright.

With respect to this horrible conspiracy, it has since been ascertained, that the people of Maroof were in league with the kafila-bashee and his camel-men. Such an outrage, and to such an extent, could not have been otherwise committed.[44]

---

[44] In August, 1839, Captain Outram was placed at the disposal of the envoy and minister, and received instructions, among other important services in the Ghilzie country, "to punish the inhabitants of Maroof, who, in May last, wantonly destroyed a caravan proceeding to Hindostan from Candahar." Describing his expedition against the Barukzye tribes of Maroof, Captain Outram says: "Arriving (17th Oct.) at day-break (having left the camp at 1 A.M.) within sight of the principal Barukzye villages, I galloped on with the cavalry, and surrounded them before a soul had time to escape. Aboo Khan and Jubbar Khan, the chiefs of the tribe, together with all their followers, were thus secured; and they informed against others concerned, whom I also apprehended; by proceeding immediately to their villages with a few horsemen. Having placed the prisoners in charge of the infantry, I crossed the valley to the fort of Maroof, which, in consequence of the approach of the Bombay column, had been evacuated some days before. To my

How many instances have occurred of an Affghan or a Belooch murdering a defenceless camp-follower for plunder of the smallest value! but a richer and more tempting prize led to this catastrophe of unspeakable horror. True, indeed, is the common remark, that an Affghan has no more compunction in taking life, than in cutting a radish!

It appears that the Lohanees, under Surwur Khan, in charge of the recently arrived kafila of grain from Mooltan for the army, had visited the robbers on the road with Affghan severity, in the way of retaliation. Every man who shewed himself armed, and seemed to meditate robbery, was cut down. Every man caught in the act was ripped up at once. At one village, the Lohanees were told that an attack would be made on them at night. "In that case, then," said the Lohanees, "we will cut the throats of every man, woman, and child in the village." No attack was made. If the people have understanding, they may see the diffrence between our conduct on the march and theirs, and it may tell hereafter. But man, as he is in this country, and looking no further than the present moment, seems to require that species of treatment which alone can control his rapacity.[45] The Lohanees lost not a camel nor a load all the way from Mooltan to Candahar, whilst we have lost hundreds "at one fell swoop," and are losing them daily, the property of individuals as well as of the state.

Our halt at Candahar extended to two months, the hottest in the year. In tents, the heat generally rose to 110°, but in a mud house at Balakerz, a small village between our camp and the city, which I occupied during the day, the thermometer was never above 82°. The room I sat in had but a very small door-way, according to the custom of the country, and over that doorway a tent-chik, of thin slips of bamboo, was hung, to keep out the glare. There was no window. It is only by such means that comparative coolness (82°) can be produced. The thermometer at the same time, mid-day, outside, in the sun, stood at 140°.

---

astonishment, it proved to be the strongest fortress that we had yet seen in the country, being constructed with *double* gates, a ditch, fausse braye, and towers of solid masonry, which might have held out successfully against all the *materiel* with which the Bombay division is provided." 18th Oct. "Remained with the Sappers and Miners and 19th Regiment, in order to destroy the fort, which before nightfall had been effectually accomplished by blowing up the gateway and principal towers. Forwarded to Candahar, under charge of Captain Walker, commanding the detachment of the Shah's 2nd Cavalry, nine prisoners selected for example, and released the remainder."-*Captain Outram's Rough Notes.*

[45] The Affghans are perhaps little altered since Baber's time, and how did he treat them? Orders were given for beheading such of them (the Affghans) as had been brought in alive, and a miuaret was erected of their heads at our next halting place!" Again: "The troops cut off a hundred or two hundred heads of the refractory Affghans, which they brought down along with them. Here, also, we erected a minaret of heads!"-*Erskine's Baber,* p. 159.

The health of the troops had suffered considerably during the long and harassing marches that had been made. Up to our arrival at Quetta, in the valley of Shaul, in the latter part of March, the sick list had scarcely exceeded the common average in cantonments, and it was not till after the army had left Quetta for Candahar that a general increase began to shew itself. The prevailing disease was diarrhrœa, often assuming the dysenteric form, and occasionally complicated with fever of the intermittent and tertian type. No age escaped, and no rank. From the Bolân Pass, and through the whole of the Pisheen Valley, the water obtained from the wells and kahreezees was of a bad quality, turbid, and with a soapy mawkish taste. Besides, the men had been unavoidably placed on reduced rations, and the want of many customary articles of food was severely felt. Those for whom the reduced allowance was insufficient were glad to add to the quantity by purchasing grain of an inferior kind, and not a few ascribed all their complaints to eating Doomba mutton, which is a richer and greasier animal diet than they had been accustomed to, and no other was procurable. The hospital tents afforded but a poor protection from the weather at Candahar; and there could be no confident hope of speedy convalescence from the disorders which had assailed both Europeans and sepoys on the march. Some relief, however, was obtained by hiring as many suitable buildings as could be found in the neighbourhood of camp for hospitals, and this measure gave the patient an atmosphere less intense, by full 20°, than under canvass.

The sick being still numerous, it became of consequence to provide against the chance of having more to carry, when the army was ordered to move, than our existing means, extensive as they were, could supply. With this view, I drew the attention of the Commander-in-Chief to the expediency of employing camels, each furnished with a pair of *kajawahs,* or panniers, a mode of conveyance common throughout Upper Asia, and always used in travelling for the females of a family; the *kajawahs* to be adjusted in such a manner as to render the motion as easy as possible to the patient. To the hospital of every corps a certain number was appropriated, in addition to its own establishment of doolies, and others from the Field Hospital; and these resources being most ample, and sufficient for about five hundred patients, not the smallest inconvenience attended our forward movement on Ghizni.

CHAPTER IX

MARCH FROM CANDAHAR TO GHIZNI

Valley of the Turnak — Refractory chiefs — The Ghilzies-Kelat-i-Ghilzie — Affghan robbers blown from guns — Failure of Dost Mahomed Khan to get up a religious war — Defeat of a band of horsemen — Source of the Turnak — Robber chiefs — Rumours of the enemy's proceedings — Arrival before Ghizni.

JUNE 29.-Marched from Candahar, towards Caubul, to Abdullah Azeez, six miles. The first division started on the 27th, the Shah on the 28th, and the Bombay column follows us tomorrow. The plains all the way quite flat, but bounded by mountains all round. Not a tree to be seen, or a speck of vegetation.

June 30. -To Killa-i-Azeem, ten miles. A number of donkeys, laden with panniers of fine purple grapes, eight seers the rupee — a refreshing treat. The weather intensely hot. The paper upon which I am writing curls up, and is as crisp as if it was before a blazing fire; even the tent table is so hot as to be unpleasant to the touch.

July 1. - From Killa-i-Azeem to Deh-i-Akhond, sixteen miles. We marched at midnight by moonlight, to avoid the heat of the morning sun. The road a fine turnpike nearly all the way, rather a phenomenon in Affghanistan. At Akhond, there is a tomb, with a cupola, to the memory of Melanda Mahomed Akber, by whose name the village is also known, he being of the *Akhond,* or learned class. In the burying-ground, full of cairns, close by, there is a circular shaft, dome-capped; but I could not ascertain to whose memory so uncommon a structure here had been erected. Half a mile before coming to the village, and within a few hundred yards of the road, flows the Turnak river; it is shallow, and only about thirty feet wide. We begin to see people on the road, villagers driving their asses, and horsemen apparently on business, with no indication of hostility, or a disposition to annoy. Our camp is contiguous to fields, in which the villagers are industriously at work. This is the valley of Turnak. Passed a dead elephant, belonging to the Shah: the red-cloth howdah and trappings on, and still untouched, a singular circumstance, and a proof that we are not surrounded, as before, by robbers. Abandoned thus, the housings would have been fair game.

July 2.-From Akhond to Shaher-i-suffa, twelve miles. The road lies parallel with the Turnak river, and is intersected by numerous rather deep watercourses. Our ascent to-day has been considerable, and the weather evidently improving.

The place called Shaher-i-suffa is a lofty mound, about fifty feet high, with sloping sides, standing in the middle of a plain. The summit was formerly fortified, and it is said that Nadir Shah used to keep in it a strong garrison. It is at present without any trace of tower or wall. There once was a village near its base, but only a few mud walls remain of it now. We are surrounded by corn-fields just cut, and encamped on the stubble land. The Turnak, within a few hundred yards of us, is running with a strong current, over a stony bed. The jhow and clover are in flower on its banks.

July 3.-To Jelowgeer, fifteen miles. At about the twelfth mile came to Teer-andaz.[46] The tradition which gives the name of Teer-andaz to this place refers to the circumstance of Ahmed Shah having one day shot an arrow from the adjacent mountains; and it was to commemorate the great distance the arrow flew, that this tower or minaret was erected by him on the spot where it fell, which is about the middle of the valley. The form is octagonal; it is about thirty feet high, and of burnt brick, unplastered. It appears to be solid, having no aperture of any kind, and is called *Minar-i-padshah,* or 'the king's tower.' At Jelowgeer, three miles further, the ground is covered with sweet-scented herbs, marjoram, thyme, &c., and affords fine grazing for the camels. The heat to-day intense.

Since we left Candahar on the 29th of June, the brigade has not once been molested by thieves or armed men carrying off camels. This is accounted for by supposing that all the fighting men have concentrated at Kelat-i-Ghilzie, to oppose our progress, which is indeed the current report, and also that Dost Mahomed Khan is actually on his way to Caubul for the same purpose. A junction of our whole force is therefore ordered to be effected, including the Bombay troops in our rear. This morning our advance and rear guards were doubled, so as to protect the whole line more efficiently.

The prospect of something to do diffuses animation everywhere, for, from information received, we may expect to encounter a set of refractory chiefs, as hostile and inveterate as Mirab Khan. Among these are Abdoo Rohman Khan and Gool Mahomed Khan, two Ghilzies of noto~ rious character. The Shah, when at Candahar, had written to them a friendly letter, inviting them to wait upon him, and sent with it a Koran, the usual token of friendship, some valuable presents, and money to the amount of 10,000 rupees. The rapacious Ghilzies kept the cash and the presents, but returned the Koran, which was tantamount to a declaration of war. This unexpected and timely supply infused additional vigour into their councils, and improved their means of defence . A threat soon followed, that 50,000 Ghilzles were ready to check the progress of the infidel army at Kelat-i-Ghilzie.

The Ghilzies are of ancient descent, their ancestors having been in high authority, both in Persia and Affghanistan, long before the accession of the Suddozye dynasty, or of Nadir Shah, and they have, on that account, looked upon themselves as superseded in power, and felt jealous of, and were always openly inimical to, the new race of kings. They form a numerous tribe in Affghanistan,

---

[46] * *Teer-andaz* means the 'archer,' or 'thrower of arrows.'

being, according to Sir A. Burnes, rated at twenty thousand families, extending from Candahar to Gundumuk, between Caubul and Jellalabad. In the reign of Shah Mahmood they made an attempt to recover their consequence, but entirely failed, and left no proof of the vigour or efficiency of their combinations, but rather strong evidence of their utter unfitness for any such comprehensive enterprise. Dost Mahomed, with the view of strengthening his power, has allied himself by marriage to this tribe, as well as his son, Mahomed Akber Khan, who once held the appointment of chief of the Eastern Ghilzies. He was also himself affianced to the sister of Abdoo Rohman, to whom the fulminating letter just quoted was addressed; but the restoration of Shah Shoojah put off the celebration of his nuptials *sine die*![47]

July 4. - From Jelowgeer to Julduk, full eighteen miles, though said to be only fourteen. The road bad, crossed by deep ravines, and broken ground all the way. Still in the Turnak valley, between the hills, and mostly on the stony slope of those on our left, where, in many places, large fragments of rock, which have tumbled down from the heights, lay on the ground. Came up with the Shah's force, part of which was just leaving the ground of encampment, a number of tents still standing. The Shah was in his palankeen, surrounded by horsemen, and followed by an elephant ready caparisoned. Crowds of Affghan cavalry, dressed in every sort of colour, and every sort of fashion, among the natives of this country, were trotting, galloping, and curvetting about in all directions. The weather oppressively hot. We are in fact carrying the summer season with us to Caubul, and must expect it to be hot for some time. Our camp is now in advance of the Shah's, leaving a few hundred yards between. From Candahar to Julduk we have ascended about 1,900 feet.

July 5.-The distance from Julduk to Kelat-i-Ghilzie is twelve miles. Julduk is the last village in the Candahar state. The valley now becomes more compressed, and the road lies along the low mountains on our left, the river winding down the middle space. The whole scenery sterile and rugged, dotted over with detached tufts of vegetation, like the mountains of the Kojak Pass, except a few patches of cultivation here and there. The Shah and his force followed an hour after us. On coming to our ground, instead of fifty thousand Ghilzies being assembled to check our progress, not one was to be seen! When the first brigade arrived here yesterday morning, about two hundred men on foot, and twenty-five horsemen,

---

[47] Multiplied alliances are common in Affghanistan. The sister of Dost Mahomed is the wife of Shah Shoojah. Nor is this the only relationship, for the two daughters of Hajee Rehmut-oolah are married severally to the Shah and Dost Mahomed, and the wife of the latter exercises the greatest influence over him, and is the mother of Mahomed Akber Khan, the favourite son of the Dost. The mother of Shahzada Timoor, eldest son of Shah Shoojah, was a Ghilzie. Dost Mahomed also espoused a daughter of Shah Abbas, and niece of Shah Shoojah, to his majesty an inexpiable offence.

were observed moving out of a fort, distant about a mile, and have not since been seen or heard of, but they are supposed to have gone off to Dost Mahomed. Abdoo Rohman and Gool Mahomed had long held their territory at Kelat-i-Ghilzie, and had been in the habit of levying black-mail in every quarter, from Candahar to Caubul, so that the restoration or the introduction of a regular system of government into Affghanistan would be of no possible benefit to them, but highly prejudicial to their interests. Dost Mahomed was too limited in his power to keep them in any thing like subjection; indeed they were wholly independent, acknowledging no supremacy but their own; and now that his own political existence was becoming extinct, he urged them with promises of impossible things, to harass us by unceasing attacks, on the silly plea of our being a race of infidels, of cannibals, and our great aim — the destruction of the Mussulman faith! But, notwithstanding the vituperations poured forth, and the overwhelming excitement intended to be produced, the cowardly assassins performed no higher feat than that of putting to death our helpless followers, and stealing our camels.

At Kelat-i-Ghilzie, we obtained further information on the subject of the massacre at Maroof, but we had not the means of apprehending the murderers. Punishment is only delayed for a more favourable opportunity. Great numbers of Ghilzies are in camp, selling sheep, goats, and flour.

July 6.-Sir John Keane, with the 1st Brigade, marched this morning. We follow to-morrow, with the Shah and his forces in the rear. After all, the old trade is going on again; horses carried off from the picquets, and yesterday several Ghilzies were brought in prisoners, and also the heads of three men, who were found in the act of driving away the Shah's camels. Took especial care to place Toorkee close to my sentry, to whom I gave particular instructions to thrust his bayonet into any hostile intruder, who attempted to take him away!

July 7.-Moved at two A.M. to Ser-i-Asp, twelve miles. The waning moon had risen about half an hour, and shed only a very dubious light. The road bad, scarcely any road at all, and crossed frequently by ravines and deep watercourses. The valley is now wider, and near our encampment it is covered with fresh verdure. The Shah's camp nearly a mile in our rear. Heard in the afternoon that three Affghans, found guilty of carrying off camels, and wounding and killing some of the sarwans, had been sentenced by the Kawzee to be blown from a gun. Ripping up the belly is said to be the usual punishment among the Affghans. At a little before sunset, three of the horse artillery guns were drawn out, and presently the three criminals were brought to the ground, led by an old man, with a long beard, stained of an orange colour, and wearing a long conical red cap, garnished with four perpendicular rows of black horns, pointing out horizontally. After they had stood awhile, another functionary came in a different shaped cap, also red, the form of a crab's claw, with a black horn stretching out on each side, and asked if all was ready. "All ready," was the reply; whereupon the said functionary went to make his report to the Shah, whose *sera purda,* or pavilion tent, was not above a hundred yards from the place. In ten minutes he returned, and repeated the order to proceed to execution. The three men were then tied with ropes to the guns, their backs against the muzzle. The rope, fastened to one of the spokes of the wheel, passed with a knot round the arms, over the muzzle of the gun, round the other arm, and then to the spoke of the opposite wheel, which kept the body fixed. The prisoners, with their wrists tied together, kept crying incessantly, "There is no God, but God, and Mahomet is the Prophet of God!" Just as every thing was ready, the prisoner in the middle was let loose, having been pardoned by the Shah, and the noise made the other two turn their heads. At that instant, the priming was fired, and the explosion took place. I could only see the body nearest to me, for the thick clouds of smoke. One arm and shoulder blade was driven perpendicularly upwards, at least a hundred feet; the other arm and part of the body were found right forward, — thirty yards off, with the hand torn away. The explosion produced a shower of blood, and small particles of flesh. On going to the gun, I found the head separate, as if it had been purposely severed from the body, and lying between the wheels: close to it were the lower limbs, trunkless, upturned on the ground, with part of the intestines twisted round one leg. The criminal was a man of muscular form, and about twenty-five years of age. The other, with felon marked on his countenance, could not have been more than nineteen. His head and legs also fell under the gun. Neither of the miserable wretches betrayed any emotion, or spoke a word more than declaring that they were innocent, and repeating the ejaculation" *Lâ Illâh Illilâh Mahomed Russool Illah!"* till they were blown to atoms.

July 8.-Left Ser-i-Asp at two A.M. in the dark, the thin moon just appearing, and then being obscured by black clouds. The road crossed by deep hollows and precipitous banks, eight miles.

July 9.-On approaching the new ground, at Abi Tazee, found the first brigade halting, in consequence of the road ahead being reported impassable, and the sappers and miners had gone on to remove the difficulties. The Turnak is here wider and deeper than lower down, and contains plenty of fish; but only of one kind, which is full of bones. The valley too is widening, and we have a rather fine view between the rugged sterile hills that encompass us. The plains below and all round are dotted over with thousands of our camels grazing. In the distance are several fort-like villages, each with a tope of mulberry trees, and the river, glittering in the sun, is seen winding its serpentine way through the fields of corn yet uncut, which vary the prospect with bright tints of green and yellow. A Ghilzie chief came in yesterday, and joined the Shah, a man of considerable influence. He, with all the others, had been proclaimed a rebel by the Shah, and he would have submitted sooner, he said, but was afraid of punishment. He was, however, well received.

July 10.-The 1st Brigade proceeded in advance this morning. In future, it is said, our marches are not to exceed ten miles, which will be a great relief to the troops, as it will not then be necessary to start much before daylight, and thus the night's rest will be less broken. The European soldiers have suffered greatly of late, both Queen's and Company's, and shorter marches may enable them to recover their strength, especially as the climate is improving, as we proceed to a higher latitude and a loftier region. The native troops have also suffered, but in a much less degree. A man, who arrived from Mukoor last night, reports that Dost Mahomed had moved *one* march out of Caubul to meet us, and that his son, Gholam Hyder Khan, had also moved *one* march on this side of Ghizni, each with five or six thousand men; also that Dost Mahomed had tried to get up a religious war in the name of the Prophet to destroy the infidel Feringhees, but that he had failed. He had repeatedly written to Abdoo Rohman Khan and Gool Mahomed Khan, the two principal Ghilzie chiefs, to aid him against the accursed Kafirs. But what has been, and what is, the extent of their co-operation? Their followers lurk about and steal our camels, first murdering the sarwans, and in this sanguinary vocation they are wonderfully expert, being utterly destitute of one jot of human feeling. Another Ghilzie chief has deemed it his interest to join the Shah to-day.

July 11.-Marched from Abi Tazee to Shuftee, eight miles. Had to pass four or five deep ravines with abrupt sides, which the pioneers had sloped down for the passage of the troops, and the artillery wheel-carriages. They were got over with less difficulty than was expected. The road, for the most part, half-a-dozen parallel foot-paths, was generally good, without one atom of cultivation on either side, the whole prospect being tufts of the memorable jungle, with high, bleak, and peaked mountains around us. Our camp is about a mile from the Turnak, which has here very steep banks, and we observe on each side of the river long lines of waving corn nearly ripe.

July 12.-Marched to Chushma-i-Shadee, called also by the natives Mulla Shadee, eight miles. Only one deep ravine, which had been sloped down by the pioneers. The skirts of the hills, about six miles apart, are full of villages and cultivation, but in the middle part only Jowassa, which, however, is excellent forage for the camels. The natives selling doomba sheep in camp. It was at this place that ten thousand Ghilzies were defeated on the 11th May, 1802, by the troops of Shah Mahmood, and it was the last united effort of that tribe to recover their independence.

July 13.-To a place called Punjuk, and also by the natives on the spot, Shumazee, six miles. Still numerous villages at the foot of the mountains on each side.

July 14.-The march from Punjuk to Aghojan, twelve miles. Road good all the way. Two or three steep hills and hollows, and others with a fetlock of water in them. The plains between the mountains much widened, in the midst of which Aghojan is distinguished by a lofty conical hill, standing alone, and near it is our encampment. A great number of villagers with eggs, fowls, flour, asses, &c., for sale, in much more abundance than on any former occasion.

July 15.-From Aghojan to Mukoor, twelve miles. At about the tenth mile, closed upon a conical mountain of the great range to the left, and passing along its base, with the envoy, we heard the firing of muskets ahead. We soon perceived that a number of Ghilzies were on a high rock, which overlooked the road, casting down stones on the Shah's troops as they passed, and that several suwars had moved from the line, and were firing at them, but without effect, as the distance was too great. They, however, succeeded in taking two prisoners. We then passed on, and met Captain McSherry, an officer of the Shah's force, returning to inform the envoy that a body of horsemen, five hundred strong, was ahead, to the left, concealed in a deep ravine, and that it would be necessary to detach a reinforcement to protect the baggage in the rear, and prevent its being cut off. This was done. Soon after I arrived at the new ground, a sharp firing was heard for some time, apparently from the spot where tIle two prisoners had been taken. We afterwards learnt that the men on the hill had again assembled, and in considerable force, fancying, no doubt, that their position was as impregnable as it was commanding. But they were mistaken: the Shah's regiment, which was then assailed by stones, immediately rushed towards the hill, and, ascending the rocks (they were Ghoorkas), succeeded in killing nineteen of the enemy, and the rest ran off with the utmost precipitation. The chief, named Adam Khan, was among the slain. He had been the terror of the country for many years, having had under his influence and authority a numerous band of merciless robbers. He is said to have followed the army all the way from Candahar, and only a day or two ago, several horrid instances of wounding and killing occurred among the camp-followers of the first brigade, which may be attributed, without doubt, to the unceasing cruelty of these barbarians. Some of the headmen of the villages at Mukoor have waited on the envoy to express their gratitude on the extinction of Adam Khan, by whom they had suffered so long and so deeply.

We are in the midst of villages, fort-fashion, with their customary accompaniment of groves of mulberry trees, at least a dozen within a mile of us. On our left, and close to our camp, is the mountain from whence the river Turnak springs. The water, transparent as glass, bursts from the rock at a considerable height, in a sparkling cascade. It descends in a beautiful meander on the plain, and the stream formed there is full of fish. The mountain itself is peculiar, abounding in rough projections, and nobbed over like vitrified brick. At its base, and on the margin of the road, is an extensive burying-ground. Mukoor appears a most fertile spot, and promises to be the harbinger of more pleasing prospects in advance.

Sir John Keane, with the first brigade, halted here on the 15th, and marched again this morning, the 16th. We now find that Abdoo Rohman Khan, the Ghilzie chief, has been hanging on our flanks ever since we entered the Kelat territory, with two hundred horsemen. The Shah, having got intimation of his position yesterday, sent of his own accord a body of his men to surprise and attack him, but the Khan had received intelligence of the movement, and was prepared. A smart encounter took place, which ended in favour of the Shah's men, who dispatched eight of the enemy, and took several prisoners. They had, however, two killed. The Shah is said to be fond of a little independent enterprise of his own. A troop of our cavalry would probably have produced a more decisive result, and caught the Ghilzie chief. No accounts of his confederate Gool Mahomed.

July 17.-From Mukoor to a Kahreez, in the district of Obah, fourteen miles. Starting at three A.M. in the dark, great delay was experienced in crossing the river, and some deep ravines, within the first few miles. The road afterwards good, with corn-fields on both sides, the grain just cut; and the stacks lying on the ground. Numerous villages appear, and the trees fuller of foliage than hitherto. The space between the mountains eight or ten miles. Water is here obtained from a Kahreez; it abounds, and is excellent. The natives, with poultry, fire-wood, grass, ghee, and goats for sale, were ready on the ground. The immediate jurisdiction of Dost Mahomed commences at Mukoor. The appearance of the country is certainly improving, and agricultural industry more conspicuous. Two or three villages in sight are, notwithstanding, deserted, and the mud walls in ruins. Increased rations, which were reduced at Quetta to half, are now restored to the troops and camp-followers.

July 18.-Last night we had a storm of thunder and lightning, with as heavy rain as ever I experienced in the lower part of Bengal. It lasted two hours, and the tents of the whole camp were all completely soaked through with water; in consequence of which, as the camels were unequal to carry their increased weight, our march was postponed till the sun had in some degree dried them. In the afternoon we arrived at Chahar-Deh, twelve miles. Passed several beautifully clear springs: the country, for the most part, well cultivated; some corn was standing, and the people were quietly occupied in reaping. They have little hooped sheds, covered over with jungle grass, to protect themselves from the sun occasionally, when they rest. The plain is now wider than at the last ground; and along the sloping margin of the mountains, on either side, we have counted a hundred fort-like villages on picturesque situations. The mountains are still of a reddish-brown, and barren, and only rendered agreeable to the sight, now and then, by the varieties of tint, produced by the sun and atmospheric changes. The Hazareh tribe inhabit those on the left.

July 19.-Made two marches in one, to join Sir John Keane at Urghesan, twenty miles. At the twelfth mile, Mooshakee or Karabagh, where there is a large burying-ground, extending to a considerable distance on both sides of the way, the graves, as usual, piled up with stones; and there are four or five of a more important character, with high walls, and roofed in, close to the road. The most considerable one is said to be that of a chief named Hajee Khan, a notorious robber; and another of a Sultan Mahomed Khan, equally distinguished for his depredations in these parts. Fakeers were stationed there, and while they pray for the souls of the defunct, enlarge on their achievements, and cherish their fame. Thus it is, where civilization and moral culture are little known, and less appreciated, the greatest ruffian is the greatest man. The peasants brought for sale ass-loads of peaches, very rich and ripe, but small, and with crimson cheeks. It is needless to say that, in a moment, the panniers were emptied! The plain is now more wide, and two-thirds of the way wholly corn-fields under the sickle. Great numbers of the people, quitting their occupations, assembled on the road-side to see us pass, and seemed to be commenting on our foreign appearance in a good-humoured spirit. We have passed several mountain streamlets, rapid, and clear as crystal, and delightfully cool to drink. The villages still numerous, but many of them are deserted. Abdoo Rohman and Gool Mahomed are said to be behind the mountains with a ragged rabble, some with matchlocks, some without, and some without powder.

July 20.-Marched to Nanee, eight miles, the 1st and 4th Brigades together. The road sandy and stony over small hills. From a hill close to the encampment, Ghizni is visible through a telescope. This morning, Abdul Rusheed Khan, a nephew of Dost Mahomed, joined the Shah on the march, with a few men. He made his escape from the fort of Ghizni last night. The accession of this man is of great importance, bringing, as he does, accurate information on the existing state of things. The ditch had been widened and deepened, two of the three gates built up, and it appears that Dost Mahomed's two sons, Afzul and Hyder Khan, have with them about five thousand men within the walls, well equipped with arms, and determined to oppose us to the last extremity. Fine ripe apples are brought into camp, eight seers the rupee; horses also for sale, and fowls twelve the rupee.

July 21.-In consequence of a rumour yesterday afternoon, that a party of two thousand men from Ghizni intended to make a night attack upon the camp, the cavalry and infantry were ordered to be under arms at 9 P.M., and they remained on the ground all night; but, after all, nothing occurred. The Bengal column having come up at midnight, the whole force began to move on Ghizni at four in the morning, in four parallel divisions. The road was at the foot of undulating hills, some of considerable height, stony and barren, till we were near Ghizni. Looking from one of the highest, the concourse appeared immense — prodigious. Far as the eye could reach, front and rear, the ground was covered with lines of troops, camels, and baggage, more than half-obscured with the dust, which ascended in clouds, so that, as Firdousee says, "the heavens and the earth seemed not to exist." The amount of human life could not have been less than a hundred thousand, and nothing but the moving mass was to be seen.

As I was passing along, I was told by the people I met, that Dost Mahomed's son, Afzul, had quitted the fort, with four thousand men, and gone to the mountains; others said he had gone to our rear, but that the younger son, Hyder Khan, remained to defend the fort; others again said the fort had been evacuated. Those whom I spoke to seemed to be going about their own business, and apparently felt no interest whatever in what was taking place.

CHAPTER X.

ATTACK AND CAPTURE OF GHIZNI.

Ghazees or fanatics — Defeated by Shah's troops and Lancers — Execution of some of them — Assault of the fortress — Rapidity of the achievement — Desperate resistance of the garrison — Visit to the fort — The gun called Zubur-jung — Appearance of the slain — The governor of Ghizni deceived as to the intentions of the British — His conduct and behaviour — The two minars of Ghizni — Tomb of Sultan Mahmood — His invasions of India — Plunder of Somnat — The idol of the temple, a lingam *— Dexterity of Affghan pickpockets.*

WHEN I arrived, at a quarter past nine A.M., within a little more than a mile of Ghizni, I heard the enemy's fire without being able to see the smoke, the long walls of several gardens shutting out the view. These gardens had been occupied by parties from the garrison, but they were driven back by our corps in advance. On coming up to higher ground, I observed the 1st Brigade on the north-west side of the fort, and the guns of the Horse Artillery returning the fire. While standing in front of one of the gardens, where the 2nd Cavalry, dismounted, were looking on, but ready to move in any direction, I could see many shot from the citadel strike the ground, and knock up the dust, at least a quarter of a mile over and beyond the Horse Artillery and troops on that side; others struck near, and a few men were wounded. This continued for some time, and then the firing on our part ceased, another course of operations being resolved upon. In the meantime, a party of us had taken possession of one of the walled gardens, where, not exactly *sub tegmine fagi,* but under the shade of some large fruit-trees right in front of the fort, we could see with a glass all that was going on, and where, not the least agreeable part of the business, our camels and servants having come up, we enjoyed a good breakfast *à la fourchette,* the guns still thundering from the fort, at the distance of less than a mile. The 2nd Cavalry were just outside the south wall, and whilst engaged at our pleasant repast, for hunger had whetted our appetites, we heard the loud whizzing of a ball near us, and found, on inquiry, that it had struck off a troop-horse's leg, and done other damage, about ten yards from where we were seated. The ball proved to be a shell of iron filled with lead, and weighed fifty-four pounds. The Shah and Envoy had taken up their quarters in another garden a little way to the north of us, and the royal *cortège* being discovered by the enemy, the firing from the fort soon made it too hot for them too.[48]

---

[48] The word *garden* must not present to the imagination of the reader any thing like a European garden. The middle part of that we were in consisted of numerous deep furrows for the convenience of irrigation. The ridges between each furrow were planted with the vine, then in full foliage, an uninterrupted mass of which covered the whole surface, and the area was surrounded by a high mud wall. Bordering the wall inside were rows of

No tents of course had been pitched for the troops, and orders were now given to change ground at three P.M., and to take up a position on the Caubul road, eastward of the fortress, on which side the only gate is situated. The day was blazing hot, and we had to make a long *détour* beyond the range of the fort guns, crossing numerous deep canals with slippery banks, so that it was night before we reached the new ground. The cavalry, with Shah Shoojah and his contingent, rounded the fort on the south, and the infantry on the north, meeting and forming a crescent to the south-east, about a mile and a quarter from the walls. This movement was viewed with great joy by the garrison. Hyder Khan and his chiefs deemed it conclusive of our inability to make an impression on the fortress, and fully expected that we would abandon Ghizni, and proceed at once to Caubul, giving them the opportunity of attacking our rear, aided by Abdoo Rohman and Gool Mahomed, while the Dost, who was reported to have left the capital on the 16th, and supposed to be close at hand, checked our progress in advance.

July 22.-The garrison kept firing all yesterday afternoon and all night. About eleven this morning, a body of armed men, horse and foot, amounting, it is estimated, to about four or five thousand men, was suddenly discovered upon the ridges of the hills, immediately in the rear of the Shah's camp, which was at the south end of the crescent, and at some distance from the corps of cavalry posted on that side. This was a legion of fanatics, headed by Mihter Moosa, whose sister was one of the wives of Dost Mahomed. They called themselves *Ghazees,* or defenders of the Mussulman faith, and endeavoured to promote a sanguinary crusade against the Kafir English, as well as against him whom they deemed a renegade king. They carried green banners, were in continual motion, and by their gestures, for I saw them distinctly through a telescope, were on the point of making a descent from the mountain; but the prompt appearance of the Shah's own troops, with two guns, and a party of Lancers, soon changed their purpose, and in the course of an hour the whole of the rebellious champions of the faith were chased from the hills, with the loss of more than one hundred killed and wounded. Several prisoners were taken, but upon their declaring that they had been forced into the enemy's ranks, they were released by the Shah. In the afternoon, however, others were brought in, thirty-eight in number, and shewn to be, on sufficient evidence, of most atrocious character, and his majesty was determined to make an example of them all, by having them beheaded on the spot. They had been captured whilst fighting against the Shah's troops, and when led before his majesty, they bitterly denounced him as an infidel, who had brought an army of infidels to pillage and destroy their country, and they only longed for the opportunity to put his majesty himself to death. The ferocity of

---

plum and peach trees, but none of the fruit was ripe. Every mud inclosure with fruit-trees is called a bagh, or garden. There was just open space enough for our cold collation.

one of them was carried to such an extreme degree, that, in the presence of the Shah, he struck a dagger into the breast of one of his personal attendants. The Envoy, on being informed of the determination of the Shah, suggested that, instead of putting so many to death, a selection might be made, and immediately communicated the circumstance to Sir John Keane, through Sir Alexander Burnes. His Excellency's opinion was, that the most summary example should be made of all such dastardly ruffians. They were known to be robbers and murderers, and to have been among those who committed such inhuman excesses on our line of march. The fanatic band, which finally assembled on the hills to attack the royal camp, had hung upon our flanks during the whole route from Kelat-I-Ghilzie, and were ever on the watch to plunder and destroy unprotected stragglers. The Shah was satisfied that both justice and policy demanded their execution. Two were spared, one on account, it is said, of his being a Syud, and the other merely because he begged for his life. The whole remaining number would doubtless have been pardoned, had they exhibited any symptoms of a desire to be forgiven; but they continued to utter threats of vengeance to the last moment of their existence, having sworn on the Koran to take the life of the king.[49] There existed a strong impression in our camp, that the Shah had been

---

[49] This transaction exhibits another instance of the discordance of evidence given by different individuals in their several publications, when a moment's inquiry, all being in the same camp, might have enabled them to state the number. Captain Outram says, about fifty men were executed, Major Hough twenty-five, and Dr. Kennedy upwards of sixty. Great indignation, too, has been expressed at the cruelty and injustice of the act, whether the lives sacrificed amounted to twenty-five or sixty-five. However much humanity may lament over such a catastrophe, war has its laws, and, after all, is but a cut throat business. The Shah was paramount, supreme; and although it has been the fashion to call him a puppet in our hands, he has a full knowledge of his rights, and fails not to put those rights in force. We were bound by solemn treaty, before he entered upon the campaign, not to interfere between him and his subjects, and that point was tested whilst we were at Candahar. "Four Affghans tried by a native general court-martial for having stolen and carried away, on the 2nd of June, twenty-three camels belonging to the Bombay army (they were said to be Sir John Keane's), and sentenced to be hanged, were to have been executed on the 7th of June, on the spot where Lieutenant Inverarity was murdered, but the king claimed them as his subjects. His majesty was not satisfied with the trial, and appointed a Mirza to re-hear the evidence, when the king pronounced them not guilty, upon the evidence taken by the Mirza." This fact is from the narrative of Major Hough, Deputy Judge Advocate General, who conducted the proceedings at the native general court-martial. The Shah appears to be borne out in his resolution, to put to death the rebellious Ghazees, by the following extract from Vattel's Rights of Nations, or the Principles of the Natural Law, applied to the conduct of Nations and Sovereigns. Our position at the time was certainly a critical one. "When the number of prisoners is so great as not to be kept or fed with safety, is there a right of putting them to death? Or shall they be sent back to the enemy, at the hazard of thus strengthening him, so as on another occasion to gain the advantage? At present the case is plain. These prisoners are

merciful to a fault in several instances, pardoning men who, to the full conviction of others, had been guilty of the most flagrant crimes. And this feeling prevailed before we had reached the Bolân Pass.

Whilst the Shah was thus occupied in his own camp, preparations were all day actively in progress for the morrow's operations. The party employed in the reconnoissance on the north-east angle had been continually fired upon, but the garrison was not able to frustrate in any degree the object of the engineers.

July 23.-This was the glorious day. An immediate attack having been decided upon, "the only feasible mode of proceeding, and the only one which held out a prospect of success, was a dash at the Caubul gateway, blowing the gate open by bags of powder." Accordingly, about midnight, as soon as the moon went down, the different corps left camp, and silently took up their several positions. Four companies, from Her Majesty's 2nd, 13th, and 17th Foot, and the Bengal European Regiment, formed the advance of the storming party, led by Brigadier Dennie, which were followed up by Brigadier Sale, in command of the remainder of the Europeans. The Reserve, consisting of the 16th, 35th, and 48th Bengal Native Infantry, was under Major-General Sir Willoughby Cotton, and the Cavalry, under Major-General Thackwell, were distributed in various situations round the fort, to be employed as circumstances required.

The field-hospital tents of the Bengal army were about the middle of the crescent, and on the south-east angle of the fort. The distance being great, and anxious as I was to see as much of the operations as possible, I repaired with the field surgeon and medical storekeeper (R. M. M. Thomson and M. Ross), at two P.M., in front of the lines, so far indeed as to be within the range of the guns, for a few shots whistled over us. The spot where we stood was on the road over which the *doolies,* with the wounded, would have to pass, and we were therefore in the way of our duty. It was quite dark, and only the outline of the lofty citadel visible against the sky, except when lit up for a moment by the guns fired at random by the garrison. The false attack commenced at three, which had the intended effect of drawing the Affghans from the quarter they expected to be assailed to the south-western ramparts, and afforded the engineers the opportunity of placing the bags of powder against the gate and arranging the train, though that was not done without some annoyance from the wall-pieces. At a quarter before four, the gate was blown open with a tremendous crash. Silence ensued, and at this period of breathless interest, our suspense was most painful. Then, nothing could be seen

---

sent back on their *parole,* not to carry arms for a certain time, or to the end of the war. But if we are concerned with a formidable nation, savage and perfidious, shall we send back its soldiers by whom it may be enabled to destroy us? When our safety is incompatible with that of an enemy, though subdued, it is out of all question but that in cold blood a great number of persons should be put to death." Book 3, chap. 8, sec.151. Such is Vattel's interpretation of the law of nations on the point under consideration.

or heard but the flashing and thundering of the guns, with no appearance to satisfy us of the success or failure of the explosion. In this anxious state, some time elapsed; at length, an electrical soul-exhilarating "huzza!" and a volley of musketry, assured us that the storming party had got inside. That was enough. In half an hour more, as the darkness was wearing away, we perceived a *dooly* coming up to us, the bearers hurrying on with the greatest speed. It contained a soldier of the European Regiment, and to our inquiry, "What news?" "We have done 'em!" was the ready and gratifying reply. Our attendance on the wounded then commenced, and happily the cases were surprisingly few.[50]

The first gleam of dawn displayed the British flag flying on the tower of the citadel. It is universally allowed that nothing could exceed the skill or the bravery with which the conquest was obtained in so short a time. The overwhelming rapidity of the achievement, however, must in some measure be ascribed to the general consternation of the garrison on finding the gate blown open, although the admirable gallantry of our troops could not be surpassed, and must have been triumphant however long the contest might have been maintained. While the powder-bags were being cautiously laid down, a light was visible through the crevices of the gate; and so little was the nature of our operations apprehended — so complete the surprise — that the guard were heard in undisturbed conversation within. And it is not improbable that the sanguinary struggle made by the Affghans immediately after the storming party had got inside, arose more from despair and anxiety to escape, attempting to cut their way through our ranks, than from any hope of defending the place, or repelling our efforts. A body of the

---

[50] Only thirty-eight wound-cases were received into our field-hospital; six of them belonged to H.M.'s 13th Light Infantry, two to H.M.'s 2nd or Queen's, twenty-seven to the European Regt., and three sepoys of the 48th Regt. N.I. Three men of the European Regt. died in the hospital, one from a matchlock-ball passing through his chest; and injuring the back-bone, and the two others from matchlock-balls penetrating the abdomen, so as to occasion the protrusion of the bowels. Happily, the gunshot wounds, the most dangerous, were few. All the sword-cuts, which were very numerous, and many of them very deep, united in the most satisfactory manner, which we decidedly attributed to the men having been without rum for the previous six weeks, the Commissariat having none to give them. In consequence, there was no inflammatory action to produce fever, and interrupt the adhesion of the parts: a strong argument in favour of tee-totalism, but the soldier's love of his dram is too potent to be extinguished. The case of Thomas Jones, after the famine in spirits had ceased, is an apt illustration of this enduring love of grog. Jones, who belonged to the European Regt., was a hard drinker. He had a severe attack of pneumonia, of which he was cured for the time and discharged. Nearly three weeks afterwards, he was again taken to the hospital, still under the influence of liquor, and labouring under the same complaint as before. On the second day he was seized with convulsions, having again had access to spirits in excess. When the spasms left him, he was still unable to swallow; but the last words he uttered, in a voice scarce audible, were "more grog!"

enemy rushed impetuously down the steep descent towards the gate, and were actually between the advanced party and the column under General Sale, when the conflict was most severe. The bayonets of our men were driven home with such force, that they could not be withdrawn for want of room; and one of our brave fellows, desperately wounded, told me afterwards, when in hospital, that he, among others, was compelled to relinquish his musket on that account. Many, however, did escape through the gate, and hundreds lowered themselves down with ropes from the ramparts; but great numbers of them were either shot by the infantry or pursued and cut down by the cavalry. Several, when overtaken, called out for quarter, and it was invariably given. The official despatch of the Commander-in-Chief, and the full reports of the engineers, in the Appendix, furnish a complete description of the splendid manner in which this important victory was obtained.

Meer Afzul Khan, who left the fort before we arrived, with two thousand men, was within three miles of us on the morning of the assault, and, hearing the result, immediately went off to Caubul, abandoning his tents and elephants about six miles from Ghizni, the whole of which fell into our hands.

July 24.- Visited the fort, to select a proper place for the accommodation of the wounded, and fixed upon a number of apartments in the citadel. In approaching the walls, there is a considerable ascent across the bridge to the base of the rampart, on the east side. The gate was lying in fragments, and the explosion had been so tremendous, that the beams of the roof were precipitated to the ground, and had greatly impeded the advance of the storming party. A bastion to the right of the gateway had also been demolished. Fortunately, there was no inner gate. The ascent, inside, is very abrupt to the citadel, which is spacious, with a large quadrangle, and buildings on three sides, of two stories, a room and a verandah in breadth. The windows have wooden sashes, made of mountain-fir, which slide up and down. They are curiously carved, in open net-work fashion, for the admission of air. The roof commands a most extensive prospect over the country, which is full of vineyards and mulberry groves in patches, at present variegated by the yellow stubble and the bright green clover-fields. The whole is built on a hill, which slopes down more gradually towards the south-west, where the town is situated. Each house with its premises is distinct: all built with sun-dried brick or mud, containing endless little rooms, or holes, generally with light from very small apertures; and the streets are filthy and narrow. The north-east angle of the citadel is commanded by a hill not many hundred yards from it, and behind which our batteries were placed, which did considerable execution. To protect this point, a new curtain had been raised at the time we were at Candahar.

A new *fausse braye*[51] had also been carried round the greater part of the fort, by forced labour from the people.

Half-way up the ascent from the gate to the citadel, was placed the brass 68-pounder, called Zubur-Jung, — 'the mighty in battle.' It turns upon two huge solid trucks, and a third at the end of the carriage, which is of most unwieldly construction. About a foot in length of the nosle, or mouth, had been blown off, perhaps by an overcharge, and it had been repaired and faced with plates of copper with some skill. It was from this gun that the ball was thrown which struck off the troop-horse's leg on the 21st. The whole was embossed with leaf ornaments, and "Sirdar Gholam Hyder Khan" was newly engraved upon it in Persian, the line of every letter shewing the clean metal. A Hindoostanee, *Golandaz,* had charge of this highly-prized gun, which was worked by him a few times on the 21st and 22nd; but foreseeing the result, he escaped from the fort in good time, though it was said, that a guard with drawn swords had been placed over him, and some other Hindoostanee gunners, to see that they did not flinch, but performed their duty.

At the time I was in the fort, the dead bodies stripped perfectly naked were being dragged down from the ramparts to be buried in deep pits, ready prepared, about fifty paces south-east of the gate. It was a dreadful sight; some of them in strange attitudes produced by the spasms and agonies of death; scarcely one stretched out, as in the usual position of exhausted nature, but all stiff, sharp, and angular, as if still animated with the wild ferocious spirit which inspired their living efforts.[52] The number, too, huddled together and buried to-day, was appalling. They were said to amount to four hundred and fifty. Apprehensive that the interment of so many near the surface, for the pits were not more than ten feet deep, might be productive of dangerous consequences to the troops left in garrison, and the town-people, by vitiating the air, I recommended the bodies being burnt, but it was impossible to procure wood enough for that purpose at Ghizni. I then suggested that the surface should be heaped well up with earth, so as effectually to prevent any bad effects from the decomposition of such a mass; but the three pits were left nearly level with the surrounding ground, and I was afterwards informed that nothing offensive or unpleasant had ever been noticed

---

[51] *Editor's note:* A second rampart which is outside, and parallel to, the main rampart, and considerably below its level.

[52] Quintus Curtius notices a similar result, but from a different cause, when describing the storm on Alexander's march to Gabaza. "Tradition," he says, "represents that some of the men frozen to death looked as if they were alive in conversation; stiff in the attitude in which death had surprised them." The retreat of Napoleon from Moscow has similar pictures. "None seems to have been frozen in a composed state, each was fixed in the last action of his life. Even the eyes returned the last expression of anger, pain, or entreaty."- *Narrative of the Campaign,* &c.

by those who remained in charge of the fortress.

Many fine horses were lying dead in the dust, having got loose during the assault, and been shot to prevent accident. There were about fifteen hundred in the fort at the period of the capture.

The wives and families of Gholam Hyder Khan,[53] the Governor, and of the garrison, in all about three hundred, were found collected together in the citadel, and as soon as the firing ceased, they were conveyed to a place of safety in the lower part of the fort, and afterwards sent to their friends. Those belonging to Hyder Khan were kept as state prisoners.

When, on the 21st, we moved round to the Caubul road, it was supposed, as before observed, that we had given up all thoughts of reducing the fort, and were proceeding to Caubul. The operations of that day on our part bad impressed the garrison with the belief that, consistent with their own notions, the walls were really impregnable. And Gholam Hyder Khan, with the same sort of conviction, felt not the least apprehension or uneasiness, because, according to his father's opinion, Ghizni could not be taken in less than a year. The first proof of the fallacy of this opinion, however, was shewn to the astonished governor, by the apparition of the storming party, after the gate had been blown open. This latter circumstance he had never dreamt of, and it filled him with confusion and terror. He then, seeing the game was up, with a few followers valiantly made the best of his way from the citadel, and secreted himself in the uttermost verge of the fort, the farthest from the scene of conflict. The dark recess in which he took inglorious refuge was at the bottom of some steps, which lead up to the rampart on the west side, close to what was called the Kinak gate. Its privacy was rendered perfect by an intervening court-yard, with a small door in the wall, facing the narrow filthy street. He was traced and discovered there in the course of the morning, crouching down, with a few matchlock-men in front of him. Upon information of his "whereabout" being given to Captain A. W. Tayler, of the Bengal European Regiment, and Captain Macgregor, Assistant to the Envoy and Minister, application was instantly made to Brigadier Roberts, to detach a strong party of sepoys with them to the spot. The matchlock-men offered resistance, but were overpowered, and the hero was withdrawn from his nest! I was anxious to see the place, and, accompanied by Captain Tayler, made a sketch of it, so nicely situated as it was for a *refugium!*[54] When brought before the king, Hyder Khan

---

[53] Sir John Keane, in his despatches, calls him erroneously *"Prince Makomed Hyder."*

[54] After his panic was over, he appears to have been ashamed of his conduct, and made out a very different story. The following, in Major Hough's narrative, is "the account given by himself while a prisoner. When he heard our first firing from the false attack, he went to that quarter; but when he heard that the British troops were entering the fort, he galloped back to the gateway, where he met some of the Europeans. He had a bayonet run through his *kumerbund* (waistband)! and one of his attendants had a shot through his

was in great agitation and alarm. The young warrior expected nothing but death on being taken, and wept with joy on finding himself pardoned by his majesty. "I do not blame your conduct," said the Shah to him mildly; "you have only acted in obedience to your father's will."

Yesterday evening I visited the two Minars, which bear strong marks of former beauty and elegance. They are well built of red brick, and do not appear to have been ever plastered. Indeed, the exquisite finish of the brick-work, adjusted in various minute forms, highly curious and ornamental, shews that plastering was never intended, and it is surprising that so large a portion of them remains so fresh and sharp, particularly some of the devices, which look as clean and pointed as if they were just out of the artist's hands. The inscriptions executed in various parts of the columns are in the Togra-Arabic character, the letters strangely mingled, so as to produce an agreeable combination, according to Mussulman taste. The style is common in all Mahomedan buildings of consequence, and the language generally Persian.[55] I regret that I had not the means of deciphering the inscriptions, which probably mention the period in which the Minars were erected, and by whom. There is no evidence on the subject in any author I have consulted; but they are supposed to belong to the bright period of the Sebuktageen monarchy. They stand along the Caubul road, the first or smaller one about half a mile from the fort, to the east, and the second a quarter of a mile further, in a direct line. Whether they formed parts of palaces, or mosques, or baths, or tombs, or were originally detached structures, cannot now be ascertained. But the holes in the lower part, and pieces of timber, laid horizontally, so as to form a connecting medium, would seem to justify the conclusion that they were either surrounded by porticoes or attached to other buildings. It is remarkable that the smaller one has the well-known Etruscan fillet or border, surrounding the column near the top, neatly cut, which would indicate European workmanship or a European model. The other parts are, however, essentially Oriental. From the shadow of the largest, at eight A.M., I calculate the height to be about one hundred and eighty feet, the other is not so high by twenty feet at least. The foundation of both is octagonal, not in the common octagon

---

turban! At this moment, his horse reared, and he was almost falling; if he had, his life was gone. He recovered himself, and dashed away up to the citadel. He saw the place was lost, and he resolved to give himself up to the first British *officer* he saw, fearing the *men* would kill him. Captains A. W. Tayler and Macgregor passing by, he sent to tell them that he was in the *citadel,* and ready to give himself up on his life being spared!!!" The citadel was in our hands many hours before the place of his concealment was discovered.

[55] In my published account of Dacca, in Bengal, I have given a fac-simile of an inscription in the same Togra-Arabic character taken from the *Great Kuttra* in that city, built by Abdool Kasim Tubba Tubba Hussainee Ulsumanee, in the year of the Hejira, 1055.

form, but every point or projection like a star. This polyangular shape runs about half-way up, and is surmounted by a round column of similar height. A broken part of the building shews an inner shaft, round which the stairs run to the summit.[56]

It is curious that Bâber, in his Memoirs, when describing Ghizni with so much minuteness, does not mention the two Minars, from which it might be inferred that they were not in existence in his day. Forster, however, so late as 1783, is equally silent on the subject, which is most strange and surprising, for they must have been standing in his time; objects, too, one would think it quite impossible to be overlooked, and yet he distinctly says, that, excepting a few mounds of ruins, there is not a vestige of the past grandeur of Ghizni. A similarly singular omission appears in Tavernier, who visited Dacca in January, 1666. "Dacca," he says, "is a large city, extending more than two koss along the banks of the Ganges, and the distance is entirely occupied by a line of detached houses, which are in fact nothing but miserable huts, built of bamboo, grass, and mud." He mentions no public buildings, excepting those of the Europeans; although the great Kuttra, a most magnificent edifice, as well as the beautiful mosque of Syuff Khan, had been erected many years, and the small Kuttra more recently, but still a considerable time before the celebrated French traveller visited Dacca. These splendid buildings, and several others, had unaccountably eluded the observation, or escaped the memory, of Tavernier.

After viewing the Minars, I proceeded to the tomb of Sultan Mahmood, which is situated in a garden in the village called Rouzah, on the Caubut road, famous for its excellent grapes, and about three miles from the fortress of Ghizni. The garden is walled round, and full of mulberry trees. Passing through the gate, there is a path of flat stones leading to the brick building which contains the tomb. Fronting is a pointed arch-way, covering a narrow sort of portico, or rather vestibule, with stone seats on each side; and mounting a few steps at the further end, you enter the room, about twenty-four feet by fourteen. The tomb is in the middle, of polished white marble, nine feet by four feet six inches, and of the usual Mahomedan shape. The inscription gives the date of his death, Hejira 421, or A.D. 1005. At each end is a wooden pillar or post, adorned with peacock feathers, which support a silken canopy of pale blue, variegated with gaudy colours, but now faded, and in a very tattered condition. Upon the white-washed walls are written sentences and distichs in Arabic and Persian, apparently the enthusiastic outpourings of pilgrims, who had come to visit the shrine, for shrine it is, of great sanctity among the Mussulmans, whose Moolahs are daily in attendance, reading the Koran in honour of the illustrious dead. All sorts of

---

[56] The fourteenth drawing in my collection represents the fortress and citadel of Ghizni, and the two Minars, taken from the Caubul road.

votive, offerings are hung up, and spread out on the wall; at the further end is the preserved skin of a Buber, a tiger of the largest kind, measuring about ten feet long, without the tail. The door is part of the spoil brought by Mahmood himself from the Hindoo temple of Somnat in Guzerat, said to be made of cedar or sandal wood; but the smell is entirely gone, if it ever had any. It is in pannels, carved and well put together. Two folds, hinged, form one-half of the door, which seems to be about eight feet wide by fourteen feet high. It is a massive door, and the same which Runjeet Sing coveted so much, that he at one time demanded it as his part of his recompense for aiding in the cause of Shah Shoojah's restoration. He coveted it, because he wished to rescue it from the Mahomedans, and to restore it to the temple of Somnat, thereby hoping to merit the gratitude and admiration of the Hindoo world. But the trophy of Mahmood was not to be given up. Ferishta makes no mention of this door, but thus specifies the booty obtained by the conqueror: " Among the spoils of the temple was a chain of gold, weighing two hundred *muns* (four hundred pounds), which hung from the top of the building by a ring; it supported a great bell which called the people to worship. The king of Ghizni found in this temple "a greater quantity of jewels and gold than it is thought any royal treasury ever contained before." Describing such enormous wealth, a wooden door must have been beneath Ferishta's notice.

Above the pointed arch-way just mentioned, are three lozenge-shaped ornaments, suspended from a cross beam. They are painted red, with white lines, resembling bricks in a wall. Nobody could tell what they were intended for, but they are looked upon as mysterious symbols, and regarded with great veneration. I fancy, however, that the solution is very easy. In an old copy of Persian verses, they are called *Seh Kungar, sernagoon sar,* — three *Kungars* turned upside down.' *Kungar,* in Persian, means 'battlement, parapet wall,' and this mysterious device, in imitation of brick-work, seems to be no other than the representation of a portion of the serrated lozenge-shaped upper line of a battlement, turned upside down, as an ornament to the building. Strings of large ostrich eggs, interwoven with peacock feathers, embellish the upper and outer part of the door-way. Several pieces of Hindoo sculpture, in white marble, carried off from India, the Pagan trophies of Mahmood, some of them said to be fragments of the idol at Somnat, lie scattered in the vestibule. I forgot to observe that the mace of the conqueror was not to be found. It was whispered that it had been secreted by the Moolahs, under the apprehension that it might be carried off during the presence of the army at Ghizni; but if so, it has not yet been restored. It was described to me as an iron bar, with an iron globe at the end, studded with sharp angular points, and of great weight.

According to Ferishta, the Sultan was buried with great pomp and solemnity in the Kisr-Feroozee, the Palace of Victory, and as there is no probability of the tomb having been removed, the little that now remains must be a portion of that palace. The dome of that portion is still standing, but the interior of it is shut in by rafters, which form a flat ceiling to the room below.

The victorious Mahmood invaded India on ten different occasions. In his first invasion (1001), he defeated Jypal, Rajah of the Punjab; in the second (1004), he conquered Bhootea; in the third (1005), he re-conquered Mooltan; in the fourth (1011), Tahnesur, a city near Delhi; in the fifth (1013), Nindoona, in the Punjab; in the sixth (1015), Lokate; but he was obliged to abandon the enterprise. In the seventh invasion (1017), he subdued the Rajah of Kanooj, and took Meerut and Muttra. Of the latter place he gives the following account, in a letter to the governor of Ghizni: "There are here a thousand edifices as firm as the faith of the faithful, most of them of *marble,* besides innumerable temples; nor is it likely this city has attained its present condition, but at the expense of many millions of dinars; nor could such another be constructed under a period of two centuries. Among the temples at Muttra were found five golden idols, whose eyes were of rubies, valued at 50,000 dinars (£22,331). On another idol was found a sapphire weighing 400 miskals, and the image itself, being melted down, produced 98,300 miskals of pure gold; besides these images, there were above one hundred idols of silver, which loaded as many camels."[57] In the eighth expedition (1023), Mahmood again invaded the Punjab; in the ninth, Kaleenjur, and in the tenth (1024), he marched against Guzerat, to plunder the Hindoo temple at Somnat.

Ferishta merely represents that celebrated shrine as abounding in riches; and the researches of Gibbon enabled him to state that the pagoda: of Somnat "was endowed with the revenue of two thousand villages; two thousand brahmins were consecrated to the service of the Deity, whom they washed each morning and evening in water, from the distant Ganges: the subordinate ministers consisted of three hundred musicians, three hundred barbers, and five hundred dancing girls, conspicuous for their birth and beauty." Wealth, therefore, probably constituted the greatest attraction to Mahmood, who never failed to load himself with the spoil of captured provinces. But the traditions of the people on the spot, given by Sir A. Burnes, who visited Pattan Somnat in October, 1830, ascribe the expedition of the conqueror to another cause. "The Caliph," they say, "had heard with indignation that the infidel prince, ruling in Pattan, and great in his own estimation, slew a Mahomedan daily, and had the *tika,* or mark, on his forehead, renewed day by day from the gore of a fresh sacrifice; that he even ground the victim in an oil mill, or pounded him in a mortar. Magool Isa, a man pious and devout, was despatched to remonstrate against these inhuman practices; but his advice was of no avail, and the durwesh transmitted the particulars to the Sultan Mahmood, of Ghizni, who, in his zeal for the propagation of the faith, besieged Pattan with an army for twelve years, massacred or converted its inhabitants,

---

[57] See Briggs's *Ferishta.*

annihilated its great temple, and put to death its prince, by name Jypal; since which period Pattan has continued, with one or two temporary successful usurpations, a Mahomedan settlement. The temple of Somnat was at once converted by the Sultan into a mosque; its cupolas were overlapped with minarets, which still remain, and the minar temples in the city shared a like fate." The traditions stated above are evidently of the Mussulman stamp; they furnish an adequate cause for the invasion of Mahmood, which a brahmin would not be disposed to acknowledge. According to Ferishta, the capture of Somnat was only the work of three hard-fought days, and not of twelve years! Mahmood started on his expedition in 1024, and returned to Ghizni in 1026, which, considering the great distance, must limit the operations to a short period. The story which relates to Mahmood's breaking the idol is still current in Somnat. Having struck off its nose, a crowd of brahmins offered a quantity of gold, if the Sultan would desist from further mutilation; but Mahmood replied, "If I should consent, my name would be handed down to posterity as the idol-seller, instead of what I am, Mahmood, the idol-destroyer.'" The next blow, says Ferishta, broke open the belly of Somnat, which was hollow, and discovered a quantity of diamonds, rubies, and pearls, of much greater value than the amount which the brahmins had offered.

In speaking or writing of an idol or image formed for pagan warship, the object naturally presented to the mind of the reader is a human form, especially when nose and belly are described as its component parts. But it would appear that this celebrated image of Somnat was nothing more nor less than a Lingam of the usual shape, composed of a single piece of rough stone, hollow, and containing the ùdiamonds, rubies, and pearls," mentioned by Ferishta. Indeed, the description by that author fully bears out the Lingam interpretation, for it says:- "In the centre of the hall was Somnat, a stone idol, five yards in height, two of which were sunk in the ground." It is not likely that, if the idol was of the human form, two yards of its stature would be sunk in the ground. This of itself shews, that it must have been a Lingam, and the words nose and belly are obviously used metaphorically.

I may now advert to a little circumstance illustrative of Affghan skill and dexterity. On my arrival at the village of Rouzah, I was met by several natives, who gave me the *salâm aliekum,* and joined me. The path lay up two or three narrow streets, and my followers soon increased to about a hundred and fifty of all ages, but all very respectful. Still, so far from camp, and alone, the fort too having been taken by storm that very morning, I was not quite easy, and I began to think that my impatience to see the tomb of Mahmood had led me into some danger; when fortunately observing a party of our sepoys on duty at a well, I called one of them off guard to attend me. Two of the Affghans, one on each side, stuck close to me all the way, and were vociferous in their complaints against Dost Mahomed, expatiating bitterly on the oppression they had suffered, and the extortion that had been practised throughout the country. The coming of the Shah, they hoped, would put an end to all the tyranny that had been so long exercised among the people. They shewed me the tomb, and accompanied me back to the place where I had dismounted, still sticking close to me, — one in particular. He had seen the silver pencil with which I had made several sketches, and where I put it away. *Salâm aliekum* marked our parting, and when I got to my tent, I found that my pencil was gone!

Beloochees in the Bolân Pass

The title page of this Work represents a Den in the Mountains of the Bolân Pass, with a party of Beloochees ready to commence a cowardly and murderous attack on the British troops.

Scene on the River Sutledge, near Pauk-Puttun in the Punjaub

This Drawing represents a scene on the river Sutledge, not far from the Pauk-Puttun in the Punjaub, a country in the north-west of Hindoostan Proper. A number of the Punjaubees occupy the fore-ground, some of them are busily engaged in cooking, others in conversation, while the boatmen, in the boats peculiar to the Punjaub, are seen to the left. On the middle bank is a faithful delineation of "the Persian Wheel," used for irrigating the fields, and which is turned by a couple of bullocks, and when in motion, its shrill and squeaking noise may be heard miles off, indicating a village at no great distance; the driver is on a seat carried forward at the end of a beam, supported over the horizontal wheel. At a short distance are two females in crimson dresses, the usual color in this part, carrying water-pots on their heads, this drudgery, among the lower orders in the East, being usually performed by the *softer sex*.

The Town of Roree and the fortress of Bhukker, on the Indus.

About a mile east of Roree, the encamping ground of the British Army, a fine view presents itself of the town, the island, fortress of Bhukker, and the further shore of Sukkur on the Indus. Bhukker was formerly the capital of Scinde. The fort stands on a flint rock, upwards of twenty feet above the level of the river, and the walls are between thirty and forty feet high; its extent is about eight hundred yards by four hundred. The garrison stationed here consisted of the 35th N.I. commanded by Col. Monteath, who resided in the Killadar's house. The jutting out of Roree into the stream, and the centre space being so extensively occupied by the fort of Bhukker and the other islands, esteemed of peculiar sanctity, it has but two comparatively narrow channels, and over which the bridge of boats was thrown to enable the British troops to pass. One of the islands is consecrated to the renowned saint, Khaja Khizzer, and *a hair*, plucked from the beard of that prophet, is there exhibited as a most sacred relic; indeed, such is the veneration in which even a hair from the Prophet's beard is held in Mahomedan countries, that at Cudapah a temple was erected in honor of one which was preserved in a golden casket, with a crystal lid.

The Encampment at Dadur, with the entrance to the Bolân Pass.

This view represents the encampment of the troops at the entrance of the Bolân Pass, about a mile from the town of Dadur, where they halted, by command of Lord Keane, on their march from Nowshera, a distance of twenty-six miles, over a road the most rugged and harassing. Two hundred camels were dispatched from this spot by Captain Watt, with one thousand gallons of rum, to Lord Keane (who had now assumed the command of the Army of the Indus) to enable him to march from Gundava. The mountains at Siriab, covered with snow, are seen in the extreme distance, and between them and the encampment the road winds between huge sand-hills to the Bolân Pass, which is hidden by the immense mountain in the front. On the fore-ground is Khalik Dad, Belooch, governor of Dadur, and his attendant, and some of the wearied camp-followers, preparing their scanty meal. As far as the eye can reach from the camp, desolation has marked this arid spot, and the progress to it was a most arduous one; water rarely met with, but in small quantities, and forage equally scarce. Major Reed, as appears by the latest news, had succeeded in reaching Dadur, having with him a valuable convoy of treasure, and 4,000 Camels, with which he is now preparing to ascend the terrific Pass of Bolân.

View of the mountain Baba-Naunee

This Drawing was taken from Kutl-gah, or the Place of Slaughter. In the fore-ground is a camp-follower asleep, and three Beloochees, eager to wreak their cowardly vengeance on the unprotected, are stealthily approaching him, with the intention of committing murder; a piece of ordnance is also introduced, drawn by camels, on the line of march. It was under the mountains of Baba-Naunee the British forces were encamped, and from which they marched to Abigoon, a distance of eight miles and a quarter, over a road of loose stones and pebbles, affording but little hold for the feet, and very fatiguing both to man and beast, and this was the case for nine-tenths of the distance.

Entrance to the Bolân Pass from Dadur.

Leaving the encampment at Dadur for Kundye, a distance of eleven miles and a half, the troops then entered the Bolân Pass, which is represented in this drawing, the road being rough and pebbly, between sand-hills, studded with flint and lime-stones of all sizes, the space in breadth between the mountains varying from three to four hundred yards to about thirty. As the torrent in the Pass runs deviously from one side of the gorge to the other, the Army was compelled to cross it six or seven times, thereby adding to the hardships already experienced during the march to this Pass; - and here too, the British troops suffered great losses, by the continual discharge of musketry from the Beloochees, who had secreted themselves in dens hewn out of the stupendous mountains overhanging the Pass and which are represented in the cover image of this work.

The wild pass of Siri-Kajoor

A den of Beloochees is exhibited in the foreground, which overhangs the road traversed by the Army. A party of Sepoys is seen on the heights above, ready to punish the murderers. This Pass lies between Abigoom and Siri-Bolân, a distance of nine miles and a half; two-thirds of the way, on the right, is the date-tree from which this Pass takes the name of "Siri-Kajoor." The road is hemmed in by wild and rugged mountains which afford numerous inaccessible positions for the predatory and murderous Beloochees, who from these haunts most skillfully use their jezails or rifles, most formidable weapons with fixed rests, and which are said to carry about eight hundred yards, being seven feet in length. A dead camel and a camp-follower with his throat cut and otherwise most cruelly mutilated, were seen lying together in the middle of the road. Here also, destruction to the Army was most unsparingly dealt out and almost with impunity, the mountains affording protection to the cowardly Beloochees from any volley directed at them.

The opening into the narrow pass above the Siri Bolân

A skirmish with the Beloochees is here represented, a circumstance by no means uncommon near this place. Not far from it the rear-guard of an European regiment was attacked by between two and three hundred Beloochees rushing down the hills, and after firing their matchlocks, were advancing sword in hand, when the officer commanding, collected his Sepoys (about eighty) and keeping them quiet till the Beloochees came within gun-shot, gave them a volley and immediately afterwards charged them with bayonets to their great discomfiture. Fifty-one killed and wounded were left on the ground, besides a number with slighter wounds, carried off by their flying companions, thus terminating for that day, the troubles of the rear-guard. The rocks on each side of this Pass are projecting and stupendous, and in the narrowest passages almost perpendicular. Immense blocks of stone are scattered about all the way and the scenery is of a more magnificently wild character and of a bolder form than any hitherto met with. Many impediments, during the march through the Pass, had been removed by the Engineers, but it was still an arduous task to surmount the many remaining difficulties which were continually appearing.

The approach to the fortress of Kwettah

Kwettah is in the province of Shaul, situated on a wide plain with interior and outer walls, and appears at a distance like a lofty mound. Lord Keane and Staff are seen occupying the middle ground. Here the state of the Army, for want of a sufficient supply of grain and ollah, became alarming, and although at this place abundant supplies had been promised and expected, it became necessary for the chief military authority, Sir Willoughby Cotton, to reduce the daily rations to one-half, which scanty allowance was continued for nearly three months. At Kwettah, Captain Golding was murdered, his corps of Jan Baz had been ordered on service towards Girisk when they mutinied and murdered their leader; - Lieutenant Pattenson of the 2nd B.M.I. escaping, but wounded in eleven places.

Entrance into Kojak Pass from Parush

The Kojak Pass is situate in the Khjeh Amraun range of mountains. At the foot of the hills on each side leading up to the Pass are regular rows of trees, giving an idea that in former times some care had been bestowed in embellishing the ground. At Parush appeared stupendous masses of perpendicular rocks, but affording two narrow paths, although only a few yards wide, that to the left was the usual Kafila route, while that on the right, although rarely trodden, had been cleared and made practicable by the Engineers for the passage of the British troops and artillery. While reconnoitering in this defile, Brigadier Arnold and his aide-de-camp were fired upon from the heights by a Pesh-Khidmut under Ibar Khan, in the service of the Candahar Sirdars. By the latest accounts received, it appears that pursuant to General Nott's orders, Brigadier England, with 2,500 men, left Kwettah for Candahar, a portion of the force at the latter place having been detached so as to meet Brigadier England, and aid him in getting the convoy through this Pass.

The troops emerging from the narrow part of the defile in the Koojah Pass.

This Drawing represents the troops emerging from the narrow part of the defile, and the old and newly constructed roads up the ascent. The road up to the defile had gradually increased in steepness, and diminished in width, and the ascent became more difficult. The tediousness of the march may, therefore, be easily conceived. The old path to the left, was so steep as to be quite impracticable for the purpose of ascent, and, in consequence, taking a wide sweep, another was cut, less abrupt, upon the brow of the hill, as seen to the right of the drawing. It was not, however, above eight or ten feet in breadth, and the upper part, owing to the projection and rocks, was still difficult of access.

The first descent through the Koojah Pass

The first descent from the point described in the last Drawing, was for a considerable distance, very abrupt, precipitous and winding, and the bottom crossed by a torrent, and here the view up to the next position of the pass was most terrific, both as regards its altitude and broken course, about to be pursued in toiling up to the summit. The first slope was strewed with dead camels, no less than sixteen lying on one precipitous spot, and the face of the whole acclivities exhibiting similar evidence of the peril which attended the progress of the army. The column here diverged, following different paths, and after much toil and fatigue, accomplished the task.

The second descent through the Koojah Pass

This descent was not less perilous than that described in the former view, threatening equal destruction amongst the camels, and it was not long before these fears were painfully realized, by a great number of the camels falling head-long into the ravines, being unable, from the soft and loose state of the earth, to obtain any secure footing. The column and innumerable camp-followers, here took three different routes, and encamped near the bottom of the hills, about two miles distant from the plain of Chumum, where the First Brigade had already encamped.

The third descent of the Koojah Pass

Looking back from three-parts downwards, where the 1st Bengal European Regiment had encamped, to assist in bringing over the artillery, is the spot from whence this view was taken, and which represents in the foreground the encampment of the 1st Bengal European Regiment, with a group of camp-followers, some asleep, while others are busily engaged in unpacking their baggage; much difficulty was here incurred, in getting over the park of artillery, which occupied no less than five days of indefatigable exertion, performed by the troops, under a burning sun, with the utmost cheerfulness. This task devolved on detachments of fatigue-men, from the European, the 13th Light Infantry, and the 48th Native Infantry regiments. Plunder, in every description of articles, was carried on during this encampment, by the mountaineers, who were continually committing outrages, rolling down heavy stones from the crags which overlooked the regimental bazaar, and firing into the camp.

The city of Candahar

This view was taken from the camp of the Fourth Brigade, about a mile and a half on the south of Candahar, a fortified town of Afghaunistan, the capital of the province of Candahar, near which Akbar Khan (by whom fell Sir W. Macnaghten) so unsuccessfully marked, when he was met by Shah Mahommed, with 6000 horse at Jakan, near Candahar, and compelled, with considerable loss, amidst confusion and defeat, to fly towards the Indus, which he afterwards crossed near Leia, taking temporary refuge in the territory of Mahommed Khan Suddozye. General Nott was in command here, with 10,000 men, having successfully repulsed the enemy before it, with a very trifling loss on his part, and to whose relief General England has now succeeded in marching. The city is situate on the north side of an extensive plain, about two miles from the lofty mountain called Baba-Wulee, and is surrounded by a mud wall, about thirty feet high, with numerous bastions; the length of the city is about five thousand feet, and four thousand in breadth, with a small stream running across the interior from north to south.

The fortress and Citadal of Ghuznee and the Two Minars

This view of Ghuznee possesses considerable interest, having been the scene of a successful attack by the British, under the command of Lord Keane, but which, alas! has since capitulated, the troops having been attacked by the Ghazees, a dreadful slaughter ensued. One hundred only of the Sepoys, with Colonel Palmer and several other British officers of the Bombay Establishment, narrowly escaping with their life. In approaching the walls of this fortress, there is a considerable ascent across the bridge to the rampart on the east side. The gate was lying in fragments, and a bastion to the right of it was also demolished. The ascent inside is very abrupt, to the citadel, which is very spacious, and built wholly on a hill, but sloping more gradually down towards the South West, where the tower is situated. The North-East angle of the citadel is commanded by a hill, no great distance from it, and behind which the British batteries were placed, which did considerable execution. Between the gate and citadel, about half-way up, was placed the far-famed brass 68-pounder, called Zabur-Jung, "the mighty in battle." It was worked by an Hindoostanee, over whom a guard was placed with drawn swords, to compel him to perform his duty. The two Minars, here introduced, bear strong marks of former beauty and elegance; they are built of red brick, with most exquisite finish, in various minute forms, highly curious and ornamental. The inscriptions executed on various parts of the columns are in the Togra-Arabic character, the letters strongly mingled, but producing an agreeable combination of the Mussulman taste. The admeasurement of the higher is computed at about 180 feet, while the other is not so high by at least twenty feet.

The valley of Maidan

At the top of the strong ghaut or pass is a round tower, or watch-house, called Buzrak, and from this eminence the Valley of Maidan is distinctly seen, although but a small portion of it is represented in this view. The beauty of this valley is highly extolled by the Afghauns, and well it may be, in comparison with other parts of the country hitherto seen. The valley is semi-circular, about a mile and a half wide, and four miles long, hemmed in by the most sterile hills, with a charming silver line of river flowing through its centre, and the trees, meadow, and plantations, always appearing bright and glowing. The troops are here seen on their march from Maidan to the village of Urghundee. The road for five miles is an ascent, most rough and rugged, and intersected with deep ravines, where numerous Camels belonging to the Brigade in advance had perished, and many left, exhausted, to die.

The village of Urghundee

To the extreme right of the drawing, at the foot of an immense mountain is the village, and across the valley are ranged the guns, twenty-five in number, of Dost Mahommed Khan, which were abandoned the night previously and afterwards secured by Major Cureton, who had been sent with his Lancers to take them. Dost Mahommed, who had, with great difficulty, persuaded his adherents, consisting of about twelve thousand fighting men of all sorts, to advance even as far as Urghandee, had placed his guns in position, with the profoundest intention of vigorously coming to action, but no sooner were the guns so ranged in battle order that the Ameer, convinced that his safety consisted in flight, discarded them, blew up the powder and moved off precipitately across the mountains towards Bamian. Some of the guns were thrown from their carriages, thousands of balls lying in all directions, and the ground literally strewed with belts and cartouche-boxes, half consumed by the explosions that had evidently taken place. Two hundred gun-bullocks had been left behind and became a part of the prize property.

The guns varied in size from three to nine pounders, the carriages of the clumsiest construction, so unskillfully put together, that a few rounds must have shattered them to pieces, and upon inspection it was found that *each* gun was loaded with *three* balls, so that the danger to the gunner would have been greater than to the enemy.

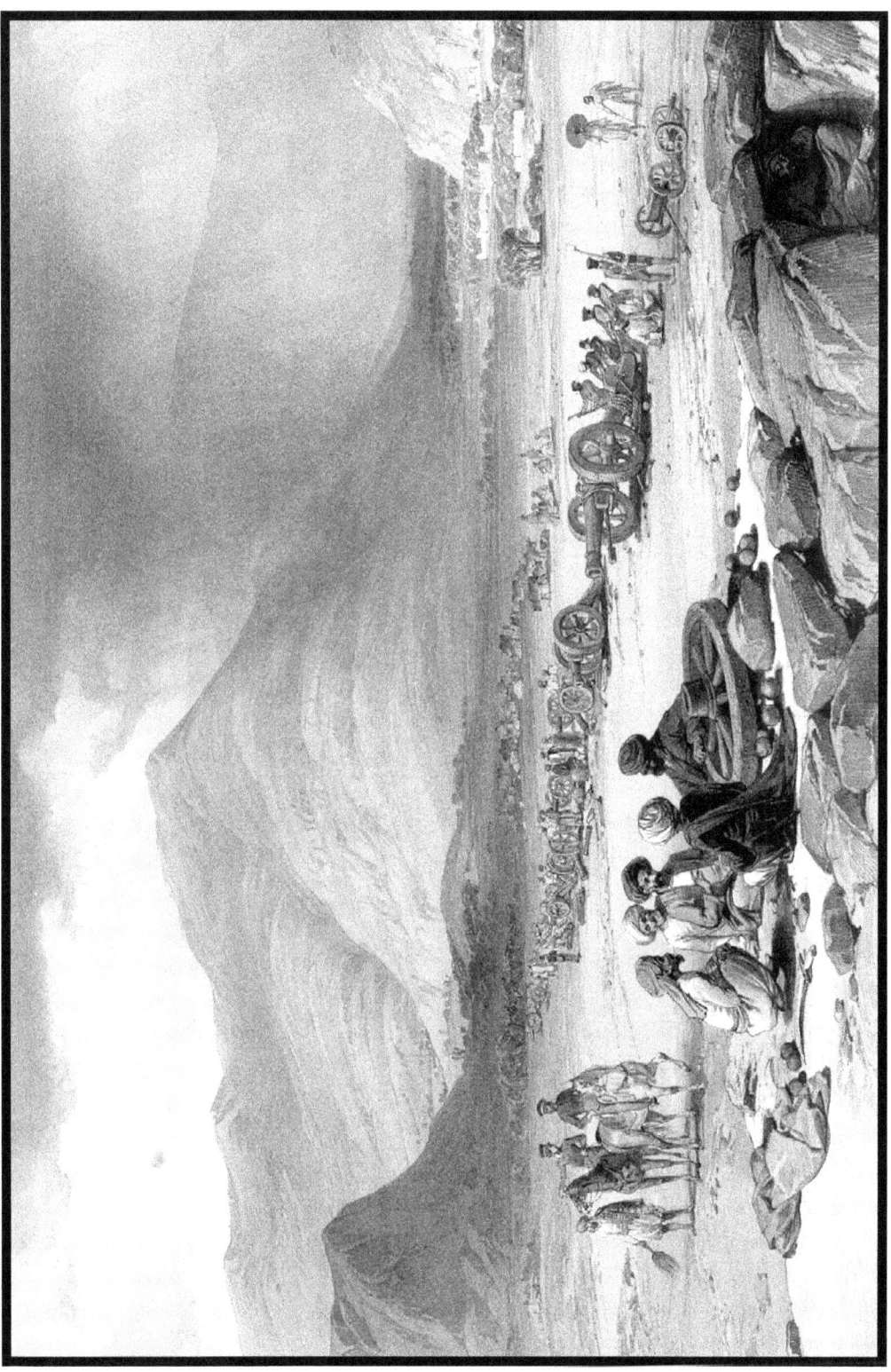

Entrance into Caubul from Killa-Kâzee

On the right of this drawing the peasants are treading out the corn, and on the left winnowing it. The small building half-way up the mountain is called the Johan Numat, which commands an extensive prospect over the valley of Killa-Kâzee; a little below this spot is the site of the Emperor Bâber's Tomb. In the narrow gap, formed by the two craggy mountains, sloping towards each other, and which is seen in the centre of this view, lies the road from the camp to Caubul, the extreme edges of those slopes, as seen from a distance, exhibit a line of fortified or rather serrated and loop-holed walls from top to bottom. The road from Killa-Kâzee is very confined, hemmed in by huge masses of rock on the left hand and dense groves of mulberry trees on the right bordering the Caubul river. In the foreground of the drawing is represented the surrender of Dost Mahommed Khan to Sir William Macnaghten. This event occurred while the British Envoy was taking his accustomed ride, attended by his staff, and totally unconscious of any intention on the part of the Dost, to surrender himself. The latest news from this part states that Captain Mackenzie was sent by Akhbar Khan to the camp at Jellalabad, on parole, as the bearer of a dispatch from Major Pottinger and to treat for the ransom of his companions.

The main street in the Bazaar at Caubul in the fruit season

The entrance into Caubul was by a narrow street, presenting to the view a scene of the most busy description. The numerous shops, little better than sheds, exhibited fruit, not only surprising for its beauty, but for its prodigious abundance; melons and grapes out of number, and this display continued for some distance, Caubul having long been famous for its fruits, more particularly in grapes, pomegranates, apricots, peaches, pears, apples, quinces, jujubes, damsons, almonds, and walnuts, all of which are found in immense quantities, as well as the orange, citron, amlook, and sugar-cane, which are peculiar to a warm climate and are brought from Laghman. Other articles are also presented for sale. Cooks are preparing kabobs and confectioners sweetmeats; cutlers and farriers, guns, swords, and horse-shoes; silk-mercers, dealers in carpets, furs, lace, chintz, saddlery, &c., all are attentive to their several occupations.

The Balla Hissa and city of Caubul, from the upper part of the Citadel.

The Balla Hissa comprehends nearly a fourth part of the city of Caubul, and is surrounded by a wall, the height being regulated according to the rise and fall of the mountains, with numerous bastions, but only two gates now open, that to the west leading to the town, and the other on the east called the Peshawer gate, both being closed at night. The upper part of the Balla Hissar is about four hundred and twenty yards by two hundred and fifty; the lower part about one thousand by five hundred yards. The garden on the right is occupied by the British Envoy, formerly the residence of Dost Mahommed Khan; the building beyond is the Harem Serai, in which the Shah resides, although in a falling state. On the left of it is the Musjid Shahee, or Royal Mosque, in ruins, founded in the time of Alumgeer. The roofs of the houses are flat, and but ill-suited to a climate in which so much snow falls. It was from Balla Hissar, the British troops were recalled to the cantonment, dispirited and illy clad, and suffering most acutely under the deprivation of food, which scanty allowance they could only obtain by bribery and plunder during the night.

Caubul from a burying ground on the mountain ridge, North-East of the city

Kaga-Suffa, from whence this view of the city is taken, is the burial-ground, remarkable for its neatness, numerous interments and tombs. Caubul has no pretensions to beauty, being huddled together and bounded on three sides by immense mountains occupying a space of about three miles in circumference with a strongly fortified wall running on the ridges. Externally, every house presents a blank mud wall, and the domestic arrangement of rooms and apertures for windows are in a court-yard totally unseen from without. It is too painful a subject to contemplate here, the result of the movements of the British Army from this city after the treaty had been entered into by General Elphinstone to evacuate the city, or to dilate on the heart-rending disasters that befell the British during their march from hence, through the mountain pass of Khyber, but, suffice it to say that there was but ONE EUROPEAN, Dr. Bryden of the 37th Bengal Native Infantry, who survived out of the 6,500 troops and about 7,000 camp-followers who left Caubul, which place still contains many of our bravest commanders with, alas! the noble-minded Lady Sale and other British ladies as hostages who were escorted back to Khan. Captain Colin Mackenzie, one of the prisoners, is now on parole to General Pollock at Jellalabad, with proposals from the Chief and Mahommed Shah Khan, the Ghilzie, for the release of the ladies and other prisoners. *The result* has not yet transpired.

The Durbar of Shah Shoojah-ool-Moolk, at Caubul

This drawing represents, immediately below the Balla Hissar and contiguous to the residence of the Envoy and Minister, the quadrangle occupied by the Durbah-Khanch and the Harem Serai. In the balcony is seen His Majesty Shah Shoojah, seated on his throne, and the manner in which the Khans and Officers of state are daily assembled before him, while the Royal Band, which is composed of huge toms-toms and long brass tubes, continues playing in the most horribly discordant manner with all the power that muscular arm and stentorian lung can give, from the deepest bass to the most shrill treble. This *music* is considered an essential part of regal state and is repeated several times during the day, and commencing at two o'clock in the morning much to the discomfort and annoyance of Christian ears.

The Avenue at Bâber's Tomb

This grove of magnificent cheenars leads to the burial-place of the Emperor Bâber, the space between, being some hundred yards, is divided into numerous terraces about twenty feet wide for the purpose of forming a line of diminutive artificial cascades. The water is supplied from the mountains, and which, after numerous falls from one terrace to another is received into a square reservoir. There is a wide path on each side of these terraces, and on every Friday – the Mahommedan Sabbath – the walks of this favorite grove are filled "from morn till dewy eve" with crowds of people in their holiday attire – the women always veiled in their boorkas, and each enjoying with apparent delight the social scene around.

The Tomb of the Emperor Bâber

To the right of this tomb appear the extensive ruins of a celebrated Mosque, which was built by Shah-Jehan. The Tower in the middle of the distance is the Killa-Kâzee, and the Fort on the extreme right the residence of Newab Jubbar Khan, brother of Dost Mahommed Khan. Ascending to the upper part of the grove, as seen in the last drawing, is a terrace, about thirty yards square, and nearly in the middle of it, is the tomb erected in honor of the Emperor Bâber, in 1650, by Shah-Jehan, after the conquest of Balkh and Budukshan, and is now in good preservation. The Emperor Bâber was descended from a tribe of Tartars, and in his Twelfth year (A.D. 1494), became King of Ferghana, a country in the North-East of the Caspian, or as he himself says, "on the extreme boundary of the habitable world." After an ambitious career, in which he experienced a variety of successes and discomfitures, he, in 1504, gained possession of Caubul; after several fruitless attempts to invade India, his fifth determination carried him to Delhi and Agra, having on his march slain Sultaun Ibrahim, the Emperor of Hindoostan, and in 1526, he ascended the throne of Delhi. He was undoubtedly one of the most illustrious monarchs of Asiatic history, and at Caubul, where his ashes repose, is held in the highest veneration.

Portrait of His Majesty Shah Soojah-ool-Moolk

Shah Soojah's ancestors commenced with Ahmed Shah. Nadir Shah the celebrated conqueror, was assassinated in 1747, upon which Abdullah Ahmed Khan proclaimed himself king, under the name of Ahmed Shah; his son, Tymoor Shah, succeeding him in 1773, and in 1793 he died, and the government was then broken up. Shah Zemaun, the son of Tymoor, mounted the throne of Caubul, whilst Humayoon seized upon Candahar; Abbass on Peshawer, and Hajee Feroz-oo-deen, and Mahmood on Herat, all sons of Tymoor, by different mothers. Political rivalry then sprung up, and Shah Zemaun dispossessed Humayoon of Candahar, took him prisoner, and cruelly put out his eyes. He also seized upon Peshawer, and compelled Abbass to relinquish, and placed him in confinement. A conspiracy amongst the nobles and chiefs at Candahar then existed, and terminated by dethroning Shah Zemaun, and placing his brother Shah Soojah-ool-Moolk on the throne.

His Majesty Shah Shoojah-ool-Moolk

Caubul Costumes

Ladies preparing for Walking, and a Lady seated at Home. The dress of the women of Caubul is simple; they wear a loose yellow, blue or red jacket of muslin or silk, hanging down below the waist, and wide trowsers; their hair is in various forms, and plaited behind in numerous long tails, hanging over the shoulder and back. The outer margin of the ear is pierced and decorated with rows of silver rings. The face is adorned with moulds of gold, silver, and vermillion, fixed on with gum. The jacket and trowsers are alone worn in the house, as represented in the seated figure, but when prepared for walking, as the ladies on the left, they put on leggings, gartered at the knee, and cover themselves with the *Boorka-posh*, which prevents their being known abroad.

A Caubul Lady – as seen in her Window in the main street.

The Governor's Place of Refuge – at Ghuznee, after the capture of the Fortress.

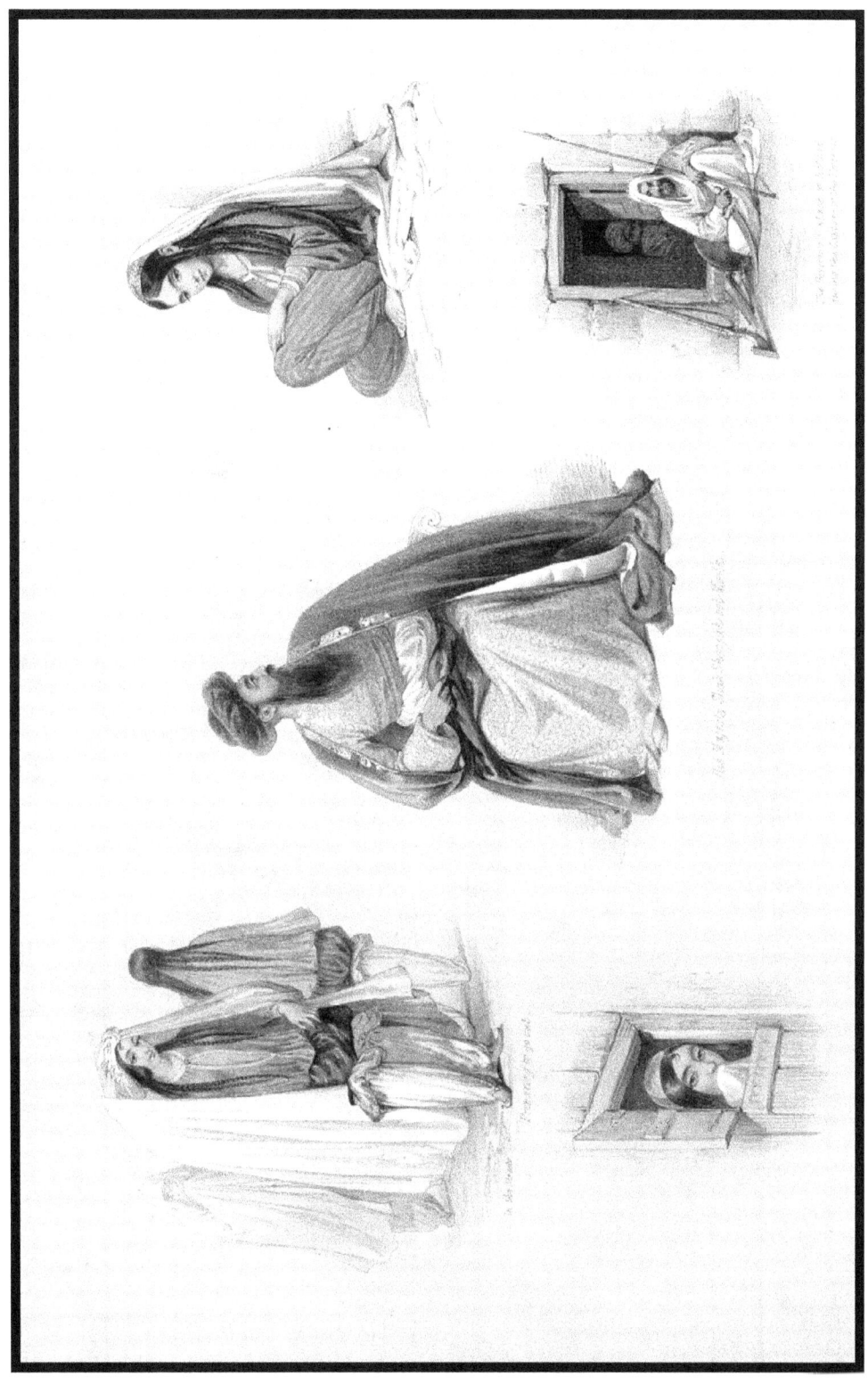

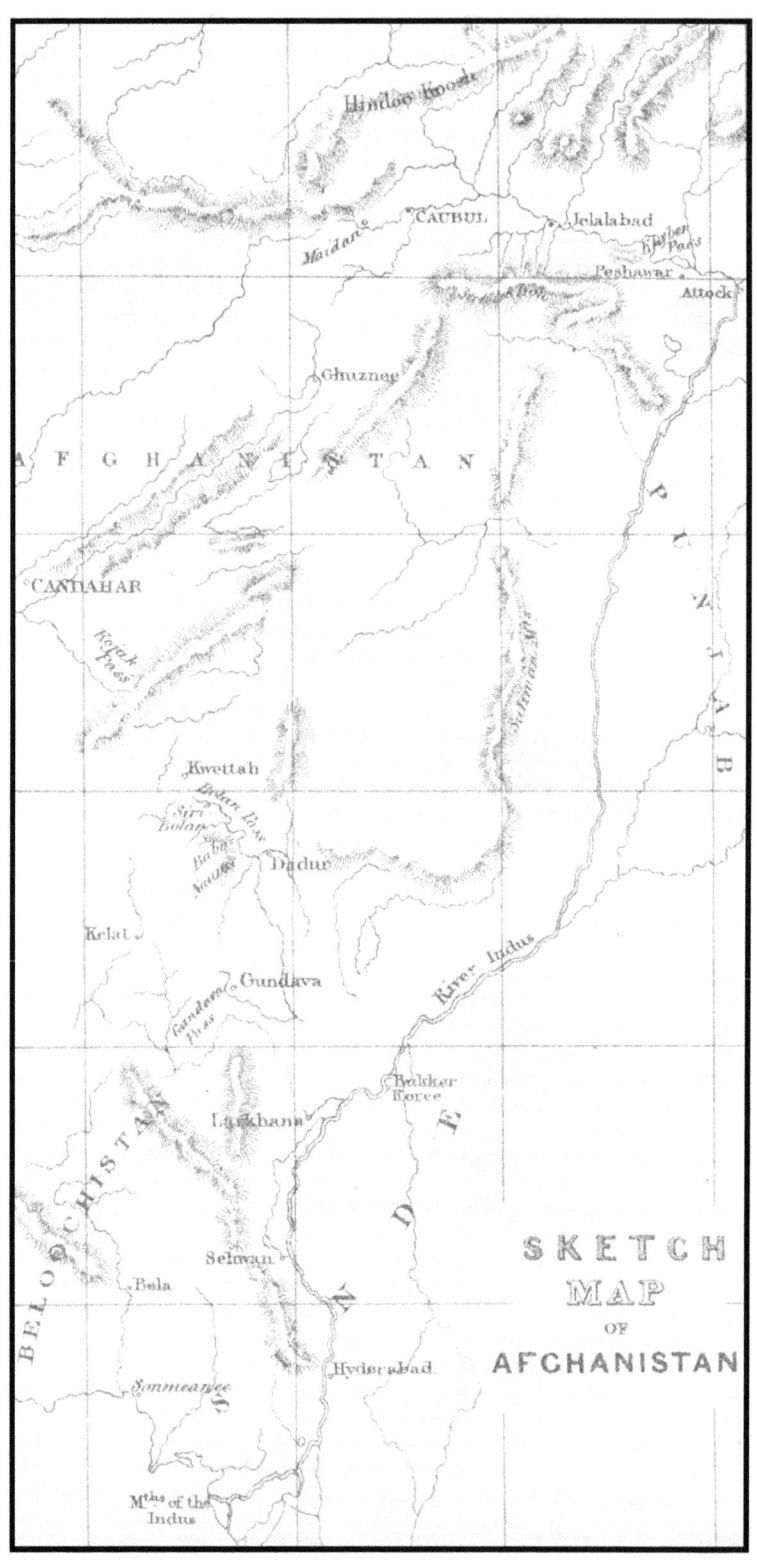

CHAPTER XI.

GHIZNI.

The sick troops — Mission from Caubul, under Nawab Jubbar Khan — Character of the Nawab — His interview with Shah Shoojah — He blackens the English character — Condition of Dost Mahomed Khan — His son, Mahomed Akber Khan — Gholam Hyder Khan, late governor of Ghizni — The town — Effects of the conflict — Wullee Mahomed executed — Former and present state of Ghizni — Mahmood and Firdousee — No indication of the splendour of the ancient city — Want of durability in the materials of the cities of antiquity.

Sir John Keane, always attentive to the comfort of the sick, was desirous of leaving all the patients in hospital at Ghizni; but this was impracticable, for, on my referring to the state of each regiment, I found that those unfit for immediate active duty would amount in the Bengal division alone to nearly six hundred, which would involve the provision of more medical officers, and a larger establishment, than could be given, preserving at the same time the efficiency of the field hospital, which indeed might still be urgently required on the march to Caubul, in the event of Dost Mahomed adhering to the uncompromising course he had threatened to pursue.[55] I therefore proposed a modification of the arrangement, and suggested that those only who could not be moved without danger should be left at Ghizni. His Excellency immediately complied with the recommendation, and issued the following order:-

"Camp, Ghizni, July 27th, 1839.-Superintending Surgeon Atkinson having represented that sufficient hospital establishment for the whole of the sick and wounded of the army cannot be left at Ghizni, without compromising the efficiency of the field hospital, His Excellency the Commander-in-Chief is pleased to direct, that such sick and wounded men as cannot be removed without risk be left in the hospital depôt at this place; and that all for whom transport is available shall move with the army."

The severe cases only of both divisions were accordingly left under the care of Mr. Surgeon Pinkey, of the Bombay establishment. The number from the Bengal column was one hundred and ten, including Major Warren, and Lieut. Hazlewood, of the European regiment, and Capt. Graves, of the 16th N.I.

In the afternoon of the 28th of July, Nawab Jubbar Khan, the half-brother of Dost Mahomed, arrived in camp, attended by a few horsemen, on a mission from Caubul.

---

[55] There was neither a field hospital nor a depôt of medical stores with the Bombay column.

At the same time, the Candahar chiefs were addressed from Shikarpore, and called upon to submit to the king: a letter was also despatched by the Envoy and Sir John Keane to Dost Mahomed, in which he was apprized that our army was about to advance with rapidity on Candahar; that his majesty Shah Shoojah was prepared to bury all feelings of animosity which had so long subsisted between the two families, and that the British Government would guarantee his personal safety, honourable treatment, and a suitable provision for his wife and family, and dependents, in number not exceeding one hundred; provided that he instantly disbanded his armed retainers, and agreed to retire to such place in Hindoostan, and by such route, as would be pointed out. To this letter no answer was given by Dost Mahomed, and his first communication with us was now entrusted to Jubbar Khan, who was escorted to the Envoy's tent by a party of our cavalry, and accompanied by Sir Alexander Burnes, who, having known him before, had gone out to meet him.

Various reports of the Nawab's proposals for the adjustment of matters were in circulation. According to one, Dost Mahomed demanded, upon relinquishing the government of Caubul, that he should be invested with the office of minister to the Shah. Another, that the English should take possession of the country, the Shah to be made viceroy and he his Vizeer. The chief object of Jubbar Khan's mission, however, seems to have been the release of Hyder Khan from the condition of a prisoner of war, preparatory to negotiation; but this was not allowed. It was then requested that Dost Mahomed should be permitted to see him, and this too was refused. But the true drift of the Nawab's proposals did not transpire. Expatriation to Hindoostan was the most unpalatable condition.

Jubbar Khan had the titular dignity of Nawab from the circumstance of his having been, many years ago, governor of the two Derabs, called Derajat, *viz.,* Dera Ghaza Khan, and Dera Ismael Khan. *Nawab* is rather an exotic designation among the Affghans, though Naib is of frequent occurrence, and *Nawab* simply the plural of *Naib.* After that, he was governor of Cashmeer, and more recently of the Ghilzie country. In none of these governments does he appear to have lost sight of his own interests; on the contrary, in the extent of his intrigues and rapacity he is said to have equalled any other member of his rapacious family. The bright spot in his character is thought to be his bias in favour of Europeans, and Englishmen in particular, to whom he has more than once shewn much hospitality and consideration during their occasional or accidental visits to Caubul. Sir Alexander Burnes speaks of him, in 1832, as "a man of amiable character, with greater moral influence, at that period, than any of the Barukzye family in Affghanistan." He calls him "the patriarch of Caubul;" but, with all these virtues conceded to him by an ardent and zealous mind, justly grateful for a friendly and kind reception in a foreign land, further acquaintance with his character has not shewn him to be exempt from the failings and feelings of his countrymen. Dost Mahomed's qualities are differently proportioned. He has more impatience and undisguised ambition, and Jubbar Khan more caution and sagacity, with a keen eye to worldly advantage, looking farther into the bearing of human events, and prone to a sort of Fabian policy in all his doings. The subtle adaptation of his conduct to times and occasions had secured him in the possession of wealth and a quiet home. In the existing crisis, the Dost could find no better instrument for his purpose than this shrewd and calculating brother.

When Jubbar Khan was introduced to the king, his deportment was not uncourteous, but he said:- "If you are to be king, of what use is the British army here? If the English are to rule over the country, of what use are you here?" The Shah, with unruffled temper, parried this observation by soothing his hurt mind, and, in a bland manner, promised him a confidential situation near his person. But Jubbar Khan had not succeeded in his object; he was disappointed and silent, and took leave, returning immediately back to Caubul. This was the first time the Nawab had seen a British camp, and the state and appearance of our army were not calculated to inspire him with much hope from the employment of any military means at the command of his brother; though one of his countrymen did say; about the same time, and a day or two after the fall of Ghizni too, looking contemptuously down upon our tents from a neighbouring mountain:- "Why, your army consists merely of camels and canvas — ours of mounted warriors, with sharp swords!" What a degradation, then, to be overcome by camels and canvas!

On his return to Caubul, Jubbar Khan had recourse to a base manœuvre, in circulating the grossest falsehoods throughout the city, for the purpose of blackening the English name and character, and exciting the inhabitants to fight against us. He stated that the most wanton and revolting acts had been committed on the families of the garrison by our troops after the storm, and that every Koran found in the fortress had been defiled and destroyed. But this denunciation was well answered by the people. "If such," said they, "had truly been the fate of the families of those who resisted at Ghizni, it was quite clear that the safety of theirs did not lie in resistance."

Dost Mahomed was now fully aware of his perilous condition, and forthwith redoubled his efforts to concentrate his means. His favourite son, Mahomed Akber, had been posted, with a considerable number of troops, about five thousand, in the neighbourhood of Jellalabad, of which place he was governor, with the intention of blocking up the Khyber Pass, and on the fall of Ghizni, was recalled to Caubul. Akber had advanced as far as Lundikana, to oppose Shah-zadeh Tymoor, who, accompanied by Colonel Wade, and a respectable force, was waiting near Peshawer, to penetrate the Caubul territory by that route. Akber deferred compliance with his father's injunctions, till he had destroyed, he said, the Feringhees in the pass. But immediately after the capture of Ali Musjid, thirteen miles from his position, he thought better of it, and consulting his own safety, bravely took to flight. After hurrying through Jellalabad, and getting as far as Gundumuk, his alarm became so great, that he abandoned every thing, and pushed on with only a few followers. Twelve guns, two of which had been taken from the Shah at Candahar, and two from the Sikhs at Jumrood, seven hundred rounds of ball, camp equipage, horses, draft bullocks, swivels, with ammunition and equipments, all fell into the hands of the troops under Colonel Wade, in full march towards Caubul.

July 29.-Whilst I was in the citadel this afternoon, making arrangements for the sick and wounded, Gholam Hyder Khan was brought from camp to be confined there as a prisoner of war, the army being under orders to march to-morrow. He is a very stout young man, about twenty years of age. He had on a loose white turban; his dress, a spotted muslin chintz, with a voluminous piece of cloth carelessly folded round his waist; wide white trowsers, no stockings, and green slippers. He was at once conducted to the rooms appointed for his accommodation, which were, however, not at all to his liking. At that time, the sick and wounded of the European regiments, intended to be left there for medical treatment, were collected in the quadrangle, previous to being placed in their several quarters. Hyder Khan, looking out at the open space in front, saw what was going on with great anxiety, and at length expressed his fears that he himself would certainly be taken ill, if he remained so near the sick. He was in a state of considerable uneasiness, and therefore permitted to occupy the southern turret, about twelve feet square, built at the corner, and on the roof of the citadel, his own choice. No sooner had he entered, than a little carpet was spread by an attendant, and he sunk down on his knees in silent prayer, going through all the prostrations enjoined by his creed before us, as unconcernedly as if he had been alone. Every proper arrangement was liberally made, in fulfilment of his wishes, that could be adopted for his convenience and satisfaction; but it is not easy to please a man who is a prisoner in what he deems his own castle!

Before leaving the fort, curiosity led me again through the town — the whole comprehended within the walls — and, like almost every other, it is one great stable, straw and the litter of horses lying thick in every street. It was now a week since the capture, and there was yet no end to the dreadful effects of the conflict. There was still a long catalogue of men who had died of their wounds, in excess of those already buried; — men who had crawled into the forsaken houses for shelter amidst the fearful and deadly strife, and perished there; remaining undiscovered till the people began to return to the homes which had been abandoned on our arrival. In one place I saw two bodies brought out in an advanced state of decomposition; and in another, four, close together, with a number of men and women preparing to remove them for burial. A succession of these sad groups met my view as I passed on. After we had got possession of the citadel, there was a sharp opposition by parties on the tops of the houses, and in the streets, which lasted some hours, and during this period great numbers must have fallen. We had several men killed. On our arrival at Caubul, information reached us, that in searching thoroughly every recess and corner, between two and three hundred more dead bodies had been found and buried; so that, together with those cut down in their flight, the total number of killed has been estimated at upwards of one thousand. Nearly all the prisoners, amounting to about sixteen hundred, were released, and allowed to go where they pleased. There was one prominent exception. Wulee Mahomed, a desperate leader of one of the parties of the enemy encountered in the streets, had surrendered, and sued for quarter, which was granted; but he thought himself at liberty, time and opportunity serving, to resume hostilities. He did so, and two or three of our sepoys were, in consequence, slain, and several wounded. This treachery, however, met with its due reward. He was taken prisoner, and executed next day, by order of the Commander-in-Chief.

We cannot quit Ghizni without a few more words on its former and present state. The reign of the Ghizni kings, from Sebuktageen to the extinction of his race, was about two hundred years; but the splendour of the capital seems to have reached its height with extraordinary rapidity under Sultan Mahmood, the second king, With the immense treasures obtained in his numerous successful wars, he was enabled to gratify a taste which he appears to have manifested at an early period of his life. Before his accession to the throne, he had erected an elegant summer-house in a garden near Ghizni, which he hoped would excite the admiration of his father; but old Sebuktageen, being "made of sterner stuff," rebuked the youth, and pointed out to him what he considered more noble objects of pursuit, and more suitable for a prince. His subsequent career fully proved, and in an eminent degree, that his cultivation of the arts which embellish and dignify our nature was no impediment to his unwearied zeal in conquering kingdoms and covering himself with military glory. Oriental poets are always great moralizers, and it was adverting to the rebuke of Sebuktageen, that Nizami Orazi, of Samerkand, wrote in substance as follows :

> Mahmood's magnificence in temple, tower —
>   Glittering adornments built by mortal hands;
> Where are they now? They stood their fleeting hour,
>   And now lie mingled with the barren sands.
> How different monuments of mental power!
>   The poet's tower of verse still fresh in beauty stands.

But though the buildings have perished, the name of Mahmood will never die. It was on his return from the conquest of Muttra, loaded with spoil, that he ordered a magnificent mosque to be built, Ferishta says, "of *marble* and *granite,* of such beauty as struck every beholder with astonishment, and furnished it with candelabras and other ornaments of silver and gold. The mosque was universally known by the name of the Celestial Bride. In its neighbourhood the king founded an university, supplied with a vast collection of curious books in various languages. It contained also a museum of natural curiosities." And it is further said, that the nobility, perceiving the taste displayed by the king, endeavoured to vie with each other in the magnificence of their private palaces, as well as in public buildings, which they raised for the embellishment of the city. Thus, in a short time the capital was ornamented with mosques, porches, fountains, reservoirs, aqueducts, and cisterns, beyond any city in the East. This was the Augustan age of Ghizni, and the court of the Sultan was not only brilliant in all things that belong to royal pomp, but crowded with men of distinguished talents and learning, statesmen, philosophers, and poets. Of the latter, Firdousee, the celebrated author of the *Shahnameh,* was the most eminent. Munificent as Mahmood was generally to literary men, his conduct to Firdousee had been less liberal than his promises led to expect, which so much irritated the poet, that he gave vent to his angry feelings in a bitter satire on the Sultan; which nearly cost him his life. The Sultan, however, at length became sensible of the injustice he had committed towards Firdousee, and endeavoured to console his own heart by sending to the author of the immortal poem, who had left the court and retired to Toos, his native town, sixty thousand pieces of gold. But it was too late. The present arrived at the very moment the remains of Firdousee were being conveyed through the city gate for interment.

Every year appears to have added something to the splendour of Ghizni, and Masaood, the successor of Mahmood, with the spirit of his father, "built many handsome mosques, and endowed several colleges and schools," and in 1036 another "new palace was finished at Ghizni; in it was a golden throne erected in a magnificent hall, over which was suspended by a golden chain a crown of gold, weighing seventy muns (135lbs.), emitting lustre from numerous precious stones, forming a canopy for the king when he sat in state to give public audience." But from time to time devastation fell upon the devoted city. It is related, that the year after the death of Mahmood, a violent flood occurred at Ghizni, which levelled a great number of the principal buildings to the ground; and in the reign of Sultan Arslan, mention is made of a thunderbolt, which in its fall set fire to and destroyed most of the houses of the city. But the next visitation was the most terrible. In revenge for his brother's murder, during the reign of Sultan Khosroo, Allah-oo-Deen Hussain Ghouri, after capturing Ghizni, and giving it up for seven days to flame, slaughter, and devastation, conveyed a number of the most venerable and learned men in chains to Feroz-koh, to adorn his triumph, where he ordered their throats to be cut, tempering earth with their blood, with which he plastered the walls of his native city. "For this," says

Ferishta, "he justly obtained the surname of Jehan-soz, the 'Incendiary of the World;' and he even carried his animosity so far as to destroy every monument of the Ghizni kings, with the exception of those of Mahmood, Masaood, and Ibraheem; but he defaced all the inscriptions, even of their times, from every public edifice."

From the time of Sultan Masaood III., the royal family of Ghizni resided chiefly at Lahore, and in consequence, the former capital must have diminished in importance, and fallen into gradual decay. Bâber, in his Memoirs, says, with respect to its appearance and position, "Ghizni is but a poor, mean place, and I have always wondered how its princes, who possessed also Hindoostan and Khorassan, could have chosen such a wretched country for their seat of government, in preference to Khorassan."

Ferishta speaks of a mosque of "marble and granite," but it is probable that the material principally used was, as in the present day throughout Affghanistan, mud or sun-dried brick. The flood already noticed, levelling most of the buildings to the ground, would seem to countenance this conclusion. The space between the fortress and Mahmood's tomb, along which runs the Caubul road, and which may be about two miles and a half, is encumbered with numerous ruins of very broad mud walls, some still from ten or fifteen feet high, and it is probable that the area in question was the site of ancient Ghizni; but I found nothing like a building-stone, and traversed the whole space. Every indication of its splendour is swept away, except the two Minars which stand intermediately between the Sultan's tomb and the fort; for the few sepulchral edifices that are now seen in ruins bear no such evidence of high antiquity, as to be considered coeval with the "palmy state" of the empire, but of a comparatively modern period.

But, as before observed, cities in the East, generally, from the materials employed, had no chance of durability. Alexander built cities on his march to conquest. We learn from Strabo, and Pliny too, that Sardanapalus built the two seaport cities of Anchiale and Tarsus, on the Ciliclan coast, in one day![56] The following, according to Arrian, ii., c. 5, was the inscription on his monument at the former place: "*Sardanapalus, Anacyndaraxis filius, Anchialem et Tarsum una die edificavi, Tu autem hospes, Ede, Lude, Bibe,*" &c., adding, "Since there is nothing in this world worth thy care."

The connection, however, between building cities in one day and a recommendation to sensual enjoyment, is not very apparent. Building a city in one day "crosseth the Proverb," as old Browne says, in his *Vulgar Errors;* "Rome was not built in a day," implying that it took years, or (as it did) ages, to complete, and the boast on the monument of Sardanapalus can only be looked upon as a little

---

[56] Strab. 14, Plin, v., c. 27.

hyperbolical, meaning merely that the cities of Anchiale and Tarsus were built within a short period. For, as Browne observes, "if strictly taken, that is, for the finishing thereof, and not only for the beginning, for an artificial or natural day, and not one of Daniel's weeks, that is, seven whole years; surely their hands were very heavy that wasted thirteene yeares in the private house of Solomon; it may bee wondered how forty years were spent in the erection of the temple of Jerusalem, and no lesse than an hundred in that famous one at Ephesus. Certainly, it was the greatest architecture of one day, since that great one of sixe; an arte quite lost with our Mechanicks, and a work not to be made out, but like the walls of Thebes, and such an artificer as Amphion!"

Tymoor, as well as Alexander, is said to have built cities in two, three, or four days, and the Soldan of Egypt insults the former by telling him, "The cities of the East are built of mud, and ephemeral; ours in Syria and Egypt are of stone, and eternal." Shureef-oo-deen. Vincent. Arrian says, "that Nicæa and Bucephalia, built by Alexander, had been partly washed away by the violence of the rains when the conqueror returned to the Hydaspes," a fate to which all mud edifices are liable,[57] and there can be no doubt, from all that is now visible, that, with the exception of a few public structures, Mahmood's celebrated city of Ghizni, extending so many miles, was built of mud.

> And this is Ghizni!
> This the imperial town,
> Which once the mighty Mahmood called his own;
> Where suppliant princes bowed to him, and high
> The banners waved of Eastern chivalry,
> Where warrior-chieftains faithful thronged around
> Their gorgeous king, through every clime renowned;
> And where Firdousee, warmed with royal praise,
> Gave the admiring world his deathless lays:
> And this was Ghizni, like a brilliant gem,
> A city worthy of the diadem;
> But now, alas! its form and spirit fled,
> We only see the ashes of the dead.
>
> How little thought I when with pleasing toil,
> I sought to foster on another soil
> The poet's flowers of beauty[58] that kind fate

---

[57] If these cities suffered so much in a few months from the violence of the rains, what hope can there be of ascertaining their site after upwards of twenty centuries? And yet almost every traveller who crosses the Punjab amuses himself with speculations of this sort, and thinks that he has discovered, from various imaginary indications, the true position of Nicæa and Bucephalia.

[58] The *Episode of Soohrab,* a poem, published at Calcutta in 1814, and the *Shahnameh,* abridged, in prose and verse, published in 1832.

Would bring me here to Ghizni, now so late
In life, with pilgrim feelings to survey
The scenes of Mahmood's glory in decay; —
To seek the spot Firdousee loved to tread,
To think him present — and by fancy led —
Wander delicious bowers and groves among,
Listening with fresh delight to his romantic song.

    And this is Mahmood's tomb, memorial frail,
Had fame not cherished his heroic tale;
The sandal doors no perfume now retain,
Brought by himself from Somnat's holy fane,
And though pure marble shields his honoured bier,
Corroding years display their footsteps here.
— A mulberry bower adorns and marks the place
Where silent sleeps the monarch of his race.

    But who has come to this far mountain-clime,
Boldly to view the changeful face of Time?
What armed host in long and bright array
Through Mahmood's realms has urged his conquering way,
Unawed by distance, or by danger? How
Amazement sits on every Affghan brow,

    To see how British power pursues its course;
Horse, foot, artillery, with electric force,
Crushing the hold, whose battlements defied
Surprise or conquest, with contemptuous pride;
And with a daring spirit all its own,
Restores the Sovereign to his ancient throne!

    And this is Ghizni, this the Sultan's tomb;
Here sleeps the conqueror in sepulchral gloom;
The din of arms is heard, and all around,
Mountain and plain, re-echo to the sound;
Blithe martial notes, glad signals to the brave,
Enough to rouse a warrior from his grave.
And lo! it seems as, in a dreamy mood,
Lingering upon the spot I musing stood;
A murmur issued from the structure near ;
I saw, or thought I saw, the dead appear,
Mahmood: the jewelled crown upon his head;
The robe imperial o'er his shoulders spread;
The buckler fasten'd by a golden clasp;
The iron mace within his vigorous grasp;
In backward attitude of sharp surprise
He seemed, displeasure gleaming in his eyes;
And gathering up a frown, with tone severe,
Accents like these assailed my wondering ear.

"Who dares the precincts of the tomb invade?
What sacrilegious robbers wake the dead?
Strange sounds are these, and men in strange attire;
Whence come they? fierce barbarians, flood and fire
Shall be their doom, the land of Candahar,
The land of Caubul, conquered in the war,
And Ghizni fallen! Crush the Kafir race,
The infidels, who would usurp the place
Of him now risen from his deep repose;
The all-conquering king, the terror of his foes
But royal Ghizni to be thus overthrown,
Can be the work of magic power alone
No human effort could effect its fall,
Circled by bastions and that towering wall,
Impregnable, till now with proud disdain
Frowning o'er all the subjugated plain;
Boast of the world — my own-upraised by me;
But the whole world is ruled by destiny."

A pause ensued, and from his pallid mien,
Where, strongly marked; portentous gloom had been,
The stern expression quickly died away,
And in an alter'd tone he seemed to say, —
"But why this fruitless anger from the grave?
Can the cold dead a conquered region save?
Still fate the living universe sustains,
By that the peasant toils, the monarch reigns;
By that the world became enthralled by me,
For empires rise and fall by fate's decree ;

Ages roll on, man seeks for wealth and fame,
Rots in the dust, and haply gains a name;
The sport of wayward fate since time began,
Poor, proud, vain mortal — supercilious man!
Conquerors of old have held unbounded sway,
And why not conquerors now, as well as they?
Now, now, I see the changes long foretold,
I see the page of mystery unfold;
And British banners, fluttering high in air,
The coming change from tyranny declare.
No desolation tracks their onward speed,
No peasant groans to pamper man or steed,
He reaps his harvest with unaltered eye,
Fearless, though thousands armed are passing by;
No despot's grasp impoverishes the towns,
Rapine and plunder British power disowns —
Look to the East, where, by its fostering care,
Moslem and Hindoo equal safety share;
Then who can dread th' approach of such a host?
Justice and mercy its distinguished boast.

Happy the king, who, 'midst that martial train
(Destined his long-lost sceptre to regain),
Holds his career victorious. As the light
Of early dawn dissolves the shades of night,
So vanish all his enemies; I see
The chiefs of various tribes, with loyalty,
Hailing his wished return; I see them bring
Oblations to their venerable king;
Each with his numerous band, with shield and spear,
Dagger and matchlock closing in the rear;
Eager to swell the multitudinous tide,
Which unimpeded rolls on every side;
The vast assemblage covers all the plain,
Promise of trust in Shoojah's coming reign."

Here ceased the voice — I gazed, and stood alone,
All save the solitary tomb was gone.

CHAPTER XII.

MARCH TO CAUBUL.

Good disposition of the peasantry — Their complaints of oppression — Affghan mode of cultivation — Flight of Dost Mahomed Khan — Beauty of the valley of Mydan — Arghundee — Spot where Dost Mahomed Khan was to have made a stand — His guns captured — Motives of his conduct — The Khans of the Khuzzilbashes and Mr. Campbell refused to fight against the Shah — Dost Mahomed flies to Bamian — Attack by an armed Alfghan — Shah Shoojah takes possession of the capital — Killa of Nawab Jubbar Khan.

July 30.-All arrangements connected with the brilliant and memorable achievement at Ghizni having been completed, the whole of the Bengal column, with the exception of the 16th Native Infantry, which was left to garrison the fort, marched to Shesh-gao this morning, *en route* to Caubul. The ascent was about 800 feet, and our increased elevation was rather sharply felt: at day-break, in the early part of the march, my hands and feet ached with the cold. The thermometer 42°. We were then on the top of the rugged defile called *Sheer Dundan,* the 'Lion's Teeth,' 9,000 feet above the level of the sea, the highest point in this quarter. From thence to Caubul the descent is said to be about 2,500 feet. No baggage being now allowed to go on in advance as before, we had to wait some hours in the sun, after reaching the new ground, till our breakfast-tents came up, which was not before noon. A high blustering wind all day covered every thing with dust. The Shah follows to-morrow with the Bombay column.

July 31.-From Shesh-gao to Heft Asyah, fine road and gradual ascent, but sandy, with stones. On approaching Heft Asyah (seven miles), we found the country in a good state of cultivation, the slopes of the hills being managed by successive flat surfaces to keep in the irrigation. The villages are all fort-fashion. Crowds on the road came forward to see us pass, and the walls were covered with people. Herds of cattle are seen grazing on the distance, while the men and women are employed getting in the harvest. The mountains are still very brown and bleak. Various reports of Dost Mahomed; some say he has intrenched himself a few miles on this side of Caubul, to oppose us; others, that he is gone off!

Aug. 1.-To Hyder-Khail eleven miles, situated in the district of Tukeea. For the first four miles, the valley is confined and barren, with a small torrent running along it, frequently to be crossed, and the road often narrow. After that the valley becomes rich with cultivation; beans in flower, the harvest in hand, and innumerable stacks of the cut grain on the ground. The peasants assembled to see us, more numerous than before, all with smiling faces, and seeming to enjoy the sight. This fertile spot is full of villages, a short distance from each other, and the same luxuriance in crops extends to our camp, near which are fields of

Indian-corn, but of a smaller kind than in Bengal. The trees are becoming taller and richer in form: the valley hardly three miles wide. The natives still bring in fowls, eggs, grass, ghee, &c., for sale. Our descent has been considerable, and consequently it is much warmer to-day than yesterday. The fields are well protected by our sentries, and great care taken to preserve the property of the villagers from the smallest degree of spoliation, a measure fully appreciated by the people, who must have sagacity enough to ponder on the different fate of Candahar and Ghizni. The former place, where no resistance was offered, became wealthy by the money expended in the city. Ghizni resisted, was conquered, and all the property in camels, grain, and horses, captured and lost to the garrison and the state. It must be remembered, however, that in the latter case the *people* had no concern; the hostile power was wholly in the fort, under the influence and direction of Dost Mahomed; outside, in the villages, no hostility, but rather confidence, prevailed; a fact sufficiently proved by the numbers of cows, goats, asses, sheep, fowls, &c., which were constantly brought into camp for sale, and by the complaint repeatedly heard from the villagers, of the oppression under which they suffered: plainly shewing that the *de facto* governor had no great hold on the affections of the governed!

A sepoy getting into quiet conversation with one of the Affghans in the fort, the latter said they had no idea of our way of fighting, otherwise they never would have attempted to stand against us. The immense destruction produced by the volleys of musketry must have taught them a dreadful lesson. They dropped by scores at a time, as the red-coats mounted the steep acclivity in front of the citadel, on the morning of the assault.

Aug. 2.-From Hyder-Khail[59] to Shaikabad, ten miles. The valley continues narrow, and with diminished cultivation. At about the third mile, came to the Caubul river, a shallow, rapid torrent, foaming over stones, and, at the crossing, fifteen to twenty feet wide. It rolls on to the right. The road was rugged and confined, for, in consequence of the proximity of the river, every inch of ground was scrupulously cultivated, which left but little space for the passage of the

---

[59] The barbarous murder of Colonel Herring, commanding the 37th N.I., took place at Hyder-Khail, on the march from Candahar to Caubul in Sept. 1839. The colonel, a most worthy and excellent man, with three of his officers, was taking a walk in the evening, unarmed, and had ascended a high hill about a mile from camp, when the party was suddenly attacked by a band of ruffians, who sprang from their ambush and began pelting them with stones. The colonel was soon brought to the ground, and a number of the miscreants then rushed upon him, and mangled him in a shocking manner; others pursued the officers, who fortunately escaped. The melancholy tidings arriving in camp, a strong party of sepoys was instantly despatched up the hill, but too late to do any good, further than that they happily recovered the body of the much-lamented colonel, which was conveyed to Caubul, and interred with military honours in the Armenian burying-ground at that place.

troops. All along, on either side of the bright, clear stream, winding in a serpentine direction, were numerous groves of trees, and among them some beautiful rows of willows. Shaikabad is marked by a great number of fort-like villages, some on the sides and projections of hills, in romantic positions. The valley is thoroughly cultivated, and there appears to be more agricultural skill manifested here than in any other part of Affghanistan I have yet seen. The road is not more than fifteen feet wide, dyked in with stones and mud, and bordered with hedge-rows of a prickly bush. The fields, too, are more in squares, and terraced, where the slope of the hills requires it. One field of Indian-corn was filled with water, half-way up the stalk, and the vegetable looked as if growing in a vat, — a mud mound on all sides keeping in the water that had been turned into it from the neighbouring hills. It would appear that agriculture could hardly be pursued to a higher limit; every spring and stream is indefatigably brought into play, to irrigate the crops. No opportunity is lost: even subterraneous passages are made, at great labour, for conveying water wherever it may be required. Crossed another torrent, said to be the Logar, about the centre of Shaikabad, which descends from the mountains on our left, and runs in a south-easterly direction. Over this torrent, thirty feet wide, is a narrow wooden bridge. In the middle of the stream there is a pile of stones, to support intermediately the thick trunks of trees laid across, and covered over with stones and earth, — a novelty in these parts. A mile further on is our encampment, upon high ground. The mountains on each side, not quite a mile asunder, all barren, the usual characteristic, or scattered over with tufts of jungle grass. Between two and three hundred of the inhabitants of Shaikabad had assembled, in front of the largest village, which we passed on the left, to see us. They had all anxious curiosity and surprise marked on their countenances. The ugly females were on the walls; their children, too, with doubly-bronzed complexions and red cheeks — pictures of the roughest health — were equally on the alert to see the Feringhees.

Halt.- This was a morning of great interest and excitement throughout camp. The Shah had come up with tidings of the flight of Dost Mahomed Khan. Khan Sheereen Khan, the chief of the Khuzzilbashes, in Caubul, passed by our tents at eight A.M., with a cortege of between fifty and a hundred horsemen, all richly dressed, to tender his allegiance to the king. A great number of other chiefs and their adherents, and several thousand Khuzzilbashes, also flocked to the royal standard in the course of the day. Three elephants, too, were brought into the Shah's camp by the body-guard of Dost Mahomed. But, stirring as the moment was, there was neither bustle nor confusion, noise nor acclamations, among the chiefs and the people, in thus coming to the support of the restoration.

Preparations were now made for the pursuit and capture of the fugitive, and a force was immediately appointed for that purpose, to be ready at noon; but, by the delays of the Affghan part of the detachment, it did not leave Shahabad before night. A strong party of the 16th Lancers, however, under Major Cureton, lost no time in proceeding to take possession of the guns left by Dost Mahonied at Arghundee, about eighteen miles on this side Caubul.

Aug. 4.- Yesterday's tidings gave fresh stimulus to a forward movement, and we started at three A.M. The valley still narrow, and more like a ravine than a valley for about six or eight miles, and then it widened a little, and cultivation began to appear again. At Shaikabad we left the Logar, and just before arriving at that place, the Caubul river had turned from us to the right. The road to-day was crossed by a few small rills from the mountains, but we observed very little of the industry of man till we reached the new ground near a village on the left, called Beni-badam, and then but in a slight degree. The rocks and mountains close to us are the wildest and most rugged imaginable; broken, detached, and projecting, the highest point said to be twelve thousand feet above the sea; the whole formed of huge distinct masses, sharp, pyramidal, bleak, and precipitous. Plenty of fine cold water rushing among stones, not over them, from the cliffs, and the lucerne on the margin in beautiful verdure. A little way above, there is a large basin of pure transparent water, with reeds and rushes growing over half of it, and scarcely a foot deep. This basin swarms with fish, about six inches long; but it is the preserve of a Hindoo, who does not allow them to be caught, consecrated as they are to some of his gods; and we were not disposed to dispute his right to keep them from us on such a plea, though a few of the pretty creatures would have been a great treat. One of our party jocularly considered our forbearance equal in moral merit to the continence of Scipio! These fish are said to know the "voice of the charmer," and swim to the margin when he calls them to be fed.[60] Even now the valley is not more than a mile and a half wide, or two at the

---

[60] In a tank in Lower Sinde it is said there are alligators, which the Fakeers appear to have tamed, and which are regularly fed by name. One of Martial's Epigrams refers to a similar circumstance;-

> Piscator, fuge! ne nocens recedas;
> Sacris piscibus hæ natantur undæ,
> Qui norunt dominum, manumque lambunt,
> Illam qua nihil est, in orbe, majus;
> Quid, quod, nomen habent, et ad magistri
> Vocem quisque sui venit citatus.

Which may be thus paraphrased:
> Angler, away! while innocent of crime
>   These sparkling fish, that swim beneath the wave,
> In playful turns are sacred from old time,
>   And know the hand that feeds them — therefore, save
> The sportive shoal; so gentle and so tame,
>   Each knows its master's call and answers to its name.

utmost. The ground covered with stones and knots of stunted underwood. There are several villages in sight, but half of them deserted and in ruins. The one nearest is built of round stones and mud for cement, but all of a similar shape, with corner bastions or towers.

Aug. 5.-Our march to-day was to Mydan, stated at seven miles and a half from Beni-badam. The Killa-i-sheer Mahomed is about two miles on the road, occupied by the peasantry, whose wheat harvest was piled up in stacks close by. Fields of rice and beans were ripening on the ground. From the Killa we descend, and cross a small rivulet from a spring on the left, and after three or four miles more, ascend a narrow craggy pass, of some difficulty, scattered with masses of rock, from the top of which the valley of Mydan bursts upon the sight in all its freshness and beauty. There was a mist upon the sterile mountains, and in part over the whole landscape; but the groves of poplars and cypresses, of varied form and extent, were lit up by gleams of the sun, and shone out brightly.

Descending about a mile from the pass, we cross the Logar river, at this place wide and rather rapid, running to the south-eastward. On our left are the ruins of a bridge, of which the brick-built piers, and a few yards of the causeway, only remain, and these are on both sides far beyond the present margin of the stream. Immediately in front is a lofty rock, once, it would seem, strongly fortified, to command the entrance into the valley; but the walls are now in a broken condition, and appear to afford a residence for Fakeers, indicated by a piece of rag, on a long pole at the top of one of the bastions. We had to ascend to the right of this rock, the more practicable path on the left being filled up with artillery waggons in progress. It was an arduous labour both for horse and camel, and the descent on the other side as bad or worse. Numerous carcases of both animals belonging to the brigade in advance were lying among the crags.

After two miles more, we were at the encamping ground, with a clear view of the whole of Mydan. The beauty of this valley is highly extolled by the Affghans, and well it may be, in comparison with what the other parts of the country, hitherto seen, can display. The eye rests upon it with delight, after being wearied with the sameness and barrenness of stony roads and mountain passes. But even here the charm lies within narrow bounds. The valley, which is not straight, but semicircular, is not more than a mile and a half wide, and four miles long. It is hemmed in by the most sterile of hills. The ranges of cultivation, too, are uniformly bordered by portions of ground covered with sand and stones, as if the genius of the barren mountain would admit of no attractive encroachment on his domain. But there is a sweet silver line of river, which flows through the middle of the valley, and near it the tree, the meadow, and the plantation are always bright and glowing with the finest tints of nature. I sat and looked over the agreeable prospects for hours, as Shakespear says, "chewing the cud of sweet and bitter fancy," delighted to dwell upon a scene so calm and refreshing. The villages, all fort-fashion, are neatly finished, and exhibit none of the broken lines of dilapidation so often seen. The inhabitants would, therefore, seem to be under better circumstances than others, or under better management as we approach the capital.

Aug. 6.-Marched from Mydan to Arghundee. The road for five miles is an ascent, most rough and rugged, and intersected with deep ravines, where numerous camels had perished, and many had been left, exhausted, to die. At the top of the stony ghaut or pass, — for the mountains, sharp and angular, are close on each side, — is a round tower, or watch-house, called Buzrak. Looking back from this eminence, the valley of Mydan is distinctly seen.[61] The space between the hills now widens a little; the ground is level, and, four miles further, is Arghundee. At about half a mile off, we discovered the guns, twenty-five in number, which Major Cureton, with his Lancers, had been sent to secure. They were ranged across the narrow valley, and it was here that Dost Mahomed proposed to make a stand, and here he was, with all the military means he could muster, on the 2nd instant. The guns were of various sizes, — three, six, and nine-pounders. The carriages, mostly new, were of the clumsiest construction, and so unskilfully put together, that a few rounds must have broken them to pieces. Each gun was loaded with three balls, so that there would have been as much danger to the firer as the fired at, if not more.[62] The dissolution of the armament had been very sudden; quantities of ammunition had been blown up; some of the guns thrown from their carriages; thousands of balls of all sizes lying about, and cartouche-boxes and belts strewed the ground, half-consumed by the several explosions that had evidently taken place. The Lancers reached the spot on the evening of the 3rd, and found the villagers busy in plundering what remained. The gun-bullocks, nearly two hundred in number, had been left be-

---

[61] The fifteenth drawing in my collection represents a part of the valley, with the watch tower in the foreground.

[62] The old gun, given to Shah Shoojah by the Khan of Bhawulpore, was, at the battle before Candahar in 1834, charged with one ball cartridge, one blank, and then grape-shot. In consequence, when fired, it burst, and killed a great number of men near it. The Affghans constantly overload their matchlocks in the same way.

In returning from Caubul through the Punjaub, in February, 1841, one of my escort purchased a new matchlock at Rawil Pindee, gaily decorated, and the barrel beautifully bright, for six rupees! The seller had fired it off boastingly, with a small charge of powder, but declared that ten times the quantity might be safely used, and then it would carry a ball a full mile. Three days afterwards, the purchaser, proud of his bargain, doubled the charge, and fired off his matchlock, when, by the explosion, the barrel burst in three places near the stock. His right hand was dreadfully lacerated, and a fragment of the iron struck his stomach, and tore open the bowels. I closed the wound with a few stitches, though all surgical aid was useless; he felt as if he was all on fire, and lived in the same torment till the following day, when he died.

hind, and became a part of the prize property. One of the guns was found afterwards in a ravine, and a large quantity of gunpowder was discovered in skins, underground, only slightly spread over with earth. It would appear that Dost Mahomed had no easy task in persuading any part of his adherents, at first reported to have been about twelve thousand men, of all sorts, to advance even as far as Arghundee, where he placed his guns in position, with the professed intention of vigorously coming to action. But all this preparation does not seem to have been carried on with the soul and energy of one, either supported by the people, or determined to defend his possessions to the last. The guns were no sooner ranged in battle order, than the Ameer, convinced that his safety consisted in flight, abandoned them, blew up the gunpowder, and moved off precipitately across the mountains, towards Bamian. But we must go a little back, to shew the circumstances under which he was placed.

Before quitting the capital, he had called the Durranees, Khuzzilbashes, and Caubulees before him, and besought them to unite with him to resist the enemy. "At this alarming crisis, you had better," said he, "bring your wives and daughters into the Balla Hissar for safety, and I myself will provide for them. I will sell all my jewels and valuable property, which will produce wealth sufficient for continuing the war, even should it last for five years." But this attempt to place so many families in the condition of hostages, and thus, in a manner, compel the services of the Khans and their dependents, in his projected opposition to the invading troops, was readily seen through, and thus replied to: "That the world would cry out shame upon him if he offered such an indignity to the families of his chiefs, as shutting them up in the Balla Hissar." They thought it would be better for him to send his own family into the Kohistan, and they promised, in that case, to send theirs to the same place of refuge. The Dost apparently agreed, but further excuses were afterwards made by the Khans, on the plea of having no means of conveyance. He then called for Mr. Campbell, and ordered him to prepare to advance with a body of troops against the Shah, observing that he would follow himself. But Campbell refused, frankly declaring, that he had *eaten the Shah's salt,* and that he could not be so ungrateful as to fight against him. In this dilemma, Jubbar Khan was sent for, and requested to proceed to Ghizni, for the purpose of obtaining the release of Gholam Hyder, as a pretended preliminary to negotiations for the surrender of Caubul. We have seen the result of his mission. It was then that the Dost resolved upon sending his family to Bamian, in charge of Jubbar Khan, and Mr. Campbell, who had no hesitation in being so employed, was sent with them. Jubbar Khan seemed anxious to avoid the journey, and said, "Let them set off, and I will follow;" but Dost Mahomed replied, "No, no, no; if you stay, you will go over to the Feringhees;" and the Nawab, says our informant, was compelled to depart.

In another conference at Caubul, Khan Sheereen Khan, Jewansheer, Bauker

Khan, Moorad Khanee, and other Khuzzilbashes, declared to him that they would not fight against Shah Shoojah, and urgently advised him to abandon all thoughts of resistance, and fly for his life. Dost Mahomed could ill brook such advice as this, whatever might have been his own apprehensions or anticipations; but he was without remedy, and, gulping the bitter draught, commenced his march from Caubul, not without hope, however, that they might still be induced to listen to his entreaties, and co-operate with him against the infidel invaders. This hope, too, was fostered by the circumstance of the Khans' proceeding along with him as far as Arghundee. But the delusion soon vanished. He now repeated his solicitations to the Khuzzilbashes, amounting to a considerable force, with all his powers of persuasion, and asked them whether they would stand firmly by him, or not; the reply was again in the negative. He then spoke to the Caubulees, who promised that they would support him at all hazards. Again he appealed to the Khuzzilbashes, and said, "he had raised them to places of trust and distinction; that he had constantly showered favours on them all, and he could not have expected, at this hour of peril, that he would have been forsaken by them." But his conduct or policy had been the very reverse of what he thus urged, and the appeal had no effect.[63] The Khans earnestly reiterated their advice to avoid the

---

[63] Dost Mahomed had, on various occasions, so much mistaken his interests, as by a course of capricious and despotic conduct, to give great umbrage to the Khuzzilbashes, though his mother was of that tribe. But what has consanguinity to do with an Affghan's proceedings? The following extract from a report by Sir A. Burnes will shew the political error he committed in exciting the animosity, instead of conciliating the good offices, of so important a body in his capital: "In the beginning of the last century, the feebleness of the Persian monarchy excited the cupidity of the Affghans, who overran the fairer portion of that kingdom, and possessed themselves of Ispahan. Their successes called forth the energies of the great Nadir, who not only drove the Affghans from Persia, but annexed the whole of their territory to his empire, and turning their swords against India, with an army of Persians and Affghans, sacked it precisely a hundred years ago. During these wars, the conqueror deemed it politic to fix some native tribes in the lands he had subdued, and to this policy we owe the colony of Persians now settled in Caubul, which, when first located, amounted to less than twenty thousand families. The people composing it consist of three divisions:-lst, Juwansheers; 2nd, the Ufsheers; 3rd, the Moorad Khanees, the whole being designated by the general name of Gholam Khanee or Gholam Shah, servants of the king. The Juwansheers are a clan of Toorks from Shresha. There are various divisions included among them, such as the Koort, the Shah Samund, the Syar Munsoor, &c., and they form the principal portion of the Khuzzilbashes. They consist of two thousand five hundred families, and occupy a separate quarter of Caubul, called the Chandoul, which is surrounded by high walls. Their chief is Khan Sheereen Khan. The Ufsheers are also Toorks, and of the tribe to which Nadir himself belonged. There are three hundred families of them, who live in a strong fort, about three miles from Caubul, under Gholam Hussain Khan. The last division, the Moorad Khanees, is composed of all the Persians who have from time to time settled in this country. Fifteen hundred families of them reside together under Mihralle Khan and five other chiefs.

conflict. "You are not equal to this extremity; escape in time." Seeing matters thus arrayed against him, and no possible chance of effective resistance to the overwhelming force about to attack him, besides the apprehension of being seized and delivered up to Shah Shoojah, he thought it most prudent to fly, and, throwing to the winds the boast that "he would sacrifice sons, relations, friends, Affghans, and himself, in the glorious cause," and also forgetting his anathema against his brothers for abandoning Candahar without a struggle, he set off on the evening of the 2nd of August for Bamian, accompanied by his son Mahomed Akber, and a few other sirdars, with one small gun and a few hundred sirdars, with one small gun and a few hundred horsemen. Khan Sheereen Khan, with the Khuzzilbahes, about two thousand, proceeded at the same time to pay homage to the Shah.

Whilst I was sketching the exact position of Dost Mahomed's guns, and the scenery of Arghuridee, a fine effect being produced by masses of deep blue clouds, surcharged with rain, rolling over the mountain opposite, I was startled by a loud screaming at a short distance behind me. Looking round, I found it proceeded from a servant in attendance on me, covered with blood, and running towards the spot where I was standing, with an Affghan weapon, called a *charra*, in his hand. In wandering about, whilst I was engaged, he had descended into a deep ravine, at about the distance of forty paces from me, where he was surprised and assailed by an armed Affghan, who first gave him a severe cut on the thigh; and afterwards knocked him down; he then, grasping his throat with one hand,

---

Besides these, there are seven hundred others in the fort of the Byats, a division of the tribe, under Mahomed Khan. It will be thus seen, that there are at this time [October, 1837] four thousand Khuzzilbash families in Caubul, from which a force of from four to five thousand men could be levied on an emergency for the purposes of war. The number has been generally considered greater than this detailed statement; but the whole of the Sheah population in and about Caubul is then included in the calculation, and among these the Hazaras, who would furnish twice as many as the Persians." And with regard to the policy of Dost Mahomed, it appears from the same authority, that he had withdrawn much of his confidence from the party, reduced the number of those in his pay to about one thousand or two thousand persons, and retrenched part of their salaries. "Even in public," says Sir A. Burnes, "he does not conceal his contempt for their creed, and, what is perhaps more bitterly felt, his avowed opinions of their wanting courage in the field, as exhibited in his campaigns with the ex-king of Candahar, and lately with Peshawer. In the former instance, he is stated to have placed the Affghans on both flanks of the Khuzzilbashes, with secret instructions to fire on them if they fled. At Peshawer it is very certain that the party were backward in fighting; none of them were killed; and a piece of pleasantry is attributed to the Ameer, who said, 'that he never remembered a Khuzzilhash to have fallen in his service!'" But Dost Mahomed Khan may have mistaken a want of inclination, originating from disappointed hopes, for a want of courage. — *Reports and Papers, printed by order of Government. Calcutta, 1839.*

was proceeding to plunge his sword into his body, when his intended victim, with the strength of a man struggling for his life, prostrate as he was, gave him such a powerful kick on the stomach, that he staggered back almost breathless. In an instant, my servant, springing to his feet, seized hold of the charra, and though it cut his hand to the bone, had the good fortune to wrench it from him and escape with it, screaming, as I have mentioned. He now told us where the miscreant was, and where, no doubt, he had been long waiting for the appearance of some straggler. In a few minutes, we saw him emerge from the ravine on the opposite side, and walk leisurely on, but looking back repeatedly, in evident apprehension of being followed.

A party of the Poonah horse happened to be near me, and, shortly, six suwars were mounted to overtake him and bring him into camp. The deep ravine with abrupt sides, however, was a great impediment to their progress, and the villain had got almost to the foot of the steep mountain, on the east side of the valley, his only resource, before they could cross it. The wretch did not appear to be of the lowest order, for he had on a clean white chupkun, and a large blue-coloured turban and kumerbund. The white chupkun made him more conspicuous and more easily distinguished, whilst climbing up the ascent of the mountain, to which he immediately had recourse; till he saw the horsemen mounted, and over the ravine, he made little exertion to get away, being already too distant for anyone on foot to approach him, and not within gun-shot. But when he did see the suwars full tilt on their way, he redoubled his speed, and clambered up the mountain as fast as he could, and with surprising activity. He had got about half-way up before the horsemen arrived at the bottom, and too far off for their carbines to reach him. One of them urged his horse up the side of the rock with great adroitness and perseverance, and had ascended a considerable height, when the crumbling and precipitous slope he now came to, obliged him to dismount, and pursue the fugitive on foot.

The Affghan now rounded a ridge, and we lost sight of him for some minutes; he was then seen approaching to the summit, with the hope of escaping down the other side, and there could be no doubt of his success without further aid to prevent him. It was, therefore, suggested, that another party of suwars should push on, and by a rapid detour get round to the other side of the hill, where he might be easily intercepted. This was instantly done, and after an hour's chase, the villain was overtaken in his descent. But, desperate still, he presented a pistol, which flashed in the pan. In a few moments he was despatched. The loaded pistol, a dirk, a sheath of the charra, and his clothes, were brought away by the suwars and delivered to their commanding officer, Major Cunningham, in camp, in proof that the pursuit had been successful, and that the ruffian had been put to death.

Aug. 7.-From Arghundee[64] to Killa-Kâzee, six miles. The road all the way full of large loose stones, and the scenery very rugged. Killa- Kâzee is situated on a beautiful plain, surrounded by lofty mountains, about six miles by four, and superior to the valley of Mydan. Large groves of poplars are very numerous, and the whole surface is in an admirable state of cultivation. All the grain is cut, and there is plenty of accommodation for an encampment on the stubble land, without injury or inconvenience to anyone. Our tents are pitched two miles nearer Caubul for the present. The Shah took possession of his capital to-day, attended by the Envoy and Minister, the Commander-in-Chief, and a numerous escort.

Last night, about one o'clock, I was awakened by a heavy dragging noise over the carpet of my tent. I sprang up and called to my servants, who quickly brought a light, and one of my large camel-trunks was found near the door-way, having been pulled about three yards from the corner in which it had been placed. The thieves had escaped. A candle was then left burning on the table, and my servants directed to sleep across each of the four door-ways, to prevent further annoyance. About two hours afterwards, I was again awakened by a ripping, sawing noise, and on calling out again, the servants started up with alacrity, but no one was to be found. In the morning we discovered the wall of the tent ripped up immediately behind another camel-trunk — the thieves hoping, no doubt, to get it through unheard, guided and assisted, as they must have been, by the light being imprudently kept burning in the tent.

August 9.-Another move, two miles; still nearer to Caubul, where the whole of the infantry will be encamped. Took an exploratory view of the vicinity of camp, and in our progress walked through "alleys green," with clear brooks murmuring among the pebbles in the middle, and hedge-rows, and hips and haws, and poplars, and walnut-trees, casting a shade over the path.

We went, "nothing loth," into several orchards, teeming with delicious apples and pears, and full of variegated flowers. The hollyhock in all its pride, and rich purple and pink coloured daisies, arrested every step. The finest orchard was said to be by the people on the spot public property, or rather appropriated to the use of the poor, for, on coming away, I offered them some money, which they refused, on the ground that property so assigned could not be sold. We were in a kind manner invited to repeat our visit, and urged to take away some of the fruit, which we declined. They, however, loaded our servants with apples. We then went to the Killa of Nawab Jubbar Khan, the brother of Dost Mahomed, which was close by. The walls are lofty with four bastions. Three-fourths of the area are filled up with low mud hovels, grain, straw, and filth, and the fourth part is a

---

[64] The sixteenth drawing in my collection represents the village of Arghundee, on the 6th of August, 1839, with the guns of Dost Mahomed Khan in position across the valley.

quadrangle, walled in, three sides of which contain small rooms in the oriental fashion, with carved open-work windows, the residence of the Nawab himself. Externally, the whole looked like a baronial castle in the feudal times of Europe, though I conclude the feudal barons of Europe never allowed the accumulation of so much nastiness within their strongholds as was found in this retreat of Jubbar Khan. There is another fort of a similar character, recently occupied by a son-in-law of Dost Mahomed, a short distance from the road. The interior contains a great number of mud dwellings, but his own quadrangle for himself and family is carved in a superior manner, the taste the same, but the execution and finish of a higher class than Jubbar Khan's. At the very top of one of the bastions, the framework of a sort of summer-house had been raised; it was about eight feet square, and at a distance looked like a bird-cage. Indeed, all the best part of the residence seemed to be in progress, shavings and pieces of wood still lying on the ground, and the work only put a stop to by the coming of Shah Shoojah! Both these forts are inferior in accommodation to the citadel of Ghizni, which, however, cannot boast of such good workmanship in the ornamental parts. The son-in-law accompanied Dost Mahomed in his flight.

My exploratory excursion this morning was not without a professional object. Sir John Keane wished the sick to be removed into houses, as at Candahar, if procurable. The search, however, was unavailing. Jubbar Khan's castle was the most promising, but its numerous small sub-divisions and high walls, which prevented a free ventilation, were not calculated for the well-being of the sick, and it was decided, that the patients were much more comfortably and conveniently situated in hospital-tents; especially at a season when the nights, from sun-set to nine or ten in the morning, were cool and pleasant, and the heat of the day not oppressive.

CHAPTER XIII.

CAUBUL

First visit to the city — The fruit — Its beauty, profusion, and order of display — The shops — The grand bazaar — Tomb of Tymoor Shah — Civility of the people — The Balla Hissar — The houses of Caubul, a mass of mud hovels — Aspect of the city from an eminence — Burial-places — The streets — Unprincipled character of the Affghan husbands — The women given to intrigue — Dress of the latter — Public baths — Heated in an offensive manner — The Affghans a dirty people — The mint — Tomb of Thomas Hicks, an Englishman, dated in 1666 — An Affghan *soirée* — Familiar footing of different ranks with each other — Dancing girls.

Aug. 10.-To-day we have got the Caubul cries; men from the city hawking about camp, grapes, apples, melons, silks, furs, &c., &c., and calling out most vociferously, as if determined to compel us to buy. In the narrow gap, formed by two craggy mountains sloping towards each other, lies the road from camp to Caubul; the extreme edges of those slopes, as seen from a distance, shewing a line of fortified wall, or rather serrated and loop-holed wall, from the top to the bottom.[65] The road is very confined, hemmed in by huge masses of rock on the left hand, and dense groves of mulberry-trees on the right, bordering the Caubul river.

I paid my first visit to the city this afternoon. The path was crowded with people, and after a pretty long ride we entered, not by a gate, as usual, but by a narrow street, which is the introduction to Caubul. There we were, indeed, astonished by the luxurious appearance of the fruit shops. Melons, grapes, pears, apples, plums; peaches, in wonderful profusion, and all ranged in beautiful order on pieces of masonry, of different heights, so as to exhibit them in the most attractive way.[66] The shops themselves are little better than sheds. It is not only the beauty of the fruit, but its prodigious abundance, which strikes the mind so forcibly. We do not see half a dozen melons, or a dozen bunches of grapes, but thousands. This display continued a great distance, the shops twin-brothers all, but still delightful. Caubul has always been famous for its fruit. The Emperor Bâber says in his Memoirs, "The fruits of the cold districts in Caubul are grapes, pomegranates, apricots, peaches, pears, apples, quinces, jujubes, damsons, almonds, and walnuts, all of which are found in great abundance. I caused the sour cherry-tree, the aloo-bala, to be brought here and planted; it produced excellent fruit and continues thriving. The fruits it possesses, peculiar to a warm climate, are the orange, citron, the amlook (a berry like the karinda), and sugar-

---

[65] The seventeenth drawing in my collection shews the entrance into Caubul from Killa-Kâzee

[66] The eighteenth drawing in my collection represents the main street in the bazaar at Caubul in the fruit season.

cane, which are brought from Lamghanat, now called Laghman. I caused the sugar-cane to be brought, and planted it here; they bring the julghuzak (the seed of a kind of pine of a large size) from Nijrow; they have numbers of bee-hives, but honey is brought only from the hill-country on the west. The rawâsh of Caubul" (rhubarb, tarts made of it have precisely the taste of goodberries) "is of excellent quality; its quinces and damask plums are also excellent, as well as its bâdrengs, a large green fruit, somewhat like a citron." He also says, that, "on his return from the conquest of Lahore, he brought plantains and planted them, and that they grew and thrived;" but I have not seen one in this country. As we moved along, other articles for sale were presented to view in succession. Cooks were preparing kabobs, and confectioners, sweetmeats: cutlers and farriers employed on guns, swords, and horse-shoes; the silk mercer, the dealer in carpets, furs, lace, chintz, saddlery, &c., all attentive to their occupations, and all in the open day. The vegetables as well as the fruit are of an excellent kind; and the mutton sold in common to the inhabitants, is much superior to any I ever saw in an Indian bazaar.

> Every joint was a picture for painters to study.
> The fat was so white, and the lean was so ruddy.

Doomba mutton, however, though it looks so well, is not sufficiently delicate for European taste. It has a strong flavour. Nothing could exceed the industry that appeared everywhere around us; everybody employed and intent upon his calling. In our way we passed over an old bridge well stocked on each side by cobblers, hard at work. This bridge crosses the Caubul river, which runs through the city, and is about thirty yards wide, but now not above a foot deep. A few naked boys were bathing in the stream.[67] A little farther on is the grand bazaar, one of the public works of Ali Merdan Khan, during the reign of Jehangeer, and it is a gem amidst the edifices of mud by which it is surrounded[68]. It is built of

---

[67] The bridge is the bazaar and the local scenery are represented in the nineteenth drawing of my collection.

[68] Lucullus was not more distinguished for his villas at Naples, Baïæ, and Tusculum, than Ali Merdan Khan for his gardens and public buildings in Affghanistan. I observe, in *Tavernier's Travels*, that Ali Merdan Khan was once governor of Candahar, under the king of Persia, but finding that Shah Suffi had resolved upon having his head for some imputed offence, — the greatest is said to have been his possession of vast treasures, and displaying a degree of magnificence in his establishment equal to that of the king's, — he, to save himself and his property from the ruin which threatened him, delivered up Candahar to the emperor Jehangeer, called the great Moghul, by whom he was received with kindness and distinction. The princes of Candahar, who were of the Tartar race, had been independent, but the last was reduced to the extremity of choosing whether he

burnt brick, and consists of nine divisions, running in the same line along the street, and is painted over with figures of trees, fruit, &c., purple, red, and green, on a whitish ground. The first and last is a Chouk or open space, a hundred feet square. The third, fifth, and seventh divisions are also open spaces, but only fifty feet square. The intermediate second, fourth, sixth, and eighth divisions are called *chuttah,* or covered passages, each one hundred and fifty feet long, by twenty-two broad, and two stories high. The lower story is a row of small shops on each side, and the upper one a range of small apartments, but at present apparently unoccupied. The Chouks, which are rather of an octagonal form, are surrounded by shops and sheds, with a sunken square, bordered with marble, in the middle, which was originally a reservoir for the supply of a fountain to refresh and gratify the passer-by. A cluster of mud huts now fills up the place, and therefore the road necessarily breaks into a circle on coming out from one covered passage till it joins the next. The motley crowd was dense, but being in constant progression and retrogression, it readily gave way as we rode along.

Returning by the bridge, we crossed the river again at a ford to the left, to see the tomb of Tymoor Shah, which is still unfinished; it is a mere shell, built of burnt brick unplastered, and without minarets or embellishment of any kind, but larger than the tomb of Ahmed Shah at Candahar, being about a hundred feet high, and the diameter of the foundation the same number of feet. The walls and cupola bear innumerable marks of cannon-balls and shot, produced in the several insurrections that have occurred at Caubul since it was erected. It is near the Chandoul, the stronghold of the Khuzzilbashes. Close to the grave was a huge Koran, bound in wood, the volume measuring about two feet and a half by four. Lazy fakeers and beggars were lying here and there asleep, and tattered clothes hanging out to dry on one of the terraces. We then passed along the right margin of the river a mile or more, the banks abounding with poplars and gardens rich in green foliage, whilst on our left was the brown, rugged, projecting, precipitous mountain, the slope and crest of which is encumbered by a useless line of fortified wall. Turning round, further to the left, we came to the foot of the high conical rock, which juts out boldly from the mountain, and upon which stands a

---

would be subject to Persia or India, and he preferred Shah Abbas to the Great Moghul, but on the condition that the government of the province should be continued in his own family. Ali Merdan Khan was the son of the last prince of Candahar, and his wealth, chiefly derived from his father, was so immense, that when he went over to Jehangeer, he refused to accept of any compensation, but contented himself with one of the highest dignities in the empire, which he enjoyed till his death. For his own residence, he built a splendid palace on the banks of the Jumna. The canal between Kurnal and Delhi, about a hundred miles long, was constructed under the orders of Ali Merdan Khan, and bears his name, which, indeed, is associated with innumerable works of public utility, in India, Affghanistan, and the Punjab.

small building erected in the time of Shah Jehan, called the *Jehan-noomah,* a name usually given to places which command an extensive prospect, as this does over the whole valley of Killa-Kâzee, the name implying literally, 'world-displayer,'

But we were now near the grove which leads to Bâber's tomb, one of the loveliest situations about Caubul, and as it was too late to go there, a movement campward became necessary, very prudently keeping in mind the murderous propensities of the Affghans where an opportunity offers. The suburbs were all in motion, being constantly traversed by the people, following their occupations, without taking much notice of the stranger as he passes by. Men riding double on ass-back is of common occurrence here. Women ride astride, man-fashion, but completely veiled from head to foot, and we frequently saw two women and a child on one pony, led by a boy. I have mentioned the atrocious calumny circulated by Nawab Jubbar Khan, on his return from Ghizni, and, notwithstanding the disbelief of it generally, it is said there was not one woman in Caubul when the first detachment of the troops arrived there. The unfounded alarm, however, soon subsided, and in a few days every woman was restored to her home. It was amusing to see such numbers on every road converging to the city.

I saw nothing but civility among the people, who appeared as if no change had happened, and nothing particular had occurred in the government of the country. Certainly, there is no apparent want of confidence in us, no apprehension of injustice or oppression, otherwise we should not see the city swarming with industrious inhabitants, still pursuing their labours, as in a state of profound peace.

Dates must now be merged in a general sketch of Caubul. The Balla Hissar is the first grand division of the city, and entitled to be first described. In Forster's Travels, the name is printed *Balausir*, which is no doubt an error of the press, but Langlès, in his translation into French, determined to explain every thing, writes the word *Bala-ser,* and says in a note, *"Ce mot composé Persan signifie 'Tête, ou cime elevée!'"* The word, however, is not *ser,* 'the head,' but *hissar,* a 'castle' or 'palace.' *Balla* means 'upper,' and, conjoined, the words necessarily imply 'upper castle, or palace'. The Citadel is often called *Arg.*[69] Elm Haukul, about the middle of the tenth century, says, "Caubul is a town with a very strong castle, accessible only by one road. This is in the hands of the Mussulmans; but the town belongs to the *infidel Indians!"* The Balla Hissar comprehends nearly a fourth

---

[69] Quintus Curtitts, speaking of Maracænda; says, "The wall is seventy stadia (nine miles) in circumference; and the citadel is not surrounded by any outwork: ARX *nullo cingitur muro.*" The citadel at Candahar is called the *Arg* or Ark, as well as the upper fort at Caubul. Indeed, it is the common name with the Persians of all such places built for greater safety and defence within a fortress.

part of the city. It is surrounded by a wall with numerous bastions. There are only two gates now open; that which is to the west, and leads to the town; and the other on the east side, called the Peshawer gate. Both are closed at night. A wet ditch surrounds the whole; except the south-west corner, which unites with the swell of the mountain on that side. The part formerly used as a state prison, in the Balla Hissar, is upon a high hill running to a cone, and overlooks the whole of Caubul. It is on the south-west side, and is separately walled round, but gateway, bastion, and rampart are now in ruins — nothing but the fragments of single walls remaining of a place which appears to have been, but a few years ago, of great strength. The surface of the hill is very unequal, and the height of the walls is regulated according to the rises and falls of the ground upon which they stand. The lowest part is to the south-west, and farthest from the town. Beyond the walls, and between them and the mountains to the south, about two miles off, is a large swamp, and yet we find that Dost Mahomed had bestowed infinite pains in newly repairing the *fausse braye,* and ramparts on that side, on which the Balla Hissar was least likely to be assailed. But it was doing something, and thus filled the minds of the people with the idea of successful resistance to any invasion or attack.

The panoramic view, from the highest spot in this upper fort, over the town, exhibits little more than an extensive mass of mud hovels, all huddled together, and not one building of much importance or value. In the whole range, the only conspicuous places are three: the residence now occupied by the Envoy, built by Dost Mahomed Khan about five years ago, and gaily painted over with various devices, the front having the appearance of coloured chintz, of a shawl pattern; the ruins of the Musjid Shahee, or Royal Mosque, founded in the time of Alumgeer; and the Harem Serai, in which the Shah now resides, and which is tumbling down. These are situated a few hundred yards from each other, and near the upper Balla Hissar. The roofs of the houses are flat, and badly calculated for a climate in which so much snow falls, especially when formed, as they are, of a thick layer of clay, strengthened only by chopped straw.[70]

I proceeded one evening half-way up the mountain to the westward, to a place called Kaja-suffa, from whence the city, which is immediately below it, has a singular effect. Bounded by the hills, it lies perfectly flat at the bottom, like a stagnant pond, and the roofs of the houses look to be pieces of square plank, thickly spread upon the surface. You would say it was a dead city, the narrowness of the streets preventing the slightest glimpse of any thing human, and the ear is not gladdened by the sound of busy life, as in other populous cities. The sun had set, and, between the place where we stood and the houses, there was a small group of Affghans, digging a grave; this added to the sombre feeling

---

[70] The twentieth drawing in my collection represents all the objects above described.

produced by the scene. We were surrounded, too, by tombs, lofty situations, as before noticed, being always selected for sepulture in Affghanistan. A small terrace is made on the slope of the mountain, walled round with loose stones, and two or three trees are planted near the grave, and constantly watered till they attain sufficient strength. Flowers and foliage are the usual embellishments of these burying-places. I may here mention a curious fact: I have seen hundreds of cemeteries — the earth fallen in from the decomposition and decay of the body, and openings left which might be expected to expose some part of the dead, — but I have never yet seen in any burying-ground a single bone, owing probably to the great depth of the graves, which I am informed are full nine feet from the surface.[71]

The upper part of the Balla Hissar is about four hundred and sixty paces, by two hundred and fifty; the lower part, a thousand paces, by half that number, in which there are innumerable shops, and where work goes on with as much activity as in other parts of the city. Immediately below the Balla Hissar, and contiguous to the residence of the Envoy and Minister, is the quadrangle occupied by the Durbah-Khaneh and the Harem Serai.[72]

The upper story of the gate-way, leading to the town, is consecrated to the Royal Band, which is composed of huge toms-toms and long brass tube, played upon ding-dong, with all the power that muscular arm and stentorian lung can give. The horrid dissonance, from the deepest bass to the most squeaking treble, is beyond description. But this is considered an essential part of regal state, and the clatter and thumping is repeated several prescribed times during the twenty-four hours, beginning at two o'clock in the morning, to the great discomfort and annoyance of Christian ears.

Passing out of this gateway over a mound which crosses the ditch, we enter the principal street of the city, which, ten or twelve feet broad, runs through Ali Merdan Khan's Grand Bazaar, over the bridge, and to the extremity of the suburb noticed. It is here and there covered over with sticks and mats to protect the shops below from the sun, but, from the tattered and flimsy nature of the construction, the European passenger underneath looks up with some degree of alarm. The two main streets are always thronged during the day; the people live, like the French in Paris, a good deal out of doors, and eat their meals constantly at the benches, where the cooks, a numerous class, fry their kabobs, and are as expert and active as a French artist in the subterraneous kitchen of a café. Then there are the ice-shops, and Falooda shops, where you see the rugged Affghan

---

[71] One of the fairest views in Caubul is delineated in the twenty-first drawing of my collection, from a burying-ground on the mountain ridge, north-east of the city.
[72] The twenty-second drawing in my collection represents Shah Shoojah on his throne, and the manner in which the khans and officers of state are daily assembled before him.

regaling on summer dainties, crunching a lump of ice, with the usual quantum of cherries, grapes, or other fruit, and a goodly portion of his brown cake of bread, every thing of the kind being what is called dog-cheap.

The middle part of the city is a collection of dwellings, two and three stories high, with almost inaccessible zig-zag streets and blind alleys, a black offensive gutter creeping down the centre of the greater part of them. Walls across, with gateways, are common in all the streets, so that, by closing the doors, the city is divided into numerous distinct quarters of defence. The roofs of the houses have commonly a parapet-wall round them, to allow the women of the family to take an airing unveiled, and they are generally also applied to the nastiest of purposes. The parapet-walls, formed of rail-work, thickly overlaid with mud, are five or six feet high, the Affghan spouses being most anxious that their females should not be overlooked. A gentleman who had gone to the upper part of the Balla Hissa to obtain a full view of the surrounding country, was supposed to be looking at some women half a mile off below, and a ball from a matchlock whistled past him. I was told that I was in danger whilst making a sketch of the city from the same elevated place. But notwithstanding this prodigious feeling on the score of being seen, and though an Affghan would think himself utterly disgraced by his wife's face being exposed in public, he does not hesitate for a moment in sanctioning her misdeeds, "keeping her purdah," all the time, for a competent consideration. Thus "keeping the purdah," is every thing to an Affghan. Behind the screen, protected by secrecy, nothing is wrong; and this mode of conjugal proceeding seems to prevail more or less among all classes. The women of Caubul are notoriously given to intrigue. They are allowed to go anywhere they please in their boorka-poshes, which completely cover the whole person. They leave their homes on the pretence of visiting mother, sister, or female friend, and remain as long as they like, but they must take especial care to "keep their purdah!" The Persian proverb says,

> A Caubul wife in Boorka-cover
> Was never known without a lover.

In some of the walls facing the streets, there are little loopholes, with tiny shutters, through which an Affghan beauty is occasionally seen glancing furtively at the stranger passing by, and as often the old long-bearded husband may be observed sitting grimly in solemn stupidity at a wider aperture below.

The dress of the women is simple enough, as may be seen in one of my sketches. They wear a loose yellow, blue, or red jacket, muslin or silk, which hangs down below the waist, and wide trowsers, of silk or other coloured material. They are particular in having their hair minutely arranged. It is plastered down stiff with gums in various forms on the head, and from the roots behind, platted into numerous long tails which hang over the shoulders and back. The outer margin of the ears, all round, is pierced and decorated with rows of small silver rings. Larger rings hang from the lobes of the ear. The neck and chest are tattooed, and dotted over with shapes of flowers and stars. The lids of the eyes are loaded with *soorma* (black antimony), and they use rouge. The face is often adorned with little round moles of gold and silver tinsel and vermilion, fixed on with gum. The jacket and trowsers are all that is worn in the house. On going out they draw on what may be called leggings, with feet, made of cotton cloth, gartered up to the knee, and cover their persons with the *Boorkha-posh*, which entirely prevents their being recognised abroad, even, it is said, by their own husbands!

Timber forms a very large proportion of the materials employed in house-building at Caubul. Generally, indeed, the skeleton is made of upright, transverse, and diagonal beams, and the intervals filled up with the sun-dried brick, as this method is supposed to be the best, where earthquakes are so frequent. The foundation too always consists of a layer of logs. In some houses, timbers are only used at the corners, and over the doors and windows; the walls simply of unburnt brick, without bands of wood to strengthen and support them, being easily thrown down on any violent concussion of the earth. This principle, however, does not appear to obtain throughout Asia. At Aleppo, famous for its tremendous earthquakes, the buildings are said to be massive, and mostly of solid stone.

The public baths, the Humaums, at Caubul are most disgusting to those who expect them to be purifiers, for they are actually heated with unmentionable fuel. Indeed, the Affghans are dirty in the extreme. They appear to have a sort of hydrophobia, a horror of water in its capacity of cleansing the person; but perhaps they have a theory of their own, that frequent ablution injures the skin, as frequent washing increases the wear and tear of their linen. But it matters not whether this practice is defended on principle, or persevered in from example; the fact remains, that they are generally an exceedingly dirty people. The whole appearance of the city in all its ramifications confirms this undoubted conclusion.

Mr. Elphinstone says, "Caubul, though not an extensive city, is compact and handsome." But it must be remembered, that Mr. Elphinstone never saw the place: compact it certainly is, for it is huddled together, and bounded and hemmed in on three sides by mountains, occupying a space of about three miles in circumference; but, unless a jumble of mud hovels can be considered handsome, Caubul has no pretensions to that epithet. Externally, every house presents a blank mud wall, and the domestic arrangement of rooms and apertures for windows are in a court-yard, totally unseen from without.

The mint at Caubul is a low mud hovel, of many rooms, in the bazaar. The workmen sit on the ground at their several occupations, and the process of coining is of the rudest description. The silver is first melted and run into bars, about eight inches long, and the thickness of the little finger; then taken from the mint and beaten into round rods, about two feet long and three-eighths of an inch in diameter, by the common blacksmiths in the bazaar. When brought again to the mint, these rods are drawn through a hole in a thick iron plate, as wire is made, by means of a small windlass, that they may be all of the same thickness, a boy oiling the rods as they pass through. This done, each rod is cut into pieces about an inch long, which is calculated to be the weight of a rupee. This cylinder is then weighed and adjusted; if too heavy, a piece is cut off, of course, and if light, a dent is made on the side, and a piece of sufficient size is laid on and beaten into it. These adjustments being made, the cylinders are immersed in live charcoal, taken out while hot, and placed perpendicularly on a small anvil, with tongs, and a few strokes of the hammer, flattened down to the thickness of a rupee. The blank is then fixed between the upper and lower die, and the impression effected by another stroke of the hammer. In this way the edges of the coin are ragged, and even the impression is defective. The standard value is about 15 per cent. less than that of the Company's rupee.

Early travellers seem to have deemed it necessary to embellish, in their descriptions, every thing they met with, especially in the Asiatic world, carrying out the idea of Milton —

> Where the East, with richest hand,
> Showers on her kings barbaric pearl and gold;

and rather than acknowledge that mud cities are mean and contemptible, they are pleased to decorate them with all the attractions of fairy-land. Few places have figured more conspicuously in description than Caubul, with its boasted thousand fountains and thousand gardens. But every thing is by comparison good or bad. Sadi, the Persian moral poet, says:-"The inhabitants of hell think purgatory, heaven: the inhabitants of heaven think purgatory, hell." And it is not wonderful that the people of a rugged and sterile country should think Caubul a paradise.

A little white marble grave-stone, of Mahomedan form and construction, situated in the burying-ground of a mosque, a few hundred yards from the Peshawer gate, on the east side of the Balla Hissar, occasioned a good deal of amusing speculation in camp. The inscription, which runs round the stone, is as follows: "Here lyeth the body of Thomas Hicks, the son of John Hicks and Judith his wife, who departed this life the eleventh of October, 1666." The stone, which is an oblong square, about a foot in length, eighteen inches high, with a broad moulding at the bottom, lies loosely upon the ground. I have been to the spot frequently, and when I last saw it, it had been removed to a considerable distance from its former position. I was told by a resident Armenian that he had seen it, some time before, in a different part of the burying-ground. The original site, therefore, cannot well be ascertained, nor, indeed, where this portable monument might have been brought from. But who was Thomas Hicks? What, it was asked, could have brought him, an Englishman, to Caubul in the time of Aurungzebe? Some thought Thomas Hicks was a solitary way-wanderer, but then, who buried him, and who wrote his epitaph? Nobody knows. From the manner of the inscription, however, it would seem that Thomas Hicks was a child. The insertion of father and mother in the epitaph gives probability to this suggestion, as it is not usual to put the names of father and mother on the tomb of a grown-up person, but always on that of a child.

Abdul Rusheed Khan, who had "done the state some service," when he joined our army and the Shah, on our approach to Ghizni, invited a party of us to an evening entertainment at his house. We were curious (Captains Outram, Macgregor, Hogg, and myself) to see an Affghan *soirée,* and left our own dinner in the chance of getting something, at least, to supply its place. Abdul Rusheed resides in the city, and we arrived at his domicile at dusk. The front door offered not a flattering presage of the interior decorations. It was like that of a stable, and not very suitable, I thought, for a Barukzye lord or chieftain. The passage through which we had to go was long, narrow, and dark as Erebus; and, having got to the end of it, we emerged into a square, open to the sky, in which there was a large heap or mound of dirt, offensive enough. Along the walls, pierced in several places for holding provender, stood his horses. A little low door was now before us, which led into another division of the premises, where the house was situated. Entering a further narrow door, we had to ascend a zig-zag and still narrower staircase, dangerous from projecting beams above, that threatened to break your head, or put out your eyes if you did not take special care, at every step. There was no light to guide us. At last, we landed in a little balcony-place about ten feet square, beyond which was an inner room, a *sanctum sanctorum*, perhaps twice the length, laid out with rich carpets and pillows for the company. We were there cordially received by our host.

He was now incessant in his attentions, with repeated *jor-astees, khoosh-astees*, 'are you strong? are you happy?' the invariable salutation after *salâm aliekum*, and motioned us to our several places without loss of time. The only lights were in this inner room, and looking round we now discovered, at the further end, six long-bearded personages, whose province it was to perform the musical part of the entertainment. Presently, several trays of fruit were brought in and put down on the carpet before us. The band then struck up most vehemently; they not only played, but sung, with voices so shrill and barbarous as scarcely to be human. After a quarter of an hour of this all-absorbing discipline, they ceased, and a further quantity of fruit and sweetmeats was brought forward, though hardly any of the former supply had been touched. Every now and then a kalyàn was presented by a domestic. When returned to him by the first smoker, after a few whiffs, according to custom, he took off the chillum of tobacco, and blew into the tube, to drive out all the smoke that might have collected on the surface of the water, so as to make the kalyàn quite pure for the next smoker. He then replaced the chillum, and handed it round to all in succession. The same kalyàn was used indifferently by Abdul Rusheed, his Affghan friends, several of whom were present, and the fiddlers, as a thing of course; a remarkable instance, among many, of the practical footing on which individuals of unequal grades stand towards each other at a feast. But great familiarity is constantly displayed by the lower orders. They never hesitate on any appeal to a superior to seize hold of his leg or bridle, and stop him on the road, to make known their wants.

After another hour, the sweetmeats and fruit were removed and pilaws were brought in, with a dozen large saucers of pickles and vegetables, mixed up with ghee and spices. In the pilaw were large lumps of mutton, and the accompaniment was some Caubul spirit, colourless, and nearly twice the strength of gin. The taste was so pungent, that comfits of sugar were used the moment after it was swallowed, to soften its effects on the mouth and throat. We had nothing but our fingers to help ourselves with at the repast, and the set-to was as amusing to ourselves as it appeared to be to those by whom we were surrounded. But I forgot to mention that, on the approach of the more substantial viands, a young lady and two old sybils, not of "the light fantastic toe," but of "the jingling toe," were brought into the apartment, and seated on one side. Thus "mine host," his visitors, fiddlers, and dancing women, were placed on the same footing, — an Affghan Saturnalia.[73] Great justice was done by the professional ladies and gentlemen to the various kinds of food before them, and they partook handsomely too of the exhilarating spirit above alluded to, but perfectly within the bounds of propriety, their taste and skill being only perhaps a little heightened by the libation.

This part of the business being settled, the young lady rose up to dance; her face was tolerably fair, but round as the full moon — the *mah-roo* of the Persians; her eyes large, and smothered with *soorma;* she had a nose-ornament of pearls, and was dressed in a pink muslin *jama*, or loose gown, garnished with gilt brocade. The crown of her head was covered with a small gold-embroidered cap; her hair behind was formed into numerous strings, platted, and of a considerable length. The hair on her temples appeared to be gummed down flat, upon which a

---

[73] In the latter years of Dost Mahomed's domination, dancing girls were not allowed in the city, and the use of wine was equally prohibited· by the Barukzye chief, so that this was an emancipation from the bondage so long endured, and perhaps the first amusement of the kind that had occurred since his fall. Indeed, Dost Mahomed would seem to have been as rigid in some respects as the Presbyterians in Cromwell's time. But did he improve the morals of the people, or did he make them worse?

square piece of gold-leaf was stuck, and another between her eye-brows; a pearl drop hung over her forehead, which was further adorned with a lock in the form of the letter C. Her action in dancing was rather graceful; it was more gesticulation than dancing, and more than once reminded me of the opera and melodrama at home. There were some touches of hurried passion and marks of sentiment, that made one wonder how they came there. The action in her had nothing of the foolery, and something worse, of Hindoostanee nautching; not a single movement to bring it to recollection, except the jingle of the anklet-bells. She sung, too, the old "*Mootriba khoosh,*" but in that she completely failed. She had now gone through her part, and retired; and in ten minutes more, one of the old sybils came in, dressed in her clothes, but the character of her exhibition was inferior, although her voice was not deficient in melody. It had now become rather late, and, with Abdul Rusheed's good leave, we rose to depart, highly pleased at having seen the novelty, to us, of an Affghan *soirée*.

CHAPTER XIV.

CAUBUL.

Pursuit of Dost Mahomed Khan — Rendered abortive by the treachery of Hajee Khan Kauker — Character of the Hajee — His arrest — And that of other traitors — Affghan chiefs reputed to be illiterate — Entertainment by a Khizzilbash merchant —Bâber's Tomb — Fête Champêtre in the Grove — Historical account of the Emperor Bâber.

I have mentioned that, on the 3rd of August, when intelligence of the flight of Dost Mahomed was received, orders were immediately given for the pursuit of the fugitive. Unfortunately for the work in hand, our own troops were not exclusively employed, but principally Affghans, who are never ready at a call, and who, in the present instance, as before stated, could not be got away till nightfall, which of course increased the chances against overtaking their flying enemy. A number of British officers volunteered on the occasion, with a hundred troopers, not only for the purpose of stimulating the exertions of the Affghans, but to prevent any insult to the person of Dost Mahomed or his family, should they fall into our hands. After an arduous and fatiguing march, the party returned unsuccessful, and arrived at Caubul on the 17th of August; but the failure was owing to the treacherous conduct of the arch-betrayer, Hajee Khan Kauker, the very man whom the Shah had "delighted to honour," and under whom the party of Affghans was placed. A brief summary of the particulars will be found in the note below.[74]

---

[74] I am indebted to a military friend for the following diary: "Aug. 3, 1839. Accounts received of the flight of Dost Mahomed towards Toorkistan; two thousand Affghans, under Hajee Khan Kauker, to go in pursuit forthwith, and the following British officers volunteered to accompany the party: Captain Outram, commanding; Captains Wheler and Lawrence, 2nd Light Cavalry; Captain Backhouse, Artillery; Captain Troup and Lieut. Broadfoot, Shah's service; Captain Erskine, Poonah Horse; Lieut. Hogg, Bombay Infantry; and Lieut. Ryves and Dr. Worrall, 4th Local Horse. With Captains Wheler and Lawrence were fifty of. the 2nd Cavalry, with Lieut. Ryves twenty-five of the 4th Local Horse, and with Captain Erskine 25th Poonah Horse.

"We were ready to start, and at the Envoy's tent, by noon; we were then told to return to our tents till four P.M., at which hour we moved to the mission camp, waited till dark, when about five hundred Affghans joined us, three hundred well mounted and armed, and the rest on yaboos (ponies), &c. A hundred and twenty-five of Christie's horse, under that officer, joined us, to make up in some degree for the deficiency of Affghans. Hajee Kauker, at starting, advised us to take the high road by Mydan, which was overruled by Outram, and into the mountains we dived, marched all night, crossing several ranges of hills, and winding along the dry beds of rivers and perfect goat-paths in many places. Halted occasionally, to let stragglers close up. 4th. At seven A.M. reached Goda, a small village in a confined but lovely valley, computed distance thirty-two miles. About one hundred Affghans up with us, the remainder dropped in by sixes and sevens, loaded with plunder of all sorts. Marched at five P.M.; the Hajee, unwilling to move, talked of bad roads and dangerous precipices, and we at once perceived that he had no heart in the cause. Road very bad, along the channels of mountain streams, and over high hills. After ten miles, laid down by our horses till the moon rose. 5th. At two A.M. started, and carried on till seven o'clock; crossed the Pughman range, a lofty and stony pass; encamped at Kalee Suf-feid, a petty village. Nothing for the men to eat but parched grain. Not fifty Affghans reached the ground with us, but they tumbled in during the day. Heard of Dost Mahomed being at Youk, one march ahead of us. The Kauker begged that we would halt, and send for reinforcements, stating that the Dost had two thousand select horsemen with him. Outram ordered the march at four P.M. Mustered the Affghans, now amounting to seven huhdred and fifty, but most of them badly mounted, and got off after much difficulty and altercation, full of the idea of overtaking the Ameer by gun-fire next morning. Our Hindoostanees were plucky and in high spirits. We had not, however, got many miles, when, after crawling down a precipitous mountain, we descended into a sort of punch-bowl, and a cry rose from the front that the guides were *goom-shud*, ' lost.' The night was pitch dark; and so there was no help for it, but each to lie down on the spot where he stood, first planting videttes, to keep a look-out, and a most comfortless bed we had, with large stones for our pillows; there we remained till day broke. 6th. At daybreak, started for Youk, and only reached it at seven A.M. Far off the Affghans, and nothing would induce Hajee Kauker to advance on to Hurza, sixteen miles, where we were told the Ameer was halting. He, however, solemnly promised to go on in the evening, if we would wait till then. To this we were obliged to agree; At four the cavalry mounted, but not an Affghan in the saddle, and after all, nothing would induce the Hajee to budge that night; so we dismounted, angry enough, as the delay would prevent all chance of our coming up with the Dost. Outram remonstrated strongly with the Hajee, who at last promised to make a double march next morning, but talked of the folly of the pursuit, — that we would be unequally matched, Dost Mahomed having treble our number of men, with fresh horses, and himself and followers fighting for their families and lives. The reply was, that we had to perform our duty, and that every thing possible *must be done.* 7th. Marched at day-break, and on arriving at Hurza, found the traces of the Ameer's yesterday's encampment. The Hajee halted, declaring that his men were famished and done up, and tried to persuade us to do the same, but we pushed on. A mile further, met some deserters from the Dost's party, who told us they had left him at Keloo early in the morning, and that he had no idea of moving. Captain Outram rode back to inform the Hajee and urge him to come on — but no, nothing would have any effect; he declared we were mad, running our necks into destruction; that if we encountered him, not a man would survive to tell the tale, and that disgrace would fall upon the Shah. Outram told him that on we would go, and if the Ameer was at Keloo, we would attack at all hazards, and if we did not succeed, he might look to his head. We arrived at Keloo at 3 P.M., found the Dost had left some hours before, and by that time must have surmounted the pass, the highest of the Hindoo Koosh. It was useless, therefore, following him; the men and horses required rest, night was at hand, and no signs of our Affghan allies, all of whom remained with Hajee Kauker. We had been nine hours in our saddles. 8th. This morning, we were joined by Captains Tayler, European Regiment, and Trevor, 3rd Cavalry, with fifteen troopers of the Bombay 1st Cavalry, and fifteen of the Bengal 3rd, and about three hundred Affghans. This accession of force induced the Kauker to come on, but no sooner had he arrived, than he resumed the old story of halting for more troops and the danger of pursuing desperate men. He said that not one Affghan would fight

It has been seen that the Hajee came into the service of the Shah, a traitor to the chiefs of Candahar, but it is difficult to fathom the depths of Affghan duplicity, for he appears to have been in correspondence with Dost Mahomed, and to have communicated to him our 'whereabout,' in the pursuit. Certainly, under all circumstances, the defection of the Hajee could not render the prospects of the three sirdars worse than they were, and very possibly, veteran as he was in all the doublings of a systematic genius for intrigue, he imagined, that his joining the Shah might ultimately benefit them, and also tend to the benefit of Dost Mahomed. Whatever his secret motives were, there can be no doubt that he contributed largely to the successful flight of Dost Mahomed, since, at starting, he recommended a circuitous route, evidently to consume time, and not the direct passage across the mountains, which was adopted. He had been governor of

---

against Dost Mahomed; but probably against us. Outram's reply was, that we had come to intercept the Ameer, and do it we must, if possible, and that if the Affghans would not fight, they must answer for their conduct to the king. The Hajee, finding words of no avail, imploringly took off his turban and laid hold of the skirt of Outram's coat, begging that he would not advance; but off went Outram and all our party. We had not got half-way up the pass before we saw the Hajee slowly following, as if ashamed of his conduct. The ascent of this pass was so steep, that we dismounted, and led our horses for a mile or more — the descent less abrupt — a deserted village at the foot. Halted, to allow stragglers to join, and rest the wearied cattle. Outram here informed the Kauker that he would mount at 2 P.M., and push on to Bamian; and again the Kauker implored him to be cautious, saying, besides, that his Affghans would not march at night, and begged. to remain till day-break, as our horses were pretty well done up. This was at length acceded to; but two officers proceeded at 5 A.M. to reconnoitre Bamian. 9th. Just as we were mounting, information came that Dost Mahomed, instead of stopping at Bamian, had passed on the forenoon of yesterday (having sent his family in advance), and that to-day he would be at Syghan, forty miles beyond the limit of the Shah's country, and to-morrow at Kemard, under the protection of the Waly. Outram then told the Hajee, if this proved true, he should be answerable to the Shah with his head for the Dost's escape. On our arrival at Bamian, twelve miles, found seventy horsemen, who had been dismissed by the Dost, and who confirmed the report, as well as two of the mission spies, who were here. They said he had two thousand men of all sorts with him, and that his sick son Akber was so much recovered as to mount an elephant. We were thus reluctantly compelled to give up the chase, and halted three days. Before closing this brief sketch, I would mention, in the highest terms, the conduct of our Hindoostanee troops, both regulars and irregulars. Nothing could exceed the patience, fortitude, and good humour with which they underwent great fatigue and constant exposure. *The Brahmin and Rajpoot vied with the Mussulman in making a joke of their difficulties and privations, and when it is known that the clothes on their backs were all the covering they had for fifteen days, with not a cooking utensil among them, too much praise cannot be given them. And yet it is the fashion to say, 'Our native soldiers are not what they used to be!'"* G. St. P. L.

Bamian under Dost Mahomed, and was familiar with every part of the country. In the progress of the pursuit, he managed, in various ways, to frustrate the very important object which he was appointed by the Shah to accomplish; at one time tampering with the guides, purposely missing the way, urging, with a beggar's earnestness, the British officers to halt, and at other times, declaring that the Affghans under him were traitors, and not to be depended upon in an encounter with Dast Mahomed, and the formidable party by which he was surrounded.

It must be allowed that his adhesion to the Shah was tendered at a most important period, and for this advantage his Majesty covered him with honours, and settled on him an estate worth three lacs per annum. It must also be observed, that the versatility of his character was well known to everybody; but all suspicion in the heart of the Shah seems to have been lulled to rest, or he thought, perhaps, that by apparently reposing the fullest confidence in the Kauker's integrity, he would cure him of any chance of relapse into his natural habits of intrigue and accustomed duplicity. As an unequivocal proof of that confidence, real or assumed, he, upon quitting Candahar, left with him two of his own guns, and a numerous band of professed adherents, about three thousand, to follow in a few days! Hajee Dost Mahomed was of the party. Every individual of the army who gave a thought to the subject, wondered at this proceeding. Hajee Kauker could have easily come up with the army, but that did not suit his purpose. He and Hajee Dost Mahomed, a man of wealth and importance, with some other equivocal characters, well knew that a vigorous opposition would be made at Ghizni, by a garrison of picked men sent by Dost Mahomed from Caubul, and they had a high opinion of the strength of the fortress. They therefore lingered on the road to await the result of our operations, and finding to their astonishment that the fortress had actually fallen, came into Ghizni that very day full of smiles and congratulations. Had we failed, we should have doubtless heard of the defection of Hajee Kaukel and Hajee Dost Mahomed, who would have, as doubtless, joined Mahomed Afzul, with his four thousand "experienced warriors," then close upon Ghizni. But the defeat and dispersion of the swarm of Champions of the Faith under Mihter Moosa, on the 22nd, and the glorious storming of Ghizni on the 23rd, happily changed the face of things.

We find, however, that the Shah, though well aware from the beginning of the perfidy and dissimulation of Hajee Khan Kauker, again trusted him in rather a momentous matter, that of attempting to overtake and capture Dost Mahomed Khan, and we have seen the result. But he had expressed himself to be bitterly hostile to the Dost, and it was believed that he would be glad to complete the ruin of the man whom he so much detested.

It was now the Shah's turn to be on the alert, and he performed his part with admirable tact. On the 19th of August, two days after the return of the party from Bamian, Hajee Kauker, his brother Khan Mahomed Khan, and two other chiefs distinguished for their disloyalty, waited on his majesty, and were received in the most courteous manner. Friendly inquiries and compliments passed among them all, and the arch-deceiver, feeling assured that his genius was still triumphant, and that his conduct in the pursuit had not been suspected, chuckled at his continued success. But that chuckle was of a very short duration. At the convenient moment, they were all pronounced to be state prisoners by the Shah, and instantly conveyed under a guard of sepoys to the place of confinement. Not a word was spoken, nor a murmur escaped their lips, till they entered the prison allotted to them, and then their only exclamation was *"Lahoul! Toba!"* expressions of wonder and lamentation.

A few days afterwards, five other noted characters, thinking themselves perfectly safe, and all their misdeeds forgotten or forgiven, made their *salâm* to the Shah. Among these were Hajee Dost Mahomed and Mulla Rusheed, a crafty, bad man, and they were all secured in the same quiet way, and with similar adroitness.

I went to see them all in prison shortly afterwards, and took sketches of the two Hajees, who both sat to me with great composure. They supposed, however, that there must be some object in such a proceeding, and sagely conjectured that their pictures would be sent to London, and themselves liberated. When I had completed the drawing of Hajee Kauker, I asked him to write his name upon it, and he readily took the pencil from me for that purpose; but Hajee Dost Mahomed, an astute, stern man, prevented him, saying, "Never sign your name — you know not to what use it may be applied." I mention this circumstance, because it has been stated that the Hajee could not write. It is probable that he could at least write his name, otherwise he would not, I think, have so readily taken the pencil from me, and leaned forward to comply with my request. But he is a consummate deceiver.

Dost Mahomed Khan and Jubbar Khan have equally the reputation of being scarcely able to read. That, however, is nothing remarkable in this part of the world, where every sort of business is done by deputy. In rulers, the will only is exerted. They have their mullahs for religious concerns, kazees for the law, meerzas for correspondence; they do nothing that can be done for them, contented to exercise command and shew their superiority, by being above the ordinary pursuits and accomplishments of mankind. An Affghan has just left me, who expressed his surprise to find me occupied in drawing.

"What! are you not the *Hakeem-i-Kelaun,* the chief medical officer, and employed in this way!" looking upon the occupation of a *Nukkash* (an artist) as something degrading. The old story told of an Asiatic, who said to a European, "Why do you play on the flute, and why do you dance? cannot you get people to play and dance for you, as we do?" illustrates the whole theory and conduct of an Eastern prince or chief. There have been and are exceptions, of course, but the general character is still the same.

Of the above-mentioned prisoners, only two were deported, Hajee Khan Kauker, to Hindoostan, and Gholam Hyder Khan, the ex-governor of Ghizni, to Bombay.[75] They were both escorted from Caubul in October, 1839. The greater part of the remainder were subsequently released.

Curiosity not being quite satisfied with the *soirée* at Abdul Rusheed's mansion, I was not unwilling to be present at one of another description, given by Naib Mahomed Shureef, of whom Sir Alexander Burnes, in his Travels, makes honourable mention, to a large portion of the staff of the army, at his residence in the Chundoul, or Persian quarter. Mahomed Shureef is a Khuzzilbash, and a respectable merchant, warmly attached to the English interests, a portly man — a very Falstaff, and fond of a cup of good sack too. The access to the interior was as intricate, dark, and uninviting, as the generality of Caubul dwellings. The tables "groaned with the weight of the feast," for the dinner was laid out in the European fashion, with plates, and knives and forks, vastly outshining the native exhibition of Abdul Rusheed; and the company had the luxury of chairs to sit upon. The wine of Caubul growth and manufacture did the duty of better, and the Caubul fiery spirit was made drinkable by being diluted with a dozen waters. The eatables of Persian cookery were redolent of fat, and whole kids roasted, with rice and spices in their bellies, pilaws of mutton, sweetmeats, fruit, and huge vessels of herb-soup, all in "most admired" confusion, swelled the catalogue of the good things which were set before us. Mahomed Shureef himself kept moving everywhere round the tables, drinking wine with his guests, and expressing the delight he experienced on being so highly honoured.

In due time, the notes of squeaking instruments, accompanied by the voices of the singing-women, were heard, and when we rose up from the tables, an extraordinary scene took place, but perhaps only extraordinary to those who were unaccustomed to native manners in India. In the shortest possible time, all the fragments, roasted, boiled, and stewed, were tumbled out of the dishes, and conveyed down-stairs, for the festival was held in the upper apartments, and spread out in the enclosure below, which was brilliantly illuminated. Looking from the balcony, all the household servants were seen collected together and banquetting on the "broken victuals," with an avidity and a satisfaction quite diverting. Our Indian Mussulman domestics viewed the revel with horror, for they would as soon take poison as defile and degrade themselves by being seen eating a morsel from a Christian gentleman's table. But the Persian Sheeah has no such prejudices, and the scramble that occurred was as novel as it was amusing to the whole party. The Naib also favoured us with an exhibition of fireworks; but the fire-works, and the dancing, and the singing, were not of a very

---

[75] He was afterwards sent round to Calcutta to join his father.

superior order, though the best procurable at Caubul. The guests, however, separated well pleased with the cordiality and hospitality of their host.

On one occasion, Mahomed Shureef sent an Affghan dinner to a small party desirous of tasting the choicest viands, upon which a Caubul gourmand delights to feed. There was a great variety of richly-seasoned kabobs, and stews, and pilaws. Among the sweetmeats, considered the most *recherchés,* were the *Feel-gosh* ('elephant-ear'), sugar cakes, the *Safeed-reesh* ('white-beard'), threads of sugar formed to look like a beard, and sundry concoctions of milk, fruit, and vegetables. He ate nothing himself, but was unceasing in his attentions, recommending to the company particular dishes, familiar as he was with their excellence and peculiar qualities, till dinner was over, and then he became more animated, libations of champaign, a new liquor to him, and exactly suited to his taste, filling him with mirth and joy. He repeated several of the Odes of Hafiz, sung the everlasting *"Mootriba khoosh"* with great glee, and the agreeableness of the evening was much increased by the good humour and vivacity of this Khuzzilbash Falstaff; this *rara avis* in Affghanistan.

We may now make a visit to Bâber's tomb. Immediately under the conical rock upon which the Jehan Numah is built, is a village, called Guzar-gah, and a little farther on are the extensive ruins of a mosque, which must have been once equal in magnitude to the Musjid Shahee in the Balla Hissar. This mosque is beautifully situated on the bank of the Caubul river, and through its crumbling arches and gateway we pass into the grove of magnificent Cheenars, which leads to the burial-place of the Emperor Babel. The ground from the mosque to the tomb is rather a steep slope of the rugged mountain, which overlooks the valley of Killa-Kâzee; and the space between, being some hundred yards, is divided into numerous terraces, about twenty feet wide, for the purpose of forming a line of diminutive artificial cascades. The clear sparkling water is supplied from the mountain above, and, after successive falls from one terrace to another, is received into a square reservoir close to the mosque. There is a wide path on each side of these terraces, and on every Friday, the Mahomedan sabbath, the walks of this favourite grove are filled "from morn till dewy eve" with crowds of people in their holiday attire.[76] The trees are lofty and umbrageous, and afford ample shade to the visitors in every part. The women, always veiled in their boorkas, are generally as numerous as the men, and everyone enjoying with apparent delight the social scene. This is unquestionably a strong mark of civilization, though contrasted, as it is, by so many instances of an opposite description. It is, however, gratifying to record every approach in this quarter to the sociabilities and amenities of European private life. Bâber himself saw nothing of this kind after he had transferred his capital to Hindoostan, where, to him, a new state of

---

[76] Represented in the twenty-third drawing of my collection.

things was presented, and he thus gave expression to his disappointed feelings: "Hindoostan is a country that has few pleasures to recommend it. The people have no idea of the charms of friendly society, or frankly mixing together, or of familiar intercourse. They have no genius, no comprehension of mind, no politeness of manner, no kindness of fellow-feeling." And then he goes on to enumerate some amusing particulars, characteristic enough of a man "born and bred" in a land so totally different to Hindoostan: "They have no good horses, no good flesh, no grass or musk melons, no ice or cold water, no good food or bread in the bazaars, no baths or colleges, no candles, no torches, not a candlestick!"

In several parts of the grove, embowered in chequered shade, there is sufficient space for pitching tents; and a *fête champêtre* in so romantic a situation, could not be otherwise than a pleasing event. This agreeable recreation was adopted by the Envoy, who with his family and friends made up a large party, that all the beauties of the spot might be fully seen and explored at leisure. The party assembled before breakfast, and the whole day was passed in various pleasant amusements, and in that spirit-stirring intercourse and social cheerfulness which give a zest to life, especially in Affghanistan, where opportunities of rural enjoyment are "few and far between."

Ascending to the uppermost part of the grove, we found a terrace surrounded by masonry, about thirty paces square, and nearly in the middle of it is Bâber's tomb. The grave, the surface of which is plain earth, is edged round with slabs of white marble, now broken and greatly displaced; and at the foot and head are two flat pieces of marble rounded at the top, and eighteen inches high. The tombstone, placed at one end, consists of a white marble slab, about three inches thick, sixteen inches wide, and five feet high, inscribed with the name of the emperor Zeheer-oo-deen Mahomed, surnamed Bâber.[77] At the other end there is a dwarf tree, called the Arghowan, which bears reddish-purple flowers; and behind the tombstone, a rude structure, on which garlands of flowers are placed, and in an aperture of which a lamp is kept burning every night in honour of the dead. There are several other tombstones to the memory of members of the royal family, of the same shape, but smaller in dimensions. A little below the terrace, and at the commencement of the artificial water-falls, there is a mosque of whitish grey marble, highly polished. It is arcaded, and the hall or interior about fifty feet by twenty; the inscription on the cornice which fronts the tomb, imports that it was erected in honour of the Emperor Bâber, by order of Shah Jehan, after the conquest of Balkh and Budukshan, in the year of the Hejira 1056 (A.D.

---

[77] The word *Buber* means a tiger of a large limb. The skin of one is hung up near the tomb of Sultan Mahmood at Ghizni. *Bâber* is the plural of *Buber,* the plural being generally adopted in the names of distinguished individuals, who are also spoken of, and to, in the third person plural.

1650), and it is specially noted, that the building cost forty thousand rupees. It has a sloping roof, studded with light pinnacles or minarets, and is almost covered with the foliage of the adjacent trees. It is in a good state of preservation, though nearly two hundred years old.[78]

Now step a few hundred yards back higher up the mountain, and turn round — on your right, still higher up, is the Jehan-numah; you look down the mass of grove, half in deep shadow, and far off, in the middle distance, is Killa-Kâzee; a little to the right is the Killa of Sultan Jan, the son-in-law of Dost Mahomed, and a little further that of Jubbar Khan, with their adjacent orchards. The intermediate spaces are covered with lines of mulberry-trees and poplars, and plots of cultivation, deep dark foliage contrasted with crops of a bright yellow green. The shadows of clouds rest upon parts of the landscape, and brilliant sunshine illuminates the rest, chequering, in endless variety, the quiet prospect. You see the towering mountain-boundary, but the valley below is flat; there are no undulations here, no rises and falls of the soil, no curving outline, no upland. The mountain lends none of its inequalities to the plain, and the valley is as resolute in adhering to its flatness!

The Emperor Bâber was descended from a tribe of Tartars, and in his twelfth year (A.D. 1494) became King of Ferghana, a country on the north-east side of the Caspian, or, as he himself says, "on the extreme boundary of the habitable world." After various successes and discomfitures in his ambitious career, he, in 1504, gained possession of Caubul and Ghizni, of which his paternal uncle Alugh Beg Mirza had been king a few years before, and which had fallen at his death into the hands of one of his ministers, who usurped the whole power in the name of the royal heir. But a band of conspirators soon put the minister to death, and the consequent tumult and confusion led the way to Bâber's easy conquest of not only Caubul and Ghizni, but Candahar and Herat. He afterwards made several attempts to invade India, but at first confined himself to short inroads. The fifth invasion, however, carried him to Delhi and Agra, having in a great battle, before reaching the former place, defeated and slain Sultan Ibrahim, the Emperor of Hindoostan. Bâber ascended the throne of Delhi in 1526. In the inscription on the Chehel Zeena, at Candahar, before alluded to, the empire, comprehending Affghanistan, the Punjab, and upper India, is said to have reached as far south as Jaggernath and Chittagong!

It is a remarkable fact, that the victories of Bâber were gained by comparatively small armies. He mentions in his Memoirs that the force of Sultan Mahmood, in conquering Hindoostan, exceeded 100,000 soldiers; that the second conqueror of Hindoostan, Sultan Mahomed Ghouree, had at least 120,000 men;

---

[78] The view downwards on these objects is represented in the twenty-fourth drawing of my collection.

and that he himself, the third, accomplished the conquest with only 12,000 men. "I do not," he says, "ascribe this success to my exertions; I refer it to the favour of the Almighty, who was pleased to aid me in my humble efforts."

Bâber was undoubtedly one of the most illustrious monarchs of Asiatic history, and at Caubul, where his ashes repose, his memory is held in the highest veneration. Inured as he was to the rugged and hardened scenes of military life, in so rude an age, and in a country so far removed from the more civilized portions of the globe, it is, indeed, extraordinary to meet with a man like him, so susceptible of sentimental delicacy, and imbued with so amiable a spirit, as is frequently displayed in the frank and amusing autobiography which he composed at different periods of his surprising career. It is delightful to see a Tartar, with a mind like his, softened down to the contemplation of the beauties of a flower or a plant, to the tender associations produced by habits of friendship, to constancy in that friendship, and to the enthusiastic cultivation of literature, for the poetry of Bâber is of no common stamp.

But notwithstanding the higher qualities of his disposition, his ambitious pursuits and fondness for letters, he is almost equally celebrated as a *bon vivant*, having been long addicted to "vinous potations" and convivial parties. One spot is still pointed out, on a mountain which overlooks the city of Caubul from the east, where he and his boon companions used to assemble in social colloquy, to enjoy the pleasures of wine. Ferishta says, that when he was inclined to mirth and festivity, he used to fill a reservoir, in a garden in the neighbourhood of Caubul, with wine; but this is probably a mere figure of speech, to illustrate the extreme conviviality and munificence of the emperor.

The following account of one of his drinking parties is curious, and characteristic:- "Next morning," says the emperor (March 5th, 1519, near Behreh on the Sinde), "after Divan was dismissed, when I had finished my ride, I went on board of a boat, and had a drinking party with Khwajeh Dost Khawend, Khasrou Nizam, Mirza Kuli, Mahomed Ahmedi, Gedai, Naaman, Lenga Khan, Rukhem-deen, Kasim Ali Teriàki, Yusef Ali, and Tengri Kali. Towards the bow of the vessel, a space was roofed in. It had a level platform above, and I and some others sat on the top of it; a few others sat below the scaffolding. Towards the stern of the boat, too, there was a place for sitting; Mahomed, with Gedai and Naaman, sat there. We continued drinking spirits till afternoon prayers," (an Affghan stops and goes through the formula at the enjoined periods, however he may be engaged). "Disliking the spirits, we then took to majùn, an intoxicating preparation made from hemp. Those who were at the other end of the vessel did not know that we were taking majùn, and continued to drink spirits. About night prayers, we left the vessel, and, mounting our horses, returned late to the camp. Mahomed and Gedai, thinking that I had been taking nothing but spirits; and imagining that they were doing an acceptable service, brought me a pitcher of liquor, carrying it by turns on their horses. They were extremely drunk and jovial when they brought it in. 'Here it is,' they said; 'dark as the night is, we have brought a pitcher. We carried it by turns.' They were informed that we had been using a different thing. The majùn-takers and spirit-drinkers, as they have different tastes, are very apt to take offence with each other. I said, 'Don't spoil the cordiality of the party; whoever wishes to drink spirits; let him drink spirits; and let him that prefers majùn, take majùn, and let not the one party give any idle or provoking language to the other.' Some sat down to spirits, some to majùn. The party went on for some time tolerably well. Baba Jan Kabùzi (a player on the Kabùz) had not been in the boat; we had sent for him when we reached the royal tents. He chose to drink spirits. Ferdi Mahomed Kepchak, too, was sent for, and joined the spirit-drinkers. As the spirit-drinkers and majùn-takers never can agree in one party, the spirit-bibbing party began to indulge in foolish and idle conversation, and to make provoking remarks on majùn and majùn-takers; Baba Jan, too, getting drunk, talked very absurdly. The tipplers, filling up glass after glass for Ferdi Mahomed, made him drink them off, so that in a very short time he was mad drunk. The party became quite burdensome and unpleasant, and soon broke up." Two days afterwards, he had another drinking bout, with nearly the same party:- "We continued drinking spirits," says he, "in the boat till bed-time prayers, when, being completely fuddled, we mounted, and, taking torches in our hands, came at full-gallop back to the camp from the river side, falling sometimes on one side of the horse, and sometimes on the other. Next morning, when I was told of our having galloped into the camp with lighted torches in our hands, I had not the slightest recollection of the circumstance."

This dissolute run of occasional dissipation, however, had its bounds, and Bâber, some years afterwards, firmly resolved upon leading a new life; and he adhered to that resolution. The subjoined passage presents no unfavourable view of the spontaneous character and sensibility of his mind. He thus writes from Etawah, in Hindoostan, to his friend Khwajah Kelàn, February, 1529:- "My solicitude to visit my western dominions is boundless, and great beyond expression. The affairs of Hindoostan have at length, however, been reduced to a certain degree of order, and I trust in Almighty God that the time is near at hand, when, through the grace of the Most High, every thing will be completely settled in this country. As soon as matters are brought into that state, I shall, God willing, set out for your quarter, without losing a moment's time. How is it possible that the delights of those lands should ever be erased from the heart? Above all, how is it possible for one, like me, who has made a vow of abstinence from wine, and of purity of life, to forget the delicious melons and grapes of that pleasant region? They very recently brought me a single musk-melon. While cutting it up, I felt myself affected with a strong feeling of loneliness, and a sense of my exile from my native country; and I could not help shedding tears whilst I was eating it." At the conclusion of the letter, he says:- "Indeed, last year, my desire and longing for wine and social parties was beyond measure excessive; it even came to such a length, that I have found myself shedding tears from vexation and disappointment. In the present year, praise be to God! these troubles are over, and I ascribe them chiefly to the occupation afforded to my mind by a poetical translation on which I have employed myself. Let me advise you, too, to adopt a life of abstinence. Social parties and wine are pleasant in company with our jolly friends and old boon companions. But with whom can you enjoy the social cup? With whom can you indulge in the pleasures of wine? If you have only Sheer Ahmed and Haider Kalee for the companions of your gay hours and social goblet, you can surely find no great difficulty in consenting to the sacrifice."

Bâber died at the Chaharbagh, near Agra, on the 24th December, 1530, and his body, according to his own directions, was carried to Caubul, where it was buried on the spot chosen by himself, and which has been already described. The close of his life exhibits a remarkable instance of paternal affection. "When Humayoon had resided at his government of Sambal about six months, he fell dangerously ill. His father, whose favourite son he seems to have been, was deeply affected at the news, and gave directions for conveying him by water to Agra. He arrived there, but his life was despaired of. When all hopes from medicine were over, and while several men of skill were talking to the emperor of the melancholy situation of his son, Abul Baka, a person highly venerated for his knowledge and piety, remarked to Bâber, that, in such a case, the Almighty had sometimes vouchsafed to receive the most valuable thing possessed by one friend, as an offering in exchange for the life of another. Bâber exclaimed that, 'of all things, his life was dearest to Humayoon, as Humayoon's was to him, and that, next to the life of Humayoon, as his own was what he most valued, he devoted his life to heaven as a sacrifice for his son's.' The noblemen around him entreated him to retract the rash vow, and in place of his first offering to give the diamond taken at Agra, and reckoned the most valuable on earth;[79] that the ancient sages had said, that it was the dearest of our worldly possessions alone that was to be offered to heaven. But he persisted in his resolution, declaring that no stone, of whatever value, could be put in competition with his life. He three times walked round the dying prince, a solemnity similar to that used in sacrifices and burnt-offerings, and retiring, prayed earnestly to God. After some time, he was heard to exclaim: 'I have borne it away! I have borne it away!' The Mussulman historians assure us that Humayoon almost immediately began to recover,

---

[79] It is said to have weighed eight miskals or 224 ruttees, or in English, 672 carats; but Aurungzebe's diamond weighed 900 carats. The famous Pitt diamond was only 137 carats, but considered the finest jewel in the world.

and that, in proportion as he recovered, the health and strength of Bâber visibly decayed. Bâber communicated his dying instructions to Khwajeh Kalifeh, Ali Beg, Terdi Beg, and Hindee Beg, who were then at court, commending Humayoon to their protection. With that unvarying affection for his family, which he shewed in all the circumstances of his life, he strongly besought Humayoon to be kind and forgiving to his brothers. Humayoon promised, and, what in such circumstances is rare, he kept his promise."

Bâber says, that in his time there were eleven or twelve different languages spoken in Caubul, Arabic, Persian, Toorkee, Mugholi, Hindee, Affghanee, Pashai, Parachi, Geberi, Berekee, and Lamghanee. "It is to be doubted," he adds, "whether so many languages could be found in any other country." At present, the Persian is almost universally used; we hear it continually in the streets, and even the beggars beg in Persian, though Pushtoo has been said to be the common dialect among the people. At their homes it may be so.

CHAPTER XV.

CAUBUL

Ruin and decay apparent throughout the country— Oppression, rapacity, and neglect, of the late government — Political weakness of the Barukzye chiefs — Arrival of the Shahzada Tymoor — His reception by the Shah — Distribution of the Order of the Durranee Empire — Insurrectionary movements of the Ghilzie chiefs — Expedition under Captain Outram — March of the Bombay force to Kelati — Nusseer — Removal of the Shah to Jellalabad — Risings in Khyber, Kooner, and Bajore — Turbulent state of the frontier near Bamian — Capture of Kelati-Nusseer — Return of the Shah to Caubul — Fresh disturbances amongst the Ghilzies — Proceedings of Dost Mahomed Khan — He communicates with the King of Bokhara, and proceeds thither — Is imprisoned by the King — The British authorities negotiate with Jubbar Khan — Surrender of Dost Mahomed's wives and family — The Khan of Kokan interferes with the King of Bokhara in favour of Dost Mahomed Khan — Employs force — Dost Mahomed escapes by stratagem to Kholoom — He proclaims a holy war — Discouraging aspect of affairs.

The miserable appearance of Caubul as a metropolis has been shewn; and where there is no refinement or civilization at the capital, neither the one nor the other can well be expected in the provinces; for whatever distinguishes the seat of government, the same qualities and tendencies never fail to be observable in the other parts of the state. Every public work, everywhere, was neglected when the empire became a prey in different quarters to numerous candidates, each only anxious about the exaction of tribute; and bigoted as they were in the Mussulman faith, even their mosques of other times were permitted to crumble in the dust. The royal Musjid in the Balla Hissar seemed to have lost its sanctity, perhaps on the ground of its being called the Musjid Shahee, and equally so the great mosque near the Emperor Bâber's tomb. Both are now "things that were." The magnificent garden at Gundumuk, and the buildings belonging to it, were destroyed by order of Dost Mahomed, and many others, because they had been constructed by Shah Shoojah. At Gundumuk, two cypresses and a few pieces of broken wall only remain. The Harem Serai at Caubul is described to have been, thirty years ago, an elegant structure, splendidly embellished. It would be as easy to trace the loveliness of a Venus in the bare skeleton, as any thing like splendour in that tottering building; and yet it continued to be the occasional crazy abode of Dost Mahomed Khan up to the period of our approach to Caubul. The wear and tear of years was allowed to go on, unnoticed.

And now the whole country exhibits nothing but ruin and decay. In every town or village, broken mouldering walls encumber the ground, the debris of thirty years of anarchy and despotism. Many towns and villages have totally disappeared. The peasant had been screwed to the uttermost, and still even the petty tyrant of the place derived no substantial or permanent benefit from his rapacity; there was, in fact, no government; it was a universal scramble, and property of every description was seized, and held by the sword. What was Dost Mahomed

Khan's observation, after his surrender to the Envoy, when asked why he permitted every thing to go to decay? He said that he had not the means to prevent it, and that, during the whole period of his rule, he never passed what he called a really happy day. He was pleased to say so. His revenue was certainly small, and obtained with great difficulty; the claims upon him by his people innumerable. No doubt, like most intruders, he was in continual apprehension of being dispossessed of what he had won by perfidy, and retained by rapacity and violence. He was assailed from morning to night with demands for money; and the current wants for subsistence, and even existence, were all that could be supplied. Mosque, tower, garden, consequently all, went to ruin. It is precisely the same from Bhukker to Jellalabad. The area of the fortress at the former place is a mass of ruins — it is covered with heaps of fallen houses. Sukkur, on the right bank of the Indus, must have once been a flourishing and an extensive city, but it now consists of massy broken walls and fragments of glazed tiles, which indicate its former importance. All the way, the same deplorable effects of time are visible. Candahar is surrounded with the remains of towns and villages. Kelat-i-Ghilzie, Ghizni, and the whole space to Caubul and Jellalabad, display the same march of desolation, the same proof of the withering and destroying influence of despotism under the Barukzye rulers. It is clear that these ambitious brothers had no real hold of the nation, or the portions over which they presided. Their strength, or rather their continuance in authority, was owing to their weakness. The chiefs of tribes paid them occasionally, domineered over them, and allowed them to reign. It was a species of compromise, tacitly felt, not expressed. When the Khizzilbashes and other nobles of the land finally fell off from Dost Mahomed, at Arghundee, the compromise was lost, and his authority terminated.

On the 3rd of September, Shahzada Tymoor, the heir-apparent, arrived at Caubul, accompanied by Lieut.-Colonel C. M. Wade. In their progress from Peshawer, they had captured the strong hill fort of Ali Musjid, in the Khyber Pass, and thus successfully contributed to the happy results of the campaign. The Shah was on his throne in full Durbar, ready to receive the Shahzada, who, before he reached the Balla Hissar, had been welcomed by Sir John Keane and Sir Willoughby Cotton, attended by an escort of dragoons and infantry. But the splendid *cortège* did not enter the Balla Hissar — the Shahzada only, supported by Colonel Wade and Captain Macgregor, the Envoy's military secretary, and two other officers. When he had passed through the inner gate, which leads to the large quadrangle, the prince dismounted and walked with measured step till he came in front of the open verandah, in which his Majesty was seated, attended only by two chowrie-burdars, standing behind him. He wore a large white turban and a purple velvet tunic, richly trimmed with gold lace, and seemed to be about forty years of age. He now moved through a street formed by the chiefs or khans of the kingdom, at a right angle with the Durbar-khana, and when within a dozen yards of the presence, made a salaam, to which the reply of the Shah was, *"khoosh amudeed!"* 'You are welcome.' The Shahzada then turned to the left, and proceeded slowly up a flight of stairs, re-appeared, and moving towards the king, kissed his Majesty's hand, and retired to a little distance, where he sat down on the carpet. Things remained in this posture, all silent, solemn, and motionless, a dumb show, for at least ten minutes, and we looked on in wonderment at what would happen next. Such is the formal etiquette observed on these state occasions by Affghan kings. The ceremony, however, was not of long duration; nothing more was to be seen or heard. The king rose up, and the assembly separated in silence.

The residence of Shahzada Tymoor adjoins the Durbar-khana; it is a small contemptible building. The prince is very much liked both by Europeans and Affghans, his manners being affable and courteous. He is said to be strictly pious, and most rigid in the regular performance of the duties of the Mussulman faith.

On the 17th of September, the Shah presented the newly-created Order of the Durranee Empire to all the officers present in the capital on whom that honour had been conferred. The ceremony took place in the court-yard of the Harem Serai, once the gaily ornamented palace of the kings of Caubul, but now a wreck, like every other public building in the country: the Shah now occupies a part of it only. On the occasion adverted to, he was seated, in compliment to the English, on a chair, and not on a carpet, supported by large pillows, according to the custom in Asiatic nations. He wore his crown, which is something like a hunting-cap, surrounded by a four-cornered brim, and from each point hung a small tassel of precious stones. The crown itself was purple velvet, his tunic yellow, and his choga or gown, left open in front, crimson purple, with no gaudy garniture. Almost every officer of the army was present, and in full dress, and the whole assemblage had a novel and brilliant effect. The Commander-in-Chief, the Envoy and Minister, Sir Willoughby Cotton, Sir Alexander Burnes, and Colonel Wade, were invested with the decorations of the first class; fourteen other officers were nominated of the second class, and thirty-six of the third class. Another year of service has extended the range of these honours considerably.

It was not long after the Shah had arrived at Caubul, that the insurrectionary movements of the Ghilzie chiefs demanded immediate attention, and an expedition under Captain Outram was promptly sent into the districts which had exhibited the strongest proofs of rebellion against the King's authority. These districts, situated between Ghizni and Candahar, were under the powerful influence of Mihter Moosa, Gool Mahomed, and Abdoo Rohman. The principal forts were destroyed, and especially that of Maroof, in which the dreadful atrocities were perpetrated upon the kafila proceeding from Candahar, which have been already described. The whole country received an awful lesson during this rapid and successful expedition, and for a time tranquillity was restored.

Mihter Moosa, the leader of the Ghilzie crusaders, who were driven from the heights at Ghizni, the day before the capture of that fortress, despairing of success, surrendered himself to Captain Outram. Several of the supposed murderers of Lieut. Inverarity and Colonel Herring were made prisoners, and sent to Candahar, and afterwards to Caubul, for trial; but, in the former case, the evidence was incomplete, and the culprits in the latter effected their escape by night from the prison in the Balla Hissar.

On the 18th September, the Bombay force, which had moved, two days before, a few miles south of the city, marched in progress towards Ghizni, and from thence by a new route, leaving Candahar on the right, to Kelati-Nusseer, the fortress of Mihrab Khan. The object of this movement was to inflict signal punishment on the Khan for the perfidious conduct he had pursued, by depriving him of his power over that province, and seating another chief of the same family in his place.

Early in November, the Shah moved to Jellalabad for the winter, and in our progress to that station, accounts were received of the rising of the tribes in the Khyber mountains, which happily was soon repressed. Then came the rebellion in Kooner, which was also, after some hard service, put down,[80] and next the disturbances in Bajore, secretly instigated and fostered, it was supposed, by the Sikhs.

Soon after the Bombay force had left Caubul, and arrangements had been made for the return of a part of the Bengal troops, leaving only two brigades in Affghanistan, information was received of the disaffected and turbulent state of the frontier beyond Bamian. It was reported that Dost Mahomed Khan had with him 1,200 well-armed and mounted followers, and was aided by the Walee of Kholoom, by Baba Beg of Hybuk, and by Murad Beg of Kundooz, with their own adherents in great numbers, all bent upon proceeding against us. It was also stated that the ex-chief was making preparations for casting cannon, and that he was improving his resources by collecting the transit duties from the kafilas in Kholoom. Clouds of most unfavourable omen seemed to be darkening the horizon in that quarter, and, in consequence, the Envoy and Minister requested Sir John Keane would permit a brigade to remain in Affghanistan in addition to the force already decided on.

---

[80] The history of the Syuds of Kooner is as full of atrocities as any other part of the Affghan dominions: one may do as a specimen. In presence of a large assembly of chiefs, at which his father presided, Syud Fakeer stabbed and put to death his brother, Mahayaoo-deen. For this murder he was confined, but almost immediately released. Shortly after, in a struggle for supremacy, he caused his aged father to be smothered to death, then eighty years of age, and who had ruled over Kooner fifty-seven years, and the fratricide-parricide continued in power for a long time afterwards.-*Capt. MacGregor's interesting Report on Kooner.*

In the propriety of this requisition, Sir John Keane entirely concurred, and well it is for our interests, considering the events of subsequent occurrence, that so much foresight was displayed.[81] Our great object was the expulsion of Dost Mahomed from Toorkistan, and the countries on this side of the Oxus. But the season was thought by the Commander-in-Chief to be too far advanced to admit of the regular troops being sent on that expedition, and considerations of political expediency therefore gave way to the military objections which were stated on the occasion. Other measures were, however, put in execution. A detachment of the Shah's disciplined troops with guns was despatched by the Envoy to Bamian, in promotion of the same views, but unavoidably on a limited scale. On arriving there, the son of the Walee of Kholoom had pushed forwards with an armed force, consisting of about eight hundred men, to Syghan, a village thirty-five miles from Bamian; but his camp was surprised by a rapid movement on the 31st of October, and his whole force driven over the hills in every direction. Syghan was thus re-annexed to the Shah's dominions. In November, positive intelligence was received at Caubul, that Dost Mahomed Khan had left Kholoom, and gone off to Bokhara.

In the midst of these occurrences, information arrived of the capture of Kelati Nusseer, by the British troops. The blow had been only delayed. The hour of retribution came like the whirlwind. The fortress was most gallantly stormed and taken by the force under General Willshire, and the desperate Khan was among the slain. This last effort of his was superior to any thing exhibited by the enemy during the war, and reflected deeply on the very different conduct of Dost Mahomed, his sons, and his brothers. It is said, that the Khan heard some of his people cry out for quarter in that sanguinary struggle, and that he instantly exclaimed — "No quarter for friend or foe!" Saying this, he rushed on, "and foremost, fighting, fell." This splendid achievement of the little army under General Willshire occurred on the 13th of November, 1839, and Shah Nawaz Khan, the nephew of Mihrab Khan, was in consequence raised to the musnud.

Shah Nawaz, however, was never popular, and being at last deserted by his people, and his garrison in close communication with the rebels who had risen

---

[81] The sudden reduction of the army and establishments was more a measure of economy than prudence. Among the reductions, the Field Hospital was wholly abolished, but upon that order being given, I officially suggested to the Commander-in-Chief the importance of at least a portion of it being retained with the remaining force, as in the probable event of corps being detached, the sick would necessarily be left behind, without any available or adequate means of providing for them, each regiment of course taking along with it its own hospital establishment. His Excellency approved of my suggestion, and at once sanctioned the modified scale I laid before him. The great utility of this resource was abundantly experienced on many occasions, especially in the subsequent expeditions into Kooner and the Kohistan.

against him, he was under the necessity of abdicating in favour of their leader, the son of Mihrab Khan. The withdrawal of so many of our troops from that quarter, for emergent purposes, made it impossible for us to prevent that catastrophe, which took place on the 30th of July, 1840. On the 3rd of November following, however, we regained possession of Kelat, without firing a shot, the rebel chief and his rabble having evacuated it on the approach of the British under Major-General Nott.

On the return of the Shah and the British troops from Jellalabad to Caubul, in April, fresh measures of coercion were required to put down the disturbances which had been renewed by the Ghilzie chiefs. For this purpose, a force was ordered from Candahar, and an engagement took place, on the 16th of May, at Tazee. About 2,000 Ghilzie horse and foot were first discovered crowning one of the heights, and prepared for action. From round the adjacent hills and up ravines, other bands of the enemy appeared, and a desperate cavalry charge seemed to be meditated; but the heavy fire of grape, poured on them on all points, disconcerted the forward movement, which was finally repulsed at the point of the bayonet:

Ultimately, the enemy took to flight in all directions. This brilliant little victory was achieved under the command of Captain W. Anderson, of the Horse Artillery, and it was one of the most conspicuous in the campaign.

Let us now turn to Dost Mahomed Khan, and trace his steps till the period of his surrender. After his arrival at Kholoom, he was received as before stated, most hospitably by the Walee, who assisted him for a brief space in his hopeless attempt to regain his lost influence and power. But he well knew that further co-operation was indispensable to any thing like success, and, incessant in his endeavours to compass his own ends, communicated at once with the King of Bokhara. He stated to the King, that Shah Shoojah had become a Kafir, an infidel; that he was leagued with Kafirs, and that he himself had been dispossessed of Affghanistan merely by fraud and treachery. He affected to be still in great force, with numerous pieces of artillery, to recover his rights. "You are a Mussulman," said he, "and the Light of Islam, and it most imperatively behoves you to aid me against the accursed Kafirs. Their spoil shall be divided between us. If you fail to share in this great enterprise, Shah Shoojah and the Feringhees will not only overrun this country, but conquer and destroy your own; and make you their prisoner. The people of Toorkistan, Budukhshan, and Kashgar, are assembling. In the good cause. I await your speedy reply, defender and protector of the Mussulman faith." In the meantime he made the most strenuous endeavours to gather together a force of Uzbeks, but with very little success. A reply at length arrived from the King of Bokhara, who requested that a vakeel might be deputed to him, to discuss the various matters in which he was interested, and then he would send an army to co-operate in the great design. The

Dost accordingly deputed Mirza Samikhan to Bokhara, with full instructions, and the vakeel, on arriving at that place, and being presented at the Durbar, was thus addressed by the king:- "Write to Dost Mahomed Khan, and give him my warmest assurances of relief and assistance; but I recommend his coming to me himself, and money and troops shall be at his command. A personal interview will be most satisfactory to both of us."

Upon this assurance, Dost Mahomed, elated with the flattering prospect, and no doubt alarmed by our operations at Syghan, set off immediately to Bokhara, with his sons, Akber and Afzul, and Sumunder Khan. This was in the latter part of November, and so urgent appeared to be the occasion, that the journey was accomplished in fifteen days. The king received him in the most cordial and distinguished manner, told him how happy he was to see him, and after countless expressions of esteem and attachment to the sacred cause in which he had so meritoriously embarked, ended by suggesting the propriety of sending for his family for protection, and intimating his desire, that intermarriages should take place between their children, so as to render more firm their bond of union, and establish their future friendship on the most secure foundation. He at the same time secretly required the Walee of Kholoom to despatch, at all risks, the family of the Dost to Bokhara. Catch a weazel asleep! The ex-ruler was not to be circumvented on this point. He addressed a letter to Nawab Jubbar Khan, requesting him to lose no time in escorting his family to Bokhara, and respectfully laid this communication open before the king for his perusal and despatch; but having fathomed the depth of the plot, and the sinister object of the king's requisition, he sent another privately to Jubbar Khan, telling him rather to put every member of his family to death than allow them to move in that direction. His Majesty of Bokhara had keenly contemplated getting hold of the family-jewels, and all such property as they might be possessed of. But the scheme was unsuccessful, and, finding, by the non-appearance of the Zenana, that his purpose had been defeated, he became highly indignant, and cast the Dost and his sons into prison, saying:- "There you shall remain till your family is brought to Bokhara."

Jubbar Khan, now acquainted with the real state of things at Bokhara, felt the difficult situation of the family at Kholoom; and being at variance, as he was, with the British Government, and having little confidence in the Walee, he was doubtful how to act. On our part, again, it was considered an important point to obtain possession of the family, and a correspondence was promptly opened with the Nawab for that purpose. The negotiations began in March, but he continued undecided; and, notwithstanding the threat of his property being confiscated, persisted in delaying, under various pretexts, his promised submission and return to Caubul. The communications he received from Dost Mahomed at this time, appear to have contained little more than complaints of the hardship and cruelty of his confinement, the severity with which he was treated, and expressions of hope that God would soon put an end to his sufferings.

Meanwhile, Jubbar Khan continued to collect the transit duties from the Bokhara kafilas passing to Caubul, to defray his expenses and those of the family, and shewed great reluctance to move, though he had been besought to consult his own honour, and that of his friends, by coming in as a guest, before we should be compelled to bring him in as a prisoner. Various demonstrations were then made to induce the belief that a strong force was proceeding to Kholoom for the purpose alluded to, and a party actually advanced to the fortified position at Bajgah, which had the anticipated effect, for towards the end of June, the Nawab and the family of the Ameer were actually on the road towards Bamian. The whole cavalcade arrived at Arghundee on the 15th of July, from whence Jubbar Khan and his own family were permitted to proceed to his fort at Killa-Kazee, near Caubul; and the wives, sons, daughters, and slaves of the Dost were escorted to Ghizni, to remain there till suitable accommodations should be prepared for them at Quetta, which had at that time been decided upon for their future residence. The number amounted to two hundred and forty-nine!

The more the King of Bokhara dwelt upon the defeat of his plans by this contemptuous opposition to his will, the more he was enraged; and he certainly would have put the Ameer to death, had it not been for the minister, who interfered in his behalf, and dissuaded him from so unjust a proceeding. The Dost had become aware of his danger, and contrived to get a letter sent to the Khan of Kokan, in which he earnestly supplicated his intercession in this extremity; and his supplication was not in vain. The Khan said, in writing to the king, "This is a stranger, who has sought your protection. He has fled from the Feringhees, and is now at your feet. He is a true Mussulman, and if you cannot assist, do not injure him. Bring not destruction on your own head by cruelty and injustice, but let him depart in peace." The king, however, was not easily to be withdrawn from his purpose; he argued that the Dost had been, and was, his bitter enemy; that he had formerly united with the Persians against him, and that even then, he observed, his brothers of Candahar were at Tehran, employed in designs inimical to his prosperity. Equally obstinate and determined was the Khan, and it was not long before he had recourse to arms to support the cause he espoused.

He soon captured the strong fort of Juzuk, and was in full march upon Bokhara, when the king, unable to cope with the force sent against him, consented to liberate the prisoner, on condition of hostilities being suspended. The terms were agreed to, but, Asiatic-like, his majesty of Bokhara still threatened the Dost with death. The means of escape, however, fell into the prisoner's hands, but probably not without the connivance of the king, who dreaded another contest with the Chief of Kokan. I am told that the escape was effected in the following manner: — Dost Mahomed was confined in a small mosque, near one of the great bazaars. He succeeded in bribing a guide to procure him a good horse, to be posted in a suitable situation, a few miles from the city, and to remain himself close by for the purpose of shewing him the way. He then assumed the Uzbek dress, and finding an opportunity of joining his conductor, an Uzbek, who was ready mounted in the thronged bazaar, jumped up behind him. The Dost and the Uzbek trotted on unnoticed, passed through the city, and reached the spot where the other horse was stationed without impediment. He then sprung upon his own horse, and eagerly pursued his journey; but in a few days he discovered that the animal had become rather lame, and, dreading the chance of being detected and chased, and unable from that circumstance to accomplish his own deliverance, he thought it more safe to have recourse to even an inferior steed, which was sound in wind and limb, than to continue on his own. Upon the urgency of the occasion, he therefore made an exchange with his guide. Proceeding onwards, the Uzbek began to repent of his undertaking, and, apprehensive of the consequences to himself, considered in what way he might avert the punishment that awaited him, if discovered. He was also anxious to turn the ex-ruler to some account, and was not long in forming the scheme of getting him back to Bokhara, and delivering him up to the king. A favourable moment soon occurred, for next day he fell in with a few horsemen, with whom he entered into conversation about Dost Mahomed and the Feringhees, and finding they were enemies of his charge, his avarice led him to hope for a high reward, not only from them, but from the King of Bokhara. In this spirit he said to them, "Perhaps you would like to gain a prize. Do you see that horseman? That is Dost Mahomed, who has just escaped from prison at Bokhara," pointing to the Caubul chief, a few hundred yards ahead of them. "No! no!" they replied, "That is impossible; Dost Mahomed would never ride on such a sorry Yaboo as that, and you, his follower, mounted on this fine horse; no, no! You are yourself Dost Mahomed in disguise. We know you well; so come along with us to Bokhara." The consternation of the guide at this blow to his cunning project was strongly depicted on his countenance, which to the horsemen was an additional proof that he was "the real Simon Pure." He was thus caught in his own trap, and, in spite of his remonstrances, borne away, Dost Mahomed being left unsuspected to pursue his own course to Kholoom.

The tidings of his arrival produced a deep sensation throughout Affghanistan, revived the spirit of the rebellious, and gave a new stimulus to our military operations against the anticipated movements of the restless Ameer, whose first measure was to collect the taxes and custom-duties levied on kafilas passing between Caubul and Toorkistan, assisted by his son Mahomed Afzul Khan, proclaiming his object to be a holy war, a crusade against the infidels, and producing for a time a strong feeling of hatred against his enemies. With these collections he raised a small force of Uzbeks, and by promising to make the

Walee his Vizier, when he recaptured Caubul! and exciting other expectations, gained the active cooperation of that chief, still insisting on the religious obligation of sweeping the infidel English from the face of the earth. The Walee himself had been previously impressed with the dread of our conquests extending beyond the Affghan frontier, and he had secretly promoted and effected a confederacy among the petty states of Toorkistan, with the view of repelling any encroachment to the north of Bamian. But of these sentiments and proceedings we were not exactly apprized at the time.

Information of the Dost's escape from Bokhara reached the Envoy and Minister on the 27th of July, but it created little inquietude, as his family were in our possession at Ghizni, and the Walee of Khooloom, on whose aid he might chiefly rely, was professing the most devoted attachment to the Shah and the British Government, and indeed had sent his prime minister and his son to Caubul, as a proof of his sincerity! But the common principle of action among Asiatics, with respect to females and children, as in the present case, was not observed. Instead of considering them any thing like hostages, or their condition as an inducement to come to terms, the Dost must have secretly rejoiced at his family being in such good hands and so well provided for, a circumstance which enabled him to turn the resources necessary for their support to another account. He never entertained a doubt about their safety.[82]

On the 6th of August, it was reported that disturbances had broken out on the Bamian frontier, but these produced little concern, as it was supposed that they had their origin in some local misunderstanding. On the 7th, intelligence was received that Kelat had fallen into the hands of the rebel Belooches; that Yar Mahomed, the Vizier of Herat, meditated a descent on Candahar, and that Dost Mahomed Khan had actually reached Khooloom. About the same time, the rebels in Bajore obtained a signal success over the party in the Shah's interest, and had captured a gun. These were untoward events, and of an alarming character; but the Envoy had taken the precaution of strengthening Candahar, by sending there another regiment of Native Infantry; he made the most liberal overtures to Dost Mahomed, which there was every reason to hope he would have accepted, and the well-known activity and zeal of Capt. Macgregor, the political agent at Jellalabad, gave assurance that the rebels would not be permitted to take much advantage of the success they had gained in that direction. About this time, arrangements were made with the rebellious Hotukee and Tohkee clans of Ghilzies, which satisfied them, and ensured their adherence to the existing

---

[82] It is the usual practice in Affghanistan to disgrace the wives of a rebellious chief by giving them to mule-drivers, if the said rebellious chief perseveres in his hostility. The mule-drivers are generally Hazarehs, and of the very lowest class, on which account they are selected, to add bitterness to the degradation.

government. Syud Hashim, too, the rebel chief of Kooner, had been conciliated by Capt. Macgregor, whilst the negotiations which had been long carrying on with other rebel chiefs were prosecuted with renewed activity.

The intrigues of the Sikh feudatories, which had never slumbered since we first got footing in Affghanistan, were observed with increased vigilance, and the most urgent representations were made to the Governor-General in Council on the subject. The intelligence received from Herat about this period was of the most unfavourable nature. Yar Mahomed had persuaded our Envoy at that place that he intended to attack Ghorean, and having on this plea extracted a large sum of money and assembled a numerous force, he all of a sudden abandoned the enterprise on the most frivolous and groundless pretences. His treacherous nature prompted him to the belief that it could never be to his interest to be sincere in his alliance with us, or to give such offence to Persia as would stop the channel of his intrigues in that quarter.

Amidst these discouraging circumstances, there was one bright, though distant gleam of comfort. Lieut. Shakespear, who had been deputed by Major Todd to Khiva, had succeeded in persuading the Khan Huzrut of that place to liberate all the Russian slaves in his country, and to issue a prohibitory order to his subjects against making any more slaves of that nation. The good people of England will perhaps regard this consummation as one of the happiest results of the campaign.

CHAPTER XVI.

CAUBUL.

Dost Mahomed Khan takes the field — Insurrections in his favour — He is defeated by Brigadier Dennie — Treachery and disaffection at Caubul and in Kohistan — Successful stratagem employed against Dost Mahomed — Activity of his partisans — Effect of his inflammatory appeals — Plot against the Shah — Operations against the Kohistan chiefs — The last effort of Dost Mahomed Khan — Dastardly conduct of the Second Cavalry at Purwan — Surrender of the ex-Ameer — Conversation between him and the Envoy — Person of the ex-Ameer — Effects of his surrender in the city — Cunning and finesse of the ex-Ameer.

In the meantime, rumours of Dost Mahomed's approach were being rapidly spread throughout the country, and indisputable evidence reached us of the fact that the ex-chief was in active correspondence with the three brothers, the triumvirate Sikh feudatories of Peshawer, who promised on the part of their superiors to supply him with the means of war.[83] Other letters were intercepted, regarding which it is needless to enter into any detail.

On the 5th of September, information reached Caubul that the whole country between Hindoo Koosh and the Oxus had risen in favour of Dost Mahomed, and that he was advancing towards Bamian with a powerful army. He made a show at Bajgah, where we had an advanced post, and from which it was deemed prudent to retire towards Bamian, which station it was considered necessary to strengthen by reinforcements from Caubul, though at the risk of leaving the capital insufficiently protected. So completely had the enemy closed up every source of intelligence, and so difficult was it to collect the least exact information of his whereabout, at the time, that Dost Mahomed actually slept about three miles from our camp at Bamian on the night of the 17th of September, and the first knowledge our troops had of his proximity was furnished next morning, by some hundreds of Uzbeks on the heights and others descending into the valley.

---

[83] The triumvirate consisted of Sultan Mahomed Khan, Peer Mahomed Khan, and Safeed Mahomed Khan; the principal jagheer was Kohat, which became a place of rendezvous, a focus of intrigue and sedition, for the Ghilzie rebel chiefs, who, compelled to abandon their own districts, took refuge there with their families, and, under the protection of the Dost's brothers, carried on their hostile designs against the Shah's authority. The Sikh government was supposed to be not a little implicated in these hostile proceedings, but on a strong representation being made by the British Government at the recommendation of the Envoy and Minister to the Lahore Durbar, the Ghilzie rebel chiefs residing at Kohat were delivered up, and they are now in confinement in the fort at Loodianah. The three brothers, too, have been dispossessed of their jagheers, which were so conveniently situated for carrying on a mischievous correspondence with the several districts of Affghanistan, and probably they may be otherwise provided for by the Sikh government in localities where they can do no harm. The snake has thus been not only scotched, but killed, in that quarter.

A small detachment, under Brigadier Dennie, immediately proceeded to oppose them, when, after driving them off to a considerable distance, he found, to his surprise, the whole of the confederated troops, amounting to several thousands, at the entrance of the defile which leads to Bamian. There was, however, no hesitation; the forward rush of our men was impetuous, and Dost Mahomed and his Uzbeks were soon completely routed, his scattered rabble being followed and cut up in pursuit by Anderson's Horse for several miles. The enemy lost his tents, baggage, kettle-drums, standards, and his only gun, the fellow to the small rifle one taken among others at Arghundee, and which he carried with him in his flight from thence to Bamian and Khooloom.

Dost Mahomed was encouraged to make this apparently bold advance by the assurances of spies that the Janbazes and other Affghans in the Shah's service, present at Bamian, would desert to a man — and one whole company did go over to him; but he shewed no disposition to dispute the ground, he and his son Afzul and the Walee retreating or rather dodging from behind one fort to another in succession, as our detachment pushed rapidly forward.

But there were dangers nearer home, which excited the most serious attention. The town of Caubul was full of traitors, and the Kohistanee chiefs, a powerful race, not forty miles from the capital, were known to be disaffected, though the greatest consideration and forbearance had always been shewn to them by the Shah. These chiefs were summoned to Caubul. The most of them obeyed the summons, but their object in doing so was merely to "spy the nakedness of the land," for it was ascertained that, immediately after they had bound themselves by the most solemn oaths of fidelity, they went to the house of one Hafiz-jee, a prime mover of sedition, and there took equally solemn oaths to devote their lives and property to the destruction of the Shah.

It became, therefore, of the greatest consequence to frustrate the secret as well as the open designs of our enemies in that quarter. Had Dost Mahomed Khan been able to make good his entry into the Kohistan at that moment, and to have got up an insurrection in the town of Caubul and the adjacent countries, our game with our handful of troops would have been, indeed, a desperate one. Great excitement prevailed everywhere. Our camp was about two miles from the Balla Hissar, and we had constantly an alarm that a night attack would be made upon us; picquets were strengthened, and a sharp look-out was kept, but nothing was attempted. In the Balla Hissar, artillery was placed, and the gates and magazine were doubly guarded. During the whole of September and October, the city continued in an extreme state of agitation; armed men in the streets, sharpening their swords at the cutlers' shops, looked fierce and threatening; and day after day a revolt was whispered to be at hand. Under such circumstances, no one could feel at ease. The Khizzilbashes and Affghans who had joined the Shah were in dismay, and with good reason, for should the conspiracy meet with even temporary success, their heads would have soon been severed from their bodies, or their bowels ript up, *secundum artem!*

The Kohistan is full of strong forts, and the chiefs could, on an exigency, have mustered forty or fifty thousand fighting men. But, happily, Dost Mahomed was distrustful of the Kohistanees; several of whose chiefs he had caused to be assassinated, under circumstances of the grossest treachery. Advantage was taken of this state of things, and the ex-chief was foiled with his own weapons in the following manner.

There was a notoriously active adherent of Dost Mahomed in the Kohistan, by name Sultan Mahomed. To this man a cunning messenger was sent, with instructions to say that he was on his road to join the ex-chief with verbal messages from certain inhabitants of Caubul, and that he would be the bearer of any letters that might be in trusted to him. The bait took, and Sultan Mahomed wrote a long letter to the ex-chief, naming to him all his supporters, and the parts they proposed taking in the forthcoming operations. This letter was brought to the Envoy and Minister; upon which a letter was prepared, as if from Dost Mahomed Khan, to the two chief conspirators in Caubul, named in the letters, asking their advice as to the course he should pursue. This bait also took; the parties addressed assembled all their brother-conspirators, and wrote a letter in their joint names to Dost Mahomed Khan, urging him to enter Kohistan at once, where he would find effectual support. This letter was not sealed, but authenticated by what in Affghanistan is termed *Nishans;* that is, each writer mentions some trivial circumstance only known to the writer and the party addressed, as thus:- "When I was riding out with you on such a day, or eating grapes with you at such a place, you praised my horse, and said you would give me one thousand rupees for it. If this really happened as I state it, then know that this letter is authentic."

When this treasure fell into the hands of the Envoy and Minister, a letter was prepared and despatched to Dost Mahomed, with all the *nishans,* exactly as in the genuine letter, but with advice of an opposite tendency. The ex-chief was warned not to think of entering the Kohistan, the chiefs of which place, he was assured, had entered into a solemn league with the Feringhees, for the sake of lucre, to seize and deliver him up, and, therefore, he was on no account to listen to their professions of friendship, however earnestly made. On the receipt of this document, Dost Mahomed Khan, as was subsequently ascertained, was sorely puzzled. "The hand was the hand of Esau," but how could he reconcile tbe advice with the almost unquestionable proofs of fidelity which he had received from the Kohistanees themselves? The effect of this letter was, that Dost Mahomed determined on advancing against our post at Bamian, where he met with the signal defeat already described.

Still the game was not lost; he had active partizans all over the country.

We have said that a whole company of the Affghan regiment had deserted to him, and his inflammatory missives amongst the bigoted population of Affghanistan had produced a most extensive and alarming effect. In the meantime, every possible precaution was taken to provide for the safety of the state at this perilous crisis. The guards over the citadel gates and magazines were further increased, and guns were mounted in the upper Balla Hissar, so as to command the principal avenues and streets of the town, whilst an active system of espionage was instituted, with a view to discover the plans of the conspirators, who were known to be meditating mischief.

The Shah was in the constant habit of repairing in the evening to a garden situated about two miles from the citadel. His road lay close under the fort of a chief named Mahmood Khan Byat, well known as an active adherent of Dost Mahomed Khan, and a plot had been laid that, on the occasion of the Shah's visit to the garden, a chosen band of two or three hundred men should rush out of this fort, seize his majesty, and convey him off to the Kohistan; whilst another band of ruffians, at the head of whom were two men of influence, named Agha Hussain and Nekoo Mamma, aided by the religious exhortations of the notorious Hafiz-jee, already mentioned, were simultaneously to raise an insurrection in the city. — "By the Lord," as Hotspur says, "a good plot as ever was laid; friends true and constant; a good plot, good friends, and full of expectation." But, by the advice of the Envoy, the Shah, on the plea of indisposition, refrained for a few days from paying his usual visit to the garden; and in the meantime, so well did his majesty concert the requisite measures, that the persons of all these conspirators were quietly secured. And, subsequently, the arch-intriguer Hafiz-jee himself was deprived of his power to do harm. The seizure of these men had a talismanic effect; and their followers, as is generally the case in Eastern conspiracies, became at once paralyzed and powerless.[84]

---

[84] Hafiz-jee is a younger son of Meer Waez, already mentioned as having released Shah Mahmood and others of the blood royal from prison in the early part of Shah Shoojah's reign, and his ambition has been to set aside his elder brother, and to be himself, like the Pope in Catholic countries, the head of the Affghan priesthood. His noiseless apprehension was another successful specimen of the tact of the Shah. Notwithstanding his known seditious practices, he was fully at large, and, like all others, regularly attended daily at the royal Durbar; he himself had no notion of being ever suspected. In conversation with Osman Khan, the minister, one evening, he said, as if conscious of innocence, and pretending to be above all worldly affairs: "These are wicked times; indeed, nothing but gross misrepresentation and malice on every side. Truly, it would hardly be surprising even if I, devoted as I am solely to spiritual matters, should be among the calumniated. Oh! that I was on a pilgrimage to Mecca, and away from the enemies that surround us!" Osman made no remark, but next morning related the interview to the king. A few days afterwards, his

Measures were next taken to chastise the treachery manifested by the Kohistan chiefs. A force proceeded against them, under Major-General Sir Robert Sale, who was accompanied by Lieutenant-Colonel Sir A. Burnes, in the capacity of political agent. Negotiation was soon found to be useless; the chiefs had previously broken the most solemn engagements of allegiance to the Shah, and intercepted correspondence had placed in full view the extensive confederacy that existed among them in favour of Dost Mahomed Khan, and the numerous difficulties he had to contend with. Our object, therefore, now was to destroy the strongholds which studded the valley, and the first that fell was Tootum-derrah, belonging to the insurgent, Ali Khan, a most violent promoter of the rebellion, although his father had been one of the victims of Dost Mahomed. The adjacent town was burnt to the ground.

Three other insurgent chiefs, terrified by this catastrophe, fled to the fort of Jool-gah, near Nijrow, distant about sixteen miles from Tootum-derrah. A rapid midnight movement enabled our troops to surprise the enemy, and surround that place at sunrise, on the 3rd of October. The rebels were hemmed in, but, fighting desperately, repulsed our attack on the breach, which unfortunately proved to be impracticable. They were not, however, disposed to await another attack, but stole away as soon as it was dusk. Jool-gah, too, was levelled with the ground.

Majesty sent for Hafiz-jee, and he immediately attended, unsuspicious of the smallest danger. "Hafiz-jee," said the Shah, "I hear that you are desirous of going to Mecca." "Me!" exclaimed the astonished Hafiz-jee, "me? not I! I do not wish to go to Mecca." "Oh yes, you do, you told me so," obserted the minister who was standing by. "But I was not in earnest," rejoined Hafiz-jee. "Oh, this is only your modesty," said the Shah; "you have not the means, you are poor. I see the delicacy of your situation; but I think the pilgrimage a very proper thing — extremely meritorious. Your sanctity will be increased, and your character made more venerable. I entirely approve of your determination; you have many enemies, and you will thus be saved from their malevolence; you shall have no difficulty about your expenses, I will defray them all." Hafiz-jee, finding himself entrapped, succumbed with a good grace, and he was kept in custody, but not treated as a prisoner. In a few days, the necessary preparations for his departure were completed, and Mehr Ali Khan, one of his bitterest enemies, but also a conspirator in favour of Dost Mahomed, was selected to convey him as far as Peshawer. Mehr Ali Khan himself, however, was not to be trusted, and the Envoy, well knowing this, to make all sure, sent a party of horsemen, called Janbaz, to accompany the cavalcade as an escort, but solely to look after Mehr Ali. All went on well, but the Janbazes had exceeded their orders, and kept a stricter look-out than was intended. On arriving at Peshawer, the political authority there, under the impression that suspicion attached to Mehr Ali, refused to let him return, till a reference had been made to Caubul. Hafiz-jee was safely passed on to Bombay in progress to Mecca; and when Mehr Ali was permitted to go back to Caubul, he was furious at the indignity he had received, but the Envoy had no difficulty in satisfying him that it was a mistake!

These results operated so powerfully on the minds of the three principal chiefs in Lower Kohistan, that they sent in hostages for their future loyalty and peaceable conduct, and remained themselves in the camp of Sir A. Burnes.

After the fight at Bamian, the Walee of Khooloom, who had been the chief supporter of Dost Mahomed Khan, was convinced of the hopelessness of his cause, and saved himself and his territory by a timely submission to the Shah. He concluded an agreement with Mr. P. B. Lord, our agent on the Toorkistan frontier, the chief condition of which was, that he renounced all connection with Dost Mahomed, who, now deserted by his Uzbek confederates, and afraid of being seized and given up for the promised reward of two lacs of rupees, retired precipitately on Ghoree, which commanded several defiles in the Ghorbund Pass, through one of which he meditated proceeding as a last venture into Kohistan. With his son Afzul, and a few followers, he made a detour towards Khinjan in the Pass, then to Purwan Tagow, and lastly to Nijrow, in Kohistan, where, as defender of the holy Mussulman Faith, he succeeded by cunning and incessant exhortations against infidels, and imputed defilers of the Koran, in collecting together a considerable number of adherents.

It was on the 11th of October that the information of his having actually arrived on the valley of Ghorbund was received in Lieutenant-Colonel Burnes' camp. He had required the surrender of the Shah's Governor of that place, who immediately fled and communicated the intelligence. This flight was productive of serious evil, for the people, seeing him abandon his post, became influenced either by alarm or the hopes of wholly avoiding the payment of their rents, at that time in the course of collection, and went over at once to the enemy. A company of the Kohistanee local corps was forthwith despatched into Ghorbund, which had the effect of compelling a change of place, and at day-break on the 13th, Dost Mahomed left the valley with only a few followers. Intelligence of this move having been received in camp, a body of Affghan cavalry, under a British officer, was sent in pursuit of him; but he had too long a start, and safely continued his rapid flight, without a moment's rest, till he arrived in Nijrow. The lateness of the season, and the inadequate strength of the force for such an operation, rendered any attack on that strongly-fortified valley impolitic; indeed, its localities had never been explored or seen by any European, and, therefore, a more practicable and efficient course was pursued.

Two other rebellious chiefs remained to be punished, Durwesh Khan of Bab-oo-koosh-kar, and Saif-oo-deen Khan of Kah-derra. Accordingly, on the 17th of October, the force proceeded against Bab-oo-koosh-kar, but the chief preferred flight to sustaining the attack, and took refuge in Kah-derrah. The fort of Bab-oo-koosh-kar was blown up. Kah-derrah was noted as a place impregnable, on account of its high walls of uncommon breadth, and of its fortified position. Negotiation was, therefore, tried, but in vain. About a thousand men were seen assembled in the gardens in front of the fort, and on the 18th they made a night attack on the camp from a ravine within forty yards of the picquets, and kept up a constant fire for nearly three hours, but without doing much damage. It was dark as pitch, and not a shot was returned, for nothing could be distinguished but the flashes of the priming. Next day, the garrison of about one thousand men were observed throwing up breast-works. On the 21st, the force advanced in three divisions, but almost as soon as this imposing movement was seen, the fort was evacuated, and the chief and his garrison fled to the hills. Kah-derrah was then set on fire, and burnt to the ground.

On the 22nd, the force advanced and took up a position at Akserai, to cover Caubul, as the activity of Dost Mahomed had gathered together, it was said, several thousand adherents, and he might attempt a surprise in that quarter. On the 27th, the Dost left Nijrow, and on the 28th was at Doornama. On the 29th, our force marched towards him, and halted at Baghi Alum, and, on the 1st November, to within twelve miles of his camp. He is reported to have had four hundred cavalry and four thousand foot, and as he proceeded, seized hostages from the principal inhabitants, to secure support and assistance. He moved on close under the hills, with great caution, gradually approaching nearer to the capital. He was now at Purwan, and, on the morning of the 2nd of November, our troops advanced direct upon the place, and arrived there, after a difficult march of about thirteen miles, at noon.

Lieutenant-Colonel Salter commanded the advance, consisting of a wing of H.M.'s 13th Light Infantry, two 6-pounders of the Shah's Horse Artillery, two squadrons of the 2nd Cavalry, Anderson's troop, two flank companies of the 37th N.I., and 1st company 27th N.I. Colonel Salter, as he approached, received information that Dost Mahomed with his army was endeavouring to retreat by a flank movement along the mountains, and the hills were covered with the armed people of Nijrow; the Dost himself and his horsemen descending the side of the hill. The two squadrons of the 2nd Cavalry were detached to intercept the fugitives — they moved up at a slow trot, but when Captain Fraser, commanding, called on them to charge, their pace was not quickened, and the urgent repetition of "charge!" "charge!" from the other officers, had no better effect. On approaching the enemy, they turned round, and leaving the officers surrounded and attacked, basely galloped back to the rear, and only stopped at Abbott's Battery, which when their flight commenced was advancing to support them.[85] Fraser and Ponsonby were severely wounded. Dr. Lord, the political agent, Lieutenant Broadfoot, Engineers, and Adjutant Crispin, of the 2nd Cavalry, were killed on the spot.

In the confusion produced by this deplorable event, Dost Mahomed escaped, whilst his infantry remained on the hill, waiting an attack; but nothing further was done on our part. Night came on, and with it the expectation of a descent on our camp; but it was afterwards found, that the enemy retreated the moment they had an opportunity of doing so unseen. They had probably discovered by that time that the Dost was not among them.

This was a most melancholy occurrence, and its probable consequence, as far as was then known or calculated, the rising *en masse* of the whole of Kohistan. This impression forced itself strongly on Sir A. Burnes. The Dost was supposed to have fallen back to Nijrow, and notwithstanding the punishment already inflicted on the chiefs by the signal destruction of their forts, it was apprehended that their hopes would be immediately revived by our disaster at Purwan. In this desponding spirit, justified no doubt by the pressure of circumstances, Sir Alexander Burnes wrote to the Envoy and Minister, and strongly advised that all the troops should be at once concentrated at Caubul, and there be prepared to resist the enemy. But happily the most melancholy forebodings, forced as they may be on the mind by disaster and disappointed hopes, are sometimes dispersed in an extraordinary way.

The event just recorded took place on the 2nd of November. On the evening of the 3rd, whilst taking his ride, the Envoy and Minister received the alarming communication made by Sir A. Burnes, which naturally produced in him a corresponding impression of gloom. He was, in this depressed state of mind, proceeding homewards, accompanied by two or three officers, and within fifty yards of the gate of his residence, when a horseman, passing his escort and the gentlemen with him, rode suddenly up to him, and said, "Are you the Envoy?" "Yes, I am the Envoy." "Then," rejoined the horseman, "here is the Ameer." "What Ameer? Where is he?" "Dost Mahomed Khan!" was the reply. The surprise, the amazement of Sir William Macnaghten at this announcement may be readily conceived, and in an instant afterwards, he beheld the very ex-chief himself alighting from his horse, and claiming his protection. The whole scene was truly electrical.

---

[85] In consequence of this dastardly conduct, the 2nd Regiment of Light Cavalry has been, by general orders of the Governor-General in Council, dated the 10th of February, 1841, struck off the list of the Bengal army. The two squadrons were dismissed with ignominy on arriving at Kurnal, and the remaining Native commissioned and non-commissioned officers and troopers of the corps drafted into the other regiments.

The Dost was requested to remount and ride on to the gateway, where both alighted. The Envoy then took his arm, and led him through the garden up to the house, saying, "Why have you persevered so long in opposing our views, and subjecting yourself to so much vexation and anxiety, aware as you must be of the good faith and liberality of the British Government, as well as of its power?" but his only reply was, in the true Asiatic spirit — "that it was his fate! he could not control destiny!" Arrived at the house, and seated in the very room where, a year before, he was "monarch of all he surveyed," the voluntary prisoner delivered up his sword into the hand of the Envoy, observing, that he had now no further use for it; but the Envoy, with becoming generosity, begged him to keep it.

I was at the Mission at the time, and the volubility with which the ex-Ameer conversed, and the remarkable self-possession he displayed under circumstances certainly embarrassing, surprised me. His first inquiry was after his family, and he almost immediately requested that a moonshee might be sent for to write some letters, which he dictated with precision and distinctness, correcting words, as the moonshee proceeded, like a man accustomed to business. These letters were to his sons. The first to Mahomed Afzul Khan, in Nijrow, requiring him to hasten forthwith to Caubul, he himself, he said, having been received and treated most kindly, most honourably. He had not his seal with him, and therefore, to satisfy his son of the authenticity of the letter, unbound a string from his waist, to which was fastened a small clasp-knife, which, he observed, would be recognized at once. He also dictated letters with the same view to his two sons, Azeem Khan and Sheer Ali Khan, who had made their escape from Ghizni on the 23rd September, and had taken up their quarters in Zoormut, in the fruitless expectation of collecting followers.

Having finished his despatches, he conversed freely, and in the most familiar manner, with the Envoy. His countenance, however, was haggard and care-worn, denoting the hardships he had undergone; but a bright eye animated his features, and diffused over them a rather pleasing expression. Yet I was disappointed in his general appearance, for report had presented to my imagination a very different man; tall, rather spare, and handsome. He is, on the contrary, robust, and large-limbed; his nose is sharp and aquiline; his eye-brows are highly arched, and his forehead falls back at a striking angle. His moustaches and beard are grey. They had not been dyed, he said, afterwards, from the time he quitted Caubul. The latter had been long and sweeping, but from want of proper attention during his imprisonment at Bokhara, and the late struggle, a great part of it had fallen off. "Why," said he to the Envoy, "they told me you were an old man; but I do not think so: how old are you?" "Nearly fifty." "Ah!" he replied, " that is just my age." But the Dost is nearer sixty!

He acknowledged to have been in the fight, but he had, he said, previously determined to surrender himself, and rode off with four horsemen, none of his adherents, whom he left, knowing whither he had gone, except Sultan Mahomed Khan; and we may fully believe his assertion, as the conduct of the two squadrons of the 2nd Cavalry, chased as they were from the field, had no effect in changing his mind. He doubled round our camp at some distance, passed along by unfrequented paths over the mountains and through the valleys, and after having been twenty-four hours on horseback, arrived at Caubul, between five and six o'clock in the evening. He cautiously avoided the city, pushed his beard under his chin, and held it there by a fold of his turban, which also half covered his face, to prevent being recognized. He passed near the new cantonments, and, by a fortunate concurrence of circumstances, he was not encountered by any of the Shah's people, from whom, assuredly, he would have had no mercy, but arrived, without the least interruption, in the neighbourhood of the Peshawer gate, at the time the Envoy was returning from his ride to the Balla Hissar. He followed at a distance, was challenged by the sentries at the gate; but declaring himself a courier, with despatches from the Kohistan, he was allowed to go on. He moved forward through the bazaar street, and by the new barracks, and then, well knowing every turn of the locality, despatched the horseman to announce his coming to the Envoy. The horseman was no other than Sultan Mahomed Khan, the notorious chief, who had long been stirring up the people of Nijrow to rebellion. He took the same opportunity of surrendering himself to the Envoy, and was allowed to accompany the messenger, to point out the place where Mahomed Afzul would be found. He did so, but remained in Nijrow, whilst Afzul came in immediately to Caubul.[86]

Dost Mahomed had not been long seated, when several of the Affghans belonging to the mission, and old acquaintances of the ex-chief, came into the room, *sans cérémonie,* and, demonstrating the "hail-fellow-well-met" system of the country, successively grasped his hands, and familiarly congratulated him on the wisdom of this last act. Moolah Ismut Ullah, Akkond-zadah, was eloquent in praise of the step that had been taken, and Sheer Mahomed, noted as the fleetest mounted messenger in Affghanistan, displayed equal gladness at meeting his old friend, and, with a strong pressure of the hand, equally applauded him for coming in. "Ah, Ameer, you have done right at last. Why did you delay putting an end to your miseries?" The cordiality of the meeting of these parties together was mutually expressed, and the Dost certainly

---

[86] He arrived on the 9th, and was then deputed to Ghizni, to bring on the women of the family.

looked like a man who had got rid of his difficulties, and accomplished an object calculated to secure his future peace and welfare.

The interview with the Envoy lasted about two hours, and Dost Mahomed was then handed to a tent pitched for him in the garden, and placed under a proper guard. The moolahs and other Affghans attached to the mission were directed to furnish him with refreshments, and Ismut Ullah and Sheer Mahomed were among the first to supply his wants. It was the month of Ramzan, during which period neither meat nor drink is touched, from sunrise to sunset, by a good Mussulman, and their evening repast was ready. The ex-chief partook of the meal with all the eagerness of a hungry man; conversed with good humour, and seemed satisfied that he had acted wisely in the course he had adopted. He also slept soundly, for the officer, who had posted himself near his tent, took an occasional peep at him during the night, and always found him in deep repose. Early next morning, the Soubadar of the guard announced to the officer a rather startling piece of intelligence, *viz.* that Dost Mahomed had called for his horse to take a ride. "To ride! perchance to fly — aye there's the rub." Convinced, however, that there was some mistake, the officer repaired to the Dost to inquire what was wanted, when he was told that his horse had not had any water for nearly four-and-twenty hours before he came in, and he wished to know if care had been taken of his "gallant steed." The answer was satisfactory, and the Ameer then rose, and heartily enjoyed his morning regale before sunrise.

More than a day had elapsed before a large proportion of the people in the city would believe that Dost Mahomed was actually in the Balla Hissar. They were sure that it was some artifice, some trick of the Feringhees, for most of them had so deeply involved themselves in treason, that they were afraid to think that such an event was possible. But the conviction, when it did come upon them, produced no result of an unfavourable tendency; on the contrary, all became quiet, and the city was totally free from the least trace of agitation.

In the meantime, Dost Mahomed continued in cheerful spirits; indeed, nothing was left undone that could contribute to his comfort or convenience. He early betrayed signs of being fond of good eating, and repeatedly inquired after a favourite cook, who was at that time employed by the Shah. His wardrobe, for he had nothing, of course, but the shabby clothes which covered him, was amply replenished with handsome apparel of all kinds; and amusing stories are told of his slyness and cunning in obtaining discount from the dealers, from money paid for the articles by the Mission! A more ingenious proceeding took place respecting the sword which he delivered to Sir William Macnaghten. When he was on his way to surrender himself, and had arrived near Caubul, he gave his own good sword in charge of an attendant, from whom he took a common one in temporary exchange, for the purpose of figuring in the scene which subsequently occurred. The sword was, as already stated, given back to him by the Envoy, and when Sir Alexander Burnes paid him his first visit, and the usual interchange of civilities on both sides was over, the Ameer warmly expressed a hope that all former differences between them would be forgotten, and that they would now be good friends again. With these sentiments he presented *the* sword to Sir Alexander, and, as customary, another was cordially given in return, to ratify the reciprocal good feeling. The sword presented by Burnes was of a superior description, whilst that of the Dost was worth only a few rupees! No doubt, the Ameer chuckled and exulted in the entire success of this double manœuvre.

CHAPTER XVII.

MARCH TO JELLALABAD.

Removal of Dost Mahomed Khan towards Hindoostan — Treated more like a guest than a prisoner — His conversation with the Author — Want of military resolution exhibited by the ex-Ameer and his family — Comments of Dost Mahomed on the state and prospects of Affghanistan — Ingratitude and intrigue the attributes of an Affghan — Treachery of Shah Zemaun — Character of Shah Shoojah — The Author's intercourse with him — Death of the Shahzada Akbar — His character — Popularity of the Shah's measures — His position difficult — Our policy to be directed by a cautious hand — Amount of sick in the Bombay and Bengal divisions.

On the 12th of November, Sir Willoughby Cotton, with part of the force under his command, moved from Caubul towards Jellalabad, to winter there, and Dost Mahomed was conducted by him so far, on his way to Hindoostan. The ex-chief was treated more like a guest than a prisoner. He was indulged in all he wished for, — horses, attendants; and the utmost respect was paid to his person on all occasions. About fifty armed Affghan horsemen were in his train, several of whom were with him at Purwan, on the 2nd of November. He is an incessant talker, and was exceedingly cheerful on the march. He had seen, whilst at Caubul, my drawings of the various interesting views in Affghanistan, and sketches of several individuals who had been remarkable in the late change of rulers; and one day, while riding along, he requested me to send them to him again, asking me at the same time if I could draw a good likeness of himself. "But," he added, "you must make my beard black. It is now much shorter than it used to be, for since my troubles began, no attention has been paid to it, and it has not been dyed." On our arrival at Jellalabad, I paid him a visit in his tent. He was then (27th November) in a gay dress, for the gaudiest colours meet with most favour in his sight. The fast of Ramzan was just over, and the festival of the Eed had commenced. There were at least forty persons sitting round him on carpets, — sons, nephews, and followers. In little more than three weeks, his haggard looks had disappeared, the effect, no doubt, of good living, for his culinary appliances were on a large scale. I took this occasion to make a sketch of him. He sat very patiently, seeming proud of the opportunity, and making inquiries every minute from the numerous Affghans who were looking over me about the progress of the drawing. When finished, all agreed that it was very like, (the bright yellow turban exciting much admiration!) and, on the sketch-book being handed to him, a small Affghan looking-glass, about three inches square, was brought for him to examine his own features in, and compare them with the drawing. The tiny glass could reflect little more than a nose or an eye at a time, but he twisted it about in all directions very gravely, and then said, looking at me, disappointed: — "You have not blackened my beard — you must make it black, quite black." But I excused myself on account of the original not being blackened. "I cannot dye it black now," he replied, "it belongs to the Envoy;" by which he meant; I fancy, if he meant any thing, that he was still in a sort of durance, and that, at least, till the journey was over, he could not alter its colour.[87] He then turned over the leaves of the sketchbook, and said to the gaping people assembled around him:- "This is Pokur, the banker[88]; this is Abdul Rusheed; *baráber,* 'exact.' This is Naib Mahomed Shureef; *baráber.* Here is Khan Sheereen Khan; *khoob, bisiar khoob, baráber.* And here is Gholam Hyder Khan, of Ghizni; and here Shums-oo-deen Khan[89] my son, and nephew *eech neest,* 'not a bit like.' Hajee Khan Kauker, *khoob ast,* 'very like.' In giving back the book, he added, with childish perseverance: — " You had better blacken my beard!" but I did not like to hazard the likeness by thus altering the character of the head.

Next day; the 28th November, his journey was resumed under a strong escort. At Peshawer he was joined by his family from Ghizni.[90]

---

[87] Not long afterwards, however, on the march to India, he conferred the usual honour on his beard, by dying it a glossy black.

[88] Pokur is a Hindoo, of the Shikarpore race, settled at Caubul; he had been useful to us, in advancing a large sum to an ally in the commencement of the campaign, on the faith of an inch square note that had been conveyed to him under the signature of Sir:A. Burnes. Dost Mahomed became acquainted with the circumstance, and put old Pokur in prison, but released him on his paying a fine of some thousand rupees. Pokur was of course reimbursed on our arrival at Caubul. There is a peculiarity about this genuine Hindoo Shylock. His jaws are locked, I never heard from what cause; and he can only receive his sustenance through the hole of an extracted tooth.

[89] Shums-oo-deen led the charge of cavalry at the fight of Jumrood, against the Sikhs. He was Governor of Ghizni, and removed to give place to Mahomed Hyder Khan, the Dost's son, who had held the situation about two years before the reduction of that fortress in July, 1839.

[90] The following document may amuse the reader:-

Received from Lieutenant Charles Burnes, in charge of the under-mentioned members of Dost Mahomed Khan's family, during the march from Ghizni to Peshawer,

Wives of Dost Mahomed		9
Younger sons		11
Sirdar Mahomed Afzul Khan	) grown up	1
Ditto Akran Khan	) sons	1
Wives of Afzul Khan		1
Ditto Akber Khan		3
Ditto Akram Khan		1
Ditto Azeem Khan		2
Ditto Sheer Ali Khan		1

It is worth while to look back at the feats of valour that have been displayed by the martial members of the Dost's family in the late campaign. Meer Afzul Khan sneaked out of Ghizni, waited in the neighbourhood till he saw the British flag flying over its turrets, and then ran off helter-skelter to Caubul, leaving his elephants, tents, and baggage behind him. Gholam Hyder, finding our troops had blown open the gate, instead of being an example of heroism to the garrison, took to flight, and ignominiously hid himself in a dark corner under the ramparts. Mahomed Akber, another son, on the approach of Colonel Wade and Shahzada Tymoor, in the Khyber Pass, also took to his heels, quitting his guns and baggage at Jellalabad and Gundumuk, in his flight to Caubul. The Dost himself and this same Akber, with the Walee of Khooloom, came down upon us as Bamian, and as our troops advanced against them, they all retreated rapidly, sheltering themselves successively under the walls of the forts which stud the country in that quarter. At Purwan, the ex-ruler appeared with a numerous force, horse and foot, and notwithstanding the misconduct of our 2nd Cavalry, abandoned the adherents who had been induced to assemble in his cause, "cast them off, as a huntsman does his pack," and ran off secretly, and surrendered himself to the Envoy and Minister at Caubul! This was at any rate discreet; and Falstaff says, "the better part of valour is discretion!" in the which better part he saved his life.

Dost Mahomed, during the march from Caubul to Jellalabad, on several occasions, felt himself competent to comment on the existing state of things, and the future prospects of Affghanistan. He recommended strongly the policy of taking the dominion of the country into our own hands. "The Suddozyes," he said, "had never been accustomed to obey, and never would

Ditto Hyder Khan	2
Daughters of the Ameer	7
Grandsons ditto	4
Granddaughters ditto	6
Sons of the late Mahomed Khan	2
Wives	4
Female slaves for the above	102
Male slaves and attendants	210
Relations	14
	381

P. NICOLSON, Lieut.
In charge of Ameer Dost Mahomed Khan.
Peshawer, Dec. 18, 1840.

On the original removal of the family from Caubul to Bamian, many slaves were left behind with their friends, and these all joined in progress to Peshawer, making an addition of 132, and the total 513!

obey, and by their intrigues under the anomalous sovereignty of Shah Shoojah, we should be involved in perpetual embarrassment. The only effectual mode of crushing them was to govern them in our own way. You will also find," he observed, "the very courtiers about the Shah, who have for years been fattening on your bounty, the most forward in plotting against you." And this, truly, is no great exaggeration. At the moment I am writing (December, 1840), the Shah has been actually assailed by the discontented, on the ground of his nothingness; and that the Feringhees are universally considered the rulers of the land. The short-sighted fools would be glad to get rid of us, never for an instant imagining that our presence is their only safety from another revolution. But intrigue and ingratitude are pre-eminently the attributes of an Affghan, of which the following is a striking instance.

At the time the Kohistan was still in agitation, a communication was intercepted, with the authentic seal of the blinded Shah Zemaun, who had been subsisting on our generosity and the kindness of Shah Shoojah for so many years. It was addressed to Sultan Mahomed Khan, the Barukzye Sirdar of Kohat, and ran laconically thus: — "The Feringhees have taken Affghanistan, and put Shah Shoojah on the throne. Do you, in co-operation with the Sikhs, proceed against them, and restore me to my kingdom." According to the system of *Nishan,* the bearer of the scrap was to enter into all the details of the plot. This is a prime specimen of monstrous perfidy and ingratitude in a man signally disqualified, from blindness, to be the ruler of an empire. On this occasion, the Shah observed: "You see what *sugs* (dogs) these Affghans are. Here is the hand of my own brother, whom I have fostered so long in my family, raised up against me. Aged, infirm, and blind, and still endeavouring to compass my destruction!"

Pronouncing Shah Shoojah to be one of the best men, if not the best, in his kingdom, may not be saying much, perhaps, with reference to the scale of moral government in European countries. But it is something to be superior to the members of his own community, though far removed from an equality with individuals of more civilized nations. Of kingly state he has, no doubt, a profound opinion, and of kings I can almost hear him say-

"There's a divinity doth hedge a king!"

With him, royalism is a rooted passion, and in etiquette, on public occasions, he is inflexible; for even when he was an exile and our pensioner at Loodianah,[91] ensconced in a corner on his throne, and playing the king there,

---

[91] It is a singular freak of fortune that the very house so long occupied by Shah Shoojah at Loodianah is now to be the allotted residence of Dost Mahomed Khan!

he would not allow the Political Agent to sit in his presence, and now even the Envoy and Minister is placed under the same prohibition or disqualification. But his practice is always to receive him standing, and he remains so, or walks about during the whole period of interview or conference, frequently of two hours' duration. At these interviews, he often stands for a long while in rather an amusing position, on one leg, the foot of the other being placed on the knee. It is the uncompromising feeling of royalism, and strict adherence to its forms (witness the cold ceremony on Shahzada Tymoor's arrival at Caubul from the Khyber campaign), which is so much disliked, and which fosters the notion, or perhaps affords the conviction, of his being arrogant and supercilious; but that is a mistake. Those who know him best speak highly of his temper and disposition, though it would not be unnatural if he had a spice of the Affghan in his nature. I can say little about him from my own personal experience, but that little may be worth stating.

I was requested by his majesty to visit his sick son Shahzada Akber, who had been some time in a precarious state. It was a little before dark when I first went to him, and he received me walking to and fro in the open square of the Harem Serai. The Pesh Khidmut in attendance had told me that it was unnecessary to uncover the head, and no ceremony was observed. I found the Shah was very much distressed on account of his son's illness, and he began the conversation with much affability, listened attentively to what was said on the subject of the disease, which was abscess of the liver, — asked me, as we walked together alone, what sort of food should be prepared for him, and in how many days he would be well. The Hakeems of the East are a sort of Brunonians, simplifying disease into two classes, and what Brown called Sthenic and Asthenic, they call hot and cold. The Shah, therefore, was anxious to know whether the prince's food should be of a hot or a cold description. On one occasion, he sent for me whilst sitting in public Durbar, which he holds in the open verandah already noticed, the Khans and officers of state standing in two rows at a right angle from the front of the building. I was conducted to the head of the line of courtiers, immediately under, and in front of, the verandah where the Shah was sitting. He then spoke to me in the same bland manner as before, and expressed great anxiety about the Shahzada, inquiring whether the change to Jellalabad was likely to be favourable to him or otherwise. The winter is severe at Caubul, and it had been customary, on that account, for the Court to remove to the former place, where the climate is temperate at that season of the year. On the 2nd of November, therefore, his majesty proceeded towards Jellalabad, accompanied by the 1st European Regiment, a squadron of the 2nd Cavalry, and one of his own corps. The head-quarters of the troops under Sir Willoughby Cotton also moved to Jellalabad. The Shahzada was carried in an easy palankeen, made as comfortable as possible, and he suffered no inconvenience from the march; but the progress of the disease was not to be checked. On the morning of the 9th we arrived at Nimlah. I went immediately to the Shah's tent, pitched in the once beautiful garden at that place, but now in a wild deserted state, and found the Shahzada still in his palankeen, and the king walking near him in great affliction. And good reason had he to be in affliction, for thirty years before he had lost his crown on that very spot, and now a favourite son was breathing his last. The youth had no pulse, and death was marked on his features. He died that day.

Akber was only nineteen, an excellent, interesting young man, of fine temper, and beloved by everybody. His anxiety to get back to his mother, the sister of Dost Mahomed Khan, at Loodianah, preyed upon his spirits, and the very mention of Loodianah, and the hope that he would soon be well enough to go there, used to light up his wasted countenance with the most pleasing expression. His remains were conveyed, attended by a numerous escort, to the burying-place on the Lughman range of mountains, about sixteen miles from Nimlah, called Zeearut-i-Mihter, Lamech, the father of Noah, traditionally said to have been buried there, and thence the reputed tomb is a shrine of the highest sanctity among Mahomedans.[92]

The Shah is well known to be a good Arabic scholar, and a poet of considerable merit. As a monarch, his aim is to dispense the strictest justice to all his subjects, tempered with mercy. He sits in Durbar every morning, except on a Thursday, for about two hours, and attends to the petitions or representations which may be made to him, and one day in the week is devoted to the hearing of appeals. He himself examines his revenue accounts, and is well acquainted with public business. At Candahar, the Shah gratified the people by an immediate abolition of many vexatious and burthensome imposts, which had been levied by the Barukzye chiefs, since the fall of the monarchy, amounting to a lac and a half of rupees per annum; and at Caubul he was equally prompt in removing or reducing all objectionable taxes, which had been imposed by Dost Mahomed Khan to a ruinous extent in the city. For these just and conciliatory measures he won "golden opinions from all sorts of people."

---

[92] In the *Asiatic Researches,* it is said that the tomb is about forty cubits in length, which was actually the stature of Lamech, according to tradition. Under it is a vault of the same dimensions, with a small door, which is never opened out of respect for the remains of this illustrious personage. They say that his body is in high preservation, and that he is sitting in a corner of the vault on his heels, with his arms crossed over his knees, and his head reclining upon his hands, a favourite posture among the inhabitants of India."— Vol. vi. p.480.

His position, however, is a difficult one; he is restored to an impoverished monarchy, without the means of either rewarding his old or satisfying his new adherents, the resources of the state having been nearly destroyed during a protracted period of tyranny and oppression. He also labours under another disadvantage; the power which raised him to the throne is the principal drawback on his popularity. It is difficult for the people rightly to comprehend the policy which influenced that measure. They can see nothing in our advance to Caubul but a scheme of conquest, and no denial can convince them that we are not now the masters and the controllers of the country. The applications and petitions constantly made to the Envoy and Minister, shew sufficiently the prevailing belief, and though he invariably refers them to the Shah, as the proper regal authority, they go away incredulous and disappointed. Jubbar Khan's taunting and plausible remark to the Shah at Ghizni will be remembered: "If you are to be a king, of what use are the English here? If the English are to be the rulers of the country, of what use are you in Affghanistan?" But Jubbar Khan well knew that the Shah could not have succeeded in the enterprise without our commanding aid, and his remark was merely an outpouring of personal hostility, occasioned by the fall of the Barukzye power and influence in the country.

The Shah has often observed — founded on the comments of others — that he is not looked upon "as the true king" — that the commanding authority is not wholly in his hands. This is no doubt true, and it cannot be otherwise, consistently with the principle upon which he was restored to the throne. We have ventured too far on the general question, connected with Indian as well as European policy, to risk a failure by delivering what we have gained into hands unequal to the task of compelling obedience among a turbulent people, so long accustomed to be their own masters. We *must* interfere in general policy, and thus preserve the country as a barrier, which it was our policy to make it. It would not answer our purpose to abandon the supremacy obtained for him, and act towards Affghanistan as the Allies did towards France, when Louis XVIII. was restored to the throne. The object in the two cases is essentially different. The Shah himself understands the present unavoidable state of things quite well, but it is the Khans about him, who would give the world to get rid of us, and therefore already harp upon the humiliating nature of our control and presence. The Affghans are the most bigoted, arrogant, and intolerant people imaginable, and they equally detest our interference, our customs, and our creed. They look upon us at once with dread and contempt; subdued and prostrate as they are by our power, they yet despise us as a race of infidels, and without one quality to warrant their being numbered generally among the class of civilized beings, they have nevertheless vanity enough to suppose that we have not sufficient penetration to detect or suspect their subterfuges and cunning, their doublings and deceit.

In conclusion, I concur fully in the opinion expressed by a competent judge, "that it is the duty of the British representative rather to watch carefully for opportunities of suggesting reform, and to treat his majesty with all possible consideration, than to urge sweeping innovations, or to assume towards him any thing like a tone of dictation. Such proceedings would reduce him to the condition of a cypher, and would afford to our enemies the means of successfully propagating reports to our prejudice, and to the effect that our design is to seize the government of his country." We know that the Envoy and Minister has on this principle invariably turned a deaf ear to all trifling complaints that have been brought to him, referring the complainants for redress to their lawful sovereign, deeming it of paramount importance to our interests that his majesty's authority should be felt and respected. There are doubtless numerous flagrant abuses to correct, and great reform required, both in his army, and in the financial arrangements — all of which can only be gradually accomplished — for "Affghanistan is not a country in which objects are to be attained *per saltum.* The Shah's wishes must meet with some consideration — the prejudices of the people must be respected — minor abuses must be overlooked, at least for a time, and our proceedings at every step must be guided by caution, temper, and forbearance."

One word more, professionally, but that shall be confined to results. Dr. Kennedy thus closes his narrative of the campaign in Sinde and Affghanistan:- "I may conclude by stating, that the summary of the history of nineteen hospitals of the force during the fourteen months, from November 1st, 1838, to December 31st, 1839, gives in the European hospital, cases treated, 4648; deaths, 273; and in the native hospital, cases treated, 7041; deaths, 135; which sufficiently indicates the hardships endured when compared with the strength of the division, and proves also that every branch of the hospital department was efficient."

The amount of sick and casualties in hospital in the Bombay division, during the campaign, being thus stated, it may be as well to offer a similar report of the hospital results in the Bengal division, that the sum total in both may be known. Cases treated in the Bengal European hospitals, 4471; deaths, 161; cases treated in the native hospitals, 12,249; deaths, 288. Dr. Kennedy's numerical statement gives nearly 6 per cent. of deaths among the Europeans, and 2 per cent. among the native troops, in fourteen months. But the Bengal division had only 3.75 per cent. of deaths among the Europeans, and 2.25 per cent. among the native troops, during the same period. The total number treated in hospital in the Bombay column was less than 12,000, but in the Bengal column nearly 17,000.

CHAPTER XVIII.

JOURNEY FROM AFFGHANISTAN, THROUGH THE PUNJAB, TO FEROZEPORE.

The Author leaves Jellalabad on his return to India — The Boorj, or Tope of Lala Beg — Ruins of an ancient city — Remains of antiquity — Jumrood — The Khyber Pass — Contrast between Sikhs and Affghans — Peshawer — Good effects of General Avitabile's severe administration — The splendour of his living — His hospitality — His improvementa in the city — Nowshera — The Afreedees — Crossing the Indus — Attok — Hussan Abdal — Shrine of Baba Nanak — Rawil Pindee — Coin-hawkers and coin-buyers — Manikyala — The Tope — Its style of architecture — Singular aspect of the plain — Rotas — The Jelum — The Chenáb — Wuzeerabad — The Author's Sikh escort — Encampment before Lahore — Arrival at the city — Insubordination of the Sikh army — Departure from Lahore — Arrival at Ferozepore.

The surrender of Dost Mahomed Khan having closed the great business of the campaign, I became desirous of quitting Affghanistan; and his Excellency the Commander-in-Chief, obligingly complying with my request to be relieved, and pointed me to a division of the army in India.

I left Jellalabad on the 15th of January, 1841. The route I had to take has often been trodden and described before, but it does not follow that every thing remarkable has been either seen or described, or described correctly. It is with reference to this consideration that I now venture upon adding to the preceding plain narrative, a brief account of scenes and objects which pressed upon my observation on the journey through the Khyber Pass and across the Punjab.

As I had to travel alone through a country still infested by banditti, I was escorted by ten horsemen called Janbaz, and twenty Khyber Rangers, in Shah Shoojah's service. The first was a short march, only seven miles, to Ali Boghan. Next day I rode twenty-two miles to Bursool, and on the 17th to Dakka, thirteen miles. The distance from thence to Lala Beg is sixteen miles. I had no previous information that Lala Beg possessed any point of interest, but when looking from the spot selected for my new ground, I observed about a mile off, close upon the road ahead, what seemed to be a watch-tower upon a lofty situation; and, inquiring of the villagers who had assembled round me its name, they told me it was a boorj, or tope, of great antiquity. As I had come on at a quick pace, my breakfast-tent had not arrived, and therefore, to occupy the time, I went immediately to view the novelty which had presented itself, and to ascertain what it was. Ghuree Lala Beg is a large stone building, erected on a high black rock, jutting over the road. The basement is square, sloping narrower upwards, of the Egyptian form. The sides are in the direction of the four cardinal points. Upon the basement is a lesser square, and above that, another, each about four feet high, and a third much higher, the facings of which are ornamented with pilasters, with bases and capitals, a plain cornice running over the whole. Above is a terrace, and from the middle of it a dome ascends, rather lofty in its proportions and somewhat conical. Only about half of its external form remains, the rest having tumbled down from age, leaving the inner structure, which is an irregular mass of materials, exposed. The summit is crowned with tufts of foliage, and also a round tower, built upon it a short time ago by a Khyber chief, named Ali Dad Khan, to overawe his neighbouring enemies, the situation commanding a pass. The dilapidations of the dome, leaving rough projections, enabled the Khyberees to ascend to the top and erect the tower, up to which a watchman, still stationed there, has now to scramble at the risk of his neck. The corners of the architecture are perfectly sharp and square, and the whole skilfully built. The stones forming the walls are not regular in shape or size, and the intervals are not filled up with lime, or other cement, but with horizontal lines of thin slate, the lengths nicely accommodated to the unequal spaces required to be adjusted, so as to preserve the rows accurate and level. The face only of the stones is chiselled and flat. On the north front are the ruins of a large flight of steps, leading to the terrace, from which the dome springs. The side walls shew that the steps were not continuous, but had three or four pretty wide landing places between the bottom and the top. On the south front, which overlooks the road, and where the foundation-rock is rather higher, an excavation has been made diagonally, downwards, through the lower part of the dome, to the centre. I passed to the bottom, but there was no chamber or recess, the whole being a solid mass broken through by some searcher after antiquities, and, from the appearance of the fracture, not long since. In constructing so huge a mass, it is clear, I think, that the builder must have been unacquainted with the art of forming an arch or hollow dome. Lime is the internal cement.

After I had examined the edifice on every side, difficult as the task was, owing to the height and uncertainty of footing over loose stones, I was told that an ancient city had existed contiguous to it, and that several images or idols *(b'hoots)* had been dug up from among the ruins. This added an exciting novelty to the adventure. A number of boys had followed me, and offered to bring me some if I wished; but not liking to depend upon any thing doubtful as to genuineness, I requested to be shewn the spot, and at about fifty yards down the slope of the rock they pointed out a succession of, apparently, foundations of buildings constructed like the tope, and covered with earth and loose stones, but not more than a foot or two above the ground. Within the area of these foundations, marks of previous excavation appeared, and I set the boys to work in places which had not been disturbed. In a short time, two small female heads were discovered — casts, in lime; two small hands fell to my own share, in digging, or rather poking the earth up with the end of my umbrella, and also many other portions of the human figure; but the material had become soft by being so long buried, and generally broke in raising it up. Several fragments of drapery, striped with red paint, were found; but as the boys had only their fingernails to work with, and the heat was becoming unpleasant, I delayed further excavation till the evening, and retired to my tent.

All the implements I could muster were a bill-hook and an axe, and before sunset I again went to the tope. In our renewed operations we came to a large figure, parts of which only could be removed. The drapery was stained red. But our career was suddenly stopped by a heavy shower of rain, which sent me back again to my canvass dwelling.

January 19.-Before resuming my march this morning, I revisited the site of the ancient city. Got up the cast of a colossal foot, of remarkably fine execution. The figure to which it belonged must have been at least ten feet high. The different parts were skillfully marked, and displayed a class of art much superior to the usual productions of Asiatic sculptors. This case of *ex pede Herculem* applied not only to dimensions, but style, and, referring to itself, there might have been good reason with some to suspect in it a Grecian leaven; but though the general character of the foot was correct, it had one peculiarity never to be seen in European sculpture: that of the nails being concave. That was conclusive; besides which, my next discovery was a Hindoo or Bhuddist female head, natural size, with all the usual characteristics of feature; the long eye, thick lids, angular profile, and full mouth. Certainly, there was nothing Greekish in these peculiarities. The head broke off from the neck in lifting it out of its bed. The hair was platted perpendicularly from the forehead, and tied in a knot on the crown. The lobe of the ear was much elongated, as if to represent its being dragged down by the weight of an ornament.

Until I met with these fragments, I was not aware that plaster *casts* were of such antiquity in this part of the world. In the large figures, the plaster is less than an inch in thickness, externally quite smooth, and the inner surface pretty even. I should have liked to dig up some more specimens, but I had not time. I, however, went over the greater part of the site of the supposed ancient city. The eminence immediately to the north of the tope is crowned with the remains of distinct buildings, constructed in the same way; the walls four feet thick, and the highest at present measuring about eight feet. Some of the rooms are twenty and thirty feet square, others small, and there are long passages between them. The ruins of this description extend for half a mile along the mountain side, on detached eminences and projections, and from the great number of idols found everywhere, the city might be supposed to have been a mart for images — the headquarters of paganism. The slope of the rock to the bottom is filled with ruins of stone-built houses, some of them on the frightful edge of a perpendicular mass. I observed below several square foundations, twelve feet by six, and four by six, parallel, and at a little distance from each other.

Coins have been found on the upper part of the tope, and I obtained a copper one from the keeper of the watch on the spot, thick, and an inch in diameter, but it is so much corroded, that neither inscription nor figure can be satisfactorily made out. Enough, however, may be distinguished to shew that it is a most rude production with respect to art. I did not hear of one having been dug up below.

Lala Beg is a new field for antiquarian pursuits, no account of it, I am told, having hitherto been published, and such extensive remains of stone edifices which would appear to have been places of residence and not temples, and in such a position, are well calculated to stimulate conjecture and speculation regarding the era of their erection, and the people by whom they were occupied.

This day's march brought me to Jumrood, the scene of the battle between Dost Mahomed Khan and Runjeet Sing, in 1837. The pass, in most parts, is very wild, narrow, and precipitous, with formidable jutting rocks, from which, by an expert enemy, detachments or travellers might be easily checked and destroyed. The defile near Ali Musjid is of this description. Emerging from the mountain, and descending to the plain, the fort of Futtyghur is seen in the distance, about six miles off. All is now flat towards Peshawer, and the difference of temperature from that of the hills is very considerable. My tent was pitched near the fort; and here a new world, contrasted with Affghanistan, opened upon me. The Sikh sepoys were making merry in sundry groups; dancing and singing, in their gay fantastic garments, beating tom-toms, and torturing the ear with "the wry-necked fife," beggars and fakeers in abundance. The Affghan dress is wide and loose, almost smothering the wearer; but the Sikh's pantaloons fit the leg to above the knee, with unwrinkled tightness, and his upper robes sit equally close to his body. He rejoiced too in a small turban, jauntily worn on one side. I was not sorry to get away from the tumult and clamour.

On the 20th, I reached Peshawer. Approaching the city, on a high spot of ground, by the side of the road along which we pass, a rather disgusting spectacle thrusts itself on the view: a lofty triangular gallows, with above a dozen criminals, in different stages of decay, dangling in the air; some suspended by the neck, and others by the heels, probably according to the nature of the crime of which they had been found guilty. General Avitabile, a native of Italy, is the Sikh governor of Peshawer, and when he was appointed; some years ago, to that post, the whole province was in a state of the greatest anarchy, and robberies and murders were of daily occurrence. By a system of uncompromising severity, founded on all active and impartial administration, exhibiting, too, *in terrorem,* the gibbeted felons in various public places, he has succeeded in establishing something like security in every part of his rule. He lives in good style, and is distinguished for his hospitality, which has been amply experienced and acknowledged by the British officers of the different regiments and convoys passing from India through Peshawer to Affghanistan, and from thence back to India. On every occasion, his table has been crowded with guests, and, according to Oriental custom, the sumptuous entertainments always concluded with a grand nautch, his figurante-company of Cashmeer women consisting of about thirty, singers and dancers, from the age of twelve to twenty-five.

I remained three days under the friendly roof of Captain Mackeson, the political agent at Wuzeeree Bagh, the news of a revolution at Lahore, in consequence of the disputed succession, after the death of Nou Nihal Sing, having thrown some doubt on the propriety of moving immediately in that direction. However, accounts were soon received of Sheer Sing's triumph, which dispelled the alarm previously felt, and enabled me to proceed, though I was strongly recommended to keep a good distance from the capital. At Peshawer, I had to discharge my Janbaz horsemen and the Khyber Rangers, who had served me faithfully and well; and the Chevalier Avitabile furnished me with another guard, of a havildar and eighteen Sikh long-bearded sepoys, armed with sword and matchlock, who were to attend me as far as Ferozepore.

The city of Peshawer has been greatly improved by Avitabile. Many rows of houses, forming narrow streets, have been pulled down, and large open bazaars erected on their site, and various other changes made for the general good. The work of destruction and renovation is daily going on, and in a few years, with the same zeal and exertion on the part of the governor, Peshawer will become an airy commodious city.

On the 23rd, I resumed my march with my new escort. At Pubbee, I came up with twenty-five Sikh horsemen, who had accompanied one of our convoys to Peshawer, and were returning to Lahore, and who had been directed by the political agent to join my party on the march, and afford me better protection through the Punjab.

At Nowshera, on the 24th, I took a walk alone in the afternoon, up the neighbouring hill, to see the country all round; but I was presently followed by four of the Sikh guard, armed, who cautioned me against ever venturing so far unattended. Avitabile had ordered them, they said, to be on all occasions ready at my side, to protect me whenever I might walk out, as the Afreedee mountaineers often came down and committed great havoc on man and property; and certainly several instances have occurred of a murderous band starting upon unwary travellers as unexpectedly as the clansmen of Roderick Dhu. Between the Khyber Pass and Peshawer, the Afreedees were in the constant habit of rushing down from their hills, and plundering and wounding the Sikh villagers, till Avitabile erected a line of towers and guard-houses, which have had a good effect in controlling the depredations of the mountaineers in that quarter. They now, therefore, often venture farther to the eastward; but my party was so strong, that nothing unpleasant occurred. At the close of the day, the Sikhs in a body kept looking anxiously to discover the new moon. At last its thin curve was seen, and then all simultaneously closed their hands in prayer. They were always most regular in their devotions.

At Akora, not far from my tent, the villagers were preparing a circular reservoir for water. The circle was about fifty yards in diameter. To effect their purpose, a pair of bullocks were yoked to a sort of plough-scoop, which they dragged up from the centre, carrying along the collected earth to the circumference line, and there depositing the loads, which by repeated accumulations formed a high ridge. Six of these plough-scoops were hard at work, diverging from the same centre, and in three days the reservoir was to be completed. The villagers, assisted by their women, were singing merrily all the while.

On the 26th, I made a long march of nineteen miles, to Shumsabad. Crossed the Attok over the bridge of boats, twenty-seven in number, fastened together. The slope from the westward to the river is gradual and sandy; but the left or eastern bank is steep and craggy and took some time to ascend. The loaded camels went by a different but circuitous route. At the time of passing the river, the sun had newly risen, and was behind the lofty range of rock and fortifications, so that the whole prospect visible below was in a mass of shadow, giving the fortress, of mixed Mahomedan and Hindoo architecture, and its surrounding scenery, a tranquil and solemn appearance. The stream was rather rapid, and did not seem to be more than one hundred and fifty yards wide. Descending eastward, no part of the fortress can be seen, on account of the high rocks left behind, and the road below becomes perfectly level.

The Sikh officer, in command of the twenty-five horsemen, informs me, tidings from Lahore to-day mention that the whole army has joined Sheer Sing, and that he was besieging the city. On the 27th, at Boorhan, further news. A battle had been fought near the Delhi gate, Lahore, between the Ranee's people, and the supporters of Sheer Sing, in which a thousand men were killed, and the old woman taken prisoner. Sheer Sing, it was added, had mounted the throne.

The march to Hussan was mostly through jungle. My tents are on the banks of a clear rivulet. One of Baba Nanuk's shrines is at this place, and the reputed mark of his hand on a white stone is held in great veneration. The attendants on the spot are singing, or rather roaring, and beating tom-toms, all day; the noise and clatter, most stunning to the ear, bearing, perhaps, some proportion to the degree of sanctity conferred on the old devotee, who is said to have resided at Hussan Abdal about a year. I was shewn a sacred tank of exquisitely transparent water, constantly renewed from a spring, in which a great number of fish, about a foot long, are kept and daily fed by the ministering priests. The stone upon which appears the hand-mark, black as if received from a hand covered with pitch or black paint, is about twelve inches above the surface of the water. There are several ruins of splendid mosques and tombs at Hussan Abdal, apparently of the time of Shah Jehan.

On the 29th, I marched to Janee-ka-Sung. At about a third part of the way, we passed over a wide stone causeway with a parapet, crossing a ravine, then thickly wooded, called Mar-gullee. My guard informed me that a great battle had been fought there in former days between the Sikhs and Mahomedans, and that ten thousand of the latter had been killed on that very spot, which is now known by the name of *Mar-gullee*, or the 'defile of slaughter.' The causeway answers a double purpose; it commemorates the event, and also makes a convenient passage over the ravine. It may be about three hundred yards in length, but the clumsy pavement affords a very insecure footing for horses Affghan-shod.

On the 30th, I arrived at Rawil Pindee. This place contains several thousand houses, and has an extensive bazaar, full of people, and full of traffic. Hindoostanee only is spoken now. The house, which was erected by Shah Shoojah, and in which he and his family resided so long, has not much the appearance of a royal abode. It is of small dimensions, and stands in the town surrounded by hovels. Rawil Pindee is a famous place for old coins, and no sooner is a tent pitched, than the dealers make their appearance with their little bags of the money of ancient days. A coin-hawker brought me a large quantity for sale. He had sold some, he said, and copper ones too, for eight and ten rupees apiece. When he found that I was indifferent about the store he possessed, for he had nothing of any value, he fell into an inquiring mood, and asked me, in a confidential way, why the Feringhee gentlemen gave such large prices for bits of copper. He thought it very strange. When I told him that coins pointed out the names of kings, and in some degree the history, of former times, and that thence they were deemed valuable by those who found delight in studying the changes of governments and countries, upon which coins alone remain to throw any light, he sagaciously observed that, such being the case, he hoped to have a good and speedy market for his collection. He had already sold an immense number. The demand had been great, for individuals, who had never seen a Greek letter before, had become decypherers of Greek names, and those of Menander, Apollodorus, or Eucratides, as familiar as the shillings and sixpences[93] of the present day.

On the 1st of February, I started early for a double march to Manikyala, nineteen miles. We are descending gradually, and the hot weather is coming fast upon us. Passed Hurmuk at the ninth mile, and soon after Robât-ke-Serai, now only the mouldering remains of an extensive building for the accommodation of travellers. From this place I first saw the dome of the Manikyala tope, on the extreme line of the horizon. Mr. Elphinstone's account of it, and the subsequent

---

[93] *Editor's note*: Britain's currency before 1971 consisted of twelve pennies to the shilling, and twenty shillings to the pound.

discoveries, had made it an interesting object, and I gazed upon it almost with as much pleasure as when I had the first glimpse of St. Peter's, at Rome, from Baccano, the dome only, as in the present case, being visible from that point, and the effect in that respect similar. On my arrival at Manikyala, I found my breakfast-tent near the tope, the mighty fabric standing alone in solemn majesty; and it was no slight gratification to contemplate, at my morning meal, its mysterious grandeur, after a march of so many hundred miles down the left bank of the Indus, through Bhukker, Shikarpore, Candahar, Caubul, Jellalabad, and Peshawer, where little else is to be found but meagre mud buildings, or edifices "of no mark or likelihood," excepting the beautiful Minars at Ghizni, and the solitary remains at Lala Beg. Considering its magnitude and its evident antiquity, grand and imposing as it is, on an extensive plain, which has hardly any thing to break its flatness, I do not think the tope has been hitherto sufficiently described. It has, indeed, been only cursorily noticed, and more interest felt about what it might contain of coins and relics, than its exact external form. On this point I will adduce two extracts.

"On the 6th of March" (1832), says Sir Alexander Burnes,[94] "We reached the village of Manikyala, at which there is *a singular tope or mound of masonry*. It has been described by Mr. Elphinstone, who gives a correct drawing of it, and tells us that 'it was, indeed, as like Grecian architecture as any buildings which Europeans, in remote parts of the country, could now construct by the hands of unpractised native builders.'"

"The tope is a circular building," says Major Hough, in 1839.[95] "It is about sixty or seventy feet high from the top of the mound to the top of the building, whose circumference is three hundred and seventy-five feet. It is arched over; the outer coating is of plain hewn large stones; the inside is of a rough stone and mud; there is a well in the centre. The stones are all polished. It is erected on a mound, about twenty or twenty-five feet high; a flight of steps[96] lead you to the top of the building."

But the *mound,* upon which it is supposed to be built, is merely the accumulation of earth and stones since its erection, almost entirely burying the lower story, which is raised upon a massive basement. At the first view, it is, I think, evident that only a part of the building is above ground, that is, above the *débris,* for it looks like a round dish-cover, all dome, as in Mr. Elphinstone's engraving, shorn of its fair proportions, which would indicate a ruder age than that in which it would appear to have been constructed. Dome, indeed, is not the correct term, as that word implies an arch or hollow within, and the Manikyala tope, as well as

---

[94] Travels into Bokhara, vol. ii. p. 56.
[95] Narrative of the March and Operations of the Army of the Indus, p. 341.
[96] A mistake: it is only the broken stones that have that appearance.

the one at Lala Beg from all that has been ascertained, is an entirely solid mass. The belt or girdle of pilasters seems to have given rise to a notion of the work being of Grecian mould; but a pilaster *per se* does not authorize such a conclusion, as pilasters are common in Hindoo architecture. Mr. Elphinstone's drawing is, I think stated to have been done from recollection, which accounts for the particular form of the pilaster not being preserved. At a distance, the belt appears to be formed of a succession of superficial or false arcades, owing to the length of the abacus, which, with the ornamented part of the capital or acanthus, nearly joins the next to it, making the upper part, between, look like an arch. I do not remember to have seen the elongated abacus anywhere, excepting in the drawings of the excavated Hindoo temples at Ellora, which, like that at the tope, is more than double the width of the capital, whilst the Greek abacus and top of the acanthus are nearly of the same measurement. Neither is the base of the pilaster at all of the Grecian order. Regarding the workmanship, the abacus is well formed, and the acanthus seems to have been highly ornamented with grotesque heads and flowers; but they are so much corroded and broken, that no distinct shape can well be traced. The entire height of the pilasters is four feet ten inches, and the distance from each other about the same. Above this belt is another, a plain one, with a moulding along the upper part of it, over which the dome ascends. At the base of the pilasters is a surrounding terrace, sixteen feet wide, never before noticed, and now on a level with the upper part of the accumulated *débris*. Under this is a lower story, about twelve feet high, part of which only has been exposed on the north-east side, and from which the form and character of the building is now ascertained. The pilasters of the lower story are six feet high, with triple bases. Thus, instead of the tope being like a round dish-cover, we find it is of a highly classical description, and in general outline displaying tiers, lessening from the bottom, not very unlike the mausolea of the ancient Romans. The mausoleum of Augustus was an ornate edifice of this kind. The dome, it must be remembered, is not a mark of Grecian architecture; it belongs to Rome, and the oldest mentioned in history is said to he that of the Pantheon. But the Roman dome is vaulted.

I examined the ground carefully all round, and on the east side discovered the remains of a broad flight of steps leading up to the terrace, similar to the one at Lala Beg, on a grand scale: I could find no trace of any other. The outer surface of the tope is formed of enormous hewn stones, admirably fitted, constituting a sort of shell, about three or four feet thick, without cement, at least I could not detect any. A great part of this outer shell has tumbled down, and the edges left have become stepping-stones, by which it is now easy to ascend to the top. The inner part consists of huge rough stones regularly laid with mud as an intermediate material, and the whole is one solid mass, with the exception of a hollow shaft about twelve feet square from the summit down the centre, which was discovered by General Ventura in 1830,[97] but filled up with stones and earth.

One of my servants walked round the building at the foot of the belt, along, but not including, the terrace, at a measured pace, and the circumference was thus

---

[97] To those who are curious in antiquarian lore, the following enumeration of relics discovered will not be uninteresting. General Ventura is a French officer in the service of the Sikh government:- "He commenced the excavation on the 27th April, 1830, at, the very bottom of the cupola, on the south side, where, having met with nothing but loose materials, the work was discontinued. On the 28th the cap of the cupola was laid open, and, at the depth of three feet, six medals or coins were discovered. On the 1st of May, at the depth of twelve feet, a square mass of masonry was found exactly in the centre of the building, and regularly formed of quarried stone in good preservation. On piercing ten feet into this, a medal was found in the middle of a clod of earth. At the depth of twenty feet, a silver coin and six copper coins were met with. On the 8th the workmen came to a box of iron (probably copper), which was broken by a stroke of the pick-axe. In this box was a smaller one of pure gold, with an ornamental top. It contained one medal of gold, weighing 122 grains — a gold ring, set with a pale sapphire stone, having characters engraven on it, apparently Pehlevi — a small bit of pale ruby, three very small silver coins, a thin silver Sassanian coin, similar to those so frequently met with in Persia, weight 60 grains, and several others. On the 12th, the perforation had reached thirty-six feet, when another copper coin presented itself. On the 22nd, as it was imagined nothing more would be found in the centre of the cupola, on account of the termination of the square building (or shaft), an opening was made on the northern side, of the height of six feet, and twelve broad; the excavations were pushed forward at both points. On the 25th, a depth of forty-five feet had been attained, when, on lifting up a large quarried stone, another similarly squared stone was found underneath, having in its centre a round hole, in which lay a copper box; the lid was decayed. Inside the box was found a little piece of cloth, a circular crystal drop, and a small cylinder of pure gold. On the 27th, at the depth of fifty-four feet, another copper coin was turned up. On the 29th, at the depth of sixty-four feet, a copper ring and a courie *(cypræa moneta)* were found. On the 31st May, the General discovered, under an immense stone slab, a small chamber or basin cut into the solid stone, a foot in breadth and depth, in which were found a cylindrical box of copper 9½ inches by 4½, filled with a brown compound liquid, and within this box and liquid, a brass cylindrical box, cast and turned on the lathe: the surface of the metal in excellent preservation. The lid fitted perfectly tight, and must have kept in, without loss by evaporation, another portion of the thick brown liquid with which it was found to be filled. Within the brass cylinder, and buried in the brown liquid, appeared a gold cylindrical box, 4 inches by 1½ in diameter. This box again was filled with thick brown liquid mixed up with fragments supposed to be broken amber, of a light yellow colour. In this box a small gold coin, 30 grains weight, was discovered. On the 8th of June, the opening perforated from above met that from the side, and reached the earth beneath the foundation. The setting in of the rains finally obliged the General to discontinue his operations." — *Journal of the Asiatic Society of Bengal,* vol. iii.

Adverting to the brown contents of the several boxes remaining in a fluid state so many years, I may remark that in the Royal Museum at Naples is the bronze cock of a reservoir, discovered at Capreæ during the excavations which were made in the palace of Tiberius. Time having firmly cemented the parts together, the water in its cavity has remained hermetically sealed during seventeen or eighteen centuries. I have seen this curious piece of antiquity, and on shaking it, heard the splashing sound of the contained fluid.

shewn to be about four hundred feet. The height from the terrace does not seem to be nearly equal to the diameter, but may be estimated at about eighty feet.

In considering the construction of the two topes — that of Lala Beg and Manikyala — they do not appear to be the work of the same people. With respect to form, the dome of Lala Beg is more conical. The belt, with its plain pilasters, is square, and the mass of masonry which forms the basement, sloping upwards and inwards, is also square. Lime is employed in the dome, but, in the walls and in the adjacent ruins, lines of slate fill up the interstices between the stones, which are only chiselled on the outer surface. The tope at Manikyala is wholly circular; no lime, apparently, used in its construction, and the parts are fitted with the nicest art. For instance, the skill of the artist is strikingly shewn in the perfect manner in which the stones are put together, so as to make the pilasters a part of the solid wall. It is a wonderful production, and the bringing to the spot, and the raising up, and the placing, of such immense blocks of stone with such accuracy, gives us no mean idea of the scientific resources which the builders of that age must have possessed. Antiquarian speculation has not yet decided for what express purpose the tope of Manikyala was built, nor, from an examination of the coins and relics discovered, to what era it belongs. By some it is supposed to be a tomb, by others a temple dedicated to the gods of pagan times. I may resume this subject at another time.

The march on the 2nd was from Manikyala to Perhano, two miles beyond Pukkee-Serai, across the Kassee river. Leaving Manikyala, the road is traversed by flat masses of rock, which ring under the horses' feet. The whole distance this day was a succession of deep ravines and eminences, all of earth, formed into the most fantastic shapes imaginable, and the vast plain on all sides seemed to be interspersed with cities, the lights and shadows produced by the slanting sun on the different masses of rifted ground, giving them at a distance the semblance of houses, towers, spires, and pinnacles, in infinite variety. I looked round with wonder, and I could not help thinking it the spectral representation of what the country might once have been, concluding, in my imaginings, that the tope at Manikyala could not be other than merely a part of a magnificent whole. The prospect in the evening had a rich landscape effect, and in the view to the west, looked like the calm, blue sea, with an unbroken line of horizon.

I was at Tamiaka on the 3rd. At this place one of the men with me was killed by the bursting of a new Rawil Pindee match lock. My next march was to the village of Chikore, thirteen miles and a half. At nine miles, Bakerala, from whence the army route goes by Udeerana, which runs off at an angle to the right along the dry, sandy bed of a stream. The short cut is over the hills to the left, but it is unfit for a wheeled carriage; and my escort took me that way. But it is a most difficult one even for horses and camels, precipitous and dangerous; rocky ledges having to be got over constantly, with craggy acclivities and steep descents, till within half a mile of Chikore, which stands on a large open plain.

On the 5th, passed what was once a splendid Serai, with gay cupolas at the four corners, one of the great public benefactions by which the Moghul monarchs rendered the line of march through the Punjab convenient and comfortable. It is situated about two miles from Rotas. The fortress of that name, built on the spur of a mountain, by Sheer Shah, with its numerous mosques and lofty battlements, has an imposing effect from below. The usual route is round the extreme point of the mountain on the left, and across the Kassee river; but we rode straight forward, ascended the acclivity by a narrow path up to the fort, passing by the great gateway; then over an extensive burying-ground, full of tombs, and down a precipitous defile, the dark and towering bastions on our right, till we descended into the bed of the Kassee, where, looking back, Rotas, like Attok, was wholly shut out from our view by perpendicular piles of mountains. The distance from Rotas to the Jelum, the Hydaspes of the Greeks, is twelve miles. I passed through the town, which is not very remarkable for cleanliness, but much less of a stable than those I had been accustomed to see. The Jelum, close under it, is a broad, beautiful stream, and plenty of boats were ready at the ferry to convey travellers and their baggage-camels across: I had not to wait a moment. Elephants cross over at the ford a mile higher up, where the water is not more than belly-deep.

Speculations on the ancient site of Alexander's Nicæa or Bucephalia, said to have been situated on the banks of the Hydaspas, would be a useless labour. In upwards of two thousand years, many cities may have been built along the Jelum and destroyed, and the extensive remains of buildings now visible, may belong to extinct towns of a comparatively modern date. Yet it is soothing and gratifying to the traveller to imagine that he can trace, with precision, the route of Alexander, and the cities he founded. But "the way of an eagle in the air, the way of a serpent upon a rock, and the way of a ship in the midst of the sea," were "too wonderful" for Solomon; and at this time of day, the exact remains, or even the site, of Alexander's cities in the Punjab, may be equally classed among the untraceables.

My tents are on the left bank, about a hundred yards from the Jelum, the first *fruit* of which is a fine large fish, two feet long. Had a consultation with Ghyan Sing, the officer in charge of the Sikh horsemen, respecting the route to be taken from this point; that laid down and pursued by our troops and convoys running to the southward of Lahore, whilst the direct road through Lahore is much nearer. Then the revolution there! Ghyan Sing's information led him to conclude that it was all over, and Sheer Sing universally acknowledged as the sovereign of the Punjab. By his persuasion, and the pleasing prospect of sooner completing my journey, I determined on the road through Lahore. Ghyan Sing, notwithstanding the orders he had received at Peshawer, proposed setting off immediately to look after his own affairs at the capital, where, by long marches, he expected to arrive in three days, leaving twenty of his horsemen to proceed at a convenient rate with me. Before starting, he requested to be favoured with a couple of bottles of brandy! following the enticing example of old Runjeet, in his devotion to ardent spirits. In the evening, the cheerful voices of the people in groups were heard distinctly across the river; children noisy at play, and the sound of our bugle was echoed most perfectly along the opposite shore.

Passed through Bhyrwal, Khasspore Serai, and arrived at Goojrat on the 8th. The town of Goojrat is much larger than that of Rawil Pindee. The kar-dar, or governor, is Rajah Golab Sing. The houses are very neatly built with a small red brick, and the population numerous. The police officer has just given me the comfortable assurance that Goojrat is notorious for thieves, and therefore recommends a strict look-out at night. *That* was never forgotten.

The country from Goojrat to the Chenab, the Acesines, is a perfect flat. We came to that magnificent river at the fifth mile, then passed along the right bank, bending south-west about a mile and a half to the ferry, through heavy sand more than fetlock-deep. The ferry is at a narrow part, and not near so wide as the Jelum; the depth ten feet. From thence to Wuzeerabad, the distance is about three miles, two-thirds of the way heavy sand. Formerly, the river ran close by Wuzeerabad, which is situated on high ground. The town has been considerably altered and improved by General Avitabile, who was kar-dar, or governor, of this district before he was appointed to Peshawer. The walls of the gateways were covered over with Hindoostanee paintings, hundreds of figures, durbars, nautches, and hunting scenes. The streets are wide, and the pavement formed of bricks placed edgeways in various compartments and shapes, sloping down to the middle, and leaving a horizontal passage two feet wide for a drain. The public road runs through Wuzeerabad, which enabled me to see at once, as I passed along, how much good Avitabile had done in demolishing the narrow filthy streets, and, by constructing large squares for bazaars, giving lungs to the city. From Wuzeerabad to Tonkul, the country all round is as beautiful as a perfect flat can be; well stocked with villages, and trees in picturesque groves of varied tint and form.

On the 10th, I was a mile to the eastward of Gujrawala. Passed Myut Khan-ke-kote, Nutt, and Lakenwala. The surface flat all the way. Numerous villages on either hand, and the whole expanse full of cultivation. The road leads through Gujrawala. Muneer on the 11th. On arriving at the ground, the Jemadar, left by Ghyan Sing in charge of the mounted guard, asked permission to go on to Lahore with his horsemen, recommending me at the same time to remain where I was, as it would be most dangerous for me to proceed without a passport from the minister, and stating that the army encamped near the capital was completely disorganized, and under no control. I reminded him that Ghyan Sing had directed him to attend me to Lahore, and declined interfering by giving him any orders.

He said, but very respectfully, that he did not consider himself under Ghyan Sing, or anybody else, and went away. I then sat down to breakfast, and was soon after informed, that the cavalcade had actually set off to Lahore. I was rather uneasy under the impression that, at this ticklish time, some of the horsemen might turn robbers, and back upon us, in the night, on the succeeding marches, with the alacrity of faithless Affghans. But the Havildar of the infantry guard, furnished by Avitabile, came forward, and assured me there was no danger in going on, the misrepresentations of the Jemadar and his men being merely an excuse to get away to Lahore at once about their own affairs. I, however, wrote immediately to General Ventura and Captain Lafant, and despatched the letters by a swift messenger, requesting them to favour me with their advice, and such assistance as they might deem necessary on the occasion, intimating my intention of moving forward next day to Baminwala, which would take me to within ten or twelve miles of Lahore.

At nine A.M. on the 12th, I arrived at Baminwala. My servants, having started very early with my breakfast-tent, overtook some of the horsemen who had left me, and who again warned them against going through Lahore. Still no answer from General Ventura or Lafont, in consequence of which I prepared to strike off directly south next morning, and get into the route sanctioned for our troops, by which I should be well clear of the capital. And yet travellers, on foot and horseback, were constantly passing by my tent from Lahore, from whom I could collect nothing to alarm. Men, loaded with parcels from India for Affghanistan, were trotting along, without having received the least interruption, and about thirty mounted Affghans, who had followed Dost Mahomed, were on their return home, halting close by me: they had passed through Lahore in perfect safety. Notwithstanding which, I engaged a guide to cross us over the southward next morning. In the evening, at sunset, whilst strolling near the village and settling with the guide about the route, I was surprised by the sudden appearance of a number of sepoys quickly advancing amidst clouds of dust towards my tent, which produced some apprehension among the people round me. They proved to be a Jemadar and twenty-four grenadier sepoys, sent by the Maharajah Sheer Sing, as a guard, with a letter from Captain Lafont, informing me that the said sepoys would conduct me in safety to his house.

On the 13th, I took with me twelve of the new, and six of the old guard, leaving the rest to accompany the camels and baggage. Road through grass-tuft jungle most of the way. At the seventh mile, came to Shahdurra, formerly a large and populous town, where stands the noble mausoleum of Jehangeer, with four lofty minars at the corners of an immense quadrangle, each side measuring six hundred yards and in the usual Mahomedan style. The Ravi (or Hydraotes) flows close to it. Passed along a westerly bend of the river for about a mile, and then came to the ferry. The width of the river here is about the same as the Chenab.

Lahore full in view; nearest is the Musjid Shahee, a magnificent building. Moved right upon it, and rounded the north-east side of the fort, containing the royal palaces, of great extent. These were on the right; on the left, an encampment as far as the eye could reach; the tents of every shape and colour, forming to me a wonderful and splendid sight, which it was worth undergoing some little annoyance to witness. My Lahore guide magnified the number of troops to a hundred thousand; but I was afterwards told that about thirty thousand was the amount. I passed on betwixt this numerous host and the city, meeting constantly crowds of horsemen, in their bright yellow silk dresses, armed to the teeth, and others on foot, all of most haughty and unpleasant aspect; but the guard and I kept "the noiseless tenor of our way," appearing to look neither to the right nor to the left, and delighted I was when I got, without difficulty, under Lafont's hospitable roof, and still more so when, in a few hours more, all my servants and camels arrived safe with the baggage. They had come on without the smallest hindrance, or a word being spoken to them.

My letters to General Ventura and Lafont did not reach them before the afternoon of the 12th. Captain Lafont was just entering the Durbar at the moment they arrived, and he lost no time in communicating to Sheer Sing the misconduct of the horsemen. The Maharajah immediately ordered fifty others to be sent off, and the minister accordingly directed an officer present to command them. But there was no subordination among the troops; every man did as he liked, and the officer declared that he had no power, for not a single individual would obey him. This, too, at the foot of the throne! Sheer Sing, hearing what was said, then appointed a young Jemadar standing near him, whom he had just promoted for good conduct, to take twenty Mussulman grenadiers to Baminwala, and escort me to Lahore. They set off without delay, and arrived, as already stated, at sunset.

On the afternoon of the 14th, Sheer Sing inspected a part of the disorderly army; the line extending, I was told, about two miles. The regiment Lafont commanded was paraded in front of the barracks, at a short distance from his house. As soon as they were ordered to march, they all broke loose, like boys rushing out of school, and each took his own course, running or walking, dragging or carrying his musket, as he pleased. In the evening, I looked out for their return, rather suspicious that something disagreeable might have occurred, and at dusk I saw them scampering back in the same loose and scattered manner, shouting and laughing all the way. At the inspection, there was said to be a deplorable falling off in numbers. On the 12th, Colonel Courtland's regiment had seven hundred present. On the 13th, they received their pay, and at the inspection, on the 14th, only three hundred men were mustered. The remaining four hundred had taken themselves off to their several homes and families, without leave, carrying along with them all their accoutrements! The commanding officer told me they would all be back again in a few days; but at the existing crisis, temporizing was the Maharajah's only course, and nothing would be done or said to them on their return. Other corps acted in the same way, and all authority was set at nought. Their indignation, however, seemed to be chiefly directed against the native officers and regimental moonshees; several of the latter they put to death in the streets, for rapacious exactions, and wringing from the poor soldier unjust contributions from his pay. These inflictions created no pity. The troops were all in favour of Sheer Sing, regarding him highly for his courage and martial character; but scenes occurred at the Durbar repeatedly, under his own eye, of the most tumultuous and disorderly kind. He is said to drink freely, though not to such an excess as his father Runjeet. But, however much he may indulge in deep spirituous potations, he certainly has, at a period of extreme difficulty, had all his wits about him, in managing such an immense military rabble as that by which he is surrounded.

This unsettled state of things prevented my accepting the offered kindnesses of General Ventura, who resided at a considerable distance, so that I saw less at Lahore than I expected; and going into the city, amidst strife and rebellion, would have been something like plunging into the Roman Curtius's gulf of destruction.

On the 15th of February, I left Lahore, with some addition to my Peshawer guard, and in the evening more men joined me, by order of the Maharajah, for my better security. On the 16th I was at Kussoor. On the 17th I crossed the Sutlege, near the spot where I had embarked for the campaign, on the 16th of January, 1839, right glad to be again in the Honourable Company's provinces. At Ferozepore, I dismissed the Chevalier Avitabile's long-bearded guard, with a very grateful feeling, for they had been most attentive and useful to me during the whole of the long march from Peshawer.

CAWNPORE, *March 10th, 1841.*

APPENDIX.

CAPTURE OF GHUZNEE.

The following are the official documents referred to in p. 106:-

Report from his Excellency Lieutenant-General Sir John Keane to the Governor-General of India.

Head Quarters, Camp, Ghuznee, 24th July, 1839.
To the Right Honourable Lord Auckland, G.C.B., &c., &c.
My Lord:

I have the satisfaction to acquaint your Lordship, that the army under my command has succeeded in performing one of the most brilliant acts it has ever been my lot to witness, during my service of forty-five years, in the four quarters of the globe, in the capture by storm of the strong and important fortress and citadel of Ghuznee, yesterday.

It is not only that the Affghan nation, and I understand Asia generally, have looked upon it as impregnable, but it is in reality a place of great strength, both by nature and art, far more so than I had reason to suppose from any description that I had received of it; although some are from officers from our own service, who had seen it in their travels.

I was surprised to find a high rampart, in good repair, built on a scarped mound, about thirty-five feet high, flanked by numerous towers, and surrounded by a *fausse braye* and a wet ditch, whilst the height of the citadel covered the interior from the commanding fire of the hills from the north, rendering it nugatory. In addition to this, screen walls had been built before the gates; the ditch was filled with water, and unfordable, and an outwork built on the right bank of the river so as to command the bed of it.

It is therefore the more honourable to the troops, and must appear to the enemy out of all calculation extraordinary, that a fortress and citadel, to the strength of which, for the last thirty years, they had been adding something each year, and which had a garrison of 3,500 Affghan soldiers, commanded by Prince Mahomed Hyder, the son of Dost Mahomed Khan, the ruler of the country, with a commanding number of guns; and abundance of ammunition and other stores, provisions, &c., for a regular siege, should be taken by British science and British valour, in less than two hours from the time the attack was made, and the whole, including the Governor and garrison, should fall into our hands

My despatch of the 20th inst. from Nannee, will have made known to your Lordship that the camp of his Majesty Shah Shoojah-ool-Moolk, and of Major-Gen. Willshire, with the Bombay troops, had there joined me, in accordance with my desire; and the following morning we made our march of twelve miles to Ghuznee. The line of march being over a fine plain, the troops were disposed in a manner that would have enabled me at any moment, had we been attacked, as was probable from the large bodies of troops moving on each side of us, to have placed them in position to receive the enemy. They did not however appear, but on our coming within range of the guns of the citadel and fortress of Ghuznee, a smart cannonade was opened on our leading columns, together with a heavy fire of musketry from behind garden walls, and temporary field-works thrown up, as well as the strong out-work I have already alluded to, which commanded the bed of the river. From all but the out-work the enemy were driven in, under the walls of the fort, in a spirited manner, by parties, thrown forward by Major-Gen. Sir W. Cotton, of the 16th and 48th Bengal N.I. and H.M.'s 13th Light Infantry under Brigadier Sale. I ordered forward three troops of Horse Artillery, the camel-battery and one foot-battery, to open upon the citadel and fortress by throwing shrapnel shells, which was done in a masterly style, under the direction of Brigadier Stevenson. My object in this was to make the enemy shew their strength in guns, and in other respects, which completely succeeded, and our shells must have done great execution and occasioned great consternation. Being perfectly satisfied on the point of their strength, in the course of half an hour, I ordered the fire to cease, and placed the troops *en bivouac*. A close *reconnoissance* of the place all round was then undertaken by Captain Thomson, the chief Engineer, and Captain Peat of the Bombay Engineers, accompanied by Major Garden, the Deputy Quarter-Master General of the Bengal army, supported by a strong party of H.M.'s 16th Lancers, and one of H.M.'s 13th Light Infantry. On this party, a steady fire was kept up and some casualties occurred. Captain Thomson's report was very clear (he found the fortifications equally strong all round), and as my own opinion coincided with his, I did not hesitate a moment as to the manner in which our approach and attack upon the place should be made. Notwithstanding the march the troops had performed in the morning, and their having been a considerable time engaged with the enemy, I ordered the whole to move across the river (which runs close under the fort walls), in columns to the right and left of the town, and they were placed in position on the north side, on more commanding ground, and securing the Cabool road. I had information that a night attack upon the camp was intended from without. Mahomed Ufzul Khan, the eldest son of Dost Mahomed Khan, had been sent by his father with a strong body of troops from Cabool to his brother's assistance at Ghuznee, and was encamped outside the walls, but abandoned his position on our approach, keeping however at the distance of a few miles from us. The two rebel chiefs of the Ghilzie tribe, men of great influence, *viz.* Abdool Rhuman and Gool Mahomed Khan, had joined him with fifteen thousand horse, and also a body of three thousand Ghazees from Zeinat under a mixture of chiefs and Moolahs, carrying banners, and who had been assembled on the cry of a religious war. In short, we were, in all directions, surrounded by enemies. These last actually came down the hills on the 22nd, and attacked the part of the camp occupied by his Majesty Shah Shoojah and his troops, but were driven back with considerable loss, and banners taken.

At daylight on the 22nd, I reconnoitred Ghuznee, in company with the chief Engineer, and the Brigadier commanding the Artillery, with the Adjutant and Quarter-Master-General of the Bengal Army, for the purpose of making all arrangements for carrying the place by storm, and these were completed in the course of the day. Instead of the tedious process of breaching (for which we were ill prepared), Captain Thomson undertook, with the assistance of Captain Peat, of the Bombay Engineers, Lieutenants Durand and MacLeod, of the Bengal Engineers, and other officers under him (Captain Thomson), to blow in the Cabool gate (the weakest point) with gunpowder; and so much faith did I place in the success of the operation, that my plans for the assault were immediately laid down, and the orders given.

The different troops of Horse Artillery, the camel and foot batteries, moved off their ground at twelve o'clock that night, without the slightest noise, as had been directed, and in the most correct manner, took up the position assigned them, about two hundred and fifty yards from the walls; in like manner, and with the same silence, the Infantry soon after moved from their ground, and all were at their post at the proper time. A few minutes before three o'clock in the morning the explosion took place, and proved entirely successful. Captain Peat, of the Bombay Engineers, was thrown down and stunned by it, but shortly after recovered his senses and feeling. On hearing the advance sounded by the bugles (being the signal for the gate having been blown in), the Artillery, under the able directions of Brigadier Stevenson, consisting of Captain Grant's troop of Bengal Horse

Artillery, the camel-battery under Captain Abbott, both superintended by Major Pew, Captains Martin's and Cotgrave's troops of Bombay Horse Artillery, and Captain Lloyd's battery of Bombay Foot Artillery, all opened a terrific fire upon the citadel and ramparts of the fort, and in a certain degree paralyzed the enemy.

Under the guidance of Captain Thomson of the Bengal Engineers, the chief of the department, Colonel Dennie, of H.M.'s 13th Light Infantry, commanding the advance, consisting of the Light Companies of H.M.'s 2nd and 17th Foot, and of the Bengal European regiment, with one company of H.M.'s 13th Light Infantry, proceeded to the gate, and with great difficulty, from the rubbish thrown down, and the determined opposition offered by the enemy, effected an entrance and established themselves within the gateway, closely followed by the main column, led in a spirit of great gallantry by Brigadier Sale, to whom I had entrusted the important post of commanding the "storming party," consisting (with the advance above mentioned) of H.M.'s 2nd Foot under Major Carruthers, the Bengal European regiment under Lieutenant-Colonel Orchard, followed by H.M.'s 13th Light Infantry under Major Tronson, and H.M.'s 17th Regiment under Lieutenant-Colonel Croker. The struggle within the fort was desperate for a considerable time; in addition to the heavy fire kept up, our troops were assailed by the enemy sword in hand, and with daggers, pistols, &c.; but British courage, perseverance and fortitude overcame all opposition, and the fire of the enemy in the lower area of the fort being nearly silenced, Brigadier Sale turned towards the citadel, from which could now be seen men abandoning their guns; running in all directions, throwing themselves down from immense heights, endeavouring to make their escape, and on reaching the gate, with H.M.'s 17th under Lieutenant-Colonel Croker, followed by the 13th, forced it open. At five o'clock in the morning, the colours of H.M.'s 13th and 17th were planted on the citadel of Ghuznee, amidst the cheers of all ranks. Instant protection was granted to the women found in the citadel (amongst whom were those of Mahomed Hyder, the Governor), and sentries placed over the magazine for its security. Brigadier Sale reports having received much assistance from Captain Kershaw, of H.M.'s 13th Light Infantry, throughout the whole of the service of the storming.

Major-General Sir W. Cotton executed, in a manner much to my satisfaction, the orders he had received. The Major-General followed closely the assaulting party into the fort with the "reserve," namely, Brigadier Roberts with the only available regiment in his brigade, the 35th N.I. under Lieutenant-Colonel Monteath; part of Brigadier Sale's brigade, the 16th N.I., under Major McLaren, and 48th N.I., under Lieutenant-Colonel Wheeler; and they immediately occupied the ramparts, putting down opposition wherever they met any, and making prisoners until the place was completely in our possession. A desultory fire was kept up in the town long after the citadel was in our hands, from those who had taken refuge in houses, and in desperation kept firing on all that approached them. In this way, several of our men were wounded, and some killed; but the aggressors paid dearly for their bad conduct in not surrendering when the place was completely ours. I must not omit to mention that the three companies of the 35th N.I., under Captain Hay, ordered to the south side of the fort, to begin with a false attack, to attract attention to that side, performed that service, at the proper time, and greatly to my satisfaction.

As we were threatened with an attack for the relief of the garrison, I ordered the 19th Bombay N.I., under the command of Lieutenant-Colonel Stalker, to guard the Cabool road, and to be in support of the cavalry division. This might have proved an important position to occupy; but as it was, no enemy appeared.

The cavalry division under Major-General Thackwell, in addition to watching the approach of an enemy, had directions to surround Ghuznee and to sweep the plain, preventing the escape of run-aways from the garrison. Brigadier Arnold's brigade (the

Brigadier himself, I deeply regret to say, was labouring under very severe illness, having shortly before burst a blood-vessel internally, which rendered it wholly impossible for him to mount a horse that day), consisting of H.M.'s 16th Lancers, under Lieutenant-Colonel Persse (momentarily commanding the brigade and Major McDowell, the junior major of the regiment, the senior major of the 16th Lancers, Major Cureton, an officer of great merit, being actively engaged in the execution of his duties as Assistant Adjutant-General of the Cavalry Division), the 2nd Cavalry under Major Salter, and the 3rd under Lieutenant-Colonel Smyth, were ordered to watch the south and west sides. Brigadier Scott's brigade were placed on the Cabool road, consisting of H.M.'s 4th Light Dragoons, under Major Daly, and the 1st Bombay Cavalry, under Lieutenant-Colonel Sandwith, to watch the north and east sides. This duty was performed in a manner greatly to my satisfaction.

After the storming, and that quiet was in some degree restored within, I conducted his Majesty Shah Shoojah-ool-Moolk, and the British Envoy and Minister, Mr. Macnaghten, round the citadel, and a great part of the fortress. The king was perfectly astonished at our having made ourselves masters of a place conceived to be impregnable, when defended, in the short space of two hours, and in less than forty-eight hours after we came before it. His Majesty was of course greatly delighted at the result. When I afterwards, in the course of the day, took Mahomed Hyder Khan, the Governor, first to the British Minister, and then to the king, to make his submission, I informed his Majesty that I had made a promise that his life should not be touched, and the king in very handsome terms assented, and informed Mahomed Hyder, in my presence, that although he and his family had been rebels, yet he was willing to forget and forgive all.

Prince Mahomed Hyder, the Governor of Ghuznee, is a prisoner of war in my camp, and under the surveillance of Sir A. Burnes; an arrangement very agreeable to the former.

From Major-General Sir W. Cotton, commanding the 1st Infantry Division (of the Bengal Army), I have invariably received the strongest support, and on this occasion his exertions were manifest in support of the honour of the profession and of our country.

I have likewise at all times received able assistance from Major-General Willshire, commanding the 2nd Infantry Division (of the Bombay Army), which it was found expedient on that day to break up, some for the storming party, and some for other duties; the Major-General, as directed, was in attendance upon myself.

To Brigadier Sale I feel deeply indebted for the gallant and soldier-like manner in which he conducted the responsible and arduous duty entrusted to him, in command of the storming party, and for the arrangements he made in the citadel, immediately after taking possession of it. The sabre wound which he received in the face did not prevent his continuing to direct his column until every thing was secure; and I am happy in the opportunity of bringing to your Lordship's notice the excellent conduct of Brigadier Sale on this occasion.

Brigadier Stevenson. in command of the Artillery, was all I could wish; and he reports that Brigade Majors Backhouse and Coghlan ably assisted him: his arrangements were good, and the execution done by the arm he commands was such as cannot be forgotten by those of the enemy who have witnessed and survived it.

To Brigadier Roberts, to Colonel Dennie (who commanded the advance), and to the different officers commanding regiments already mentioned, as well as to the officers and gallant soldiers under them, who so nobly maintained the honour and reputation of our country, my best acknowledgements are due.

To Captain Thomson, of the Bengal Engineers, the chief of the department with me, much of the credit of the success of this brilliant "*coup-de-main*" is due: — a place of the same strength, and by such simple means as this highly talented and scientific officer recommended to be tried, has perhaps never before been taken; and I feel I cannot do sufficient justice to Captain Thomson's merits, for his conduct throughout: in the execution he was ably supported by the officers already mentioned, and so eager were the other officers of the Engineers of both Presidencies, for the honour of carrying the powder-bags, that the point could only be decided by seniority, which shews the fine feeling by which they are animated.

I must now inform your Lordship, that since I joined the Bengal column in the valley of Shawl, I have continued my march with it in the advance, and it has been my good fortune to have had the assistance of two most efficient staff officers, in Major Craigie, Deputy Adjutant-General, and Major Garden, Deputy Quarter-Master-General. It is but justice to those officers, that I should state to your Lordship the high satisfaction I have derived from the manner in which all their duties have been performed up to this day; and that I look upon them as promising officers to fill the higher ranks. To the other officers of both departments I am also much indebted for the correct performance of all duties appertaining to their situations.

To Major Keith, the Deputy Adjutant-General, and Major Campbell, the Deputy Quarter-Master-General, of the Bombay army, and to all the other officers of both departments under them, my acknowledgments are also due, for the manner in which their duties have been performed during this campaign.

Captain Alexander, commanding the 4th Local Horse, and Major Cunningham, commanding the Poonah Auxiliary Horse, with the men under their orders, have been of essential service to the army in this campaign.

The arrangements made by Superintending Surgeons Kennedy and Atkinson, previous to the storming, for affording assistance and comfort to the wounded, met with my approval.

Major Parsons. the Deputy Commissary-General in charge of the department in the field, has been unremitting in his attention to keep the troops supplied, although much difficulty is experienced, and he is occasionally thwarted by the nature of the country and its inhabitants.

I have, throughout this service, received the utmost assistance I could desire from Lieutenant-Colonel Macdonald, my Officiating Military Secretary, and Deputy Adjutant-General, H.M.'s forces, Bombay; from Captain Powell, my Persian Interpreter, and the other officers of my personal staff. The nature of the country in which we are serving prevents the possibility of my sending a single staff officer to deliver this to your Lordship, otherwise I should have asked my Aide-de-Camp, Lieutenant Keane, to proceed to Simla, to deliver this despatch into your hands, and to afford any further information that your Lordship could have desired.

The brilliant triumph we have obtained, the cool courage displayed, and the gallant bearing of the troops I have the honour to command, will have taught such a lesson to our enemies in the Affghan nation, as will make them hereafter respect the name of a British soldier.

Our loss is wonderfully small, considering the occasion: the casualties in killed and wounded amount to about 200.

The loss of the enemy is immense; we have already buried of their dead nearly 500, together with an immense number of horses.

I enclose a list of the killed; wounded; and missing. I am happy to say, that although the wounds of some of the officers are severe, they are all doing well.

It is my intention, after selecting a garrison for this place, and establishing a General Hospital, to continue my march to Cabool forthwith.—I have, &c

    (Signed)   J. KEANE,
                        Lieutenant-General

List of killed, wounded, and missing in the army under the command of Lieutenant-General Sir J. Keane, before Ghuznee, on the 21st July, 1839.

2nd Troop Bengal H. Artillery — 3 horses wounded.
3rd do. Bombay   do. — 2 rank and file, 2 horses wounded.
4th do. do.   do. — 1 horse killed.
2nd Regiment Bengal Cavalry — 1 horse killed, 1 rank and file wounded.
4th Bengal Local Horse — 1 rank and file and 1 horse missing.
H.M.'s 13th Light Infantry — 1 rank and file killed.
16th Bengal N.I. — 1 captain wounded.
48th do. do. — 1 lieutenant and 2 rank and file wounded.
Total killed — 1 rank and file and 2 horses.
Total wounded — 1 captain, 1 lieutenant, 6 rank and file, and 5 horses.
Total missing — 1 rank and file and 1 horse.

                        Names of officers wounded.

Captain Graves, 16th Bengal N.I., severely
Lieutenant Van Homrigh, 48th Bengal N.I., slightly.

    (Signed)   R. MACDONALD
                Lieut.-Col. Mil. Sec., and Dep. Adj.-Gen
                      H.M.'s Forces, Bombay

List of the killed, wounded, and missing in the army under the command of Sir J. Keane, K.C.B. and G.C.H., in the assault and capture of the fortress and citadel of Ghuznee, on the 23rd July, 1839.

General Staff — 1 colonel, 1 major wounded.
3rd Troop Bombay Horse Artillery — 1 rank and file and 1 horse wounded.
4th do. do.   do. —1 rank and file and 1 horse wounded.
Bengal Engineers — 3 rank and file killed, 2 rank and file wounded, 1 rank and file missing.
Bombay do. — 1 lieutenant, 1 rank and file wounded.
2nd Bengal Light Cavalry — 1 rank and file wounded.
1st Bombay Light Cavalry — 1 havildar killed, 5 rank and file, and 7 horses wounded.
H.M.'s 2nd Foot (or Queen's Royal) — 4 rank and file killed, 2 captains, 4 lieutenants, 1 serjeant, and 26 rank and file wounded.
H.M.'s 13th Light Infantry — 1 rank and file killed, 3 serjeants, and 27 rank and file wounded.
H.M.'s 17th Foot — 6 rank and file wounded.
Bengal European Regiment — 1 rank and file killed, 1 lieutenant-colonel, 1 major, 2 captains, 4 lieutenants, 1 ensign, 1 serjeant, 51 rank and file wounded.
16th Bengal N.I. — 1 havildar, 6 rank and file wounded.
35th do. do. — 5 rank and file killed, 1 havildar, 8 rank and file wounded.
48th do. do. — 2 havildars killed, 5 rank and file wounded.
Total killed — 3 serjeants or havildars, 14 rank and file.
Total wounded — 1 colonel, 1 lieutenant-colonel, 2 majors, 4 captains, 8 lieutenants, 2 ensigns, 7 serjeants, or havildars, 140 rank and file, 8 horses.

Total missing — 1 rank and file.

Grand total — On the 21st and 23rd July, killed, wounded and missing, 191 officers and men, and 16 horses.

    (Signed) R. MACDONALD
    Lieut.-Col. Mil. Sec. And Dep. Adj.-Gen.
    H.M.'s Forces, Bombay.

Names of Officers killed, wounded, and missing.

General Staff — Brigadier Sale, H.M.'s 13th Light Infantry, slightly; Major Parsons, Deputy Commissary General, slightly.

Bombay Engineers — 2nd Lieutenant Marriott, slightly.

H.M.'s 2nd Foot (or Queen's Royal) — Captain Raitt, slightly; Captain Robinson, severely; Lieutenant Yonge, severely; Lieutenant Stisted, slightly; Adjutant Simmons, slightly; Quarter-Master Hadley, slightly.

Bengal European Regiment — Lieutenant-Colonel Orchard, slightly; Major Warren, severely; Captain Hay, slightly; Captain Taylor, slightly; Lieutenant Broadfoot, slightly; Lieutenant Haslewood, severely; Lieutenant Fagan, slightly; Lieutenant Magnay, slightly; Ensign Jacob, slightly.

    (Signed) R. MACDONALD
    Lieut.-Col. Mil. Sec. And Dep. Adj.-Gen.
    H.M.'s Forces, Bombay.

Report from Captain Thomson, the Chief Engineer. The accounts of the fortress of Ghuznee, received from those who have seen it, were such as to induce his Excellency the Commander-in-Chief to leave in Candahar the very small battering train then with the army, there being a scarcity of transport cattle. The place was described as very weak and completely commanded from a range of hills to the north.

When we came before it on the morning of the 21st July, we were very much surprised to find a high rampart in good repair, built on a scarped mound about thirty-five feet high, flanked by numerous towers, and surrounded by a *fausse braye* and a wet ditch. The irregular figure of the *enceinte* gave a good flanking fire, whilst the height of the citadel covered the interior from the commanding fire of the hills to the north, rendering it nugatory. In addition to this, the towers at the angles had been enlarged; screen walls had been built before the gates; the ditch cleared out and filled with water (stated to be unfordable), and an outwork built on the right bank of the river, so as to command the bed of it. The garrison was stated variously to be from three to four thousand strong, including five hundred cavalry. From subsequent information we found that it had been over-rated.

On the approach of the army, a fire of artillery was opened from the body of the place, and of musketry from the neighbouring gardens. A detachment of Infantry cleared the latter, and the former was silenced for a short time by shrapnells from the Horse Artillery. But the fire from the new out-work on the bank of the river was in no way checked. A nearer view of the works was however obtained from the gardens which had been cleared. This was not at all satisfactory; the works were evidently much stronger than we had been led to anticipate, and such as our army could not venture to attack in a regular manner with the means at our disposal. We had no battering train, and to attack Ghuznee in form, a much larger train would be required than the army ever possessed. The great height of the parapet above the plain (sixty or seventy feet), with the wet ditch, were insurmountable obstacles to an attack merely by mining or escalading.

It therefore became requisite to examine closely the whole "*contour*" of the place, to discover if any other mode of attack could be adopted. The Engineers, with an escort, went round the works, approaching as near as they could find cover; the garrison were on the alert, and kept up a hot and well-directed fire on the officers whenever they were obliged to shew themselves. However, by keeping the Infantry beyond musket-range, and the Cavalry at a still greater distance, only one man was killed and one wounded, and the former was hit by the men sent out of the place to drive off the reconnoitring party.

The fortifications were found equally strong all round; the only tangible point observed was the "Cabool gateway," which offered which offered the following advantages for a *coup-de-main*; the road up to the gate was clear; the bridge over the ditch was unbroken; there were good positions for the Artillery within 350 yards of the walls on both sides of the road; and we had information that the gateway was not built up, a reinforcement from Cabool being expected.

The result of this *reconnoissance* was that a report to his Excellency the Commander-in-Chief, that, if he decided on the immediate attack of Ghuznee, the only feasible mode of attack, and the only one which held out a prospect of success, was a dash at the Cabool gateway, — blowing open the gate by bags of powder.

His Excellency decided on the attempt; the camp was moved that evening to the Cabool road, and next morning (the 22nd) Sir J. Keane in person reconnoitered the proposed point of attack; — he approved of the plan, and gave orders for its execution. Preparations were made accordingly; positions for the Artillery were carefully examined, which excited the jealousy of the garrison, who opened a smart fire on the party.

It was arranged that an explosion party, consisting of three officers of Engineers, Captain Peat (Bombay), Lieutenants Durand and Macleod (Bengal), three serjeants, and eighteen men of the Sappers, in working dresses, carrying three hundred pounds of powder in twelve sand-bags, with a hose seventy-two feet long, should be ready to move down the gateway at day-break. At midnight the first battery left camp, followed by the other four, at intervals of half an hour. Those to the right of the road were conducted to their positions by Lieut. Sturt of the (Bengal) Engineers, those to the left by Lieutenant Anderson (Bengal); the ground for the guns was prepared by the Sappers and Pioneers, taking advantage of the inequalities of the ground on the right, and of some old garden-walls on the left. The artillery were all in position and ready by 3 A.M. on the 23rd; and shortly after, at the first dawn, the party under Captain Peat moved down to the gateway, accompanied by six men of H.M.'s 13th Light Infantry without their belts, and supported by a detachment of the same regiment, which extended to the right and left of the road when they arrived at the ditch, taking advantage of what cover they could find; and endeavouring to keep down the fire from the ramparts, which became heavy on the approach of the party, though it had been remarkably slack during the previous operations. Blue-lights were shewn, which rendered the surrounding objects distinctly visible; but, luckily, they were burned from the top of the parapet, instead of being thrown into the passage below.

The explosion party marched steadily on, headed by Lieutenant Durand; the powder was placed; the hose laid; the train fired; and the carrying party retired to a tolerable cover in less than two minutes. The artillery opened when the blue-lights appeared, and the musketry from the covering party at the same time: so quickly was the operation performed, and so little were the enemy aware of the nature of it, that not a man of the party was hit.

As soon as the explosion took place, Captain Peat, though hurt, his anxiety preventing his keeping sufficiently under cover, ran up to the gate (accompanied by a small party of H.M.'s 13th Light Infantry) and ascertained that it was completely destroyed. There was some delay in getting a bugler to sound the "advance," the signal agreed on for the assaulting column to push on; and this was the only mistake in the operation.

The assaulting column consisted of four European regiments[98], commanded by Brigadier Sale. The advance under Lieutenant-Colonel Dennie, accompanied by Lieutenant Sturt, Engineers, moved steadily through the gateway, through a passage inside the gate, ending in a domed building, with the opening on one side, which made every thing very obscure, and rendered it difficult to find the out-let into the town. They met with little opposition; but a party of the enemy, seeing a break in the column, owing to the difficulty in scrambling over the rubbish in the gateway, made a rush, sword in hand, and cut down a good many men, wounding the Brigadier and several other officers. These swordsmen were repulsed, and there was no other regular opposition; the surprise and alarm of the Governor and sirdars being so great, when they saw the column occupying the open space inside the gate and firing on them, that they fled, accompanied by their men; even the garrison of the citadel following their example. Parties of the Affghans took refuge in houses, firing on the column as it made its way through the streets; and a good deal of desultory firing took place in consequence, by which some loss was sustained. The citadel was occupied as soon as daylight shewed that it had been evacuated by the enemy; and the whole of the works were in our possession before 5 o'clock A.M.

We lost 17 men (6 Europeans and 11 natives), killed; 18 officers, 117 Europeans, and 30 Natives, wounded; total 182. Of the Affghans more than 514 were killed in the town, that number of bodies having been buried, and about 100 outside by the cavalry; 1,600 prisoners were taken, but I have no means of estimating the number of wounded.

There were nine guns, of different calibres, found in the place; a large quantity of good powder; considerable stores of shot, lead, &c.; and a large supply of attah (flour) and other provisions.

(Signed)   GEORGE THOMSON,
Chief Engineer, Army of the Indus.
Camp, Ghuznee, 25th July, 1839.
To Colonel D. MacLeod, Chief Engineer, Bengal Army;

Observations of Captain Peat, the Chief Engineer, Bombay Column.

During the reconnaissance, the wall-pieces were particularly troublesome. This weapon is almost unknown in our service, but is a very efficient one, especially in the defence of works; and its use should not be neglected. Every fortified post should be supplied with a proportion of them, and a certain number of men in each regiment practised in firing them.

The charge recommended by Colonel Pasley, for blowing open gates, is from 60 to 120lbs., and this is doubtless sufficient in ordinary cases; but in this instance we were apprehensive that the enemy might have taken alarm at our being so much on that side of the place, and in consequence have partially or wholly built up the gateway. It was afterwards found that some attempts of the kind had been made, by propping up the gate with beams.

---

[98] H.M.'s 2nd, Queen's (1st) Bengal European Regiment, H.M.'s 13th Light Infantry, H.M.'s 17th Foot.

The charge was so heavy, that it not only destroyed the gate, but brought down a considerable portion of the roof of the square building in which it was placed; which proved a very considerable obstacle to the assaulting column, and the concussion acted as far as a tower, under which an officer's party of H.M.'s 13th Light Infantry were standing at the time, but without occasioning any casualties In cases of this nature, it is of course the first object to guard against any chance of failure, and it is impossible, even now, to say how much the charge might have been reduced with safety.

The enemy appeared so much on the alert, and the *fausse braye* was so much in advance of the gate, that we never contemplated being able to effect our object by surprise. The only question was, whether it ought to be done by day or night. It was argued in favour of the former, that the Artillery would be able to make so much more correct practice; that the defences would be in a considerable degree destroyed, and the fire so completely kept under, as to enable the explosion party to advance with but little loss and with the advantage of being able to see exactly what they were about. Captain Thomson, however, adhered to the latter, and we were afterwards convinced it was the most judicious plan; for although the fire of the Artillery was necessarily more general than it would have been in daylight, still it was so well directed, as to take up a good deal of the attention of the besieged, and draw upon their batteries a portion of the fire, which in daylight would have been thrown upon the explosion party, and assaulting columns.

It would also, even in daylight, have been difficult with our Light Artillery to have kept down the fire so completely but that a few matchlock-men might have kept their position near the gateway, and in that narrow space, a smart fire from a few pieces might have obliged the party to retire. The obscurity of the night, to say nothing of the confusion it must occasion among undisciplined troops, is certainly the best protection to a body of men engaged in an enterprise of this nature. Blue-lights certainly render objects distinctly visible, but their light is glaring and uncertain, especially to men firing through loop-holes.

The party of H.M.'s 13th Light Infantry consisted of 18 officers, 28 serjeants, 7 buglers, 276 rank and file. It was made of this strength not only to keep up a heavy fire upon the parapets, and thereby divert attention from the party at the gateway, but also, because we were not aware whether the *fausse braye* was occupied or not; and as it extends so much in advance as to take the gate completely in reverse, it would have been necessary, had a fire opened from it, to have carried it by assault, before the party with the bags could have advanced.

The party with Lieutenant Durand (Bengal) was accompanied by six men of the 13th Light Infantry, without their belts, the better to secure them from observation, to protect them from any *sortie* that might be made from the postern of the *fausse braye* on the right, or even from the gate itself; while another party, under Lieutenant P.R. Jennings, accompanied them as far as the tower, so as to check any attempts that might have been made from the *fausse braye* on the left, and at the same time keeping up a fire on such of the enemy as shewed their heads above the parapet; of this party one man was killed and a few wounded. Nothing could have been more gallant than the conduct of Lieutenants Durand and McLeod (Bengal Engineers), and the men under their command, or more efficient than the manner in which they executed their duty.

The powder being in bags of a very coarse open texture, a long hose and portfire was thought to be the safest method of firing it. The end of the hose fortunately just reached the small postern. The casualties during this operation were much fewer than was expected, being, in all, one private killed, two serjeants and twenty-three rank and file wounded.

The heaviest fire was certainly outside the bridge, for the enemy near the gateway, being marked whenever they attempted to shew their heads above the parapet, were obliged to confine themselves to the loop-holes, the range from which is very uncertain and limited, against men moving about. A high loop-holed wall, although imposing in appearance, is a profile but ill adapted to resist attacks of this nature.

The enemy were perfectly aware that we were in the gateway, but appeared to have no idea of the nature of our operations. Had they been so, they might easily have rendered it impossible to place the powder-bags, by throwing over blue-lights, of which they had a large quantity in store.

The powder-pots and other fire-works, so much used by the natives of Hindostan, would certainly have rendered the confined space leading to the gate much too hot for such an operation; but the ignorance of the besieged was known and calculated upon; the result shews how justly.

Their attempts at resistance were confined to the fire from the loop-holes, and throwing over large pieces of earth, some of which appeared to be intended to knock off the portfire.

The gateway appeared, from what I had seen from the hills to the north, to lead straight into the town. I was led to believe that the gateway had been blocked up, from seeing in front of the gate that had been destroyed, the outline of an arch filled up with brick masonry. The true entrance turned to the right, and would have been discovered by advancing a few paces, and that in perfect safety; for the interior was secure from all fire.

Lieutenant Durand, on first going up, saw from through the chinks of the gate that there was a light, and a guard immediately behind it; and from that circumstance was convinced that no interior obstacles of importance existed.

A party of Sappers, with felling axes, and commanded by Lieutenant Wemyss (Bombay Engineers), and two scaling ladders, in charge of Lieutenant Pigou (Bengal Engineers), accompanied the assaulting column, intended for the citadel if required.

Of ten Engineer officers engaged in this attack, only one, Lieutenant Marriot (Bombay), was slightly wounded. Captain Thomson (Bengal), however, had a very narrow escape, being thrown down by the rush of some swordsmen into the gateway, and nearly sabred while upon the ground.

    (Signed) A. G. PEAT
      Captain Bombay Engineers.

OUR CURRENT LIST OF TITLES

Abdullah, Morag Mary, *My Khyber Marriage* - Morag Murray departed on a lifetime of adventure when she met and fell in love with Sirdar Ikbal Ali Shah, the son of an Afghan warlord. Leaving the comforts of her middle-class home in Scotland, Morag followed her husband into a Central Asia still largely unchanged since the 19th century.

Abernathy, Miles, *Ride the Wind* – the amazing true story of the little Abernathy Boys, who made a series of astonishing journeys in the United States, starting in 1909 when they were aged five and nine!

Beard, John, *Saddles East* – John Beard determined as a child that he wanted to see the Wild West from the back of a horse after a visit to Cody's legendary Wild West show. Yet it was only in 1948 – more than sixty years after seeing the flamboyant American showman – that Beard and his wife Lulu finally set off to follow their dreams.

Beker, Ana, *The Courage to Ride* – Determined to out-do Tschiffely, Beker made a 17,000 mile mounted odyssey across the Americas in the late 1940s that would fix her place in the annals of equestrian travel history.

Bey, A. M. Hassanein, *The Lost Oases* - At the dawning of the 20th century the vast desert of Libya remained one of last unexplored places on Earth. Sir Hassanein Bey, the dashing Egyptian diplomat turned explorer, befriended the Muslim leaders of the elusive Senussi Brotherhood who controlled the deserts further on, and became aware of rumours of a "lost oasis" which lay even deeper in the desert. In 1923 the explorer led a small caravan on a remarkable seven month journey across the centre of Libya.

Bird, Isabella, *Among the Tibetans* – A rousing 1889 adventure, an enchanting travelogue, a forgotten peek at a mountain kingdom swept away by the waves of time.

Bird, Isabella, *On Horseback in Hawaii* – The Victorian explorer's first horseback journey, in which she learns to ride astride, in early 1873.

Bird, Isabella, *Journeys in Persia and Kurdistan, Volumes 1 and 2* – The intrepid Englishwoman undertakes another gruelling journey in 1890.

Bird, Isabella, *A Lady's Life in the Rocky Mountains* – The story of Isabella Bird's adventures during the winter of 1873 when she explored the magnificent unspoiled wilderness of Colorado. Truly a classic.

Bird, Isabella, *Unbeaten Tracks in Japan, Volumes One and Two* – A 600-mile solo ride through Japan undertaken by the intrepid British traveller in 1878.

Blackmore, Charles, *In the Footsteps of Lawrence of Arabia* - In February 1985, fifty years after T. E. Lawrence was killed in a motor bicycle accident in Dorset, Captain Charles Blackmore and three others of the Royal Green Jackets Regiment set out to retrace Lawrence's exploits in the Arab Revolt during the First World War. They spent twenty-nine days with meagre supplies and under extreme conditions, riding and walking to the source of the Lawrence legend.

Boniface, Lieutenant Jonathan, *The Cavalry Horse and his Pack* – Quite simply the most important book ever written in the English language by a military man on the subject of equestrian travel.

Bosanquet, Mary, *Saddlebags for Suitcases* – In 1939 Bosanquet set out to ride from Vancouver, Canada, to New York. Along the way she was wooed by love-struck cowboys, chased by a grizzly bear and even suspected of being a Nazi spy, scouting out Canada in preparation for a German invasion. A truly delightful book.

de Bourboulon, Catherine, *Shanghai à Moscou (French)* – the story of how a young Scottish woman and her aristocratic French husband travelled overland from Shanghai to Moscow in the late 19th Century.

Brown, Donald; *Journey from the Arctic* – A truly remarkable account of how Brown, his Danish companion and their two trusty horses attempt the impossible, to cross the silent Arctic plateaus, thread their way through the giant Swedish forests, and finally discover a passage around the treacherous Norwegian marshes.

Bruce, Clarence Dalrymple, *In the Hoofprints of Marco Polo* – The author made a dangerous journey from Srinagar to Peking in 1905, mounted on a trusty 13-hand Kashmiri pony, then wrote this wonderful book.

Burnaby, Frederick; *A Ride to Khiva* – Burnaby fills every page with a memorable cast of characters, including hard-riding Cossacks, nomadic Tartars, vodka-guzzling sleigh-drivers and a legion of peasant ruffians.

Burnaby, Frederick, *On Horseback through Asia Minor* – Armed with a rifle, a small stock of medicines, and a single faithful servant, the equestrian traveler rode through a hotbed of intrigue and high adventure in wild inhospitable country, encountering Kurds, Circassians, Armenians, and Persian pashas.

Carter, General William, *Horses, Saddles and Bridles* – This book covers a wide range of topics including basic training of the horse and care of its equipment. It also provides a fascinating look back into equestrian travel history.

Cayley, George, *Bridle Roads of Spain* – Truly one of the greatest equestrian travel accounts of the 19th Century.

Chase, J. Smeaton, *California Coast Trails* – This classic book describes the author's journey from Mexico to Oregon along the coast of California in the 1890s.

Chase, J. Smeaton, *California Desert Trails* – Famous British naturalist J. Smeaton Chase mounted up and rode into the Mojave Desert to undertake the longest equestrian study of its kind in modern history.

Chitty, Susan, and Hinde, Thomas, *The Great Donkey Walk* - When biographer Susan Chitty and her novelist husband, Thomas Hinde, decided it was time to embark on a family adventure, they did it in style. In Santiago they bought two donkeys whom they named Hannibal and Hamilcar. Their two small daughters, Miranda (7) and Jessica (3) were to ride Hamilcar. Hannibal, meanwhile, carried the baggage. The walk they planned to undertake was nothing short of the breadth of southern Europe.

Christian, Glynn, *Fragile Paradise: The discovery of Fletcher Christian, "Bounty" Mutineer* – the great-great-great-great-grandson of the *Bounty* mutineer brings to life a fascinating and complex character history has portrayed as both hero and villain, and the real story behind a mutiny that continues to divide opinion more than 200 years later. The result is a brilliant and compelling historical detective story, full of intrigue, jealousy, revenge and adventure on the high seas.

Clark, Leonard, *Marching Wind, The* – The panoramic story of a mounted exploration in the remote and savage heart of Asia, a place where adventure, danger, and intrigue were the daily backdrop to wild tribesman and equestrian exploits.

Clark, Leonard, *A Wanderer Till I Die* – In a world with lax passport control, no airlines, and few rules, the young man from San Francisco floats effortlessly from one adventure to the next. When he's not drinking whisky at the Raffles Hotel or listening to the "St. Louis Blues" on the phonograph in the jungle, he's searching for Malaysian treasure, being captured by Toradja headhunters, interrogated by Japanese intelligence officers and lured into shady deals by European gun-runners.

Cobbett, William, *Rural Rides, Volumes 1 and 2* – In the early 1820s Cobbett set out on horseback to make a series of personal tours through the English countryside. These books contain what many believe to be the best accounts of rural England ever written, and remain enduring classics.

Codman, John, *Winter Sketches from the Saddle* – This classic book was first published in 1888. It recommends riding for your health and describes the septuagenarian author's many equestrian journeys through New England during the winter of 1887 on his faithful mare, Fanny.

Cunninghame Graham, Jean, *Gaucho Laird* – A superbly readable biography of the author's famous great-uncle, Robert "Don Roberto" Cunninghame Graham.

Cunninghame Graham, Robert, *Horses of the Conquest* – The author uncovered manuscripts which had lain forgotten for centuries, and wrote this book, as he said, out of gratitude to the horses of Columbus and the Conquistadors who shaped history.

Cunninghame Graham, Robert, *Magreb-el-Acksa* – The thrilling tale of how "Don Roberto" was kidnapped in Morocco!

Cunninghame Graham, Robert, *Rodeo* – An omnibus of the finest work of the man they called "the uncrowned King of Scotland," edited by his friend Aimé Tschiffely.

Cunninghame Graham, Robert, *Tales of Horsemen* – Ten of the most beautifully-written equestrian stories ever set to paper.

Cunninghame Graham, Robert, *Vanished Arcadia* – This haunting story about the Jesuit missions in South America from 1550 to 1767 was the inspiration behind the best-selling film *The Mission*.

Daly, H.W., *Manual of Pack Transportation* – This book is the author's masterpiece. It contains a wealth of information on various pack saddles, ropes and equipment, how to secure every type of load imaginable and instructions on how to organize a pack train.

Dixie, Lady Florence, *Riding Across Patagonia* – When asked in 1879 why she wanted to travel to such an outlandish place as Patagonia, the author replied without hesitation that she was taking to the saddle in order to flee from the strict confines of polite Victorian society. This is the story of how the aristocrat successfully traded the perils of a London parlor for the wind-borne freedom of a wild Patagonian bronco.

Dodwell, Christina, *Beyond Siberia* – The intrepid author goes to Russia's Far East to join the reindeer-herding people in winter.

Dodwell, Christina, *An Explorer's Handbook* – The author tells you everything you want to know about travelling: how to find suitable pack animals, how to feed and shelter yourself. She also has sensible and entertaining advice about dealing with unwanted visitors and the inevitable bureaucrats.

Dodwell, Christina, *Madagascar Travels* – Christina explores the hidden corners of this amazing island and, as usual, makes friends with its people.

Dodwell, Christina, *A Traveller in China* – The author sets off alone across China, starting with a horse and then transferring to an inflatable canoe.

Dodwell, Christina, *A Traveller on Horseback* – Christina Dodwell rides through Eastern Turkey and Iran in the late 1980s. The Sunday Telegraph wrote of the author's "courage and insatiable wanderlust," and in this book she demonstrates her gift for communicating her zest for adventure.

Dodwell, Christina, *Travels in Papua New Guinea* – Christina Dodwell spends two years exploring an island little known to the outside world. She travelled by foot, horse and dugout canoe among the Stone-Age tribes.

Dodwell, Christina, *Travels with Fortune* – the truly amazing account of the courageous author's first journey – a three-year odyssey around Africa by Landrover, bus, lorry, horse, camel, and dugout canoe!

Dodwell, Christina, *Travels with Pegasus* – This time Christina takes to the air! This is the story of her unconventional journey across North Africa in a micro-light!

Duncan, John, *Travels in Western Africa in 1845 and 1846* – The author, a Lifeguardsman from Scotland, tells the hair-raising tale of his two journeys to what is now Benin. Sadly, Duncan has been forgotten until today, and we are proud to get this book back into print.

Ehlers, Otto, *Im Sattel durch die Fürstenhöfe Indiens* – In June 1890 the young German adventurer, Ehlers, lay very ill. His doctor gave him a choice: either go home to Germany or travel to Kashmir. So of course the Long Rider chose the latter. This is a thrilling yet humorous book about the author's adventures.

Farson, Negley, *Caucasian Journey* – A thrilling account of a dangerous equestrian journey made in 1929, this is an amply illustrated adventure classic.

Fox, Ernest, *Travels in Afghanistan* – The thrilling tale of a 1937 journey through the mountains, valleys, and deserts of this forbidden realm, including visits to such fabled places as the medieval city of Heart, the towering Hindu Kush mountains, and the legendary Khyber Pass.

Gall, Sandy, *Afghanistan – Agony of a Nation* - Sandy Gall has made three trips to Afghanistan to report the war there: in 1982, 1984 and again in 1986. This book is an account of his last journey and what he found. He chose to revisit the man he believes is the outstanding commander in Afghanistan: Ahmed Shah Masud, a dashing Tajik who is trying to organise resistance to the Russians on a regional, and eventually national scale.

Gall, Sandy, *Behind Russian Lines* – In the summer of 1982, Sandy Gall set off for Afghanistan on what turned out to be the hardest assignment of his life. During his career as a reporter he had covered plenty of wars and revolutions before, but this was the first time he had been required to walk all the way to an assignment and all the way back again, dodging Russian bombs *en route*.

Gallard, Babette, *Riding the Milky Way* – An essential guide to anyone planning to ride the ancient pilgrimage route to Santiago di Compostella, and a highly readable story for armchair travellers.

Galton, Francis, *The Art of Travel* – Originally published in 1855, this book became an instant classic and was used by a host of now-famous explorers, including Sir Richard Francis Burton of Mecca fame. Readers can learn how to ride horses, handle elephants, avoid cobras, pull teeth, find water in a desert, and construct a sleeping bag out of fur.

Glazier, Willard, *Ocean to Ocean on Horseback* – This book about the author's journey from New York to the Pacific in 1875 contains every kind of mounted adventure imaginable. Amply illustrated with pen and ink drawings of the time, the book remains a timeless equestrian adventure classic.

Goodwin, Joseph, *Through Mexico on Horseback* – The author and his companion, Robert Horiguichi, the sophisticated, multi-lingual son of an imperial Japanese diplomat, set out in 1931 to cross Mexico. They were totally unprepared for the deserts, quicksand and brigands they were to encounter during their adventure.

Hanbury-Tenison, Marika, *For Better, For Worse* – The author, an excellent story-teller, writes about her adventures visiting and living among the Indians of Central Brazil.

Hanbury-Tenison, Marika, *A Slice of Spice* – The fresh and vivid account of the author's hazardous journey to the Indonesian Islands with her husband, Robin.

Hanbury-Tenison, Robin, *Chinese Adventure* – The story of a unique journey in which the explorer Robin Hanbury-Tenison and his wife Louella rode on horseback alongside the Great Wall of China in 1986.

Hanbury-Tenison, Robin, *Fragile Eden* – The wonderful story of Robin and Louella Hanbury-Tenison's exploration of New Zealand on horseback in 1988. They rode alone together through what they describe as 'some of the most dramatic and exciting country we have ever seen.'

Hanbury-Tenison, Robin, *Mulu: The Rainforest* – This was the first popular book to bring to the world's attention the significance of the rain forests to our fragile ecosystem. It is a timely reminder of our need to preserve them for the future.

Hanbury-Tenison, Robin, *A Pattern of Peoples* – The author and his wife, Marika, spent three months travelling through Indonesia's outer islands and writes with his usual flair and sensitivity about the tribes he found there.

Hanbury-Tenison, Robin, *A Question of Survival* – This superb book played a hugely significant role in bringing the plight of Brazil's Indians to the world's attention.

Hanbury-Tenison, Robin, *The Rough and the Smooth* – The incredible story of two journeys in South America. Neither had been attempted before, and both were considered impossible!

Hanbury-Tenison, Robin, *Spanish Pilgrimage* – Robin and Louella Hanbury-Tenison went to Santiago de Compostela in a traditional way – riding on white horses over long-forgotten tracks. In the process they discovered more about the people and the country than any conventional traveller would learn. Their adventures are vividly and entertainingly recounted in this delightful and highly readable book.

Hanbury-Tenison, Robin, *White Horses over France* – This enchanting book tells the story of a magical journey and how, in fulfilment of a personal dream, the first Camargue horses set foot on British soil in the late summer of 1984.

Hanbury-Tenison, Robin, *Worlds Apart – an Explorer's Life* – The author's battle to preserve the quality of life under threat from developers and machines infuses this autobiography with a passion and conviction which makes it impossible to put down.

Hanbury-Tenison, Robin, *Worlds Within – Reflections in the Sand* – This book is full of the adventure you would expect from a man of action like Robin Hanbury-Tenison. However, it is also filled with the type of rare knowledge that was revealed to other desert travellers like Lawrence, Doughty and Thesiger.

Haslund, Henning, *Mongolian Adventure* – An epic tale inhabited by a cast of characters no longer present in this lackluster world, shamans who set themselves on fire, rebel leaders who sacked towns, and wild horsemen whose ancestors conquered the world.

Heath, Frank, *Forty Million Hoofbeats* – Heath set out in 1925 to follow his dream of riding to all 48 of the Continental United States. The journey lasted more than two years, during which time Heath and his mare, Gypsy Queen, became inseparable companions.
Hinde, Thomas, *The Great Donkey Walk* – Biographer Susan Chitty and her novelist husband, Thomas Hinde, travelled from Spain's Santiago to Salonica in faraway Greece. Their two small daughters, Miranda (7) and Jessica (3) were rode one donkey, while the other donkey carried the baggage. Reading this delightful book is leisurely and continuing pleasure.
Holt, William, *Ride a White Horse* – After rescuing a cart horse, Trigger, from slaughter and nursing him back to health, the 67-year-old Holt and his horse set out in 1964 on an incredible 9,000 mile, non-stop journey through western Europe.
Hopkins, Frank T., *Hidalgo and Other Stories* – For the first time in history, here are the collected writings of Frank T. Hopkins, the counterfeit cowboy whose endurance racing claims and Old West fantasies have polarized the equestrian world.
James, Jeremy, *Saddletramp* – The classic story of Jeremy James' journey from Turkey to Wales, on an unplanned route with an inaccurate compass, unreadable map and the unfailing aid of villagers who seemed to have as little sense of direction as he had.
James, Jeremy, *Vagabond* – The wonderful tale of the author's journey from Bulgaria to Berlin offers a refreshing, witty and often surprising view of Eastern Europe and the collapse of communism.
Jebb, Louisa, *By Desert Ways to Baghdad and Damascus* – From the pen of a gifted writer and intrepid traveller, this is one of the greatest equestrian travel books of all time.
Kluckhohn, Clyde, *To the Foot of the Rainbow* – This is not just a exciting true tale of equestrian adventure. It is a moving account of a young man's search for physical perfection in a desert world still untouched by the recently-born twentieth century.
Lambie, Thomas, *Boots and Saddles in Africa* – Lambie's story of his equestrian journeys is told with the grit and realism that marks a true classic.
Landor, Henry Savage, *In the Forbidden Land* – Illustrated with hundreds of photographs and drawings, this blood-chilling account of equestrian adventure makes for page-turning excitement.
Langlet, Valdemar, *Till Häst Genom Ryssland (Swedish)* – Denna reseskildring rymmer många ögonblicksbilder av möten med människor, från morgonbad med Lev Tolstoi till samtal med Tartarer och fotografering av fagra skördeflickor. Rikt illustrerad med foto och teckningar.
Leigh, Margaret, *My Kingdom for a Horse* – In the autumn of 1939 the author rode from Cornwall to Scotland, resulting in one of the most delightful equestrian journeys of the early twentieth century. This book is full of keen observations of a rural England that no longer exists.
Lester, Mary, *A Lady's Ride across Spanish Honduras in 1881* – This is a gem of a book, with a very entertaining account of Mary's vivid, day-to-day life in the saddle.
MacDermot, Brian, *Cult of the Sacred Spear* – here is that rarest of travel books, an exploration not only of a distant land but of a man's own heart. A confederation of pastoral people located in Southern Sudan and western Ethiopia, the Nuer warriors were famous for staging cattle raids against larger tribes and successfully resisted European colonization. Brian MacDermot, London stockbroker, entered into Nuer society as a stranger and emerged as Rial Nyang, an adopted member of the tribe. This book recounts this extraordinary emotional journey, regaling the reader with tales of pagan gods, warriors on mysterious missions, and finally the approach of warfare that continues to swirl across this part of Africa today.
Maillart, Ella, *Turkestan Solo* – A vivid account of a 1930s journey through this wonderful, mysterious and dangerous portion of the world, complete with its Kirghiz eagle hunters, lurking Soviet secret police, and the timeless nomads that still inhabited the desolate steppes of Central Asia.
Marcy, Randolph, *The Prairie Traveler* – There were a lot of things you packed into your saddlebags or the wagon before setting off to cross the North American wilderness in the 1850s. A gun and an axe were obvious necessities. Yet many pioneers were just as adamant about placing a copy of Captain Randolph Marcy's classic book close at hand.
Marsden, Kate, *Riding through Siberia: A Mounted Medical Mission in 1891* – This immensely readable book is a mixture of adventure, extreme hardship and compassion as the author travels the Great Siberian Post Road.

Marsh, Hippisley Cunliffe, *A Ride Through Islam* – A British officer rides through Persia and Afghanistan to India in 1873. Full of adventures, and with observant remarks on the local Turkoman equestrian traditions.

MacCann, William, *Viaje a Caballo* – Spanish-language edition of the British author's equestrian journey around Argentina in 1848.

Meline, James, *Two Thousand Miles on Horseback: Kansas to Santa Fé in 1866* – A beautifully written, eye witness account of a United States that is no more.

Muir Watson, Sharon, *The Colour of Courage* – The remarkable true story of the epic horse trip made by the first people to travel Australia's then-unmarked Bicentennial National Trail. There are enough adventures here to satisfy even the most jaded reader.

Naysmith, Gordon, *The Will to Win* – This book recounts the only equestrian journey of its kind undertaken during the 20th century - a mounted trip stretching across 16 countries. Gordon Naysmith, a Scottish pentathlete and former military man, set out in 1970 to ride from the tip of the African continent to the 1972 Olympic Games in distant Germany.

Ondaatje, Christopher, *Leopard in the Afternoon* – The captivating story of a journey through some of Africa's most spectacular haunts. It is also touched with poignancy and regret for a vanishing wilderness – a world threatened with extinction.

Ondaatje, Christopher, *The Man-Eater of Pununai* – a fascinating story of a past rediscovered through a remarkable journey to one of the most exotic countries in the world — Sri Lanka. Full of drama and history, it not only relives the incredible story of a man-eating leopard that terrorized the tiny village of Punanai in the early part of the century, but also allows the author to come to terms with the ghost of his charismatic but tyrannical father.

Ondaatje, Christopher, *Sindh Revisited* – This is the extraordinarily sensitive account of the author's quest to uncover the secrets of the seven years Richard Burton spent in India in the army of the East India Company from 1842 to 1849. "If I wanted to fill the gap in my understanding of Richard Burton, I would have to do something that had never been done before: follow in his footsteps in India…" The journey covered thousands of miles—trekking across deserts where ancient tribes meet modern civilization in the valley of the mighty Indus River.

O'Connor, Derek, *The King's Stranger* – a superb biography of the forgotten Scottish explorer, John Duncan.

O'Reilly, Basha, *Count Pompeii – Stallion of the Steppes* – the story of Basha's journey from Russia with her stallion, Count Pompeii, told for children. This is the first book in the *Little Long Rider* series.

O'Reilly, CuChullaine, (Editor) *The Horse Travel Handbook* – this accumulated knowledge of a million miles in the saddle tells you everything you need to know about travelling with your horse!

O'Reilly, CuChullaine, (Editor) *The Horse Travel Journal* – a unique book to take on your ride and record your experiences. Includes the world's first equestrian travel "pictionary" to help you in foreign countries.

O'Reilly, CuChullaine, *Khyber Knights* – Told with grit and realism by one of the world's foremost equestrian explorers, "Khyber Knights" has been penned the way lives are lived, not how books are written.

O'Reilly, CuChullaine, (Editor) *The Long Riders, Volume One* – The first of five unforgettable volumes of exhilarating travel tales.

Östrup, J, *(Swedish), Växlande Horisont* – The thrilling account of the author's journey to Central Asia from 1891 to 1893.

Patterson, George, *Gods and Guerrillas* – The true and gripping story of how the author went secretly into Tibet to film the Chinese invaders of his adopted country. Will make your heart pound with excitement!

Patterson, George, *Journey with Loshay: A Tibetan Odyssey* – This is an amazing book written by a truly remarkable man! Relying both on his companionship with God and on his own strength, he undertook a life few can have known, and a journey of emergency across the wildest parts of Tibet.

Patterson, George, *Patterson of Tibet* – Patterson was a Scottish medical missionary who went to Tibet shortly after the second World War. There he became Tibetan in all but name, adapting to the culture and learning the language fluently. This intense autobiography reveals how Patterson crossed swords with India's Prime Minister Nehru, helped with the rescue of the Dalai Lama and befriended a host of unique world figures ranging from Yehudi Menhuin to Eric Clapton. This is a vividly-written account of a life of high adventure and spiritual odyssey.

Pocock, Roger, *Following the Frontier* – Pocock was one of the nineteenth century's most influential equestrian travelers. Within the covers of this book is the detailed account of Pocock's horse ride along the infamous Outlaw Trail, a 3,000 mile solo journey that took the adventurer from Canada to Mexico City.

Pocock, Roger, *Horses* – Pocock set out to document the wisdom of the late 19th and early 20th Centuries into a book unique for its time. His concerns for attempting to preserve equestrian knowledge were based on cruel reality. More than 300,000 horses had been destroyed during the recent Boer War. Though Pocock enjoyed a reputation for dangerous living, his observations on horses were praised by the leading thinkers of his day.

Post, Charles Johnson, *Horse Packing* – Originally published in 1914, this book was an instant success, incorporating as it did the very essence of the science of packing horses and mules. It makes fascinating reading for students of the horse or history.

Ray, G. W., *Through Five Republics on Horseback* – In 1889 a British explorer – part-time missionary and full-time adventure junky – set out to find a lost tribe of sun-worshipping natives in the unexplored forests of Paraguay. The journey was so brutal that it defies belief.

Rink, Bjarke, *The Centaur Legacy* – This immensely entertaining and historically important book provides the first ever in-depth study into how man's partnership with his equine companion changed the course of history and accelerated human development.

Ross, Julian, *Travels in an Unknown Country* – A delightful book about modern horseback travel in an enchanting country, which once marked the eastern borders of the Roman Empire – Romania.

Ross, Martin and Somerville, E, *Beggars on Horseback* – The hilarious adventures of two aristocratic Irish cousins on an 1894 riding tour of Wales.

Ruxton, George, *Adventures in Mexico* – The story of a young British army officer who rode from Vera Cruz to Santa Fe, Mexico in 1847. At times the author exhibits a fearlessness which borders on insanity. He ignores dire warnings, rides through deadly deserts, and dares murderers to attack him. It is a delightful and invigorating tale of a time and place now long gone.

von Salzman, Erich, *Im Sattel durch Zentralasien* – The astonishing tale of the author's journey through China, Turkistan and back to his home in Germany – 6000 kilometres in 176 days!

Schwarz, Hans *(German)*, *Vier Pferde, Ein Hund und Drei Soldaten* – In the early 1930s the author and his two companions rode through Liechtenstein, Austria, Romania, Albania, Yugoslavia, to Turkey, then rode back again!

Schwarz, Otto *(German), Reisen mit dem Pferd* – the Swiss Long Rider with more miles in the saddle than anyone else tells his wonderful story, and a long appendix tells the reader how to follow in his footsteps.

Scott, Robert, *Scott's Last Expedition* – Many people are unaware that Scott recruited Yakut ponies from Siberia for his doomed expedition to the South Pole in 1909. Here is the remarkable story of men and horses who all paid the ultimate sacrifice.

Shackleton, Ernest, *Aurora Australis* - The members of the British Antarctic Expedition of 1907-1908 wrote this delightful and surprisingly funny book. It was printed on the spot "at the sign of the Penguin"!

Skrede, Wilfred, *Across the Roof of the World* – This epic equestrian travel tale of a wartime journey across Russia, China, Turkestan and India is laced with unforgettable excitement.

The South Pole Ponies, *Theodore Mason* – The touching and totally forgotten story of the little horses who gave their all to both Scott and Shackleton in their attempts to reach the South Pole.

Stevens, Thomas, *Through Russia on a Mustang* – Mounted on his faithful horse, Texas, Stevens crossed the Steppes in search of adventure. Cantering across the pages of this classic tale is a cast of nineteenth century Russian misfits, peasants, aristocrats—and even famed Cossack Long Rider Dmitri Peshkov.

Stevenson, Robert L., *Travels with a Donkey* – In 1878, the author set out to explore the remote Cevennes mountains of France. He travelled alone, unless you count his stubborn and manipulative pack-donkey, Modestine. This book is a true classic.

Strong, Anna Louise, *Road to the Grey Pamir* – With Stalin's encouragement, Strong rode into the seldom-seen Pamir mountains of faraway Tadjikistan. The political renegade turned equestrian explorer soon discovered more adventure than she had anticipated.

Sykes, Ella, *Through Persia on a Sidesaddle* – Ella Sykes rode side-saddle 2,000 miles across Persia, a country few European woman had ever visited. Mind you, she traveled in style, accompanied by her Swiss maid and 50 camels loaded with china, crystal, linens and fine wine.

Trinkler, Emile, *Through the Heart of Afghanistan* – In the early 1920s the author made a legendary trip across a country now recalled only in legends.

Tschiffely, Aimé, *Bohemia Junction* – "Forty years of adventurous living condensed into one book."

Tschiffely, Aimé, *Bridle Paths* – a final poetic look at a now-vanished Britain.

Tschiffely, Aimé, *Mancha y Gato Cuentan sus Aventuras* – The Spanish-language version of *The Tale of Two Horses* – the story of the author's famous journey as told by the horses.

Tschiffely, Aimé, *The Tale of Two Horses* – The story of Tschiffely's famous journey from Buenos Aires to Washington, DC, narrated by his two equine heroes, Mancha and Gato. Their unique point of view is guaranteed to delight children and adults alike.

Tschiffely, Aimé, *This Way Southward* – the most famous equestrian explorer of the twentieth century decides to make a perilous journey across the U-boat infested Atlantic.

Tschiffely, Aimé, *Tschiffely's Ride* – The true story of the most famous equestrian journey of the twentieth century – 10,000 miles with two Criollo geldings from Argentina to Washington, DC. A new edition is coming soon with a Foreword by his literary heir!

Tschiffely, Aimé, *Tschiffely's Ritt* – The German-language translation of *Tschiffely's Ride* – the most famous equestrian journey of its day.

Ure, John, *Cucumber Sandwiches in the Andes* – No-one who wasn't mad as a hatter would try to take a horse across the Andes by one of the highest passes between Chile and the Argentine. That was what John Ure was told on his way to the British Embassy in Santiago – so he set out to find a few certifiable kindred spirits. Fans of equestrian travel and of Latin America will be enchanted by this delightful book.

Warner, Charles Dudley, *On Horseback in Virginia* – A prolific author, and a great friend of Mark Twain, Warner made witty and perceptive contributions to the world of nineteenth century American literature. This book about the author's equestrian adventures is full of fascinating descriptions of nineteenth century America.

Weale, Magdalene, *Through the Highlands of Shropshire* – It was 1933 and Magdalene Weale was faced with a dilemma: how to best explore her beloved English countryside? By horse, of course! This enchanting book invokes a gentle, softer world inhabited by gracious country lairds, wise farmers, and jolly inn keepers.

Weeks, Edwin Lord, *Artist Explorer* – A young American artist and superb writer travels through Persia to India in 1892.

Wentworth Day, J., *Wartime Ride* – In 1939 the author decided the time was right for an extended horseback ride through England! While parts of his country were being ravaged by war, Wentworth Day discovered an inland oasis of mellow harvest fields, moated Tudor farmhouses, peaceful country halls, and fishing villages.

Von Westarp, Eberhard, *Unter Halbmond und Sonne* – (German) – Im Sattel durch die asiatische Türkei und Persien.

Wilkins, Messanie, *Last of the Saddle Tramps* – Told she had little time left to live, the author decided to ride from her native Maine to the Pacific. Accompanied by her faithful horse, Tarzan, Wilkins suffered through any number of obstacles, including blistering deserts and freezing snow storms – and defied the doctors by living for another 20 years!

Wilson, Andrew, *The Abode of Snow* – One of the best accounts of overland equestrian travel ever written about the wild lands that lie between Tibet and Afghanistan.

de Windt, Harry, *A Ride to India* – Part science, all adventure, this book takes the reader for a thrilling canter across the Persian Empire of the 1890s.

Winthrop, Theodore, *Saddle and Canoe* – This book paints a vibrant picture of 1850s life in the Pacific Northwest and covers the author's travels along the Straits of Juan De Fuca, on Vancouver

Island, across the Naches Pass, and on to The Dalles, in Oregon Territory. This is truly an historic travel account.

Woolf, Leonard, *Stories of the East* – Three short stories which are of vital importance in understanding the author's mistrust of and dislike for colonialism, which provide disturbing commentaries about the disintegration of the colonial process.

Younghusband, George, *Eighteen Hundred Miles on a Burmese Pony* – One of the funniest and most enchanting books about equestrian travel of the nineteenth century, featuring "Joe" the naughty Burmese pony!

We are constantly adding new titles to our collections, so please check our websites:
    www.horsetravelbooks.com and **www.classictravelbooks.com**

www.ingramcontent.com/pod-product-compliance
Lightning Source LLC
Chambersburg PA
CBHW082003150426

42814CB00005BA/208